WHAT HAPPENED TO GOLDMAN SACHS?

STEVEN G. MANDIS

WHAT

An Insider's Story

HAPPENED

of Organizational Drift

TO

and its

GOLDMAN

Unintended Consequences

SACHS?

Harvard Business Review Press

Boston, Massachusetts

The views and opinions expressed in this book are strictly those of the author and do not necessarily reflect those of any organization with which the author has been or is affiliated. The contents of this book have not been approved by any organization with which the author has been or is affiliated. Analyses performed within this book are based on theories, are only examples, and reply upon very limited and dated information and require various and subjective assumptions, interpretations, and judgments. The author's opinions are based upon information he considers reliable; however, it may be inaccurate or may have been misinterpreted. The reader should not treat any opinion expressed in this book as a specific inducement to make a particular investment or follow a particular strategy, but only as an expression of the author's opinion.

Library of Congress Cataloging-in-Publication Data

Mandis, Steven G.

   What happened to Goldman Sachs: an insider's story of organizational drift and its unintended consequences/Steven G. Mandis.

      pages cm
   ISBN 978-1-4221-9419-5 (hardback)
1. Goldman, Sachs & Co. 2. Investment banking—United States—Management.
3. Corporate governance—United States. 4. Global Financial Crisis, 2008–2009. I. Title.
   HG4930.5.M36 2013
   332.660973—dc23

201301870

The web addresses referenced in this book were live and correct at the time of the book's publication but may be subject to change.

The paper used in this publication meets the requirements of the American National Standard for Permanence of Paper for Publications and Documents in Libraries and Archives Z39.48-1992.

ISBN: 9781422194195
eISBN: 9781422194201

This book is dedicated to my devoted wife, Alexandra, and my two loving daughters, Tatiana and Isabella. They were my cheerleaders through many long days and nights of working, studying, and writing.

I would also like to thank my parents, George and Theoni, who immigrated to America from Greece with very little money and no knowledge of English. They quietly sacrificed so that my brother Dean, my sister Vivian, and I could have a better life. They taught us the meaning of values and hard work as well as the power of the combination of these two qualities. They asked for only one thing in return—for us to strive to give our children more opportunities than they had been able to give us.

Contents

PART FOUR

Goldman's Performance

Prologue

A Funeral

O N SEPTEMBER 25, 2006, I FILED INTO THE MEMORIAL service for John L. Weinberg, senior partner of Goldman Sachs from 1976 to 1990. More than a thousand people filled Gotham Hall in New York to pay their respects. John L. (as he was often referred to within Goldman, to distinguish him from other Johns at the firm) was the product of Princeton and Harvard Business School and the son of one of the most powerful Wall Street bankers, Sidney Weinberg, who had literally worked his way up from janitor to senior partner of Goldman and who had served as a confidant to presidents.

The program listed a Goldman honor roll of those who would speak, including Lloyd Blankfein, the firm's current chairman and CEO; John Whitehead, who had run the firm with John L.—the two of them were known as "the Johns"—and who had left Goldman in 1985 to serve as deputy secretary of state; Robert Rubin, who had gone from co-senior partner in the early 1990s to secretary of the Treasury; Hank Paulson, who had run Goldman when it went public on the New York Stock Exchange (NYSE) in 1999 and had just become secretary of the Treasury; John S. Weinberg, John L.'s son and current vice chairman of Goldman; and Jack Welch, former chairman and CEO of General Electric and a long-standing client of John L.'s.

Welch's eulogy stood out. His voice cracking, holding back tears, he said, "I love you, John. Thanks for being my friend." Imagine a CEO today saying that about his investment banker and almost breaking down at the banker's memorial service.

John S. tried to lighten the mood with a funny line: "My father's favorite thing in life was talking to his dogs, because they didn't talk back." But he caught the essence of John L. when he said, "He saw right and wrong clearly, with no shades of gray." John L. was a veteran, having served in the US Marine Corps in both World War II and Korea, and the recessional was the "Marine Hymn." The lyrics "keep our honor clean" and "proud to serve" seemed to provide a perfect end to the service.

From 1976, when the two Johns became cochairmen, until John L.'s death in 2006, Goldman grew from a modest, privately owned investment banking firm focused on the United States—with fewer than a thousand employees, and less than $100 million in pretax profits—to the most prestigious publicly traded investment bank in the world. The firm boasted offices all over the globe, more than twenty-five thousand employees, almost $10 billion in pretax profits, a stock price of almost $200 per share, and an equity market valuation of close to $100 billion.

I had left Goldman in 2004 after a twelve-year career, a few months after my Goldman IPO stock grant had passed the five-year required vesting period. I had moved on to become a trading and investment banking client of Goldman's. I went to John L.'s memorial service out of respect for a man I had known and admired—a Wall Street legend, although one would never have guessed that from his demeanor. I also wanted to support John S., whom I considered (and still consider) a mentor and a friend. (See appendix F for an annotated list of key Goldman partners over the years.)

I first met John L. in 1992, when I was a Goldman financial analyst six months out of college. The legend of Sidney and John L. Weinberg was one of the things that had attracted me to Goldman, and I was excited at the prospect of meeting him. I identified with John L. because we were both sons of parents who came from humble beginnings. I figured if John L.'s father could start by emptying spittoons and end up running Goldman, then anything was possible for me, the son of Greek immigrants. My father had started as a busboy at the Drake Hotel in Chicago, and my mother worked at a Zenith TV assembly factory.

I met John L. early in my time at Goldman, as a financial analyst in the M&A department, when I interviewed him as part of a work assignment. I was asked to make a video on the history of the M&A department to be shown at an off-site department outing. Goldman was enthusiastic about documenting and respecting its history and holding off-site outings to promote bonding among the employees. In the interview John L. could not have been more jovial and humble. At the time, Goldman had less than $1.5 billion in pretax profits, and fewer than three thousand employees. Steve Friedman and Bob Rubin, co-senior partners, had embarked on an aggressive growth plan—growing proprietary trading and principal investing, expanding internationally, and spreading into new businesses.

John L. told me that his father had once fired him in the 1950s for what seemed a minor offense—without the proper approvals, he had committed a small amount of the firm's capital to help get a deal done for a client—and how, lesson learned, he had groveled to get his job back. He told me about sharing a squash court as an office with John Whitehead—the second of the two Johns—because there was no other space for them. He talked about integrity and business principles and explained how his military experiences had helped him at Goldman and in life. He told me how proud he was of his family, including his young grandchildren. He took a strong interest in my own family, and I was struck by his asking me to share my father's stories about his Greek military experiences.

John L. asked why I volunteered for Guardian Angels safety patrols and also wanted to know how I had managed to play two varsity sports at the University of Chicago while simultaneously performing community service. He revealed that his two children also played college tennis. Sharing that he liked Chicago, where I was born, he advised me to work with the head of the Chicago office, Hank Paulson, because I would learn a lot from him and it would allow me to fly from New York to see more of my family, something he emphasized was important.

––––––––––––

I didn't see John L. again until 1994, after Goldman had lost hundreds of millions of dollars betting the wrong way on interest rates as the Fed unexpectedly raised them. There were rumors that partners' capital accounts in the firm, representing their decades of hard work, were down over 50 percent in a matter of months. And to make matters worse, because Goldman was structured as a partnership, the partners' liability was not limited to their capital in the firm; their entire net worth was on the line. With the firm reeling from the losses, Steve Friedman, now sole senior partner because Rubin had left to serve in the Clinton administration, abruptly resigned. Friedman cited serious heart palpitations as the reason for his unexpected retirement. John L. viewed Friedman as a "yellowbellied coward" and his departure as tantamount to "abandoning his post and troops in combat," regardless of Friedman's stated reason for leaving.[1]

Despite John L.'s best efforts to persuade them to stay, almost one-third of the partners retired within months. Their retirements would give their capital in the firm preferential treatment over that of the general partners who stayed—and would allow the retirees to begin withdrawing their capital. Many loyal employees were being laid off to cut expenses.

When John L. walked onto the M&A department's twenty-third floor at 85 Broad Street that day in 1994 to calm the troops, the atmosphere was tense. The firm seemed in jeopardy. Before he spoke, I genuinely was worried that Goldman might fold. Drexel Burnham Lambert had filed for bankruptcy a few years earlier—why not Goldman? John L.'s encouraging words meant a great deal to my colleagues and me, as did the fact that he delivered them in person. The amazing thing is that he remembered me from my video project and, in a grandfatherly way, patted me on the shoulder as he said hello.

Later, I spent time with John L. socially. We belonged to the same club in the Bahamas, and I often saw him there. Although many of the members own large, impressive vacation homes, John L. did not. He rented a cottage. He told me once how many cots he had managed to fit into a bedroom when his kids were younger—proud of how much money he saved by not having to rent larger quarters. He read voraciously, and I always remembered how much he loved to eat coleslaw with his lunch. We exchanged books, and once he even wrote a letter of recommendation for me.

One night when he was in his seventies, I had the pleasure of having dinner with him, his wife, John S., and a few others at La Grenouille, one of New York's best restaurants. John L. was in failing health, so he didn't go out often. The place was filled with prominent CEOs and other VIPs, and, as they were leaving, each stopped at our table to say hello to John L., although many had not seen him in years. He greeted each of them by name and asked about their families, deflecting any praise about himself or Goldman.

In 2004, after twelve years, I left Goldman to help start an asset management firm. But when I saw John S. after the funeral service, he offered to help me in any way he could, just as his father had done, and showed an interest in how my family was doing, even at a difficult time for him and his own family.

Yet something struck me at the service. It caused me to stop and reflect on the cultural and organizational changes I'd witnessed, first as an employee and later as a client. The service brought them into sharp focus.

It felt strange, almost surreal, to be reflecting on change. In that fall of 2006, Goldman was near the height of its earning power and prestige. But I felt that, in some weird way, I was mourning not only the loss of the man who had embodied Goldman's values and business principles, but also the change of the firm's culture, which had been built on those values.[2]

Chapter 1

What Happened

GOLDMAN IS GOING STRONG" DECLARED THE TITLE OF A *Fortune* article in February 2007. "On Wall Street, there's good and then there's Goldman," wrote author Yuval Rosenberg. "Widely considered the best of the bulge-bracket investment firms, Goldman Sachs was the sole member of the securities industry to make [*Fortune's*] 2006 list of America's Most Admired Companies (it placed 18th)."[1] Rosenberg argued that what distinguished the firm was the quality of its people and the incentives it offered. "The bank has long had a reputation for attracting the best and the brightest," he wrote, "and no wonder: Goldman made headlines in December for doling out an extraordinary $16.5 billion in compensation last year. That works out to an average of nearly $622,000 for each employee." And as if that weren't enough, "[i]n the months since our list came out, Goldman's glittering reputation has only gotten brighter."

But only two years later, Goldman was being widely excoriated in the press, the subject of accusations, investigations, congressional hearings, and litigation (not to mention late-night jokes) alleging insensitive, unethical, immoral, and even criminal behavior. Matt Taibbi of *Rolling Stone* famously wrote, "The world's most powerful investment bank is a great vampire squid wrapped around the face of humanity, relentlessly jamming its blood funnel into anything that smells like money."[2] Understandably it seemed that angry villagers carrying torches and pitchforks were massing just around the corner. (In 2011, the Occupy Wall Street protest movement would begin.) The public and politicians grew particularly upset at Goldman as allegations surfaced that the company had anticipated the impending crisis and had shorted the market to make money from it. (Goldman denies this.) In addition, there were allegations that the firm had prioritized selling its clients securities in deals that it knew were, as one deal was described by an executive in an e-mail, "shitty"—raising the question of whether Goldman had acted unethically, immorally, or illegally.[3]

Particularly agonizing for some employees were accusations that Goldman no longer adhered to its revered first business principle: "Our clients' interests always come first." That principle had been seen at the firm as a significant part of the foundation of what made Goldman's culture unique. And the firm had held up its culture of the highest standards of duty and service to clients as key to its success. A partner made this point as part of a 2006 Harvard Business School case, saying "Our bankers travel on the same planes as our competitors. We stay in the same hotels. In a lot of cases, we have the same clients as our competition. So when it comes down to it, it is a combination of execution and culture that makes the difference between us and other firms . . . That's why our culture is necessary—it's the glue that binds us together."[4]

Some critics asserted that Goldman's actions in the lead up to the crisis, and in dealing with it, were evidence that the firm's vaunted culture had changed. Others argued that nothing was really new, that Goldman had always been hungry for money and power and had simply been skillful in hiding it behind folktales about always serving clients, and by doing conspicuous public service.[5]

Meanwhile, many current and former employees at Goldman vehemently assert that there has been no cultural shift, and argue that the firm still adheres as strictly as ever to its principles, including always putting clients' interests first. They cite the evidence of the firm's leading market share with clients and most-sought-after status for those seeking jobs in investment banking. *How*, they ask, *could something be wrong, when we're doing so well?* In fact, while in *Fortune*'s 2006 list of America's Most Admired Companies, Goldman placed eighteenth, in 2010, after the crisis, it placed eighth,[6] and in 2012, Goldman ranked seventh in a survey of MBA students of firms where they most wanted to work (and first among financial firms).[7] And even with all of the negative publicity, Goldman has maintained its leading market share with clients in many valued services. For example, in 2012 and 2011, Goldman ranked as the number one global M&A adviser.[8]

So has the culture at Goldman changed or not? And if so, why and how? It strains credulity to think that the firm's culture could have changed so dramatically between 2006, when the firm was so generally admired, and 2009, when it became so widely vilified. Once I decided that these questions were worth investigating—whether Goldman's culture had changed and, if so, how and why—I chose to start from 1979, when John Whitehead, cochairman and senior partner, codified Goldman's values in its famous "Business Principles." As many at Goldman will point out, those written principles are almost exactly the same today as they were in 1979. However, that doesn't necessarily mean adherence to them or that the interpretation of them hasn't changed. What I've discovered is that while Goldman's culture has indeed changed from 1979 to today, it didn't happen for a single, simple reason and it didn't happen overnight. Nor was the change an inexorable slide from "good" to "evil," as some would have it.

There are two easy and popular explanations about what happened to the Goldman culture. When I was there, some people believed the culture was changing or had changed because of the shifts in organizational structure brought on by the transformation from private partnership to publicly traded company. Goldman had held its initial public offering (IPO) on the NYSE in 1999, the last of the major investment banks to do so. In fact, this was my initial hypothesis when I began my research. The second easy explanation is that, whatever the changes, they happened since Lloyd Blankfein took over as CEO and were the responsibility of the CEO and the trading-oriented culture some believe he represents.

I found that although both impacted the firm, neither is the one single or primary cause. In many ways, they are the results of the various pressures and changes. The story of what happened at Goldman after 1979 is messy and complex. Many seemingly unrelated pressures, events, and decisions over time, as well as their interdependent, unintended, and compounding consequences, slowly changed the firm's culture. Different elements of its culture and values changed at different times, at different speeds, and at different levels of significance in response to organizational, regulatory, technological, and competitive pressures.

But overall, what's apparent is that Goldman's response to these pressures to achieve its organizational goal of being the world's best and dominant investment bank (its IPO prospectus states, "Our goal is to be the advisor of choice for our clients and a leading participant in global financial markets." Its number three business principle is "Our goal is to provide superior returns to our shareholders.") was to grow—and grow fast.[9] Seemingly unrelated or insignificant events, decisions, or actions that were rationalized to support growth then combined to cause unintended cultural transformations.

Those changes were incremental and accepted as the norm, causing many people within the firm not to recognize them. In addition, the firm's apparent adherence to its principles and a strong commitment to public and community service gave Goldman employees a sense of higher purpose than just making money. That helped unite them and drive them to higher performance by giving their work more meaning. At the same time, however, it was used to rationalize incremental changes in behavior that were inconsistent with the original meaning of its principles. *If we're principled and serve a sense of higher purpose*, the reasoning went, *then what we're doing must be OK.*

Since 1979, Goldman's commitment to public service has ballooned in both dollar amounts and time, something that should be commended. But this exceptional track record prevents employees from fully understanding the business purpose of this service, which is expanding and deepening the power of the Goldman network, including its government ties (the firm is pilloried by some as "Government Sachs"). Some at Goldman have even claimed that having many alumni in important positions has "disadvantaged" the firm.[10]

For example, a Goldman spokesman was quoted in a 2009 *Huffington Post* article as saying, "What benefit do we get from all these supposed connections? I would say we were disadvantaged from having so many alumni in important positions. Not only are we criticized—sticks and stones may break my bones but words do hurt, they really do—but we also didn't get a look-in when Bear Stearns was being sold and with Washington Mutual. We were runner-ups in the auction for IndyMac, in the losing group for BankUnited. If all these connections are supposed to swing things our way, there's just one bit missing in the equation." The spokesman added that government agencies have bent over backward to avoid any perception of impropriety, explaining that when the firm's executives would meet with then-Treasury Secretary Paulson, "it was impossible to have a conversation with him without it being chaperoned by the general counsel of Treasury."[11]

The vast majority of the employees, who joined Goldman decades after the original principles were written, do not really know the original meaning of the principles. Always putting clients' interests first, for instance, originally implied the need to assume a higher-than-required legal responsibility (a high moral or ethical duty) to clients. At the time, the firm was smaller and could be more selective as it grew. However, over time, the meaning slowly shifted (generally unnoticed) to implying the need to assume only the legally required responsibility to clients. As the firm grew, the law of large numbers made it harder for Goldman to be as selective. A legal standard allowed Goldman to increase the available opportunities for growth.

In accommodating this shift, those within Goldman, including senior leaders, increasingly relied on the rationalization that its clients were "big boys," a phrase implying that clients were sophisticated enough to recognize and understand potential risks and conflicts in dealing with Goldman, and therefore could look out for themselves. And in cases when the firm was concerned about potential legal liability, it even had clients sign a "big boy letter," a legal recognition of potential conflicts and Goldman's various roles and risks by the client in dealing with Goldman. This is in keeping with Goldman's general explanation of its role in the credit crisis: it did nothing legally wrong, but was simply acting as a "market maker" (simply matching buyers and sellers of securities), and it responsibly fulfilled all its legal obligations in this role. This argument is also reflective of a shift in the firm's business balance to the dominance of trading, as generally the interpretation of the responsibilities to a client are more often legal in nature, with required legal disclosures and standards of duty in dealing in an environment in which there is a tension in a buying and selling relationship of securities in trading, versus a more often advisory relationship in banking.

It's important to note in examining the change at Goldman that, as we'll explore, certain elements of the firm's organizational culture from 1979, like strong teamwork, remain intact enough that the firm is still highly valued by clients and potential employees and was able to maneuver through the financial crisis more successfully than its competitors. The slower and less intense change in certain elements is a factor in why many at Goldman seem to either miss or willfully ignore the changes in business practices and policies. Also complicating the recognition of the changes is that some of them have helped the firm reach many of its organizational goals.

While many clients may be disappointed and frustrated with the firm, and many question both its protection of confidential client information and its rationalizations for its various roles in transactions, at the same time they feel that Goldman has the unique ability to use its powerful network and gather and share information throughout the firm, thereby providing excellent execution relative to its competitors. As for ethics, many clients reject Goldman's general belief that it is ethically superior to the rest of Wall Street; nonetheless, many clients consider ethics only one factor in their selection of a firm, albeit one that may make them more wary in dealing with Goldman than in the past.

The frustration with the kind of analysis I've undertaken is that it's tempting to ask who or what event or decision is responsible. We want to identify a single source—something or someone—to blame for the change in culture. The desire is for a clear cause-and-effect relationship, and often for a villain. The story of Goldman is too messy for that kind of explanation. Instead, we need to ask what is responsible—what set of conditions, constraints, pressures, and expectations changed Goldman's culture.

One thing I learned in studying sociology is that the organization and its external environment matter. The nature of an organization and its connection to the external environment shape an organization's culture and can be reflected through changes in structure, practices, values, norms, and actions. If you get rid of the few people supposedly responsible for violations of cultural or legal standards, when new ones take over the behavior continues. We need to look beyond individuals, striving to understand the larger organizational and social context at play.

I don't intend my analysis as a value judgment on Goldman's cultural change. I purposely set aside the question of whether the change was overall for the better or worse. My primary intent is to illuminate a process whereby a firm that had largely upheld a higher ethical standard shifted to a more legal standard, and how companies more generally are vulnerable to such "organizational drift."

———————

This is the story of an organization whose culture has slowly drifted, and my story demonstrates why and how. The concept of *drift* is established, but still developing, in the academic research literature on organizational behavior (what I refer to as organizational drift is sometimes described as *practical drift* or *cultural drift*).[12] *Organizational drift* is a process whereby an organization's culture, including its business practices, continuously and slowly moves, carried along by pressures, departing from an intended course in a way that is so incremental and gradual that it is not noticed. One reason for this is that the pursuit of organizational goals in a dynamic, complex environment with limited resources and multiple, conflicting organizational goals, often produces a succession of small, everyday decisions that add up to unforeseen change.[13]

Although my study focuses on the Goldman case, this story has much broader implications. The phenomenon of organizational drift is bigger than just Goldman. The drift Goldman has experienced— is experiencing, really—can affect any organization, regardless of its success. As Jack and Suzy Welch wrote in *Fortune*, "'Values drift' is pervasive in companies of every ilk, from sea to shining sea. Employees either don't know their organization's values, or they know that practicing them is optional. Either way the result is vulnerability to attack from inside and out, and rightly so."[14] And leaders of the organization may not be able to see that it is happening until there is a public blow up/failure or an insider who calls it out. The signs may indicate that the culture is not changing—based on leading market share, returns to shareholders, brand, and attractiveness as an employer—but slowly the organization loses touch with its original principles and values.

Figuring out what happened at Goldman is a fascinating puzzle that takes us into the heart of a dynamic complex organization in a dynamic complex environment. It is a story of intrigue involving an institution that garners highly emotional responses. But it is more than that. It raises questions that are fundamental to organizations themselves. Why and how do organizations drift from the spirit and meaning of the principles and values that made them successful in reaching many of its organizational goals? And what should leaders and managers do about it? It also raises serious questions about future risks to our financial system.

The impressive statistics of Goldman's many continuing successes, and of clients' willingness to condone possible conflicts because of its quality of execution, doesn't mean that the change in the firm's culture doesn't pose dangers both for Goldman and for the public in the future. For one thing, if Goldman's behavior moves continually closer to the legal line of what is right and wrong—a line that is dangerously ambiguous—it is increasingly likely to cross that line, potentially doing damage not only to clients but to the firm, and perhaps to the financial system (some argue the firm has already crossed it). We have seen several financial institutions severely weakened and even destroyed in recent memory due to a drift into unethical, or even illegal, behavior, even though this is often blamed on one or a few rogue individuals rather than on organizational culture. Obviously this would be a terrible outcome for the many stakeholders of Goldman. However, Goldman is hardly an inconsequential or isolated organization in the economy; it is one of the most important and powerful financial institutions in the world. Its fate has serious potential consequences for the whole financial system. This doesn't go for just Goldman, but for all of the systemically important financial institutions.

I am not arguing or predicting that Goldman's drift will inevitably lead to organizational failure, or an ensuing disaster for the public (although there are those who believe that this has already happened), I am saying that the organizational drift is increasing that possibility. This is why it's important to illuminate why and how the organizational drift has come about.

A Little History

In considering how and why Goldman's interpretation of its business principles has changed, it's important to consider some key aspects of the firm's history, and why the principles were written.

According to my interviews with former Goldman co-senior partner John Whitehead, who drafted the principles, there was something special about the Goldman culture in 1979, one that brought it success and kept it on track even in tough times. He thought codifying those values, in terms of behaviors, would help transmit the Goldman culture to future generations of employees. The business principles were intended to keep everyone focused on a proven formula for success while staying grounded in the clear understanding that clients were the reason for Goldman's very existence and the source of the firm's revenues.

Whitehead emphasized the fact that he did not invent them; they already existed within the culture, and he simply committed them to paper. He did so because the firm was expanding faster than new people could be assimilated in 1979, and he thought it was important to provide new employees a means to acquire the Goldman ethic from earlier generations of partners who had learned by osmosis. Though by no means the force in the market the firm is today, Goldman had grown and changed a great deal from its early days and its size, complexity, and growth were accelerating.

Goldman Sachs was founded in 1869 in New York. Having made a name for itself by pioneering the use of commercial paper for entrepreneurs, the company was invited to join the NYSE in 1896. (For a summary timeline of selected events in Goldman's history, see appendix G.)

In the early twentieth century, Goldman was a player in establishing the initial public offering market. In 1906, it managed one of the largest IPOs of that time—that of Sears, Roebuck. However, in 1928 it diversified into asset management of closed end trusts for individuals who utilized significant leverage. The trusts failed as a result of the stock market crash in 1929, almost causing Goldman to close down and severely hurting the firm's reputation for many years afterward. After that, the new senior partner, Sydney Weinberg, focused the firm on providing top quality service to clients. In 1956, Goldman was the lead adviser on the Ford Motors IPO, which at the time was a major coup on Wall Street. To put Goldman's position on Wall Street in context at the time, in 1948 the US Department of

Justice filed an antitrust suit (*U.S. v. Morgan* [Stanley] *et al.,*) against Morgan Stanley and eighteen investment banking firms. Goldman had only 1.4 percent of the underwriting market and was last on the list of defendants. The firm was not even included in a 1950 list of the top seventeen underwriters. However, slowly the firm continued to grow in prestige, power, and market share.

The philosophy behind the firm's rise was best expressed by Gus Levy, a senior partner (with a trading background) at Goldman from 1969 until his death in 1976, who is attributed with a maxim that expressed Goldman's approach: "greedy, but long-term greedy."[15] The emphasis was on sound decision-making for long-term success, and this commitment to the future was evidenced by the partners' reinvestment in the firm of nearly 100 percent of the earnings.[16]

Perhaps surprisingly, although it's had many triumphs, over its history Goldman has had a mixed track record.[17] It has been involved in several controversies and has come close to bankruptcy once or twice.

Another common misperception among the public is that today Goldman primarily provides investment banking services for large corporations because the firm works on many high-profile M&A deals and IPOs; however, investment banking now typically represents only about 10 to 15 percent of revenue, substantially lower than the figure during the 1980s, when it accounted for half of the revenue. Today, the majority of the revenues comes from trading and investing its own capital. The profits from trading and principal investing are often disproportionately higher than the revenue because the businesses are much more scalable than investment banking.

Even though the firm was growing when Whitehead wrote the principles, its growth in more recent years has been even more accelerated, particularly overseas. In the early 1980s the firm had a few thousand employees, with around fifty to sixty partners (all US citizens), and less than 5 to 10 percent of its revenue came from outside the United States. In 2012, Goldman had around 450 partners (around 43 percent are partners with non-US citizenship) and 32,600 employees.[18] Today about 40 percent of Goldman's revenue comes from outside the United States and it has offices in all major financial centers around the world, with 50 percent of its employees based overseas.

Once regulations were changed in 1970 to allow investment banks to go public on the NYSE, Goldman's partners debated changing from a private partnership to a public corporation. The decision to go public in an IPO was fraught with contention, in part because the partners were concerned about how the firm's culture would change. They were concerned that the firm would change to being more "short-term greedy" to meet outside stock market investors' demands versus being "long-term greedy," which had generally served the firm so well. The partners had voted to stay a privately held partnership several times in its past, but finally the partners voted to go public, which it did in 1999. Goldman was the last of the major investment banking firms to go public, with the other major holdout, its main competitor Morgan Stanley, having done so in 1986. In their first letter addressing public shareholders in the 1999 annual report, the firm's top executives wrote, "As we begin the new century, we know that our success will depend on how well we change and manage the firm's rapid growth. That requires a willingness to abandon old practices and discover new and innovative ways of conducting business. Everything is subject to change—everything but the values we live by and stand for: teamwork, putting clients' interests first, integrity, entrepreneurship, and excellence."[19] They specifically stated they did not want to adjust the firm's core values, and they included putting clients' interests first and integrity, but they knew upholding the original meaning of the principles would be a challenge and certain things had to change.

Although the principles have generally remained the same as in 1979, there was one important addition to them around the time of the IPO—"our goal is to provide superior returns to our shareholders"— which introduced an intrinsic potential conflict or ambiguity between putting the interests of clients first (which was a Goldman self-imposed ethical obligation) and those of outside shareholders (which is a legally defined duty), as well as the potential conflict of doing what was best for the long term versus catering to the generally short-term perspective from outside, public market investors. There's always a natural tension between business owners who want to make the highest profits possible and clients who want to buy goods and services for as low as possible, to make their profits the highest possible. Being a small private partnership allowed Goldman the flexibility to make its own decisions about what was best in its own interpretation of *long term* in order to help address this tension. Having various outside shareholders all with their own time horizons and objectives, combined with Goldman's legal duty to put outside shareholders' (not clients') priorities first, makes the interpretation and execution of long term much more complicated and difficult.

When questioned about the potential for conflict, Goldman leaders have asserted that the firm has been able to ethically serve both the interests of clients and those of shareholders, and for many years, that assertion for the most part was not loudly challenged. That was largely due to Goldman's many successes, including leading market position and strong returns to shareholders, and rationalized by the many good works of the firm and its alumni, which served to address concerns about conflicts, even most of the way through the 2008 crisis.

At the beginning of the crisis, Goldman was mostly praised for its risk management. During the credit crisis, Goldman outperformed most of its competitors. Bear Stearns was bought by J.P. Morgan with government assistance. Lehman Brothers famously went bankrupt, and Merrill Lynch was acquired by Bank of America. Morgan Stanley Dean Witter & Co. sold a stake to Mitsubishi UFJ. But the overall economic situation deteriorated very quickly, and Goldman, as well as other banks, accepted government assistance and became a bank holding company. The company got a vote of confidence with a multi-billion-dollar investment from Berkshire Hathaway, led by legendary investor Warren Buffett. But soon after, things changed, and Goldman, along with the other investment banks, was held responsible for the financial crisis. The fact that so many former Goldman executives held positions in the White House, Treasury, the Federal

Reserve Bank of New York, and the Troubled Asset Relief Program in charge of the bailouts (including Hank Paulson, the former CEO of Goldman and then secretary of the Treasury) even as the bank took government funds and benefited from government actions, raised concerns about potential conflicts of interest and excessive influence. People started to question if Goldman was really better and smarter, or wasn't just more connected, or engaged in unethical or illegal practices in order to gain an advantage.

In April 2010, the Securities and Exchange Commission (SEC) charged Goldman with defrauding investors in the sale of a complex mortgage investment. Less than a month later, Blankfein and other Goldman executives attempted to answer scorching questions from Senator Carl Levin (D-Mich.), chair of the Permanent Subcommittee on Investigations, and other senators about the firm's role in the financial crisis. The executives were grilled for hours in a publicly broadcasted hearing. The senators pulled no punches, calling the firm's practices unethical, if not illegal. Later, after a Senate panel investigation, Levin called Goldman "a financial snake pit rife with greed, conflicts of interest, and wrongdoing."[20] But lawmakers at the hearings made little headway in getting Goldman to concede much, if anything specific, that the company did wrong.[21]

In answering questions about whether Goldman made billions of dollars of profits by "betting" on the collapse in subprime mortgage bonds while still marketing subprime mortgage deals to clients, the firm denied the allegations; Goldman argued it was simply acting as a market maker, partnering buyers and sellers of securities. Certain Goldman executives at the time showed little regret for whatever role the firm had played in the crisis or for the way it treated its clients. One Goldman executive said, "Regret to me is something you feel like you did wrong. I don't have that."[22]

There does seem to have been some internal acknowledgment that the culture had changed or at least should change. Shortly after the hearing, in response to public criticism, Goldman established the business standards committee, cochaired by Mike Evans (vice chairman of Goldman) and Gerald Corrigan (chairman of Goldman's GS Bank USA, and former president of the Federal Reserve Bank of New York), to investigate its internal business practices. Blankfein acknowledged that there were inconsistencies between how Goldman employees viewed the firm and how the broader public perceived its activities. In 2011, the committee released a sixty-three page report, which detailed thirty-nine ways the firm planned to improve its business practices. They ranged from changing the bank's financial reporting structure to forming new oversight committees to adjusting its methods of training and professional development. But it is unclear in the report whether Goldman specifically acknowledged a need to more ethically adhere to the first principle. The report states, "We believe the recommendations of the Committee will strengthen the firm's culture in an increasingly complex environment. We must renew our commitment to our Business Principles—and above all, to client service and a constant focus on the reputational consequences of every action we take."[23] The use of the word "strengthen" suggests that the culture had been weakened, but the report is vague on this. According to the *Financial Times*, investors, clients, and regulators remained underwhelmed in the wake of the report by Goldman's efforts to change.[24]

A Goldman internal training manual sheds some more light on whether the firm acknowledged its adherence to its first business principle has changed. The *New York Times* submitted a list of questions in May 2010 to Goldman for responses that included "Goldman's Mortgage Compliance Training Manual from 2007 notes that putting clients first is 'not always straightforward.'"[25]

The point that putting clients first is not always straightforward is telling. It indicates a clear change in the meaning of the original first principle.

The notion that Goldman's culture has changed was given a very public hearing when, on March 14, 2012, former Goldman employee Greg Smith published his resignation letter on the op-ed page of the *New York Times*. In the widely distributed and read piece, Smith criticized the current culture at Goldman, characterizing it as "toxic," and specifically blamed Blankfein and Goldman president Gary Cohn for losing "hold of the firm's culture on their watch."[26]

Years ago, an academic astutely predicted and described this type of "whistle blowing" as being a result of cultural change and frustration. Edgar Schein, a now-retired professor at the MIT Sloan School of Management, wrote ". . . it is usually discovered that the assumptions by which the organization was operating had drifted toward what was practical to get the job done, and those practices came to be in varying degrees different from what the official ideology claimed . . . Often there have been employee complaints identifying such practices because they are out of line with what the organization wants to believe about itself, they are ignored or denied, sometimes leading to the punishment of the employees who brought up the information. When an employee feels strongly enough to blow the whistle, a scandal may result, and practices then may finally be reexamined. Whistle blowing may be to go to the newspapers to expose a practice that is labeled as scandalous or the scandal may result from a tragic event."[27] The publishing of Smith's letter certainly resulted in a scandal and an examination.[28]

Goldman and Me

The question of what happened to Goldman has special resonance for me. I have spent eighteen years involved with the firm in one way or another: twelve years working for Goldman in a variety of capacities, and another six either using its services as a client or working for one of its competitors. I still have many friends and acquaintances who work there.

In 2010, I was about to start teaching at Columbia University's Graduate School of Business and shortly would be accepted to the PhD program in sociology at Columbia. The sociology program in particular—which required that I find a research question for my

PhD dissertation—provided me with many of the tools I needed to start to answer my question. I decided to pursue a career as a trained academic instead of relying solely on my practical experiences. The combination of the two, I thought, would be more rewarding and powerful for both my students and myself. When I began the study that would become this book, my hypothesis was that the change in Goldman's culture was rooted in the IPO. I conjectured that what fundamentally changed the culture was the transformation—from a private partnership to a public company. As I learned more, I realized that the truth was more complicated.

My analysis of the process by which the drift happened is deeply informed by my own experiences. Though some may think this has made me a biased observer, I believe that my inside knowledge and experience in various areas of the firm—from being based in the United States to working outside the United States, from working in investment banking to proprietary trading, from being present pre- and post-IPO—combined with my academic training gives me a unique ability to gather and analyze data about the changes at Goldman. My close involvement with Goldman deeply informs my analysis, so it's worth reviewing the relationship. A brief overview of my career also reveals how Goldman's businesses work.

In 1992, fresh from undergraduate studies at the University of Chicago, I arrived at Goldman to work in the M&A department in the investment banking division. M&A bankers advise the management and boards of companies on the strategy, financing, valuation, and negotiations of buying, selling, and combining various companies or subsidiaries. For the next dozen years, I held a variety of positions of increasing responsibility. My work exposed me to various areas, put me in collaborative situations with Goldman partners and key personnel, and allowed me to observe or take part in events as they unfolded.

I rotated through several strategically important areas. First I worked in M&A in New York and then M&A in Hong Kong, where I witnessed the explosive international growth firsthand with the opening of the Beijing office. Next, I returned to New York to assist Hank Paulson on special projects; Paulson was then co-head of investment banking, on the management committee, and head of the Chicago office. Also, I worked with the principal investment area (PIA makes investments in or buys control of companies with money collectively from clients, Goldman, and employees). Then I returned to M&A, rising to the head of the hostile raid defense business (defending a company from unsolicited take-overs—one of the cornerstones of Goldman's M&A brand and reputation) and becoming business unit manager of the M&A department. Finally, I ended up as a proprietary trader and ultimately portfolio manager in the fixed income, commodities, and currencies division (FICC)—similar to an internal hedge fund—managing Goldman's own money. My rotations to a different geographic region and through different divisions were typical at the time for a certain percentage of selected employees in order to train people and unite the firm.

Throughout my career at Goldman, I served on firm-wide and divisional committees, dealing with important strategic and business process issues. I also acted as special assistant to several senior Goldman executives and board members, including Hank Paulson, on select projects and initiatives such as improving business processes and cross-department communication protocols. Goldman was constantly trying to improve and setting up committees with people from various geographic regions and departments to create initiatives. I was never a partner at Goldman. I participated in many meetings where I was the only nonpartner in attendance and prepared analysis or presentations for partner meetings, or in response to partner meetings, but I did not participate in "partner-only" meetings.

As a member of the M&A department, I worked on a team to advise board members and CEOs of leading multinational companies on large, technically complex transactions. For example, I worked on a team that advised AT&T on combining its broadband business with Comcast in a transaction that valued AT&T broadband at $72 billion. I also helped sell a private company to Warren Buffett's Berkshire Hathaway. As the head of Goldman's unsolicited take-over and hostile raid defense practice, I worked on a team advising a client involved in a proxy fight with activist investor Carl Icahn.

When I joined Goldman, partnership election at the firm was considered one of the most prestigious achievements on Wall Street, in part because the process was highly selective and a Goldman partnership was among the most lucrative. The M&A department had a remarkably good track record of its bankers being elected—probably one of the highest percentages of success in the firm at the time. The department was key to the firm's brand, because representing prestigious blue chip clients is important to Goldman's public perception of access and influence that makes important decision makers want to speak to Goldman. M&A deals were high profile, especially hostile raid defenses. M&A was also highly profitable and did not require much capital. For all these reasons, a job in the department was highly prized, and the competition was fierce. When the New York M&A department hired me, it was making about a dozen offers per year to US college graduates to work in New York, out of what I was told were hundreds of applicants.

While in the department, I was asked to be the business unit manager (informally referred to as the "BUM"). I addressed issues of strategy, business processes, organizational policy, business selection, and conflict clearance. For example, I was involved in discussions in deciding whether and how Goldman should participate in hostile raids, and in discussing client conflicts and ways to address them. The job was extremely demanding. After a relatively successful stint, I felt I had built enough goodwill to move internally and do what I was more interested in: being an investor. I hoped to ultimately move into proprietary trading or back to Principal Investment Area (PIA), Goldman's private equity group.

Many banking partners tried to dissuade me from moving out of M&A. However, I wanted to become an investor, and a few partners who were close friends and mentors helped me delicately maneuver into proprietary investing. I was warned, "If you lose money, you will most likely get fired, and do not count on coming back to banking at Goldman. But if you make money for the firm, then you will get more money to manage, which will allow you to make more money for the firm and yourself."

Today people ask me whether I saw the writing on the wall—that the shift to proprietary trading was well under way and would continue at Goldman—and whether that's why I moved. To be honest, I didn't give it as much thought as I should have. My work in helping manage the M&A department and assisting senior executives on various projects exposed me to other areas of the firm and the firm's strategy and priorities. When you're in M&A, you work around the clock. You don't have time for much reflection or career planning. (This may be, upon reflection, part of the business model and be a contributor to the process of organizational drift.) You're working so intensely on high-profile deals—those that end up on page 1 of the *Wall Street Journal*—that you're swept up in the importance of the firm's and your work. Your bosses tell you how important you are and how important the M&A department is to the firm. They remind you that the real purpose of your job is to make capital markets more efficient and ultimately provide corporations with more efficient ways to finance. So you rationalize that there's a noble and ethical reason for what you and the firm are doing. In general, I greatly respected most of the investment banking partners that I knew. And I certainly didn't have the academic training, distance, or perspective to analyze the various pressures and small changes going on at the firm and their consequences. I do remember simply feeling like I should be able to do what I wanted and what I was interested in at Goldman—an entitlement that I certainly did not feel earlier in my career, and maybe one I picked up from observations or the competitive environment for Goldman-trained talent.

Paulson, a banker, was running the firm, and several others from banking whom I considered mentors held important positions. So even though it was no secret that revenues from investment banking had declined as a percentage of the total, I didn't think very much about that, nor did I consider its consequences. One longtime colleague and investment banking partner pulled me aside to tell me that moving into proprietary trading was the smartest thing I could do and that he wished he could take my place. When I asked why, he said, "More money than investment banking partners, faster advancement, shorter hours, better lifestyle, you learn how to manage your own money, and, one day, you can leave and start your own hedge fund and make even more money—and Goldman will support you." I assured him I was only trying to do what interested me, but I agreed it would be nice to travel less, work only twelve-hour days, and spend more time with my wife and our newborn daughter. When I asked why he didn't tell me this before, he said, "Then we would have had to find and train someone else."

I became a proprietary trader and then a portfolio manager in Goldman's FICC Special Situations Investing Group (SSG). We built it into one of the largest, most successful dedicated proprietary trading areas at Goldman and on Wall Street. Created during the late 1990s, SSG initially primarily invested Goldman's money in the debt and equity of financially stressed companies and made loans to high-risk borrowers (although we expanded the mandate over time). SSG was separated from the rest of the firm, meaning we sat on a floor separate from the trading desks that dealt with clients. We were called on as a client by salespeople at Goldman and the rest of Wall Street as if we were a distinct hedge fund. We did not deal with clients.

Even separated as we were, we had the potential for at least the perception of conflicts of interest with clients. For example, we could own the stock or debt of a company when, unknown to us, the company would hire Goldman's M&A department to review strategic alternatives or execute a capital market transaction such as an equity or debt offering. In that case we could be "frozen," meaning we were restricted from buying any more related securities or selling the position, something that would place us at a potential disadvantage because we could not react to new information. If we wanted to buy the securities of a company, and unbeknownst to us Goldman's bankers were advising the company on a transaction, we could be blocked from the purchase.

The biggest advantage I believed we had over our competitors—primarily hedge funds—was that we had a great recruiting and training machine in Goldman; we could pick the very best people in the company. Most had heard that we were extremely entrepreneurial, that we gave our people a lot of responsibility and ability to make a larger impact, that we were extremely profitable, and that we paid very well. Those from SSG also had an excellent track record of eventually leaving to set up or join existing hedge funds. We also had infrastructure—technology, risk management systems, and processes—that was unmatched by Wall Street banks, because Goldman invested heavily in it, recognizing the strategic importance of the competitive advantage it gave us.

We were trained to run investing businesses (for example, evaluating and managing people and risk or setting goals and measureable metrics). We had access to almost any corporate management team or government official through the cachet of the Goldman name and its powerful network. We also had a low cost of capital, because Goldman borrowed money at very low rates from debt investors, money that we then invested and generated a return a good deal higher than the cost of borrowing. We had one client—Goldman—and this was good, because it meant we did not have to approach lots of clients to raise funds. However, it was also a bad thing, because all the capital came from one investor. If Goldman (or the regulators, as later happened with the Volcker Rule) decided it should no longer be in the business, you were out of a job, although it was likely many others would want to hire you.

When I started in proprietary trading in FICC, I immediately noticed one big difference from the banking side. Although my new bosses were smart, sophisticated, and supportive, and as demanding as my investment banking bosses, there was an intense focus on measuring relatively short-term results because they were measurable. Our performance as investors was *marked to market* every day, meaning that the value of the trades we made was calculated every day, so there was total transparency about how much money we'd made or lost for the firm each and every day. This isn't done in investment banking, although each year new performance metrics were being added by the time I left for FICC. Typically in banking, relationships take a long time to develop and pay off. A bad day in banking may mean that, after years of meetings and presentations performed for free, a client didn't select you to execute a transaction. You could offer excuses: "The other bank offered to loan them money," "They were willing to do it much cheaper," and so on. It was never that you got out-hustled or that the other firm had better people, ideas, coordination, relationships, or expertise, something that would negatively reflect on you or the firm (or both). In proprietary trading, there were no excuses for bad days of losses. We were expected to make money whether the markets went up or down. There was another thing I learned quickly. One could be right as a trader, but have the timing wrong in the short term and be fired with losses that then quickly turned around into the projected profits. In addition, relative to banking, in judging performance the emphasis seemed to tilt toward how much money one made the firm versus more subjective and less immediately profitable contributions. The fear of this transparency and the potential for failure kept many bankers from moving to trading.

I later discovered that Goldman's proprietary trading areas actually maintained a longer-term perspective than did most trading desks and hedge funds, where a daily, weekly, or (at most) monthly focus was generally the norm. Our bosses reviewed information about our investments daily, but they tended to have a bias toward evaluating performance on a quarterly and even yearly basis (but much shorter than evaluating a client relationship in banking, which could take years). We were held accountable and were compared on risk-based performance against hedge fund peers, as well as other Goldman desks. If we found good opportunities, we got access to capital and invested it. Theoretically, when we didn't see attractive opportunities, we were to sell our positions and return the money to Goldman, with the understanding that we had access to it when we felt there were attractive opportunities.

However, I learned there was a perverse incentive to keep as much money as possible and invest it to make the firm as much money as possible—and yourself as much money as possible—even if the risk and reward might not be as favorable as other groups' opportunities. There was a feeling that we were "paid to take risks," and the larger the risks you took, or were able to take, the more important you were to the organization. We did have a critical advantage over most banks—we knew that many of our bosses and those at the very top of the firm understood, and were not afraid of, risk. Many had managed risk and knew how to evaluate it. They also would sometimes leave us voicemails or discuss in meetings their feelings or perspectives on the current environment and risks.

In my conversations with former competitors, I later learned that Goldman's approach to managing proprietary traders was substantially different from theirs. For example, if we lost a meaningful amount of money in an investment while I was at SSG, we would sit down with our bosses (and sometimes other traders not in our area) to rationally discuss and debate alternatives, such as exiting all or some of the position, buying more ("doubling down"), hedging the downside, or reversing our position and making an opposite bet. I learned that traders from other firms generally did not sit down with others to discuss alternatives. Rather, most often they were simply told to sell and realize the loss of money-losing investments ("cut your losses"), because their bosses or their bosses' bosses didn't understand the risks. Competitors' traders told me they couldn't comprehend the idea of our getting together with someone as senior as the president of the firm, and especially traders outside our area, to discuss and debate the attractiveness of an investment. For this reason, traders at other firms did not get as many great learning opportunities or would make poor decisions.

When I left in 2004, the firm was very successful in reaching certain organizational goals. It had the best shareholder returns and continued to recruit the best and brightest people in the industry. It had access to almost any important decision maker in the world. The culture and working environment were such that a motivated, creative person felt as if he or she could accomplish just about anything; all one had to do was convince people of the merits of the idea. But the firm felt different: it was much larger, it was more global, and it was involved in many more businesses. One could certainly start to feel the greater emphasis on trading and principal investing. The bureaucracy had grown, and as SSG grew and diversified we were increasingly encountering turf wars with other areas. I knew fewer people, especially senior partners, many of whom had retired by 2004, so I also felt a weaker social tie to the firm.

At the same time, there was great demand from outside investors (including Goldman Sachs Asset Management) to give money to Goldman proprietary traders to start their own firms and invest. Also the firm's prime brokerage business and alumni network had a great track record for helping former proprietary traders start their own firms. I felt I had a good track record and reputation, and enough support from Goldman and many of its employees and alums who were friends, to start my own investment business.

With my savings from bonuses, and with my 1999 IPO stock grant and other shares fully vested on the fifth anniversary of the IPO, I left Goldman in 2004 to cofound a global alternative asset management company with an existing hedge fund that already had approximately twenty people and $2 billion in assets under management. Shortly after, several Goldman investment professionals joined me. Less than four years later, I had helped expand the firm to 120 people and $12 billion in assets under management.[28] I was the chief investment officer and helped manage and oversee over $5 billion, about half of the firm's assets, through multiple vehicles focused on the United States and Europe. Also, I helped start several other funds while also serving on all of the firm's major investment committees. In my position, I saw firsthand the competitive, organizational, technologi-cal, and regulatory pressures facing an organization (also a private partnership) as well as the organizational challenges of growth. I maintained a close relationship with Goldman, becoming a trad-ing and prime brokerage client and coinvested with Goldman. My partners and I also hired Goldman to represent us in selling our asset management firm. In early 2008, we announced a transaction valu-ing the firm at $974 million.[29] So I also experienced what it meant to be a trading and banking client of Goldman's and am able to compare the experience versus other firms.

I have also worked for one of Goldman's competitors at a very senior level, as an executive at Citigroup from 2010 to 2012 in various roles, including chief of staff to the president and COO, vice chair-man and chief of staff to the CEO of the institutional clients group (ICG), and member of the executive, management, and risk manage-ment committees of that group.[30] When I joined Citi, it was under political and public scrutiny for taking government funds, and the government still owned Citi shares. It was a complex business with many organizational challenges; it was an intense experience, with me starting work at 5:30 a.m. almost every day to be prepared to meet with my boss at 6 a.m. My experience at Citigroup was criti-cal in my development of a new perspective on Goldman and the industry. Citigroup has approximately 265,000 people in more than 100 countries. In addition to being much larger (in total assets and number of employees) than Goldman, Citigroup is much more com-plex, because it participates in many more businesses (such as con-sumer and retail banking and treasury services) and locally in many more countries. In addition, unlike Goldman, Citigroup was created through a series of mergers and acquisitions. At Citi, I had the chance to compare the practices and approaches of a Goldman competitor that had a big balance sheet (supported by customer deposits to lend money to clients) and that had grown quickly through acquisitions—two things Goldman did not really do.

Before working at Citigroup and during the financial crisis, I advised McKinsey & Company on strategic, business process, risk, and organizational issues facing financial institutions and related regulatory authorities worldwide. McKinsey is one of the most prestigious and trusted management-consulting firms in the world, with some fifteen thousand people globally. There are many differences between the firms, but as with Goldman (before Goldman became a public corporation), McKinsey is a private partnership that has a revered partnership election process. Goldman and McKinsey compete for the best and brightest graduates every year, and there are elements of the McKinsey culture that are similar in many ways to Goldman's, especially to the Goldman I knew when I started. When attending McKinsey training programs, I could have closed my eyes and replaced the word *McKinsey* with *Goldman*, and it would have been like my 1992 Goldman training program all over again. McKinsey has an intense focus on recruiting, training, socialization of new members, and teamwork. It also has long-standing, revered, written business principles. Lastly, it has an incredible global network.

The people at McKinsey are incredibly thoughtful and hard working and have very high standards of integrity, and I learned a great deal about how they built and grew the business globally and added new practices while trying to preserve a distinct culture. McKinsey provided me the context of a large, global, growing advisory firm. McKinsey emphasized "client impact" over "commercial effectiveness" in evaluating its partners. With McKinsey, I also gained exposure to many other financial institutions, along with their senior management teams, their processes, and their cultures, and this exposure also helped put my experiences at Goldman—and the reaction of its management teams to various pressures—into context. Lastly, I had hired and worked with McKinsey as a client, and am able to compare that experience as a client versus being a client of other firms, including Goldman.

Subtle Changes Made Obvious

To give you a better sense of the shift I noticed and the organizational drift I'm talking about, I want to offer a set of comparative stories—"before" and "after" snapshots—to illuminate the differences. They illustrate the shift in the client-adviser relationship as well as in Goldman's practice of putting the clients' interests first.

This post-1979 historic commitment to always putting clients' interests first and signifying more then a legal standard is demonstrated by a 1987 event. Goldman stood to lose $100 million, a meaningful hit to the partners' personal equity at the time, on the underwriting of the sale of 32 percent of British Petroleum, owned by the British government. The global stock market crash in October had left other investment banks that had committed to the deal trying to analyze their legal liability and their legal rights to nullify their commitment, but Goldman stood firm in honoring its commitment despite the cost and despite Goldman's legal claims. Senior partner John L. Weinberg explained to the syndicate, "Gentlemen, Goldman Sachs is going to do it. Because if we don't do it, those of you who decide not to do it, I just want to tell you, you won't be underwriting a goat house. Not even an outhouse."[30]

The decision was not a simple matter of altruism. The principle of standing by its commitment had long-term economic benefits for Goldman. Weinberg was able to see beyond a short-term loss, even a large one, and to consider Goldman's longer-term ambition to increase its share of the privatization business in Europe. That could be achieved only by living up to its commitments to clients, even beyond the legal commitment. His decision was consistent with the standard of the original meaning of the first principle: "Our clients' interests always come first." In addition, it illustrates the nuance between "long-term greedy" and "short-term greedy."

More than twenty years later, this standard of commitment to clients beyond legal responsibility has largely been lost. Goldman policy adviser and former SEC chairman Arthur Levitt has challenged the "clients first" principle because "it doesn't recognize the reality of the trading business."[31] He points out that Goldman's sales and trading revenues outstrip those of the advisory businesses, financing, and money management, and there are no clients in sales and trading—only buyers and sellers. There should be transparency, Levitt suggests, but no expectation of a "fellowship of buyers and sellers that will march into the sunset" together. Goldman should stop using "clients first" in promoting itself, Levitt argues, because of the conflicts inherent in trading—the natural and ever-present tension between buyers and sellers.

This argument hit home for me when I compared one of my first experiences as an analyst at Goldman with my later experience as a Goldman client. When I was a first-year financial analyst in 1992, I was assigned to work with Paulson and a team of investment bankers to advise the Chicago-based consumer goods company Sara Lee Corporation. The project was to review Sara Lee's financial and strategic alternatives related to a particular management decision. Paulson was demanding, and he instructed us to leave no stone unturned.

We worked 100-hour weeks, fueled by Froot Loops and Coca Cola for breakfast and McDonald's hamburgers and fries for lunch and dinner. We performed all sorts of financial analysis, trying to make sure we thought of every possible alternative and issue. We also collected ideas from all the experts Goldman had. In the end, we had a presentation book 50 to 70 pages long for the client, plus another 100-page backup book. We made sure that every *i* was dotted and *t* was crossed, every number corresponded to another number, every financial calculation was accurate, and every number that needed a footnote had one. Perfection and excellence were expected—not only by Paulson but also by everyone else at the firm—no matter the personal sacrifice.

At Sara Lee's offices, all five of us from Goldman, including Paulson, waited anxiously to go into the meeting. When we were ushered into the boardroom, we took seats across the table from Sara Lee's CEO,

John H. Bryan, who would one day join the board of Goldman. After saying our hellos, we started putting our material out on the table. However, Paulson sat down next to Bryan, across the table from the rest of the Goldman team. After Paulson made some introductory remarks, speaking to Bryan as if no one else was in the room, we started presenting our analysis, the pros and cons of the alternatives, and our recommendations. (I had no speaking role; I was at the meeting in case someone asked any questions about the numbers. This was customary at Goldman—to watch and learn.)

Throughout the meeting, Paulson asked questions that he felt should be on Bryan's mind, challenging us—grilling us, really—and posing follow-up questions to Bryan's own. I wondered, *Which one is the client—Bryan or Paulson?* That's when I learned an important lesson: they were one and the same. To Paulson, and therefore to Goldman, Bryan was not a client; rather, he was a friend. This was Goldman's first business principle in action. In that meeting, Paulson embodied the spirit of that principle and of Goldman at its best. He didn't just walk a mile in the client's shoes; he ran a marathon. This rigor of service, along with his Midwestern work ethic and values, led not only to his own many professional successes but also to the many successes for his clients and for the firm he would one day lead.

Flash-forward to 2008. After I left Goldman and my partners and I decided to review strategic alternatives for our firm, I moved to the other side of the table as a Goldman banking client. After interviewing several investment banks, I voted to hire Goldman because it had the best overall team, knowledge about the markets, understanding of how to present our firm, and access to the key decision makers at potential buying firms. However, I noticed a contrast with my early years at Goldman. I certainly did not feel as though anyone from Goldman was looking at things from my perspective in the same way Paulson had at Sara Lee. No Goldman banker sat on my side of the table and raised the questions I should have been considering. In fact, I was concerned that Goldman cared more about its larger and more important clients that might consider buying our firm (and would remain Goldman clients) than about us. I had the same sense with most of the other banks that pitched for the assignment. Maybe I held Goldman to a higher standard. When we hired Goldman, I requested that John S. Weinberg—the grandson and son of former Goldman senior partners, and someone I had worked for at Goldman—help oversee the project. I felt he embodied the spirit and standards that had been in effect when I had joined the firm. Goldman was highly professional and extremely capable, but for some reason the shift was enough for me to want John S. Weinberg involved. (For more information about the Weinberg family and other key Goldman partners, see appendix F.)

The Study

While my experiences at Citigroup and McKinsey, as well as in helping build a firm, combined with distance, time, and maturity, helped put my experiences at Goldman into perspective, my insider experience also made me aware of how difficult it can be to perceive this kind of change from within, even though examples such as these may seem to suggest that the change should be obvious. Also, recognizing that change had occurred and understanding why and how that's the case are very different propositions. This is why the perspective from sociological theory is so helpful. Personal perspective isn't enough.

The analysis of Goldman that I offer here is based on established sociological approaches to studying organizational change, behavior, and innovation, an approach I've learned at both the sociology department and the business school at Columbia University. It doesn't come naturally to me. Having been a banker, consultant, and investor, typically I try to understand problems quantitatively. Those in the financial industry seem to share this trait, because they have a certain comfort with quantifying things and using numbers and metrics to hold people accountable. This approach is also followed by many regulators, policy makers, and economics and finance professionals. They focus on quantitative measures—such as imposing regulatory capital requirements or limiting activities to certain percentages—as the best way to prevent other crises.

The quantitative approach is reasonable, but it is not complete. Those trying to regulate Goldman and similar financial institutions have focused relatively little on the social activity, structures, and functions of their organizational culture—the hallmarks of the socio-logical approach—and I believe this focus will help get us closer to the root of the issues.

This book is based on my doctoral dissertation in sociology at Columbia, work that I started in 2011. It is the result of more than 100 hours of semistructured interviews with over fifty of Goldman's partners, clients, competitors, equity research analysts, investors, regulators, and legal experts.[32] I also researched business school case studies, news reports, and books about Goldman; quotations from those sources are peppered throughout the book. In addition, I ana-lyzed publicly available documents filed by Goldman with the SEC (including financial data), congressional testimony, and legal docu-ments filed in lawsuits against Goldman.

The purpose of going beyond interviews was to challenge, support, and illuminate the interviewees' and my own conclusions. I suspect that many of the people to whom I spoke are bound by nondisclosure agreements, but I never asked. I did agree that I would keep their par-ticipation confidential and not quote them. I did not take notes during the interviews, nor did I use a recording device. The only interviewee whose name I disclose, with his permission, is John Whitehead. He worked at Goldman from 1947 to 1984. Since he wrote the original business principles, he was able to clearly describe what he meant when he wrote them and what the culture was like at the time.[33]

It is not my intent to glorify or vilify any individual, group, or era in Goldman's history, although I suspect parts will be used to do so. I've tried not to be influenced by nostalgia for the Goldman that once was, and I've tried to recognize that the people I interviewed were looking back in hindsight and may have had agendas or other issues, something I tried to overcome by speaking to many different people and by balancing the interview data with other information and analysis. I've tried not to be affected by many people's contempt for the firm or by the recent economic recovery. I have relied on publicly available data to confirm and disprove various claims and theories advanced by those I interviewed.[34]

I do not wish to assert that the change in culture at Goldman I've analyzed is necessarily change for the worse, or that the changes will lead to an organizational failure or a disaster (though some would argue that it does). The concept of drift, loosely defined, has often been used to study how a series of small, seemingly inconsequential changes can lead to disaster, such as the explosion of the space shuttle *Challenger* or the accidental shooting of two Black Hawk helicopters over Iraq in 1994 by US F-15 fighter jets. Though the change at Goldman is different in a number of regards from both of those examples, they do nonetheless offer important insights into why and how Goldman's culture has drifted. In both cases—analyzed by Columbia University sociologist Diane Vaughan and Harvard Business School professor Scott Snook, respectively—pressures to meet organizational goals generally caused an unintended and unnoticed slow process of change in practices and the implementation of them, which in those cases led to major failures.[35] Each tiny shift made perfect sense in the local context, but together they created a recipe for disaster.

My analysis also draws on the sociological literature about the normalization of deviant behavior, which illuminates processes by which a deviance away from original values and culture can become socially normalized and accepted within an organization. Another factor that clearly comes through is that Goldman's business has become more complex, and that there is less cross-department and other communication, which contributed to what Diane Vaughan calls *structural secrecy*—the ways in which organizational structure, the flow of information, and business processes tend to undermine the understanding of change that may be taking place.[35] (For more on these concepts and an academic study of organizational cultural drift, see appendix A.)

My argument, in essence, is that Goldman came under numerous types of pressure—organizational, competitive, regulatory, techno-logical—to achieve growth, and that pressure, from both inside and outside of Goldman, resulted in many incremental changes. Those included changes in the structure of the firm, from a partnership to a public company, which in turn accelerated many changes already occurring at the firm. The change in structure also limited execu-tives' personal exposure to risk, as well as ushering in changes in compensation policies, which led to different incentives. The pres-sure for growth resulted in the mix of business also shifting over time, with trading becoming more dominant, which carried its own impetus for change. The growing complexity of the company's busi-ness also led both to more structural secrecy and to more potential for conflicts of interest. At the same time the external environment was also rapidly changing and impacting the firm.

These and many other changes, added up over time, caused Goldman to drift from the original interpretation of the firm's prin-ciples, most notably from the first principle of always putting clients' interests first. As the firm got larger and growth became more chal-lenging because of the law of large numbers, there was even more pres-sure to change the standards to allow the maximum opportunities. Those within Goldman were unable to appreciate the degree of change at the time, and are unable to now, due in part to a process of normalization of the deviance from the firm's principles that occurred as those changes unfolded. That blindness (or willful blindness) to the degree of change was enabled in part by rationalization and also by the sense that the firm serves a higher purpose because of the good works of the firm and its alumni, which mitigated against recogni-tion from within that the firm was engaging in conflicts.

Whether or not this process of drift is a harbinger of potential fail-ure at the firm is an open question. Certainly there is reason to worry that the many interdependent and compounding pressures that led

Goldman to slowly change and adopt its new standard of ethics from one that was a higher than legal requirement to meeting only the legal requirements will combine with its increasing size, more complexity, and greater interrelatedness, and the consequences will be an increasing risk of conflicts and organizational failure.

Since Goldman plays such a prominent role in the economy, as do other investment banks, this is an urgent issue for further exploration. Maybe even more so because I believe that Goldman is becoming even more important and powerful in our economic system. Goldman almost went bankrupt in the late 1920s, was struggling in 1994, and took government money directly and indirectly in order to hold off possible collapse in 2009 (Goldman denies this), even despite the profits or protection (depending on one's view) from the infamous "hedging" bets taken against toxic mortgage assets. Many other financial firms disappeared, of course; the economy was near collapse, and taxpayers were left with an enormous bill. I hope the analysis in this book can demonstrate that sociology can contribute to the public understanding and debate about risks in the system.

I also hope the book will help leaders and managers consider the dangers that can accompany the responses to organizational, competitive, technological, and regulatory pressures in striving to meet organizational goals.

Finally, I hope the book is an interesting journey inside Goldman, with which I'll also seek to answer a handful of questions that continue to nag other observers: why Goldman performed so well (relatively speaking) during the financial crisis, what role Lloyd Blankfein and the trading culture he is associated with played in the change, and why clients continue to flock to Goldman.

This book isn't intended as a history of Goldman—there are several authors who have admirably tackled that job (and without which this study would not be possible)—but I have also included a Goldman timeline and short biographies on selected Goldman executives in the appendices to help a reader unfamiliar with Goldman's history or people.

Part One

HOW GOLDMAN SUCCEEDED

Chapter 2

Shared Principles and Values

I N 1979, GOLDMAN CO-SENIOR PARTNER JOHN WHITEHEAD wrote down the firm's principles "one Sunday afternoon." Whitehead explained, "In the first draft, there were ten principles, and somebody told me that it looked too much like the Ten Commandments, so I made it into twelve. I believe it's up to fourteen now, because the lawyers got hold of it and they've changed a few words and added to it a little bit."[1] Although he helped bring in deal after deal and helped make strategic decisions for Goldman, Whitehead said that committing the firm's values to words on paper was his greatest contribution.[2] More than anything else, it was a statement about the perceived power of the codified values to nourish and support the partnership culture.[3]

From my interviews with those who were partners in the 1980s, it is apparent that all of them thought the principles reflected the culture and agreed with and relied upon them, which they believed allowed the firm to be less hierarchical than its peers.[4] Although many firms now have codified principles of ethical behavior (some more revered than others), Whitehead's commandments were revolutionary for the Wall Street at the time.[5] The principles promoted cohesiveness in a firm with decentralized management, among Goldman partners who were owners and managers of businesses.

The list of twelve principles was approved by the management committee—which is responsible for policy, strategy, and management of the business and is chaired by the head of the firm—and was then distributed to every Goldman employee. A copy was sent to each employee's home as well to help family members understand and cope with the long hours and extensive travel demanded of their loved ones.[6] Whitehead's hope was that family members would be proud of their association with an ethical firm that espoused high standards, and that employees—especially new partners with heavy travel schedules—would feel less guilty about spending so much time away from home.[7] Goldman managers were expected to hold quarterly group meetings for the sole purpose of discussing the firm's values and principles as they applied to the group's own business.[8] When I started at Goldman in 1992, it was typical, when introducing ourselves and the firm in initial meetings with clients, to include the "Firm Principles" on the first page of the presentation (essentially a sales pitch), letting the clients know what differentiated Goldman from its competitors.[9]

By the time of the tech boom in the late 1990s, the practice of managers holding regular meetings to specifically discuss the principles seems to have been discontinued, although they were certainly discussed in general meetings and in training sessions. One current Goldman partner told me that the principles are still talked about and discussed.[10] They have not been abandoned, but he believes they are not as revered as they once were. He told me he could not recall seeing the principles hanging on the walls like they used to, although they can be found in annual reports and on Goldman's website. However, the partner explained that with the recent regulatory and legal scrutiny, along with media attention, there is a renewed focus and more training sessions on the business principles.

Goldman's principles were modified slightly over the years when, as Whitehead put it, the lawyers got hold of them. I also remember when a fellow analyst wrote a memo in 1992 pointing out grammar and punctuation errors in the principles and sent it to a member of the management committee. I believe a few of his recommended changes were made. As mentioned earlier, the most significant modification to the list of principles, made just before Goldman went public, was the addition of the principle related to returns to shareholders, which was given prominence by being listed third.

Here are the principles (as updated, now including fourteen):

1. *Our clients' interests always come first.* Our experience shows that if we serve our clients well, our own success will follow.

2. *Our assets are our people, capital and reputation.* If any of these is ever diminished, the last is the most difficult to restore. We are dedicated to complying fully with the letter and spirit of the laws, rules and ethical principles that govern us. Our continued success depends upon unswerving adherence to this standard.

3. *Our goal is to provide superior returns to our shareholders.* Profitability is critical to achieving superior returns, building our capital, and attracting and keeping our best people. Significant employee stock ownership aligns the interests of our employees and our shareholders.

4. *We take great pride in the professional quality of our work.* We have an uncompromising determination to achieve excellence in everything we undertake. Though we may be involved in a wide variety and heavy volume of activity, we would, if it came to a choice, rather be best than biggest.

5. *We stress creativity and imagination in everything we do.* While recognizing that the old way may still be the best way, we constantly strive to find a better solution to a client's

problems. We pride ourselves on having pioneered many of the practices and techniques that have become standard in the industry.

6. *We make an unusual effort to identify and recruit the very best person for every job.* Although our activities are measured in billions of dollars, we select our people one by one. In a service business, we know that without the best people, we cannot be the best firm.

7. *We offer our people the opportunity to move ahead more rapidly than is possible at most other places.* Advancement depends on merit and we have yet to find the limits to the responsibility our best people are able to assume. For us to be successful, our men and women must reflect the diversity of the communities and cultures in which we operate. That means we must attract, retain and motivate people from many backgrounds and perspectives. Being diverse is not optional; it is what we must be.

8. *We stress teamwork in everything we do.* While individual creativity is always encouraged, we have found that team effort often produces the best results. We have no room for those who put their personal interests ahead of the interests of the firm and its clients.

9. *The dedication of our people to the firm and the intense effort they give their jobs are greater than one finds in most other organizations.* We think that this is an important part of our success.

10. *We consider our size as an asset that we try hard to preserve.* We want to be big enough to undertake the largest project that any of our clients could contemplate, yet small enough to maintain the loyalty, the intimacy and the esprit de corps that we all treasure and that contribute greatly to our success.

11. *We constantly strive to anticipate the rapidly changing needs of our clients and to develop new services to meet those needs.* We know that the world of finance will not stand still and that complacency can lead to extinction.

12. *We regularly receive confidential information as part of our normal client relationships.* To breach a confidence or to use confidential information improperly or carelessly would be unthinkable.

13. *Our business is highly competitive, and we aggressively seek to expand our client relationships.* However, we must always be fair competitors and must never denigrate other firms.

14. *Integrity and honesty are at the heart of our business.* We expect our people to maintain high ethical standards in everything they do, both in their work for the firm and in their personal lives.

The emphasis on the principles helped distinguish the firm, and over the years, most successful interview candidates were very familiar with them. The principles guided thousands of interactions each day—interactions that put the firm's reputation and partners' capital at risk.[11] One senior partner said, "As a small firm, we passed on our shared ideals and culture in an avuncular style. Everyone sat next to someone who was very experienced and had been there a long time. We were very small, concentrated in a few offices around the United States, so it was easy to do . . . Every boss I ever had worked harder than I did . . . This is a really good business and it's also a pleasant place to work, if you select the right people on the way in."[12] Goldman's principles also provided a way to substantiate the firm's trustworthiness in the eyes of clients and potential candidates.

The principles, combined with actual strategic business practice and policy decisions (such as not representing hostile raiders, as I discuss later), created for Goldman a powerful "good guy" image—both internally and externally. In 1984, a Morgan Stanley banker even publicly conceded that the principles and resulting practices made clients perceive Goldman as "less mercenary and more trustworthy than Morgan Stanley."[13]

The ultimate fate of the Water Street Corporate Recovery Fund provides a good example of Goldman's sensitivity to the potential impact of its strategic business decisions on the firm's reputation after the principles were written. In 1989, two Goldman partners convinced the management committee to commit as much as $100 million of the firm's money toward starting Water Street, a fund that bought controlling blocks of distressed high-yield junk bonds. The fund began soliciting outside investors in April 1990, with the goal of raising $400 million. Within a few months, Goldman had raised almost $700 million and stopped accepting investments. The partners were willing to give Water Street four years to see whether it could produce an annual return of 25 percent to 35 percent.[14] However, several corporate executives and large money-management firms complained to Goldman that the fund was a "vulture" investing business, claiming it was in direct conflict with the firm's reputation for acting at all times in the best interests of clients. The executives were particularly concerned that the fund was also being run by someone who was actively involved in Goldman's corporate finance advisory business. The dual roles would potentially allow the Water Street Fund to access confidential information from investment banking clients that it could use to benefit its investing. Nine of the twenty-one Water Street investments were in current or former clients. Even though the fund was making a lot of money for Goldman, the management committee, advised by John L. Weinberg, shut it down. At the time, investing clients who bought stocks and bonds also were threatening to boycott Goldman's trading desks because of their concern about potential conflicts (although many discounted that would actually happen). John L. was concerned that clients thought the fund violated Goldman's number one principle. According to partners I interviewed, the firm's decision to shut the fund down sent a powerful message, internally, especially considering how profitable the fund was. Many clients at the time also felt it sent a powerful message differentiating the firm from the principles of its competitors.

Best and Brightest

Goldman's corporate ethos, its common value system, John L. called "the glue that holds the firm together."[15] Goldman executives were conscious of sustaining this culture when recruiting and tried to hire the best of the best, but not just for their intelligence, drive, or experience. The partners looked for people who fit a certain profile: people who had all the requisite skills and knowledge, were hardworking and driven, and also espoused a value system consistent with Goldman's.[16] New hires were immersed in the Goldman culture and encouraged to apply their preexisting values and principles in a business context.

Goldman was not known as the highest payer on Wall Street for entry-level positions, and yet talented people often prioritized working for Goldman. Interviews revealed that they were attracted by the allure of partnership and the feeling that the firm's culture of putting clients' interests first and being long-term greedy was different from the other firms on Wall Street. They pointed to the principles and the firm's actions and policies, along with stories and lore that reinforced this differentiation.

Although many firms had high hiring standards, they did not as regularly send senior executives to college campuses to interview potential recruits. In the 1980s and 1990s, this was a critical part of a Goldman executive's job, an outward expression of the company's passion and culture. It was one of the roles of a *culture carrier*— someone who always put the firm and clients first, had the right priorities, cared about the firm's reputation, and put the firm's principles and long-term goals before short-term profits.[17]

Whitehead described Jimmy Weinberg, brother of John L. Weinberg, as "one of the most important culture carriers . . . He was an advocate of team play, no internal ugly competition, service to customers, putting the customers' interests before the firm's interests and all of those good things that make a partnership."[18] In a speech to the partnership, a partner stated, "Hiring the right people is the most important contribution you can make. Hire people better than yourself."[19]

Partners wanted people smarter even than they were, but they also wanted recruits who shared their values. The relatively low wages paid during employees' early years, partners thought, fostered an appropriately long-term perspective.[20] To this end, sometimes twenty or more employees, including several partners, often interviewed successful candidates. Whitehead told me that during his time, a potential candidate also had to be interviewed and approved by at least one secretarial assistant, because how one treated assistants was considered important. It showed one's values. Sometimes the interview process itself weeded out candidates better suited to a firm where "individual performance was applauded and assimilation was less important."[21] Author Charles Ellis notes that "extensive interviewing was becoming a firm tradition . . . It gave the firm multiple opportunities to assess a recruit's capabilities, interests, and personal fit with the firm . . . 'You could say that our commitment to interviewing was carried through to a fault.'"[22]

Whitehead was clear that, as a service business, Goldman needed to select the best people if it was to be the best firm: "Recruiting is the most important thing we can ever do. And if we ever stop recruiting very well, within just five years, we will be on that slippery down slope, doomed to mediocrity."[23] Active participation by the most senior partners underscored Goldman's emphasis on hiring the best people.[24]

Goldman also made sure that the future leaders devoted a "material" amount of time to recruiting. Rob Kaplan—who joined Goldman in 1983, went on to run investment banking, and retired as a vice chairman—credits Goldman's recruiting process with helping build a "powerhouse operation." He describes his impressions of the process: "I grew up [at Goldman]. We identified attracting, retaining, and developing superb talent as a critical priority. As a junior person, I was enormously impressed that the very senior leaders of the firm were willing to interview candidates and attend recruiting events on a regular basis. I learned from their example that there wasn't anything more important than recruiting and developing talent."[25]

As evidence of his commitment to recruiting, Whitehead personally conducted on-campus interviews. The qualities he looked for in potential recruits were "brains, leadership potential, and ambition in roughly equal parts."[26]

During a meeting I challenged him, saying that every firm claims to look for these qualities. "What about values?" I said.

Whitehead told me that he had overlooked the word *values* because it should have been obvious that Goldman would hire only people who exhibited values like the firm's. To him, it was the first prerequisite for employment—and the firm dedicated senior people to the task. Most importantly, he wanted people who shared the Goldman values and were willing to act in concert with its ethical principles both within the firm and in interactions with clients. For example, the boasting and displays of ego common on Wall Street were not welcome at Goldman; offenders were quickly reminded that their accomplishments were possible only because of everyone's hard work and contributions. Whitehead once admonished an associate for saying "I" rather than "we."[27] When I interviewed him, Whitehead himself used "we" instead of "I." To this day, my wife and non-Goldman friends tease me for the same subconscious substitution—it is that ingrained.

Goldman's practice was to hire directly from top business schools rather than from other firms because recent MBAs were more malleable; the "plasticity" of a young MBA's character made it easier to inculcate the Goldman ethos.[28] The firm's recruiting focused on merit rather than pedigree.[29] A privileged background was often a strike against a candidate: it was thought that perhaps he or she might not work as hard or be as careful with money as someone who had not come from wealth.

My own experience in interviewing for my job at Goldman in 1992 told me, in no uncertain terms, exactly what Goldman valued in an employee. A partner who interviewed me explained that I would regularly have to work one hundred hours a week—until two or three o'clock in the morning, Saturdays and Sundays included, and most holidays.[30] I was then asked what I had done that demonstrated my ability to maintain that pace and still excel, so I explained that I had done well academically while playing two sports in college and performing community service.

Playing team sports in college, serving in the military, performing public service, or being involved with the Boy Scouts or Girl Scouts were seen as big advantages at Goldman, because they demonstrated teamwork, discipline, and a sense of community and obligation to society. Teamwork is codified in Goldman's principle 8 ("We stress teamwork in everything we do"), and discipline is implicit in principle 9 (regarding the "dedication of our people to the firm and the intense effort they give their jobs"). Interestingly, a sense of community and obligation to society is not written as a business principle, but it is so ingrained that almost every internal and external communication about the firm prominently describes and displays its "citizenship." (For examples, see appendix E.)

At the close of the interview, the partner asked me whether I had any questions as he filled out a form for human resources. "If I work until two or three o'clock in the morning, how will I get home?" I asked. "Are the subways open at that hour?"

He chuckled. "There are always Lincoln Town Cars lined up outside the building. You can take one of them home."

Coming from a middle-class Midwestern background, I had never heard of such a thing (I couldn't contemplate someone else driving a car with me in the backseat), so I asked what I thought was a practical question: "So do I drive the car back when I come back in the morning?"

He burst out laughing. While having trouble to stop laughing, he then explained that I would be "chauffeured" and dropped off at home.

There he sat, with his sleeves rolled up on his white shirt, top button undone and back of his shirt slightly untucked, Brooks Brothers striped tie loosened a little. It was the standard look in M&A. You looked as if you were working hard. He leaned over and said, "Let me read what I wrote on your review form: 'Lunch pail kind of guy—knows nothing but will kill himself for us—and smart enough so we can teach him.'" That was me in a nutshell—and just the kind of person Goldman wanted.

I was surprised that other candidates and I were interviewed by the people they would work with, not human resources people.

After completing ten or fifteen interviews, I got an offer the next day.

Soon after I was hired, I was asked to review résumés from Midwestern schools for candidates to interview. When I was given hundreds of them bound in three-ring folders, I asked the vice president who had given me the assignment, "How should I go about choosing?"

He shrugged and told me to take anyone who didn't have a certain grade point average and SAT score and throw them out, and then get back to him.

I did that, but I was still left with what still seemed like hundreds of résumés. So I asked, "Now what do I do?"

"Take out anyone who doesn't play a varsity sport or do something really exceptional or substantive in public service," he told me, waving me out of his office.

Once again I culled the folders, but still I had too many. So I went back again.

"Now throw out any that don't have both sports and public service, and raise your grade and SAT requirements."

After this round, I came up with the thirty people we would interview to select the one or two who would get an offer.

It seemed to me that a large percentage of people hired by Goldman in the United States had roots in the Midwest or in Judaism, and when I discussed this with Whitehead and others, they said that there was no conscious effort to hire to a certain ethnic or regional profile;

it was most likely only that people are attracted to people who have similar values and backgrounds. The similarities in backgrounds can be seen in this list of the past five CEOs or senior partners:

- Lloyd Blankfein: Jewish; raised in New York public housing in the Bronx

- Hank Paulson: Christian Scientist; raised in Barrington Hills, Illinois, on a farm; played football in college; Eagle Scout; worked in the government before joining Goldman

- Jon Corzine: Church of Christ; raised on a farm in Central Illinois; football quarterback and basketball captain in high school

- Stephen Friedman: Jewish; on his college wrestling team

- Robert Rubin: Jewish; Eagle Scout

Partners modeled and reinforced the desired behaviors and delivered "sermonettes of perceived wisdom" as deemed appropriate.[31] French sociologist Pierre Bourdieu argued that in analyzing any society, as well as a firm's culture, what matters "is not merely what is publicly discussed, but what is *not* mentioned in public . . . Areas of social silence, in other words, are crucial to supporting a story that a society is telling itself."[32] The written principles were important, but it is how they were interpreted and put into action—brought alive each day—that really mattered. The Goldman partners reinforced the importance of the values by their actions; they didn't need to be specifically mentioned because they were understood by watching. The way these CEOs and partners acted, dressed, and behaved reinforced unwritten norms or uncodified principles. The men at the top wore Timex watches and not Rolexes (and this is before Ironman watches were fashionable). Partners did not wear expensive suits or drive fancy cars (most drove Fords because it was such a good client and many partners got a special discount). They lived relatively modestly, considering their wealth. It was simply not in the ethos to be flashy but rather to be understated, with Midwestern restraint.

The archetype for proper behavior was John L. Weinberg: "Revered by his partners and trusted by the firm's blue-chip corporate clients, he was entirely without pretension, he spoke blunt common sense, [and] wore off-the-peg suits."[33]

The unwritten commandment to keep a low profile was not, until rather recently, violated casually. In the early 1990s, an analyst was riding in a taxi past the famous and pricey Le Cirque restaurant in New York when he spotted a low-key Goldman vice president standing outside. To tease the VP in a funny, friendly way, the analyst rolled down the cab window and yelled out several times, "VP at Goldman Sachs!" Clearly, the subtext was, "VP at Goldman Sachs dining extravagantly at an elite restaurant!" The VP took it so seriously that the next morning he called the analyst into his office, along with a few of the analyst's friends (including me), who, he correctly assumed, had already heard the funny story. The VP explained that he had been invited to Le Cirque by his girlfriend's parents and that he would never have gone there on his own. Then he asked us to please not tell anyone or discuss (or joke about) the matter further.

The low-key imperative extended even to the modest Goldman offices. Goldman did not want clients to view an ostentatious display of corporate wealth, fearing it would be seen as an indication that the fees for the firm's services were too high or that the firm had the wrong priorities.[34]

When I started at the firm, there was no sign bearing the name Goldman Sachs when one entered 85 Broad Street; behind the reception desk there just was a list of the partners' names and floor numbers. There was even a floor for retired partners, but their names were not listed individually, the label for that floor just said, "Limited Partners" and a floor number. Even the twenty-second-floor offices of the senior partners were relatively modest, with the elevator doors opening to a gallery of senior partners' portraits. It all served to reinforce the message: keep a low profile, respect the history, and remember whose money is at risk here. Such organizational humility, combined with the business principles and a drive for excellence, helped Goldman develop strong client relationships and allowed the firm's culture to hold materialism at bay for a long time.

There was also an ethic that talking about compensation was taboo, although no one ever actually said so. Almost all of us had our sights set on partnership, and we were certainly curious about how our compensation stacked up against that of others, but no one ever directly asked.

One class of vice presidents had an interesting approach. Each year, all the members of that class got together and anonymously wrote their compensation figures on a slip of paper and dropped the paper into a bowl. The slips were then extracted randomly and read aloud to the group. In that way, no one knew exactly how much each person was making, but they knew the range and could figure out where they fell within it. I learned the range was less than 5 percent to 10 percent from the highest to the lowest (a remarkably narrow range by today's standards), and this represented that the firm equally valued each person's contribution and the equally high level of talent and hard work. I remember thinking the firm's policy on compensation range was almost "socialist."

Family Values

The firm also instilled a feeling of "family." Goldman inculcated its values in other ways as well. When I started, I was assigned a "big buddy" who had graduated from business school and worked at Goldman for a few years to work with me on my first few projects. Big buddy relationships could be traced like a family tree: my big buddy had a big buddy, and so on. He also had little buddies like me. We were "related," and one could essentially trace his "ancestors." It was an informal network, and people had a sense of pride in their lineage of buddies.

Fortunately, my big buddy was great (as were my several little buddies). He had been an athlete at a small college, worked as an accountant, and pushed his way through to an Ivy League business school and into Goldman. Someone told me that when my big buddy had been a summer associate, he essentially slept under the desk in his cubicle because he wanted to make sure he would get a full-time offer. When I sheepishly asked another associate whether the story was true, he scoffed and said, "Of course not."

I was relieved.

Then he walked me to the other side of the floor, to the office of Peter Sachs (a descendent of the original Sachs). He pointed, smiling, to a worn leather couch and advised me to take short naps there when pulling all-nighters, adding, "It's a lot more comfortable than a cubicle."

In addition to teaching me financial analysis, my big buddy gave me hints about what to wear and how to act. His general advice was don't do or wear anything to draw attention to myself.

I also was assigned a mentor—a vice president—who was supposed to speak to me about my career and give me a senior connection to the firm. If my big buddy was like an older brother figure, my mentor was like a father figure. He took me to lunch or dinner periodically and told me which projects I should work on and with whom. He also spoke to other senior people to get me assignments that would help me improve. In addition, I sat in a cubicle right outside a partner's office, and we shared the same assistant.

My mentor told me that everyone was expected to accept any social invitation from another Goldman employee (not to mention attending every department or firm meeting or function). He told me there was no excuse for missing a wedding, funeral, bar or bat mitzvah, or christening. My London wedding in 1998, when I was an associate, was attended by the head of my department, one of the co-heads of banking, and a member of the management committee.

After seeing how my mentor and the partners worked, I certainly didn't need codified business principles to understand the ethic. One partner literally had holes in the soles of his shoes. My mentor had holes in the elbows of his shirt. Both worked twelve- to fourteen-hour days and on the weekends. I once had to call a partner at his home on Christmas Day to ask him a question and got no complaints. My mentor had an L.L.Bean canvas briefcase, and one of the partners carried his things and paperwork in a large brown paper bag. I was afraid to carry the new leather briefcase my parents had given me for college graduation. And I made sure I was in the office before my mentor and the partners, and I left after they did.

When I started at Goldman, I was handed a two-hundred-page, green-covered directory with every employee's and partner's home address and work and home phone numbers (cell phones were not widespread, and e-mail was years away from being used at Goldman) as well as summer or weekend contact information. Obviously, having readily available contact information increased efficiency, but the other message was that you were expected to be reachable at all times—no matter who you were. The directory seemed like a club book, and it reinforced the feeling of being in a family, adding to the flatness of the organization.

One implication of the value of keeping a low profile was that there were to be no superstars.[35] The implicit proscription of displays of ego extended beyond office walls. Unlike other investment banks, which allowed their bankers to be quoted by the media, Goldman preferred its M&A bankers to be "anonymous executers of transactions." The unspoken message was clear to all: "No one is more important than the firm."[36]

Goldman also invested serious time and effort in training. Most analysts and associates joining Goldman from school are trained over weeks to learn the firm's history, expectations, processes and procedures, and organizational structure. The primary intent is the socialization of new members. During my training, various Goldman executives came and spoke about the Goldman history and their departments. Junior people gave talks about their jobs and explained how to be successful at Goldman. There were group dinners and cocktail parties. We learned specifics that would help us in our day-to-day jobs, such as Excel spreadsheet-modeling skills, but it was also a way for new people to gain exposure to various people and departments that would help trainees think about problems or provide information to help clients. The people we were in training with were our "class," and we developed a strong identity as members of our class. You would also be evaluated by comparison to those in your class. Even with the implicit competition, we felt a great cama-raderie. My twenty-year class reunion party in 2012, sponsored by Goldman, drew people from all over the world. Retired senior part-ners also attended.

After the initial sessions, Goldman provided constant formal training: tools to do the job better, updates on product innovations or trends, information about how to be a better interviewer or men-tor, training on how to better provide clients with full solutions and not only a product solution, and updates on compliance and legal issues as well as best practices. Not a month went by without some sort of formal training. We also had outside guest speakers to talk about specific topics. As we progressed in our careers, we received specialized training for any promotions—usually followed by a cock-tail party in which partners congratulated us, perhaps followed by handwritten notes of congratulations from various partners. In addi-tion to training, we attended many department functions, includ-ing holiday parties, strategy sessions, outdoor bonding exercises, and picnics—even group trips to the beach or skiing (often, spouses were invited).

Goldman also strongly encouraged participation in community and public service. Most people looked up to and admired Goldman employees who went on to public service, and those who were hired from government. You were expected to participate in Goldman's Community Teamworks program, an initiative that allows employ-ees to take a day out of the office and spend it volunteering with local nonprofit organizations. The firm also matched the charitable con-tributions of employees, and partners generously gave to their alma maters and other nonprofit organizations. In some interviews, part-ners explained that citizenship had multiple purposes: to do good, to make people feel good about where they worked, and, admittedly, to extend Goldman's network.

Long-Term Greedy

Goldman's foremost principle—of "clients' interests first"—entails doing what is best for the client, regardless of the size of the fee (whether it will be received now or later) and never suggesting deals to clients specifically to generate fees. Putting clients first requires a commitment to the honesty and diplomatic candor that enable clients to trust Goldman to honor confidentiality of information, provide reliable advice, and not pull any punches. This honesty was a hallmark of Goldman's earlier days, and the firm's reputation for ethical behavior distinguished it among Wall Street firms.[37]

When I was a financial analyst, we were asked to review the strategic alternatives for a division of an industrial company. Internally, we informally gathered about a dozen M&A bankers and debated the best courses of action for the client. During the discussion, a young associate revealed something the CFO had said: that the client CEO thought the division in question should be sold, and pointed to the data and analysis that would substantiate this point of view. Goldman would collect a fee if the division sold.

The vice president who was assigned to advise the company patiently listened and then snapped, "The CEO hired us for our unbiased advice, and not to justify what he thinks."

We incorporated the group's suggestions and then spent days going from one partner's office to another, discussing the merits of various courses of action. I was impressed that all these partners would take the time to listen to discussions about a situation in which they were not involved—to help us get to the best advice and teach us how to think about the issues.

In the meeting with the client CEO, the Goldman vice president presented the various alternatives. He concluded by recommending that the CEO not sell the division at that time, because there was a good probability it would be worth more in the future. Then there was an awkward silence. The client CEO complimented the team for the quality of its work and then said Goldman was the only bank that did not recommend a sale. Unexpectedly, he called a few days later. He decided to wait and continue executing the business plan.

A few years later, that same division had doubled its profits, and Goldman was hired to sell the entire company.

The Goldman approach in this case was consistent with Steve Friedman's description of Jimmy Weinberg: "He just had a great demeanor, and people would develop confidence in him because he wasn't pandering to them, he would tell them what he thought."[38] I interviewed several Goldman clients from the 1980s, and there was a general consensus that typically Goldman did emphasize unbiased advice.

Devotion to Client Service

The values of integrity and honesty are codified in the last of Goldman's business principles as being "at the heart" of the business. In the eyes of the partners during the Weinberg and Whitehead days, the firm's reputation for ethical behavior was a competitive asset and crucial to the firm's success. It was the right thing to do, and it made good long-term business sense. They recognized the value of their reputational capital.[39]

Integrity was the favorite word of longtime Goldman head Sidney Weinberg, and he defined it as a combination of being honest and putting the interests of clients first. As one partner observed, "Mistakes were quite forgivable, but dishonesty was unpardonable."[40] John Whitehead explains: "Our industry is one in which the services of the leading investment bankers are all pretty much the same. So, I've always believed that one's reputation is extremely important and that decisions are often made according to the general reputation a firm has, not so much by the fact that they will perform a service a little cheaper and a little faster. Reputation is what matters."[41]

When describing Jimmy Weinberg, Tom Murphy, former chairman and CEO of Capital Cities/ABC, said, "His clients were his friends . . . His whole reputation in the business world was as a person of honesty and integrity."[42]

Whitehead expressed the strategy behind the philosophy this way: "We thought that if our clients did well, we would do well."[43] Together with the emphasis on maintaining a "steadfast" focus on the long term, this almost religious devotion to clients' interests and service was largely responsible for Goldman's success.

Gus Levy, a senior partner at Goldman from 1969 until his death in 1976, originated the maxim, mentioned earlier, that expressed the proper attitude for Goldman partners: "greedy, but long-term greedy."[44] These words helped remind partners to focus on the future, as evidenced by the nearly 100 percent reinvestment of partners' earnings. One author interprets Goldman's long-term greedy mantra to mean that "while the firm worked in its own interest, it did so in a manner consistent with the long-term health of its industry, business, and clients."[45] This was not purely a matter of altruism. Goldman existed to make money for its partners, not only at the moment but also for years to come. Goldman cultivated an image of responsibility, trust, and restraint by intimating that the firm held itself to a higher standard than other firms.[46]

The emphasis on long-term greedy also explains in part why employees were willing to work grueling hours for relatively modest wages. In the long term, if they made partner they would more than make up for the sacrifice. Lower wages in one's early years with the firm were part of Goldman's strategy for success—part of the business model—because the less that was paid to nonpartners, the more the partners got paid.[47] Goldman got its employees to buy into long-term greedy for themselves, and the Goldman culture was distinctive enough that people wanted to work there even if they worked harder and for less money than did competitors.

Many of the partners I interviewed cautioned me that Goldman was not *always* all about teamwork, collaboration, and shared values. Hiring mistakes were made. Indiscretions were dealt with. Politics did enter into the picture the further one moved up, and there were sharp elbows. But in the end, the principles generally won out. People came and went, but generally the culture and principles remained.

Just as the policy of not advising hostile raiders (see chapter 5) and keeping the client first were good business decisions, so was getting people to buy into a culture and a purpose—it made the partners (who were certainly greedy) more money over time and helped sustain the money machine for the next generation.

Very few people left Goldman voluntarily. When I was an analyst, in the early 1990s, a respected associate decided to leave and join his father's business, and we had a department meeting to discuss this shocking event. The purpose of the session was to make us feel that in this one instance, it was acceptable; he was going to work with his family, and that was just barely excusable. I would have thought that many people would leave because of the lower pay than peers and the slim chances of becoming a partner. But voluntary turnover was less than 5 percent, I was told—significantly below the industry average in the 20 percent range.

Generally, Goldman bankers obsessed more about making partner and their relative compensation than they did about their absolute compensation. Their social identity was so bound up, through their socialization at the firm, with what Goldman valued, that bankers routinely turned down multiyear guaranteed contracts for significantly more money at other firms, even when the possibility that they would make partner at Goldman was, according to my interviews, less than 5 percent to 10 percent.[48] After their socialization into Goldman, working at any other firm, regardless of the title or compensation, would seem to them a step down, according to many of the people I interviewed.[49]

Goldman bankers were also generally convinced that they were the best—that they worked at the best firm, with the best people, and with the best brand. At the same time, they were convinced that teamwork and a team relationship with clients were so important that their own value as bankers outside Goldman would be diminished. The socialization process made well-educated, thoughtful, talented people believe that Goldman made them better bankers than they could be elsewhere. Blankfein summarized the culture as "an interesting blend of confidence and commitment to excellence, and an inbred insecurity that drives people to keep working."[50] Although it seems he was talking about an insecurity that motivated people to keep working harder and longer, this inbred insecurity is a paradox.

Nostalgia

I do not want to wax nostalgically about the good old days. I did on occasion observe vice presidents and partners acting in a way that might not be considered in the best interests of clients, though those were exceptions to the rule. For example, I remember working with an associate on a project advising a company that was buying a small subsidiary of another company. The partner was extremely busy and traveling, and although we sent him our analysis and kept scheduling calls to speak to him, he always canceled our discussions. He showed up less than a few hours before our client meeting, and, based on his questions, it appeared as if he had not read anything we sent him and was not prepared. This surprised me, because usually partners were highly detail oriented and well prepared.

He asked us for our valuation analysis, the value of the synergies, and the price the seller wanted. The asking price was higher than our valuation analysis (a breakdown that is more art than science). More-over, our estimates of the potential synergies (the cost savings and revenue enhancement resulting from the deal), which meaningfully impacted the value, were highly subjective. When we met with the client CEO, the Goldman partner claimed that he had "been poring over the numbers all day and night" and he thought that if the com-pany could buy the business at X price (coincidentally, the asking price we'd told the partner), then it was a good deal for strategic reasons.

When he said this, the associate and I looked at each other and then looked down. I reasoned that he might have been poring over the numbers without my knowledge, or maybe he meant "the team" had been. The deal ultimately got done; Goldman was paid a fee; and the partner was right—it was a strategic success, and the synergies justified the price. But it was one of the few times when I was junior that I privately questioned the approach. As for the other junior associate, we never really discussed what the partner had said.[51]

A few times I questioned coworkers directly when I felt it was appropriate. For example, I was tangentially helping a team led by a vice president in selling a company, and when the final bids and contracts were due from all the potential buyers at the same time in a sort of sealed auction process, only one buyer submitted a bid, and the bid price was less than the amount our client was willing to sell for. It seemed to be a delicate situation, because we had little negotiating leverage to persuade the only potential buyer to pay more. Also, the bidder was a good client of Goldman's. However, the vice president called the sole bidder and said, "We had a number of bids" and told the bidder that to win the auction, he would have to raise his bid.

I questioned him, and based on his facial expression and the tone of his response, I don't think he appreciated my inquisitiveness. He pointed out to me that he had said "a number of bids," and "in this instance, the number is one."

Ultimately, the bidder raised his price and ended up buying the company. When the vice president told the client exactly what he had done and said, the client chuckled approvingly.[52]

Then there are things I was uncomfortable with that I never raised through the proper channels—by speaking with vice presidents, partners, my big buddy, or my mentor, or by writing about the issues in "confidential and anonymous" reviews and surveys. Maybe it was because I didn't trust the system or didn't know how people would react. Maybe I was worried about developing a reputation as a tattletale or, worse, losing my job—something I couldn't afford. Stories were quietly discussed and passed down—stories of people having challenged behavior or things said in confidence that got back to the wrong people, and then slowly and subtly those people would be "transitioned out." Ironically, sometimes the guilty parties were characterized as not being team players or not embodying the culture when he or she left or was demoted. I was trying to figure out what was right and what was wrong—what was acceptable and what wasn't—which, it seemed, wasn't always black and white. In the story just related, the client seemed happy and the vice president didn't "technically lie." Technically, one could rationalize, we did put our client's interests first.

But, as said, these examples were exceptions. The vast majority of the time that I worked in banking, the people with whom I worked did not rely on technicalities to determine what was right or wrong. I once joked to a friend that if someone found a nickel on the floor of the Goldman M&A department in 1992, he or she would go so far above and beyond what was required as to put up a "found" poster with a nickel taped to it, something that seems crazy anywhere, let alone on Wall Street. But in retrospect, "a number of bids" should have alerted me to the fact that there were multiple moralities or interpretations and that sometimes people might be obeying the letter of the law while violating its spirit, and rationalizing their behavior.[53]

Old School

At its best, Goldman enjoyed a reputation for honesty, integrity, and unquestioned commitment to serving the best interests of its clients, and at the same time enjoyed superior financial results. Critical to the firm's success were the principles and values, both codified and uncodified, intended to guide behavior, communicate the essence of the firm, and aid in the socialization of new employees, and a partnership culture that emphasized social cohesion and teamwork. Recruitment sought to bring in people perceived to share the values, and the meaning of "long-term greedy" was taught and practiced. Sharing information and getting input from others were important, as was the socialization that the firm was a part of you and your success.

In chapter 3, I discuss the importance of the partnership structure and explain how it supported financial interdependence and provided opportunities for productive debate and discussion—all of which also supported the Goldman culture.

Chapter 3

The Structure of
the Partnership

WHEN I WAS A GOLDMAN ASSOCIATE IN THE LATE 1990S, I was asked to prepare materials for and attend a meeting with a senior partner and an unhappy client. It was unclear whether the client was not happy with the firm or with the junior partner in charge of the relationship, so the junior partner was asked not to attend.

During the meeting, the client, a CEO, said he thought very highly of Goldman but that he felt the junior partner in charge had acted inappropriately by speaking to one of his board members about something that the client felt should have been directed to him first. And when the board member called the CEO, the client was caught off guard. The client told us that if that junior partner continued to work on his Goldman banking team, Goldman would get no more business from him. At this point the senior partner, to appease the client, could easily have thrown the junior partner in charge under the bus and agreed to remove him from the team. Instead, his actions defined for me what partnership meant.

The senior partner told the client that he had known and worked with the junior partner in question for more than fifteen years and that he had the highest respect of his clients and the other partners. There must have been, he asserted, some sort of misunderstanding. He would be willing to consider replacing the partner only if the client would agree to have a cup of coffee with the junior partner in question to discuss in person what happened. And if the client would not agree to this, he said, then there was no reason for Goldman to have a relationship with him.

The client had paid the firm millions of dollars over the years, and now the senior partner was willing to walk away from the relationship and sacrifice future fees because his partner's integrity was being questioned. That was what partnership meant at Goldman.

Today, Goldman, a public company for more than a dozen years, states on a document on its website, "Our culture is rooted in our history as a partnership when business decisions were conducted by consensus." In a diagram on a page titled "The History of Our Culture: Our Governance Foundation," the partnership culture is shown at the center of Goldman's structure, guiding behavior through formally stated business principles and corporate governance practices.[1] Surrounding this are four quarter-circles—labeled "Values," "Ownership," "Teamwork," and "Public Service"—connected, respectively, with arrows suggesting their relationships. Clearly, Goldman's leaders recognize how important the partnership legacy is to the firm's success. (See appendix H.)

The elements of its value system were embodied in the firm's organizational structure of ownership and culture. Because the two things went hand-in-hand, both were inextricably bound with the concept and practice of partnership. Values, public service, teamwork, and ownership were interconnected.

Goldman's partnership structure helped create and sustain its culture in several ways, including:

- A formal process through which people became partners (or left the partnership)

- A social network based on mutual trust and financial interdependence[2]

- Opportunities for disagreement and discussion that informed decision making ("dissonance")

- Ownership of the firm by its partners

- Having personal capital at risk

Although each of these structural characteristics is discussed sequentially here, they are interrelated.

The Goldman Career Path

When I started in investment banking in 1992, Goldman typically hired new college graduates as financial analysts. Financial analysts, who made a two year commitment to the firm, did very junior work, usually supporting more-senior people. In their third year, excellent performers were sometimes offered an opportunity to stay for a year, and top performers might be invited to work in another group or geographic region of interest. However, to become an associate, the next step on the typical career path at Goldman, one had to leave, attend business school or law school, and then apply to return as an associate. Occasionally, financial analysts were directly promoted to associate, meaning that no graduate school or reapplication was necessary (that's the path I was invited to take).

Associates were typically hired right out of top business schools or law schools, and most of them spent their summer vacations working at Goldman, thereby allowing the firm to make sure there was a cultural as well as a performance fit. Associates did financial analysis but also spent time with clients and thinking more broadly about what was required for the client. After four years (if they hadn't been transitioned out of the firm or to another group), most associates were automatically promoted to the title of vice president ("executive director" outside the United States). Vice presidents spent most of their time with clients and reviewed work done by analysts and associates. Typically, VPs worked with partners on larger deals or with larger clients. One way Goldman maintained its culture was through an elaborate employee review process begun in the early 1990s.[3] The anonymous 360-degree reviews were so extensive, even for analysts completing their first year, that they sometimes filled a binder the size of a phone book. As many as twenty people (managers and peers) contributed to the meticulous preparation, which included quantitative rankings, areas for comments, and also a self-review and statement of goals. The review meeting, conducted annually, was scheduled far enough in advance of decisions about compensation that it was not a discussion about compensation, but rather about per-formance and improvement.

When I gave reviews as a business unit manager, people typically asked where they ranked in their class. By sitting in on reviews and in training sessions about giving reviews, I had learned to maneu-ver the discussion to methods for improvement and not relative class rankings or compensation. My understanding was that employees were supposed to leave the review feeling positive but, at the same time, with some degree of insecurity, knowing that they had things to work on, though no one ever formally discussed with me the ratio-nale for (and the consequences of) delivering this mix of positive and negative messages. In my experience, most people heard only the negative message, thus socializing the idea that they needed the firm more than the firm needed them. We also had less-formal six-month reviews, especially with more junior employees, to give timely feed-back for improvement.

Reviews became more sophisticated, quantitative, and profession-alized during my years at Goldman. When I started in 1992, I never heard of a policy or ritual to cull the bottom 5 to 10 percent of a class. The classes were very small, and there seemed to be little differen-tiation among the members. However, as classes became larger and some people were viewed as stronger than others, Goldman seemed to informally adopt the 5 to 10 percent policy (a policy often credited to Jack Welch, then CEO of General Electric). People who did not perform well enough were told in the annual review that they were in "the bottom quartile," which at Goldman was interpreted as a professional way of saying one should start looking for a job elsewhere. At the time, Goldman tried not to fire people outright but instead to give messages tactfully through reviews and compensation so that people could find another job. The trick in many ways was to convince the people not in the bottom quartile, but in the middle of their class, that they were on track for partner so that they were motivated, stayed focused, and did not leave. Though nearly all professionals at Goldman thought they were on the partnership track, in the back of their minds, typically they knew the chances were slim. Nonetheless they stayed.[4]

Typically, it took four to six years as a vice president in investment banking to be considered seriously for partnership election. The election process served as a sort of "up or out" mechanism, because being up for partnership a few times and not making it was essentially a public message about one's future with the firm. Being denied partnership too many times could damage one's external market value, so getting turned down for partnership the first time presented a difficult decision. One rejection could be rationalized, but failure to make partner two or three times was far more difficult to explain away to a potential employer, and by then one's compensation and responsibilities probably reflected diminished prospects at Goldman.

After 1986, when Goldman's primary competitor, Morgan Stanley, went public, Goldman was the only comparable firm that was a partnership and still used the title "partner." Partnership election happened every two years. Until 1996, when the firm changed to a limited liability corporation (LLC) and adopted the title managing director, the progression was from analyst to associate to vice president to partner. Unlike now—when titles have proliferated at Goldman and on the rest of Wall Street—the head of a department or specialty area in the early 1990s typically was a partner. That was it—only four titles (analyst, associate, vice president, and partner)—making Goldman a very flat organization.[5] The cubicles where analysts and associates sat were right next to the partners' offices, and they worked directly with the partners and shared assistants. In fact, some partners tried to sit in cubicles to make themselves more accessible and approachable. They abandoned this approach because the partners had so many meetings with so many people it distracted the junior people around them. Also, the junior people who sat next to the partners felt their personal lives and comings and goings were becoming too transparent. One banking partner instituted trading desks instead of cubicles in his department to facilitate communication. This approach didn't work, either, for much the same reasons.

Being a partner at Goldman was one of the most sought-after positions on Wall Street in part because of partners' prestige and because Goldman partners generally were the highest-paid people on Wall Street. A Goldman partnership was "about as close to a sure thing as there is anywhere in the business world—a ticket to wealth and prestige."[6] Partners tended to manage departments or work with the most important clients and had responsibilities other than working on deals. For example, in the M&A department several partners would have to agree to sign something called a *fairness opinion*, a document issued by Goldman to a public company's board of directors stating that the M&A transaction in question was "fair from a financial point of view" to shareholders. This "opinion" gave the board members confidence in the deal and was thought to protect them if they were to be sued or their judgment was questioned by shareholders.

Issuing an opinion was risky, because it could be challenged in court and Goldman could be subjected to legal and financial liability. In fact, Goldman's IPO prospectus stated, "Our exposure to legal liability is significant," citing "potential liability for the 'fairness opinions' and other advice we provide to participants in corporate transactions." Before the IPO, the partners personally shared this liability. (After converting to a LLC and the IPO, partners did not have personal liability in the event of a successful lawsuit; any financial consequences would be borne by the firm and not the private partnership.) So partners in the trading business had to trust that the M&A partners were being very careful and thoughtful in issuing fairness opinions.

The Partnership Prize

Compensation can certainly send a message, but typically it is a private message to the employee from the company. Partnership, however, is a public recognition of the value of one's contribution and ability to uphold the principles. It worked together with the culture to motivate people to accept lower compensation and work grueling hours. In addition, it served as a mechanism related to financial interdependence.

In a 2009 op-ed letter about the debate over bonuses and Wall Street pay, Peter Weinberg, son of Jimmy Weinberg and nephew of John L. Weinberg, described Goldman partnership and financial interdependence this way:

> The only private partnership I can talk about authoritatively is the one in which I was a partner from 1992 to 1999, when the firm went public: Goldman Sachs. Partners there owned the equity of the firm. When elected a partner, you were required to make a cash investment into the firm that was large enough to be material to your net worth. Each partner had a percentage ownership of the earnings every year, but the earnings would remain in the firm. A partner's annual cash compensation amounted only to a small salary and a modest cash return on his or her capital account. A partner was not allowed to withdraw any capital from the firm until retirement, at which time typically 75%–80% of one's net worth was still in the firm. Even then, a retired ("limited") partner could only withdraw his or her capital over a three-year period. Finally, and perhaps most importantly, all partners had personal liability for the exposure of the firm, right down to their homes and cars. The focus on risk was intense, and wealth creation was more like a career bonus rather than a series of annual bonuses.[7]

The partners knew an elected partner's actions and performance would reflect on them, and if they made an unwise choice, that could have serious financial and reputational consequences for them all. Partners also had to believe that transferring a percentage of profits from themselves to incoming partners would be advantageous—that the potential dilution of their own wealth and the added risk were worth the potential gain.

Consequently, the Goldman partnership process was carried out in painstaking detail, and that was generally understood throughout the firm. Partnership election was taken seriously, as shown by the personal involvement of senior executives. The partners judging a candidate's merit and suitability were the very people with whom the candidate would be financially interdependent if granted partnership. Written nominations were solicited from the partners; from those nominations, the partnership committee created a preliminary list of potential candidates.[8]

During the months preceding partnership elections, it was difficult to get time with the partners because they had so many phone calls and meetings about candidates. Goldman held its partnership elections every two years rather than annually, in part because the process was so arduous and time-consuming.

Although the process was shrouded in secrecy outside Goldman and discussed in hushed voices or behind closed doors, some people knew what was going on from off-the-record conversations with partners with whom they were close. The conversations were supposed to be confidential, but rumors were quietly passed on. People knew who was a "lay-up" (a basketball term for an easy score), who was "on the bubble" (not sure to be elected), and who did not have "a prayer."

Written nominations were solicited from Goldman's partners, and from those nominations the partnership committee created a preliminary list of potential candidates, kicking off a paper chase. Endorsement letters were filed, and internal former FBI and CIA employees conducted background checks on all serious contenders. An internal investigation (called "cross-ruffing," a term borrowed from the card game bridge) took place, led by a partner not in the candidate's division. Then the list was narrowed during the meetings to discuss the would-be partners, a photo of the candidate was displayed on a screen, and from this list, a committee selected names to be placed before the partnership for a vote. The partners generally wanted to keep the percentage of partners to total employees about the same, so the number elected would be carefully chosen depending on retirements and growth.

The process might seem coldhearted, but it was viewed as essential to maintaining the culture, and everyone knew it.[9]

The behavior you needed to exhibit to make partner was clear: make money for the firm while embodying its principles. Everyone knew that becoming a partner required the support of people outside your division and region. Someone in banking needed support from asset management or trading. Someone in North America needed support from people in Asia. This was a key tenet of teamwork; to make partner, you had better help people across the firm. This meant that if you were asked to be on a 4:00 a.m. call with a Japanese client, even if it had nothing to do with your clients, you would set the alarm and do it without question, knowing that if you did not rise to the occasion, it could hurt your chances of becoming a partner (or staying a partner). If you were asked to bring someone from another area into a project because it could help improve the firm's advice, then of course he or she was invited. And the new person participated even though the revenues of the project might not be attributed to you or your group. Candidates' behavior was being vetted as much as their ability to contribute financially to the partnership.[10]

I was surprised when very senior partners asked—in a roundabout, casual way—my opinion of vice presidents who were widely known as being considered for partnership, and as I got more senior they privately told me why someone had or had not been elected—with the implied messages such information carried. Once a partner showed me the standard form used to evaluate candidates. The blank form included numerical rankings of listed qualities related to the Goldman principles.

Former Goldman vice chairman Rob Kaplan says that many of his most stressful and difficult moments at Goldman occurred during partner promotions, particularly when he had to deliver the news to a highly qualified person that he or she would have to wait another two years for reconsideration. It was little wonder that Kaplan writes in *What to Ask the Person in the Mirror* that this message of failure to make partner was often met with "expressions of betrayal."[11]

One person I interviewed—a managing director (now at another firm) who was passed over for partnership at Goldman in the 1990s before the IPO—said that of course he was furious. He had done everything he could—he had given up weekends, birthdays, anniversaries, and vacation time with his family—and then had not been elected in spite of what he thought were positive indications (assurances that he felt were essentially promises) that he would be. Not making partner was devastating to him, he said. He told me that, for people at Goldman, who you are, and what you think about yourself, was ultimately decided at that moment. The thing he feared most was the public embarrassment and humiliation, even more so than the loss of potential riches. When he failed to receive the customary, congratulatory expected call from the senior partner of the firm on the appointed morning, he explained, he felt betrayed. He did not want to hear that he might very well become a partner the next time, in two years. He felt that people wanted him to stick around so that they could get two more years of relatively cheap labor from him and that they would say anything, just as they had assured him before, to keep him. But he was determined not to stick around while his peers from business school were called managing directors at other firms and he was called a vice president for another two years. His staying would be "a cheap option" for Goldman, so he swallowed his pride and successfully cashed in his pedigree by leaping to another firm.

In a 1993 interview, Steve Friedman, then a senior partner, explained that the partnership election process was used as a way to convey that people would be rewarded for doing what was best for Goldman and would be denied the ultimate reward—partnership—if they paid more attention to their own agenda than to the firm's. Friedman described delivering that message to one disappointed banker: "I have looked people in the eyes and said, 'You did not become a partner this time despite your basic abilities, your candle power, your energy. You had all the goods to have achieved it, but you did not become a partner because you were perceived as having too damned much of your own agenda, and you were ignoring what we were telling you was in the broader interests of the firm.'"[12]

The flip side of the partner election was that, to add partners, Goldman had to discreetly ask others to retire, for the simple reason that maintaining a greater number of partners would mean each would own a smaller percentage of the firm.[13] If someone was *departnered*, it was only after careful deliberation by the most senior partners and usually resulted from making too small a contribution relative to ownership (Goldman could get someone else to do it for less) or from doing something that jeopardized the firm's reputation and put the partners at financial risk. Thus, the pressure was on for performance and proper behavior, even for partners, and the pressure was intense.

Generally, there have consistently been more partner additions than departures, but the ratio of partners to the total number of employees has stayed relatively constant because of continued growth. For example, the total number of partners noticeably increased from 1984 to 2011, which corresponded to the increase of total employees: both nearly doubled from 1998 to 2011. However, the percentage of partners to employees (the partner ratio) remained steady at 1.5 percent to 2.0 percent. Growth was important to provide more opportunities for partnership and for the partnership to be financially attractive.

A retired partner I interviewed said that he never worked harder at Goldman than when he was a partner. He had partner responsibilities and obligations on top of his regular job. He explained that he had done everything by the book and was relieved when he made partner.

"Why were you relieved—was it the money?" I asked.

He explained, when he got to that point, it was less about the money than it was because everyone knew he was being considered for partnership—his wife, his clients, his business school classmates, everyone at the firm. He retired after the IPO, despite having been a partner for only a short time, because he was burned out, even though he knew that each year he could "hold on" represented millions of dollars. The pressure was taking a toll on his health and his family, he told me. Today he still values the social status of having been a partner, and that is how he is usually introduced in social contexts: "a retired pre-IPO partner of Goldman Sachs."

No one was exempt from performing or from upholding the firm's values. The departnering conversations were held discreetly and privately with the senior partner of the firm, but when the internal memo came out, there were almost always rumors, typically related to performance. The former partner hadn't pulled his weight or wasn't doing the expected culture-carrying tasks, such as recruiting. Or the outcast had done something harmful to the Goldman image, such as having an extramarital affair with someone at the firm or saying something inappropriate, or had subjected the partnership to unnecessary financial risk. Even if a partner left voluntarily for primarily personal reasons, there was almost always speculation about the "real" reasons.

A current partner told me that the organization looks for an explanation beyond the desire to leave because he or she may simply feel he or she has made enough money. That's not acceptable, because it might send a message that money is the primary driver. If the reason for leaving is that the partner no longer enjoys the work, then people would wonder what there is about Goldman not to like, this partner told me. The firm convinces people that being a Goldman partner is something one would never want to surrender; it gives one social identification, prestige, money, and access, and it is perceived as serving a higher good. That is what is sold to potential and current employees. So if a partner leaves, something has to be wrong with him, and the firm perpetuates that belief through whispers. The partner explained that the only acceptable answer is that the partner is retiring to serve a higher purpose, which is to go into community and public service—and many do. He said it wasn't the money, it was that their work ultimately needed a higher meaning.

Historically, Goldman's process of partner election and departnering are exemplary of what sociologists term closure, the tight coordination within a group, which ensures that people comply with the organization's norms.[14] According to sociologist Ronald Burt, "closure increases the odds of a person being caught and punished for displaying belief or behavior inconsistent with the preferences in the closed network."[15] In his view, closure strengthens organizations by ensuring that people not adhering to expected norms can be removed.[16] Making partner was so lucrative and the identity meant so much to people that they modified their behavior to enhance their chances of being elected, and, once they were partners, it became an integral part of their social identity.[17] Rewarded behavior helped the firm as a whole. Partners worked hard to make more money but also were pressured to promote teamwork, the culture and the principles, and to stay within the firm's rules and values.

Meanwhile, the close scrutiny of each partner's contributions and adherence to the mandate during the partnership election provided closure by removing partners whose continued tenure was not to the advantage of the firm, thus ensuring trust among those who remained. In this way, partnership election and departnering reinforced the distinction between insiders and outsiders. The effectiveness of this practice is best seen, according to Charles Ellis, the author of *The Partnership—The Making of Goldman Sachs*, in the "speed and clarity with which long-serving partners who left went from being insiders to outsiders and were soon forgotten."[18]

A Social Network of Trust

While the partnership election at Goldman was grueling, partnership offered camaraderie to those who made it.[19] A retired partner explained to me that there were regularly heated disagreements among partners over business decisions. He felt the partners were in fact like a family or club. As in many families, the partnership was "dysfunctional" and had "black sheep"; there might be questions of motives or agenda; and sometimes there were even sharp elbows or personality mismatches, but there was a good deal of trust and familiarity among the members.

Most partners had spent their entire careers at the firm, and many senior partners had mentored the newer partners over years. They had gone through the same election process and knew how tough it was to make partner and how demanding the job was. Partners had outings together as well as annual dinners. Many lived in the same suburbs. Generally, they knew each other well. Some ties were stronger than others because of business school friendships, experience in working in the same department or the same part of the world, or location in the same neighborhoods. However, all of them were financially interdependent and needed to trust one another. Several partners agreed when I interviewed them that the phrase "social network of trust" was a fitting description.[20] In 1994, a partner, addressing a gathering of new partners, highlighted the relationship between the partnership structure and the cultural view it promoted: "We own this business . . . We are partners—emotionally, psychologically, and financially. There can be no borders between us, no secrets."[21]

Partners also created stronger networks because of the trust. Building a network involves connecting the dots, or rather connecting Goldman people to each other and to important people outside the firm. Almost a decade before he crafted the firm's business principles, John Whitehead wrote a set of guidelines for the investment banking services area, one of which was, "Important people like to deal with important people. Are you one?"[22] Gaining access to important people requires introductions from people willing to make the call. Partners were more willing to do that for the partners who were in their social network of trust and with whom they had financial interdependency.

For example, an investment banking partner explained to me that he was at ease connecting fellow partners to his contacts outside the firm, more so than connecting a vice president or regular managing director. Partners, he said, wouldn't leave the company and take the relationship to a competitor. He trusted his partners in private banking to use good judgment and not to put his investment banking relationship at risk. This kind of trust made it easy to offer multiple perspectives to help a client. It also aided the firm in *cross-selling*: providing a full solution to clients. For example, Goldman might provide the merger advice to sell a company, and then the M&A partner would introduce a Goldman private banking partner to help the client manage the proceeds from the sale.[23] "Cross-selling" significantly improves a firm's financial performance, maximizing revenue opportunities.

A virtuous reinforcement loop was erected; partnership was enhanced by the trust fostered by the social network and financial interdependence, and the social network was enhanced by the trust.[24]

Productive Dissonance

The emphasis on shared values in the Goldman partnership model might lead to the impression that the Goldman culture was rigid, monolithic, and intolerant of diverse opinions. Generally this was not the case. Although the partners held common values and many of them came from similar backgrounds, Goldman recognized that different people had different ideas and perspectives and that a diversity of people and ideas was important to the firm's vitality and productivity.[25] Diversity was also important in its making the right decisions and giving clients the best service and judgment. Such diversity of experiences and expertise gave Goldman the flexibility to deal with constant change.

Goldman promoted cross-function communication and organizational cohesion through rotational programs for employees into other departments and regions and firmwide committees consisting of people from different departments.[26] This "small-world network" of people who built ties, had financial interdependence, and trusted one another led to innovation and high performance. Committees drew together partners or potential partners from different areas to work together on partnership election, capital commitments, risk, culture, lifestyle, brand, and more. These committees, together with partnership meetings, served as places of exchange like those Ronald Burt describes as essential for optimizing the number of brokerage opportunities for networks.[27] This practice created valuable networks, as well as a systematic, structured way to bring people together to discuss ideas, challenge each other, and seek solutions.[28] Goldman's flat organizational structure also encouraged people to interact, bringing their diverse opinions to the table.[29] The biennial change in partnership, with a balance of new partners joining and old partners leaving, kept the ideas fresh, but generally it did not introduce so many differences that cohesion was lost.[30]

Goldman's partnership culture allowed for disagreement in part because the partners have a stake in more than only their own areas of responsibility. They were financially interdependent. Banking partners had nothing to do with trading and vice versa, but trading partners were affected if a banking partner hurt the reputation of the firm, and banking partners were affected if trading partners didn't properly manage risk, because they are risking the capital of all the partners. In a typical big bank, by contrast—one without a partnership ownership structure—compensation is based primarily on departmental and individual performance (and peer group compensation averages); what others do or think in another department or divison is typically of little concern to anyone else, because one's own bonus is not materially threatened. The lack of financial interdependence typically limits the amount of productive disagreement you find at most Wall Street firms. Even with compensation in stock vesting over years, the attitude is much different because what one does typically has limited impact on the earnings or stock price of the entire firm.

The disagreement at Goldman was described by several Goldman partners as valuable.[31] Rob Kaplan indicated that "irritating, distracting, and uncomfortable" discussions were "extremely good medicine for a healthy organization."[32] For example, one seemingly contentious relationship was that between senior executive John F. W. Rogers, considered by many to be one of the firm's most powerful people, and Lucas van Praag, Goldman's public relations spokesman from 2000 to 2012. Jack Martin, CEO of the PR firm Hill and Knowlton, said that he had seen the two "disagree aggressively, but that at the end of the day they [came] together as one."[33] Although others may see friction between Rogers and van Praag as unhealthy, Blankfein expressed confidence in them and asserted that "dissent and disagreement is healthy."[34]

Whitehead described how he and his co-leader, John L. Weinberg, strove to maintain an environment conducive to productive disagreement within the management committee: "We met every Monday morning. We had an agenda, we went down the agenda, we made decisions as a group, and John and I tried not to dominate the committee because we wanted their input. It was very important to have the input of everybody on the management committee. There were seven of us, then nine of us, and then eleven. It got bigger as the firm's diversity grew."[35]

A Harvard Business School case study about Goldman's training found that Goldman used the Socratic method to explore questions through discussion and debate. One senior manager described a typical discussion: "That was a good argument. But next time, it would actually be really interesting if you also added these three things."[36] One partner expressed his delight in this learning environment: "Goldman Sachs when I started was a fantastic place to be planted and grow. They treated me the right way, encouraged me the right way . . . It's a Socratic, collaborative style. Bouncing things off of each other is fun, and you encourage that at every turn."[37]

According to a former management committee member, the dialogue was predicated on collaboration: "We were always taught that the odds are high you'll have better outcomes with a shared work effort than with that of a single individual. At Goldman Sachs it's pretty rare that an additional perspective doesn't give you a better outcome. As problems become more complex, the ability for a single individual to have the best perspective declines dramatically."[38]

David Stark, a Columbia University sociologist, argues that *dissonance*, or friction, over competing values promotes an organizational reflexivity that makes it easier for a company to change and deal with market uncertainty.[39] Dissonance prevents *groupthink*: what happens psychologically when a group is so concerned with maintaining unanimity in the face of opposition that alternatives and options fail to be identified or properly evaluated.[40] Stark notes that dissonance can become resonance, a "dangerous form of cognitive interdependence," when too many people overlook a key issue, giving "misplaced assurance" to those who think similarly.[41] A partnership structure seems to mitigate against this phenomenon in part because of the financial interdependence and social network of trust among partners. One researcher explained this effect well in describing the era of the private investment banking partnerships as one in which "no one could take excessive risk with the firm's capital, because of the vigilance of the partners. If Partner A wasn't comfortable with a new business or a new client, Partner B would have to convince him of the merits of the business—and to do so, partner B would have to go well beyond the argument that it would generate a lot of short-term fees."[42]

Stark points out that the "ability to keep multiple evaluative principles in play and to exploit the resulting friction of their interplay" is a competitive advantage. Organizations typically try to avoid the perplexing situations that arise "when there is principled disagreement about what counts," when, in fact, they should embrace such situations and "recognize that it is legitimate to articulate alternative conceptions of what is valuable, what is worthy, what counts."[43] Partners I interviewed generally agreed that this is a good description of the productive dissonance that characterized Goldman's partnership culture model.

Goldman excelled at adapting to change and dealing with market uncertainty not so much because of specific individuals but because the organization's partnership structure and culture sustained ongoing and productive discussion and disagreement. Stark notes that when faced with uncertainty, "instead of concentrating their resources for strategic planning among a narrow set of senior executives or delegating that function to a specialized department, heterarchical firms [flat organizations or those with a limited hierarchy] embark on radical decentralization in which every unit becomes engaged in innovation."[44] Therefore, hierarchical firms—those with a long chain of command—are less supportive of innovation and entrepreneurship. Dissonance—supported by the flat organizational structure that facilitated interaction and information transfer, and the financial interdependence of partnership that fostered trust and aligned interests—gave Goldman a significant competitive advantage. Based on my interviews, dissonance of this degree did not exist at most Wall Street firms, because there was no financial interdependence, earnings were distributed, or the partnership was dominated by a few individuals, decreasing the financial interdependence. Goldman's culture of debate took on special significance during the credit crisis, as discussed in a later chapter.

If dissonance encourages entrepreneurship, innovation, or flexibility in meeting competitive pressure, why was Goldman in the 1980s not considered innovative? For the most part, Goldman had a long history of watching and waiting while others did the innovating; then it moved in with an improved or enhanced version. Whitehead said, "[As] far as new products were concerned, I never felt that we had to be first when we did something. We had a reputation for being absolutely first-class in everything we did, but we didn't have to be first with every idea. In fact, I enjoyed it when our competitors had the new idea and tried it out first."[45]

Whitehead pointed out to me another reason Goldman was not the first to innovate: constrained capital limited what the firm was willing and able to do, something that changed as it first began raising more outside capital and then accelerated when it went public. It took bigger financial risks and grew more quickly. When I discussed innovation with partners and competitors, most said they did not see Goldman as an innovator in the 1980s and early 1990s, but they thought that dissonance added to the firm's superior financial and competitive performance and allowed it to get to the best answers for the firm and for clients.

When I asked Whitehead about the perception of Goldman in the 1980s of not being an innovator, he pointed out a nuance that many people were missing: Goldman's strength was not a matter of investing in and potentially taking new risks by developing new products per se. Instead, its strength lay in the ability for people to come together as an organization to figure out how to change and adapt and market products that were better for clients, no matter who created them. To Whitehead, that practice was as innovative as developing products or investing in innovations that might not work or benefit clients—but much harder to execute because of the barriers to getting people to work together, and a lot less risky.

Another significant innovation in the late 1980s and early 1990s was the heavy use of the emerging technology of voicemail, adopted much earlier and used more effectively at Goldman than at other firms. Voicemail helped improve coordination and teamwork, because multiple people could be given information simultaneously and they could hear the tone of a message. The technology resulted in better execution for clients and gave Goldman a competitive advantage. Goldman continued to rely on voicemail heavily even after it had e-mail capability, because e-mail lacked the inflection and expressive capacity of the human voice and was less effective in maintaining the firm's social network.

Goldman people responded quickly to voicemail (and later e-mail messages) because the culture demanded that they do so. A quick and comprehensive response was and still is the norm; it would be culturally unacceptable not to respond as soon as possible. No matter the hour, you can get a partner or junior person on the phone to help you think about a problem or speak to a client. That was true when I was at Goldman, and my interviews confirm it is still the expectation.

Many people from other firms were (and are) shocked at the speed and amount of information shared, often mentioning their need to adjust to Goldman's urgent voicemail (e-mail) culture.

Financial Interdependence and Risk Management

As a private partnership, if Goldman suffered large trading losses, lost a lawsuit, or received fines for criminal or illegal practices, then the partners were personally liable. Their equity was at risk every day. Even with the protection afforded personal assets by the LLC structure, which Goldman changed to in 1996, partners still faced the risk of losing their invested capital, which for many represented the bulk of their wealth.[46]

When one's own money is at stake, management of risk, both financial and reputational, is a key concern.[47] According to the partners I interviewed, managing risk for one's entire net worth, and that of all the partners, brings a higher level of intensity than managing risk for shareholders and a longer-term orientation than today's typical three-to-five-year equity vesting period. That is probably why, in Goldman's own accounts of its culture, risk management often is not included: it was so obviously a no-brainer that it was assumed.[48] As mentioned earlier, Peter Weinberg stressed this issue in his *Wall Street Journal* op-ed, "right down to their homes and cars," noting that "[t]he focus on risk was intense."[49]

The firm's culture and principles, combined with the partners' financial interdependence and the risk to their own capital, ensured that collective risk management and reputational risk management would be a priority. The structure of Goldman's pre-IPO partnership resulted in financial interdependence and a social network of trust, virtually ensuring teamwork and dissonance; in turn, the business practices, policies, and values supported it.

Part Two

DRIFT

Chapter 4

Under Pressure, Goldman Grows Quickly and Goes Public

A T A GOLDMAN PARTNER MEETING, THE STORY GOES, A SENIOR partner asked the new partners to identify the two men who were most important to the firm's business. The new partners responded with last names: Goldman, Sachs, and Weinberg. The senior partner then revealed the answer: Senator Carter Glass and Representative Henry Steagall.[1]

Congress passed the Glass–Steagall Act (formally known as the Banking Act of 1933) to provide Depression-era deposit bank customers protection against the additional risks involved in trading and investing.[2] Its intent was to separate the consumer deposit–based commercial banking industry from investment-banking activities by prohibiting well-capitalized commercial banks from getting involved in the securities business. It also had the unintended effect of protecting the profitable underwriting business of the investment banks.[3] The act explains why both a J.P. Morgan and a Morgan Stanley now exist.[4] J.P. Morgan had to spin off its investment banking business, creating two entities: J.P. Morgan became the commercial bank, whose business was deposits and lending, and Morgan Stanley was spun off as the investment bank, handling the securities and underwriting businesses.

However, in 1999 the act was repealed. Such deregulation and other external pressures—such as competition and technology—as well as pressures from within the organization, had a transformative effect on how Goldman did business and on the organizational culture. From then on, Goldman had to compete more vigorously for scarce resources—capital, talent, clients, reputation, and more—against larger, publicly traded competitors (discussed later). In addition to having limited personal liability or capital constraints, these publicly traded competitors had more, and permanent, capital and didn't espouse the same business principles or have the same financial interdependence.

These combined pressures had one major effect: the leaders of Goldman felt that the firm needed to grow—and grow fast.

I have had lengthy, spirited philosophical discussions with Goldman and McKinsey partners about growth. Growth in itself is not a bad thing. But as Goldman navigated its environment, the rapid pace of its growth had dramatic (and often unintended or unanticipated) consequences—many of which were not fully understood inside the firm or out—and they compounded over time. In essence, Goldman's response to the various pressures in a dynamic environment—in particular, rapid growth—made it even more difficult to notice that the firm was drifting away from its traditional interpretation of its principles. The rapid growth, combined with multiple, conflicting organizational goals, resulted in a series of many small everyday decisions happening so quickly that most people didn't notice (or were too busy to notice, or didn't care).

Regulatory Pressures

A great many rules and regulations govern banking in the United States: the Glass–Steagall Act, the Sarbanes–Oxley Act, exchange rules, and so on.[5] I focus here on the key regulatory changes that had a particularly strong influence on Goldman.

Public Trading of Investment Banks in 1970

Even before the repeal of Glass–Steagall, Goldman was facing increasing competitive and other pressures, and those combined pressures led ultimately to the decision to go public, which the partners voted to do in 1998, before the act's repeal (the IPO didn't actually happen, though, until 1999). Much emphasis has been placed on how the IPO affected Goldman's culture, and that's true, but the organizational drift had started well before that. Goldman had been feeling the increasing heat of competition and other external forces for years.

The public listing of investment banks is a relatively new development. Investment banking, for most of its history, was conducted by firms organized in partnerships. But before the 1970s, some partnerships decided they wanted to go public to raise capital, reduce the risk of loss of partner capital, and improve liquidity, sparking a significant change in the organizational structure of the banks.

In 1970, the NYSE repealed provisions that had prevented publicly listed companies from being members of the exchange, and the floodgates opened. That year, Donaldson, Lufkin & Jenrette was the first to list on the exchange, with Merrill Lynch, Reynolds Securities, and Bache & Co. following in 1971. Salomon Brothers listed a decade later, and Morgan Stanley went public in 1986. Goldman, in 1999, was the last major full-service investment bank to be publicly listed.[6]

Goldman followed much later for two key reasons: first, unlike most of the others, it had no retail banking business, wherein banks deal directly with consumers on smaller transactions like mortgages and personal loans rather than big institutional clients or corporations executing large transactions. Second, Goldman didn't distribute the firm's profits to partners annually, as the others did. The differences between Goldman and the others were illuminated by a 2004 study by Alan Morrison and William Wilhelm Jr.[7] In the decade before the banks started to go public, because of increasing technological and regulatory pressure to scale up (an example of the interrelationship between these pressures), those with retail business units increased the number of partners, the capital employed per partner, and the number of employees per partner, according to the study. They also needed to raise considerable sums to invest in computers and data management technology to facilitate faster handling of administrative activities to support the smaller size, but higher volume, of transactions.

Going to the market (to the outside equity capital markets or private investors) to raise this cash was considered the best, if not the only, option. Without outside capital, the only ways to infuse new capital into a partnership were to admit more partners or to increase the amount of capital contributed by each new partner (while balancing the retiring partners' capital withdrawals). Each approach has limits. Also, because these banks typically distributed their profits to the partners annually, they had less capital to work with. Going public offered the cheapest cost of capital, because equity investors in the public markets were willing to receive a lower return on their capital, in part because their investments are so liquid, than private equity investors. But it was appealing for one other crucial reason. Under a partnership model, all partners are personally responsible for all the firm's liabilities. As a public corporation, it is all of the shareholders who are liable (and liability is not personal liability).

According to interviews I conducted, Morgan Stanley had no retail banking at the time, but it generally distributed a meaningful portion of its profits to partners annually, and this meant that it faced pressure to go public earlier than Goldman. As a Goldman partner explained to me, because Goldman required partners to keep their capital in the firm until they retired, the firm had more capital to invest to stay competitive.

In 1986, when Morgan Stanley went public, Goldman had about $1 billion of equity capital, twice that of Morgan Stanley. Even so, the competitive and other pressures were such that the Goldman partners gave consideration to an IPO at that time. The first serious proposal to go public was presented by the management committee at Goldman's partnership meeting that year. It was championed by Bob Rubin and Steve Friedman, who at the time were on the management committee, and it was met with serious opposition from the partners. John L. Weinberg distanced himself from the proposal, remaining silent during the meeting. After Jimmy Weinberg spoke against it in the meeting, it was not brought to a vote.[8]

Although the proposal was set aside, it was clear from the meeting that Goldman's decision to expand to pursue a global business strategy "placed additional capital pressures on the firm, making its remaining a partnership less and less feasible."[9] In my interviews, however, some partners said the firm had enough capital at the time to fund international expansion, albeit at a slower pace, or that it could continue to take outside private capital. Although outside private capital was more expensive than capital from the public markets, it would allow the firm to stay a private partnership.

Ultimately in 1986 the partners decided to accept a $500 million private outside equity investment from Sumitomo Bank in exchange for 12.5 percent of the firm's annual profits and appreciation of equity value. The deal with Sumitomo was appealing because, according to the terms of the deal and the Bank Holding Act of 1956's preclusion, Sumitomo could not have any voting rights or any influence over the firm's operations.[10]

Goldman was growing rapidly in both size and complexity at this time. The firm ballooned from a few thousand people in a few offices in 1980, to thirteen thousand at the time of the IPO, with much of that growth overseas. At the time Whitehead codified the firm's values, Goldman's business was entirely within the United States. It was strictly a New York firm. By 1996, international employees constituted 35 percent of Goldman's workforce. Further, the total number of international employees was now larger than the total number of employees in the previous decade.

In 1987 a member of the management committee voiced a common opinion: "Everyone is uncomfortable with the rate of growth. We all feel that if we don't keep expanding, we'll lose our position. But if we keep growing at a certain rate, we'll lose control."[11] As early as the late 1980s and early 1990s, Goldman was having meetings, even hiring a consulting firm, to discuss the consequences of hypergrowth.[12] However, Goldman's growth was phenomenally successful.

Earnings nearly doubled between 1990 and 1992, funding the opening of new offices in Frankfurt, Milan, and Seoul. In 1992, the Kamehameha Schools/Bishop Estate, a Hawaiian educational trust, invested $250 million for around a 5 percent stake.

In 1994 Goldman suffered big trading losses and the unprecedented wave of resignations among the partners that followed, starting with the sudden resignation of then senior partner Steve Friedman, who cited health reasons. Making Friedman's departure all the more disruptive and unsettling was that it followed Bob Rubin's abrupt resignation after a short tenure (1990–1992) as co-senior partner with Friedman to become assistant to President Clinton on economic policy. Friedman had refused to accept a co-leader in running the firm and left the choice of successors in the hands of the management committee.[13]

Almost every partner I interviewed who worked at the firm in 1994 said that, in hindsight, the sudden departures of Friedman and Rubin, who had been handpicked by Weinberg and Whitehead to lead the firm, had significant unintended consequences for Goldman. Some even believe that the timing, circumstances, and handling of the departures caused a greater impact on culture than the IPO and were one of the main reasons behind the IPO itself.

The 1994 departures also raised serious issues of trust among the partners. In addition to the senior partner, almost one-third of the other partners retired, giving their capital preferential treatment and more protection than that of the general partners who stayed and allowing the retirees to begin cashing out their capital. The resignations would remove hundreds of millions of dollars of partners' capital from the firm, requiring a larger influx of new partners than in the past. This situation upset what had been a stable, cohesive group that traditionally had seen just enough partner turnover to balance junior and senior partners. The fifty-eight new partners, the largest partner class Goldman had ever announced, now also formed a large voting bloc on key firm decisions, and they had just seen the firm at its worst with the old partners jumping ship.[14]

Discussing the resignation of a senior partner who had been running the financial institutions group and was generally considered one of the most knowledgeable about the financial sector and the firm's prospects, one partner expressed the sentiment of many of them: "Aren't these the guys that I've been slaving with—not for? I mean really working hard with for a long time, and they are quitting? I don't get that. How can you leave? I mean, just how does that square? When it gets tough, you are supposed to get tougher."[15]

Based on the accounts of partners at the time, when the old guard—many of them viewed as culture carriers—started bailing and looking out for themselves, it shook the belief in the core values and principles of the firm. The resignations caused people to think more about themselves, their own interests, and their own personal ambitions—and materialism began to grow.[16] With Friedman's sudden resignation and no succession plan, a fierce power struggle ensued, increasing the instability and prompting personal reflection.

Corzine, a trader in the FICC department who also had a CFO-type role (which at the time was typically the head of fixed income and chief risk allocator), aggressively announced to the management committee that he wanted to be senior partner (and be given the title of CEO) and for Paulson to be the number two, with the title of COO. In recent memory there had always been co-head senior partners, reflecting a culture of teamwork. There were "the two Johns" and then "Steve and Bob." Many divisions and departments had co-heads. The firm had never had CEOs or COOs (it had senior partners or co-senior partners); the CEO title didn't make sense in the context of a partnership (it typically was used in public corporations with a hierarchy and organization charts). Although the people with the senior partner titles were everyone's bosses, everyone on the management committee had a vote, so no one person could dictate.[17]

In the end, Corzine got what he pushed for. Paulson did not have enough support on the management committee to push for a co-senior partner role. Some people said it was in part because Paulson was not based in the New York office 100 percent of the time and lacked experience in trading, where the greatest profits and risk were. But the partners I interviewed said that they recognized the need for a balance or compromise between banking and trading (and a few said they needed someone to "watch" Corzine, who they worried could be too aggressive). In hindsight, partners said, the precedent of having no co-senior partner, along with the power struggle, sent a poor message to the troops, especially in view of the defections.

Interviewees explained that once he became CEO, Corzine convinced some partners to stay, rather than retire, by leading them to believe they would get rich when the firm went public in the near future.[18] For a variety of reasons—including alleged promotion promises, guilt, and John L. Weinberg's pleading—more partners stayed than initially had been predicted. But they told me the trading losses, combined with the defections, dramatically affected the culture.

In addition to significant trading losses in 1994, throughout that year the firm worked to settle suits with a number of pension funds related to Goldman's involvement with publisher Robert Maxwell.[19] Eventually it was settled for $253 million.[20] This cost was borne by those who had been general partners between 1989 and 1991, and the size of this settlement surprised many of them.[21] A November 1994 AP article made this prediction: "The general partners may find themselves sitting with a smaller capital account at year's end than they had starting off. That rude and unfamiliar prospect explains why persistent rumors have been circulating on Wall Street that Goldman's management has recently put pressure on the firm's general partners to ante up additional capital. (One partner's capital account was reportedly wiped out completely.)"[22]

Layoffs were announced for traders, analysts, and support staff.[23] An unintended consequence was the emergence of "a culture of contingency . . . a sense not only that each day might be your last, but that your value was linked exclusively to how much revenue was generated for that firm on that day—regardless of its source."[24] Between 1987 and 1994, the firm had downsized six different times in different divisions in response to different earnings.[25]

Despite the instability, the partners opposed going public at the time. It was commonly thought, however, that there was an IPO in Goldman's future: "Down the road Goldman will surely revisit the idea of going public, thereby gaining permanent capital. But Corzine has said that a stock offering isn't 'practical' right now. You need profit updrafts, not downdrafts, to go public."[26] Goldman had been stressed by the events of 1994; it would recover, but the partnership showed signs of vulnerability.

Goldman's problems at that time were not related only to costs and "bad bets"; one partner noted, "[A] culture of undisciplined risk taking had built up over many years."[27] That same partner named other "stuff [that] built up," such as "the lack of a risk committee, trusting individual partners, model-based analytics, [thinking] that by God, you can be smart and figure it all out, and letting traders become too important and being afraid to confront them if they've been money makers."[28] When I asked partners about this, they said the statement was probably relative. They admitted that changes in business practices needed to be addressed, but they believed Goldman was still much better than its competitors. And, more importantly, the adjustments to the losses helped Goldman "strengthen" its risk management culture, and that is one reason Goldman did better than its competitors in the credit crisis, discussed later.

Corzine sought to open offices around the world during this time. "Jon wanted to do business in every country, everywhere, and wanted to be big," one partner said. "He was like the guy going through a cafeteria and he wanted to take everything and put it on his tray. That concerned people."[29] In 1995, Goldman opened offices in Shanghai and Mexico City and created joint ventures in India and Indonesia. Paulson and many others thought Corzine was moving too fast. Lloyd Blankfein, the current Goldman CEO, used to joke that "he was going to go away someday and wake up and find out we were opening up an office in Guatemala."[30] (I discuss selected other organizational changes during Corzine's leadership and their intended and unintended consequences later.)

From Partnership to LLC

Corzine raised the idea of an IPO in January 1996, and it was again rejected. But in lieu of an IPO, the management committee took several steps to shore up the firm's capital base and limit the partners' legal and financial liability. The firm became a limited liability partnership in 1996.[31] The potential liability to partners was now restricted to their capital in the firm. The "partner" title was formally abandoned. It was believed that the term could be misinterpreted or could place implied personal partnership-like liability on the partners. Equity-holding partners were now called managing directors, as were almost one hundred of the thousands of vice presidents (the more experienced ones). Those who were partners in the firm were internally called partner managing directors, or PMDs. Nonpartner managing directors were referred to as "MD-lites."

Partners told me they believed that the title change for the chosen vice presidents conveyed practical management responsibility on par with that of their peers at other firms. According to news reports, "The 128-year-old investment-banking partnership created the title of managing director last year and elevated 87 employees to the rank. They get a boost in pay and benefits, but unlike Goldman's 190 partners, they don't own a share of the firm's $5.8 billion in capital. Goldman executives say the new title recognizes able bankers and traders who face tough competition rising to partner, considered the pinnacle of Wall Street. Non-partner managing directors are likely to earn $2 million or more each, recruiters say."[32] The addition of so many people at once and with the same titles now started to impact the social network of trust.

Additionally, the firm changed its compensation practices. All MDs received *participation shares*, whose value was tied to the overall profitability of the firm and not to individual or departmental performance. Several partners told me that their change in title altered their perspective. They no longer had the cachet and status of the title "partner," something they believed differentiated them from peers at firms like Morgan Stanley; there were now many "managing directors" at Goldman.

As a result of this change, only the capital partners retained in the firm, and not their personal assets, could be used to repay the firm's creditors.[33] Although the change would greatly reduce the risk of personal bankruptcy, the retained capital was estimated to be around 70 percent to 90 percent of a partner's assets, capital that could not be accessed until retirement. Along with limited liability, however, the firm instituted changes to the capital obligations of those leaving the partnership; under the new regime, retiring partners were required to keep their capital in their firm for a longer period, on average six years.[34]

The change in legal structure was accompanied by other changes in the firm's organizational structure, processes, tasks, and systems. Goldman became a bit more hierarchical.[35] In 1995, the firm revamped its governance structure, forming two new eighteen-person decision-making groups: the partnership committee and the operating committee. The operating committee focused on coordination of strategy and operations among the firm's departments, divisions, and geographies. The partnership committee oversaw the firm's capital structure as well as the selection of partners. Soon afterward, the firm established an executive committee—the ultimate decision-making group—which was much smaller than its predecessor, the management committee. The executive committee's charter included all issues that did not require a vote by the full partnership or a partner's individual consent.[36] In addition, two new eighteen-person committees were formed. The six individuals on the executive committee had much more power than the management committee had enjoyed, including the ability to change the leadership. When I asked partners why they went along with these changes, some admitted that some were promised committee appointments, elevating their own status, or some were afraid they might be departnered if they didn't go along with the changes. (Ironically, the organizational change by Corzine to a smaller and more powerful group would lead to a coup against Corzine; this is discussed later.)

Many things changed as a result of and around the time of Goldman's transformation into an LLC. The competitive and other external pressures fueling the demand for growth did not.

From LLC to Public Company

Some of the firm's senior partners did not share Corzine's enthusiasm for abandoning the partnership structure. Corzine was strongly in favor of an IPO, but Paulson insisted on a cautious, well-informed decision-making process. According to my interviews, three of the six members of the operating committee were in favor of an IPO, and Paulson, John Thornton, and John Thain were against the idea. A strategy committee, led by Paulson, was charged with determining what Goldman should look like down the road and how best to ensure it remained on top. Input was actively solicited from partners, and Corzine tried to speak personally to most. After six weeks of study in 1998, the strategy committee submitted a plan for "vigorous expansion."[37] The study supported Corzine's conviction that Goldman needed to go public to take advantage of competitive opportunities in businesses other than traditional investment banking. Although Corzine and Paulson did not get along, Corzine eventually gained Paulson's support.

Some people in the press have speculated that Paulson's ultimate agreement to support the IPO was connected to his being made co-head of the firm. The operating committee and partnership committee, which together accounted for 39 of the 189 partners, supported an IPO for reasons related primarily to the perceived pressures to grow, and grow quickly, citing the threat posed by larger competitors and the ability "to bind more employees to the firm through equity ownership."[38] After the executive committee agreed to pursue an IPO, co-senior partners Corzine and Paulson released a statement that reflects both capital and liability concerns: "As a public company, Goldman Sachs will have the financial strength and strategic flexibility to continue to serve our clients effectively as well as respond thoughtfully to the business and competitive environment over the long term. This action will also meet a fundamental objective of the partners—to share ownership, benefits and responsibilities more broadly among all of the firm's employees."[39]

During hours of discussion over a two-day general meeting in 1998, the partners registered their opinions with the executive committee, which was empowered to recommend for or against an IPO.[40] In the end, they reached consensus, and the partners voted to go ahead. (See table 4-1; for more details on the value of partners' stock at the time of the IPO, see appendix D.)

Again, the change in structure was described as a direct response to competitive and external pressures to expand.[41] Expansion required large amounts of capital—more than the partners could or would contribute personally. The partners concluded that the best alternative was to raise capital by offering shares of the firm for sale to the public. I asked partners why they didn't push to raise more outside private capital while remaining private, following up with the question, Wouldn't the higher cost of capital be worth the benefits of maintaining the partnership structure? Most of them didn't have a

TABLE 4-1

The top eleven: percentages, shares, and value at IPO

Name	Percentage	Implied shares outstanding	Value at IPO price ($53)	First closing price ($70.38)
Henry M. Paulson Jr.	1.100%	2,915,210	$154,506,120	$205,172,466
Jon S. Corzine	1.100%	2,915,210	154,506,120	205,172,466
Robert J. Hurst	1.100%	2,915,210	154,506,120	205,172,466
John A. Thain	1.050%	2,782,700	147,483,114	195,846,445
John L. Thornton	1.050%	2,782,700	147,483,114	195,846,445
Daniel M. Neidich	0.900%	2,385,172	126,414,098	167,868,381
John P. McNulty	0.900%	2,385,172	126,414,098	167,868,381
Lloyd C. Blankfein	0.900%	2,385,172	126,414,098	167,868,381
Michael P. Mortara	0.900%	2,385,172	126,414,098	167,868,381
Richard A. Friedman	0.900%	2,385,172	126,414,098	167,868,381
Robert K. Steel	0.900%	2,385,172	126,414,098	167,868,381

good answer, but they said it was considered and dismissed. A few said that only a limited group of outside private minority investors and capital would be willing to invest without gaining a say in management into perpetuity. A few disputed this argument. They also said that by then the culture had changed enough for the IPO to go forward because of everything that had happened in the 1990s. One former partner went so far as to insinuate that in the end the real pressures were enough, and enough had changed, that their decision to vote for the IPO could be rationalized both to the outside world and to themselves. He thought this did mark a change in the culture because previous generations could have made the same rationalizations, especially in 1986.

Soon after the decision to go public was made, economic conditions took a sharp turn for the worse. The stock market was experiencing erratic swings, the economic chaos in Russia carried the prospect of enormous losses to investment banks, the stock prices of Goldman's competitors were falling, and there was virtually no market for IPOs. The firm's earnings took a nosedive in the last quarter of 1998 as trading losses soared. Goldman put its IPO on hold, but there was no doubt it was coming. The prospect of enormous personal gain from the IPO prevented another mass exodus of partners like in 1999, who would have had difficulty withdrawing their capital if they had wanted to leave the firm. However, suddenly and unexpectedly, in January 1999, Corzine, whose working relationship with Paulson had always been uneasy, resigned as co-CEO, remaining as co-chairman—but only to help the firm get through the IPO.

Another sign that the culture had already changed significantly was a Hank Paulson–orchestrated management coup that forced Corzine out and put Paulson in charge. According to interviews, he and other partners were worried that Corzine "was going off the reservation." They had found out that Corzine had merger/sale conversations with other parties without the direct consent of the executive committee. Over the Christmas holiday in 1998, while Corzine was away, Paulson made his move. Corzine had made the organizational change of consolidating power into a small executive committee versus the larger management committee, and there were some recent changes in the membership, which together opened up the possibility for a coup. In what was eerily similar to Paulson's alleged quid pro quo support for the IPO to be named co-head of the firm, allegedly Thain and Thornton agreed to support Paulson in return for what they believed was an informal promise: Paulson would be the CEO for only a few years (the time was debatable) and then transfer the CEO job to both Thain and Thornton. Thain was a longtime lieutenant and friend of Corzine. According to interviews, he justified the decision with the argument that he was doing what he thought was best for the firm in the long run. In early to mid-January, Goldman partners received an e-mail from Paulson and Corzine: "Jon has decided to relinquish the CEO title."[42] Corzine remained co-chairman, but only to help the firm complete the IPO. Several partners I interviewed said that in hindsight they believed the alleged coup sent a bad message regarding behavior and highlighted how much the firm's culture had changed. It would also affect how the next CEO would organize the firm (discussed later).

With the markets and Goldman's earnings recovering, Goldman went public on May 3, 1999, pricing the stock at $53 per share, implying an equity market valuation of over $30 billion. In the end, Goldman decided to offer only a small portion of the company to the public, with some 48 percent still held by the partnership pool, 22 percent of the company held by nonpartner employees, and 18 percent held by retired Goldman partners and Sumitomo Bank and the investing arm of Kamehameha Schools in Hawaii. This left approximately 12 percent of the company held by the public.

Less than six months after Goldman went public, in 1999 certain provisions of the Glass–Steagall Act were repealed by the Gramm–Leach–Bliley Act, and President Bill Clinton signed the legislation that year. Former Goldman co-senior partner Bob Rubin was secretary of the Treasury at the time, and he later joined Citigroup.

The repeal meant that commercial banks, investment banks, securities firms, and insurance companies could be combined.[43] Commercial banks started to buy investment banks, spawning a massive consolidation in the banking industry. Some believed it was inevitable that Goldman would be bought. The firm suddenly looked small compared to its new direct competitors, and, with its market position, brand, and relationships, it would have been a prize. It turned out that Goldman CEO Jon Corzine and others held merger discussions at the time, talks that were disrupted by Hank Paulson's ouster of Corzine (to be discussed more later). Rather than be taken over, the partners decided to grow.[44]

The dismantling of Glass–Steagall led to many changes in the ways banks competed, changes that put a great deal of pressure on Goldman to rapidly evolve its own ways of operating. The changes in practices and in the firm's culture were greatly accelerated. These new powerhouses began challenging Goldman with "margin-reducing, risk-heightening competition."[45] The impression was that competitors like J.P. Morgan or Citigroup would tell their clients, "If you want a corporate loan, you have to hire our M&A bankers." This bundling of low-margin commercial banking product offerings (such as revolving lines of credit) with higher-margin investment banking products (such as M&A work and equity underwriting) threatened Goldman's most lucrative businesses. In short, the investment banking business was becoming commoditized. In addition, clients put a premium on retail distribution—that is, selling securities to the general public, who were willing to pay ridiculous prices for tech stocks to cash in on the technology boom.

Even before the repeal of Glass–Steagall, in 1997, Morgan Stanley had responded to this pressure by merging with Dean Witter Reynolds. Morgan was considered a "white shoe" firm, referring to white buck shoes—laced white suede or buckskin shoes with red soles, which stereotypically were worn at Ivy League colleges, while Dean Witter Reynolds was a firm with strong retail distribution: nine thousand stock brokers serving more than 3 million customers.

Dean Witter also owned Discover Card. Generally, white shoe investment bankers often looked down on retail stock brokers, whose alma maters typically were not the elite schools. I remember when the deal was announced, a Goldman associate called his Ivy League business school classmate working in investment banking at Morgan Stanley and teasingly asked him if he could now help him get a Discover credit card. Little did he know that I had worked on a project to evaluate whether Goldman should buy a retail distribution firm or build a scalable internet-based technology platform to access retail investors for distribution.

In the early 2000s Goldman divided most of its M&A department into industry groups. A lateral M&A partner told me that client CEOs couldn't tell the difference between excellent and average M&A advice or banks' business practices, but they could tell whether you knew their industry.

Competitive pressures forced Goldman to reexamine and modify its strategy. For example, Goldman redesigned and restructured into industry groups. Industry knowledge was so valued that, for example, I worked on projects evaluating whether Goldman should buy a consulting firm with deep industry knowledge and CEO contacts, or a boutique investment bank focused on an industry-like technology. Goldman also put greater emphasis on expanding its powerful network of key decision makers (CEOs, chief investment officers, government officials, etc.) and on trying to ensure that the relationships and information were highly coordinated and selectively and tactically shared. Access and information were strengths of Goldman's, as they required a culture of serious teamwork. This was highly valued by clients and a key distinguishing factor in hiring Goldman. In addition, Goldman focused more on coinvesting with clients. A coinvestment relationship was seen to have many advantages, including establishment of a closer relationship than did a merely advisory one.

The industry consolidation brought about in part by the changes to Glass–Steagall resulted in fewer but much larger banks—banks that many would later argue were "too big to fail," so large that their failure was deemed a risk to the stability of the entire banking system. Another result was that the pace at which these companies now had to grow in order to stay competitive challenged their organizational cultures. Companies growing via acquisition have significant cultural and integration challenges.

Pressures Intensify

Following consolidation, the financial services industry became intensely competitive, and Goldman now faced competition for scarce resources not only from other banks but also from insurance companies, investment advisers, mutual funds, hedge funds, and private equity firms.[46]

To gain market share, commercial banks aggressively offered highly competitive pricing for services, resulting in additional pressures for Goldman. Commercial banking competitors also had access to cheaper financing, and they could take a longer-term view in pricing assets and loans on their balance sheets than could those who remained strictly investment banks. That's because investment banking firms must mark to market or use fair-value accounting (which means that the fair value of an asset is based on the current market price), compared with commercial banks, which can use historical cost accounting for assets held for investment.

Some Goldman partners often privately complained about this advantage, in addition to accusing the commercial banks of illegally tying lending to investment banking business. Goldman faced increasing pressure to retain market share by committing more capital to important clients and conducting transactions on terms that often didn't offer returns commensurate with the risks or didn't meet Goldman's internal return hurdles. Moreover, consolidation significantly increased the capital base and geographic reach of some of its competitors. It wasn't only Goldman's US competitors; foreign banks were buying US banks (Deutsche Bank bought Bankers Trust/Alex

Brown, UBS bought Warburg and Dillon Read, etc.). Goldman also faced competition from the advent of electronic execution and alternative trading systems, lowering commissions. It also faced disintermediation by hedge funds, alternative asset management companies, and other unregulated firms in providing or raising capital.

Goldman also began facing stiff competition in attracting and retaining employees. "We live in a competitive environment," said David Viniar during his tenure. "We still have people leaving for multiyear offers away from us, some from our competitors, some from other industry participants."[47]

Goldman's client base also began to change. Its traditional banking clients were corporations, which were typically relationship oriented. In the early 1990s, there weren't many private equity firms. For example, in 1992, when I started, I worked on the sale of one of a company's divisions to a private equity firm. We must have contacted fewer than a dozen private equity firms, because there were not many of them around. Nor were there many large hedge funds. Later in the 1990s, however, private equity firms and hedge funds began to boom. Generally, these firms were much more transactional and generated large fees in the short term compared with Goldman's traditional corporate clients or "buy and hold" mutual funds. People at hedge funds tended to be more transaction oriented than relationship oriented. Similarly, private equity firms tend to be transactional; buying and selling companies and taking them public are shorter-term transactions than traditional corporate client business. Goldman executives decided to focus on this growing industry and even started a group in the mid- to late 1990s to cater to this client base.

Reflecting on the shift, a Goldman partner I spoke with said that perhaps Goldman's emphasis on doing the right thing was too extreme to be practical in the competitive business environment and that an emphasis on more transaction-oriented clients, like private equity firms, was needed in banking. He felt that too many Goldman people were focused on maintain unproductive client relationships and were being rewarded simply for their internal Goldman relationships or caretaking historically loyal Goldman clients and contributions to recruiting and mentoring.

Because private equity firms and hedge funds valued and treated Goldman differently than did traditional corporate clients, Goldman's approach to clients began to change. The private equity firms valued any investment bank that could get them the inside track on deals and could provide the best financing terms (including guaranteed or bridge financing, which puts the investment bank at risk if it can't sell or distribute the loan to other lenders or investors). Many of the private equity firms felt they already had people (many of them former bankers) who were smarter and more skilled than those in the banks in the kinds of deals the firms were doing. In an interview, one private equity client described most investment bankers who maintained a relationship with his firm as "order takers."

Hedge funds also changed the landscape. Unlike many traditional mutual funds, which had a "buy and hold" mentality, many hedge funds went in and out of securities with high frequency. They typically borrowed money from investment banks to buy securities, and they shorted securities. All of these activities generate significant fees, and so Goldman organized groups to focus on these growing clients and their special needs.

I remember working on a special project to analyze Goldman's top fee-paying clients, and I was shocked by how many were hedge funds. They, along with private equity firms, quickly became the largest fee payers on Wall Street. The hedge funds were sharp and sophisticated. In trading, there is an inherent tension between buyer and seller. Because of the sophistication of the hedge funds, they also typically viewed Wall Street firms as "places of execution" that provided liquidity and securities. They valued "the edge"—receiving special access to decision makers who gave them a competitive advantage, or to traders who were willing to take the risk and provide them with liquidity, better execution, or a better balance sheet and who offered low-cost, easy financing terms so that the hedge funds could leverage their investments and improve their returns. The private equity funds and hedge funds generally treated Goldman more like a necessary counterparty than a trusted adviser for the long term. Most of these funds were under intense pressure to produce short-term results and did not value long-term relationships in the same way that many corporate clients did.

As Goldman grew its proprietary investing activities and became a more active competitor to its investing clients, some hedge funds and private equity firms suggested that Goldman was introducing too many conflicts of interest into its operations—as when Goldman had the Water Street Fund in the late 1980s and early 1990s—causing mistrust. They felt Goldman had access to proprietary information from clients and had the potential to use it to Goldman's advantage. According to most of my interviewees, these accusations began in the mid-1990s and accelerated as the hedge fund and private equity industry became more competitive and added players, and at the same time Goldman dedicated increasing amounts of capital to these competing activities.

Many hedge funds came and went, gaining a few years' worth of great returns and growth and then hitting a rough patch or falling out of style and shrinking as investors fled. Hedge fund traders also tended to move around. So there was not the same traditional long-term relationship mentality with hedge funds as with corporate relationships. But even corporations changed in this regard in the 1990s as pressure for performance increased on corporate boards and CEOs. Boards came under pressure to replace underperforming CEOs, a trend that continued in the 2000s. The average tenure of a CEO has consistently declined.[48] So relationships with corporate CEOs were also becoming short-term propositions.

Technological Pressures

Technological innovation was another source of significant pressure on Goldman and the whole banking sector. New technology has added transparency to financial markets, as with electronic trading, while also making them less transparent, as with the design of increasingly complex investment products, such as the mortgage securities behind the 2008 crisis. Generally, more transparency in markets and electronic execution hurts investment banks' profitability, and the hit on profits drives banks to seek greater scale and a higher volume of transactions to offset the losses. This is happening today, for example, with the sale of treasury notes. More than 20 percent of the $538 billion of treasury notes auctioned this year have been awarded to bidders who bypassed the traditional dealers at the banks by using a website to place their orders.[49] That's almost twice the amount as in 2011 and up from 5.6 percent in 2009. This direct-bidding system has eaten into the profits of government bond traders at investment banks. Typically, low-transparency/high-complexity products have the highest margins. So it's understandable that banks focus on developing and selling complex products, especially to offset the negative impact of transparency from technology.

Technological pressure contributed to the change in Goldman's culture in various ways. For one thing, technological changes increased the emphasis on trading, both within Goldman and generally. Traditionally in investment banking, information was exchanged primarily by word of mouth—in person or over the phone in the context of long-standing relationships. It was a labor-intensive, human capital–intensive business, as well as an apprenticeship business, more art than science. In *Information Markets*, William Wilhelm Jr., a professor of management, and Joseph Downing, an investment banker, point to technological pressures as being so powerful that they were key reasons that Goldman went public. Information technology provides a lower cost, more reliable way of disseminating, aggregating, storing, and analyzing information, and it has diminished the role of long-standing relationships and human capital in banking. In response, Goldman began to put less emphasis on selecting its human capital, and on mentoring, training, and developing the culture to support the maintenance of relationships.

Ironically, the technological advances have also put a higher premium on star players. According to one part of Wilhelm and Downing's theory, there are a few exceptional "human capitalists" or "stars" who have an ability to transcend technology and utilize their skills and talents to build relationships to bring in the kind of money that technology-driven trading does. And these stars require outsized compensation. The way this affected Goldman was that its relatively tight bands for compensation for people at the same level started to widen, and the partners decided that exceptions in hiring, compensating, and promoting "stars" must be made, further impacting Goldman's culture.

Technological innovation also required greater specialization by employees at the firm. People needed to be specialists in order to add more value to clients. This also created more silos—and the conditions of structural secrecy, where information isn't completely shared or understood by all of the appropriate people.

More Than the IPO

Too much emphasis has been placed purely on the IPO as the force of change at Goldman; as this analysis shows, the change began well in advance of the IPO. John Whitehead had pointed to issues related to Goldman's earlier growth as his motivation for writing down the business principles. The pressure to grow was there at the time the principles were written—organizational drift was already in motion—and the principles were intended as one way to manage or constrain the change. In fact, the agreement of the partners to finally go public after resisting for so long was one of the products of the cultural changes that preceded the IPO.

Some may object to the argument that competitive and external pressures to grow were behind the change at Goldman as overly simplistic. The truth is indeed more complex. For one thing, the increased complexity in management and systems that often accompanies growth must be factored in as well.[50] Charles Perrow notes that institutional complexity prevents people from understanding the consequences of their behavior.[51] Certainly, complex systems pose greater control challenges than do simple ones. And the faster an organization grows, the more the pressures and reactions to them compound and become interconnected, leading to increasing complexity and difficulty in seeing change.

In addition to accelerating certain changes, Goldman's structural change into a public company initiated a cascade of significant changes to other aspects of the organization. Now it had a board of directors that included independent directors (people from outside Goldman); a new partnership compensation program, with voting rights, as spelled out in the shareholder agreement (to help replicate some elements of the partnership); additional layers of processes, controls, and management needed by a public company; new compensation processes and consideration (stock in addition to cash) and more.

But there were also pressures from within to grow revenues. During my interviews with partners, one of the recurring themes was the need for Goldman to "increase the size of the pie." This means that revenues, and consequently the firm, had to expand for the firm to be successful in recruiting and retaining talented people. If the pie stayed the same size, then as more people became partners, each partner would keep getting a smaller slice of the financial rewards, making partnership less attractive. In this way, the external competition for people, combined with financial incentives, pressured the firm to increase revenues—not only to stay competitive but also to shore up the partners' wealth. As we'll explore in more detail in the next chapter, the acceptance of a number of changes in practices at the firm that deviated from the traditional values, and the normalization of that deviance—or what could be described as rationalization that they weren't really deviations from the original meaning of the principles—were also crucial in the process of continuing drift.

Chapter 5

Signs of Organizational Drift

I N THEIR FIRST LETTER TO SHAREHOLDERS IN THE 1999 ANNUAL report, the top Goldman executives wrote, "As we begin the new century, we know that our success will depend on how well we change and manage the firm's rapid growth. That requires a willingness to abandon old practices and discover new and innovative ways of conducting business. Everything is subject to change—everything but the values we live by and stand for: teamwork, putting clients' interests first, integrity, entrepreneurship and excellence."[1]

Changes were happening, and the partners seemed to be making it clear that they wanted any changes carefully managed to maintain Goldman's core values. But as the firm encountered decision-making dilemmas related to change and growth, managers found it difficult both to acknowledge what was happening and to confront the conflicting needs and desires that underlay the issues. The Goldman partners I interviewed, even some of those who initially said there had been no change in culture, conceded that some changes had occurred, but they described them as "one-offs" or "special circumstances," and others said the industry was growing and changing so quickly and becoming so complex that they hadn't seen the changes clearly.

It is important to understand certain unique mechanisms at Goldman that formerly had helped slow the pace of change. The pressures on these mechanisms provide a lens into the firm's policies and business practices and how they evolved.

Constrained Capital

One inescapable reality of a private partnership is that capital is somewhat constrained by its being contributed by the individual partners—and there are, after all, only so many partners. This constraint acts as a check on growth. A second factor is the personal liability of the partners, which requires the maintenance of large capital reserves to cover potential losses as well as the adoption of business practices that help the firm avoid large regulatory fines or lawsuits.

For most of Goldman's history, these capital constraints provided a measure of self-regulation that not only limited growth but also helped maintain cultural stability and led the firm to emphasize client relationships. John Whitehead observed that "limited capital forces an investment banking firm to be careful in deciding what kinds of business it should be involved in and to what extent."[2] With restricted capital, the firm had to emphasize client-oriented businesses, rather than trading, because they required less capital and often entailed relatively less risk. That is one of the reasons why the M&A department was highly valued.

Whether or not the lack of capital was a drawback is debatable, and it was debated by the partners at the time. Not only did Whitehead believe that capital constraints forced the firm to make better decisions, but also many competitors thought Goldman was at no disadvantage. As one commented, "I wish I could find a business where Goldman is capital-constrained."[3] But the stark fact was that in 1998, Goldman had roughly half the capital base of Morgan Stanley or Merrill Lynch—this, after having twice the capital base of Morgan Stanley in 1986. The increasing pressure for growth led the partners to seek outside capital in order to remain competitive, even though acknowledged Goldman culture carriers voiced concerns, fearing the impact on the firm of outside investors' goals as well as the impact that more capital would have on the firm's business mix, tolerance for risk, culture, and management.

Another key loosening of the constraints on organizational change came from the changes in liability for losses, the dangers of which many partners were also well aware of.

Partners' Liability

Earlier investments—the $500 million private equity investment of Sumitomo Bank in 1986, and the $250 million private investment made four years later by the Kamehameha Schools/Bishop Estate, had loosened the constraints on growth, but they had not relieved partners of personal liability. But first with the transition to LLC and then with an IPO, they would be freed from this liability, which a number feared would lead to a stronger appetite for growth and risk and would quicken change. They had already seen evidence of greater risk-taking even before the IPO.

In my interviews, many of the partners pointed to their personal liability as having been a constraining factor on "doing stupid things." Some pointed to the risk Goldman took in bailing out the hedge fund Long-Term Capital Management (LTCM) in 1998 as an early case of taking on more risk than the firm had traditionally been comfortable with. LTCM was a speculative hedge fund that used a lot of leverage and faced failure that year. As LTCM teetered, Wall Street feared that its failure could have a ripple effect and cause catastrophic losses throughout the financial system. Unable to raise more money on its own, LTCM had its back against the wall.

Goldman, AIG, and Warren Buffett's Berkshire Hathaway offered to buy out the fund's partners for $250 million, provide capital of $3.75 billion, and operate LTCM within Goldman's own trading division. The situation was so serious and the pressures on LTCM were so intense that the offer was made with a one-hour deadline. But at the beginning of the year, LTCM had $4.7 billion in equity, so its partners regarded the offer as stunningly low. They did not accept Buffett's offer within the required one-hour deadline, and the deal was off. Ultimately, the Federal Reserve Bank of New York organized a bailout of $3.625 billion by the major creditors to avoid widespread financial collapse. Goldman and the rest of the top-tier creditors each contributed $300 million.[4]

For some Goldman partners, getting involved in the bailout subjected their personal capital in the firm to too much risk. The investment banking partners, in particular, according to my interviews, generally were not happy about the potential risks to their personal capital and were worried about Corzine's aggressiveness in pursuing the deal. To some of them, that the firm went ahead was a sign of both the pressures and the changes.

As the risk rose—when the firm grew and invested its own money more aggressively—it subsequently changed the way the partners interacted with the firm.

The IPO Debate

Even though many Goldman partners now say that the culture hasn't changed, at the time the IPO was decided, some of the partners were quite vocal about their concerns about cultural change. In fact, when people at Goldman—not only partners but also employees—discussed among themselves the idea of the firm going public, most of the concerns they expressed were about how Goldman's culture might change rather than about financial or personal repercussions. Partners talked about their responsibilities as stewards to leave the next generation a stronger business with smarter people than the one they had inherited. In discussions, most IPO opponents expressed the concern that going public could "destroy what makes Goldman Sachs Goldman Sachs."[5]

A contemporary report described the process of debating and then postponing the IPO as "a wrenching experience that has bruised the firm."[6] It created tensions between the firm's active general partners and retired limited partners, between Goldman's investment bankers and traders, and between Corzine and Paulson.[7] The discussion was personal, because people had to consider their own self-interest as well as the interests of the firm.[8] Partners screamed and cried during one meeting in what one observer described as a "cathartic experience."[9] Conflict arose between new partners and those who had been at the firm longer and had a much greater stake in the firm and were about to retire. Partners with longer tenure, whose Goldman equity and percentage had gained greatly in value and now would get multiples of their book value, had a greater personal financial incentive to favor an IPO.

Some partners were rumored to believe they should be compensated, through the IPO, for staying in 1994, turning the firm around, and taking the risk when others left. But John L. Weinberg said, "I always felt there was a terrific risk and still do, that when you start going that way [an IPO] you are going to have one group of partners who are going to take what has been worked on for 127 years and get that two-for-one or three-for-one. Any of us who are partners at the time when you do that don't deserve it. We let people in at book value, they should go out at book value."[10]

While I was at Goldman, one partner privately told me that he felt terrible that an IPO would make him worth more money than the management committee partner who had helped build the firm and helped get him promoted to partner. He estimated that this man, who had worked at the firm for more than twenty years and retired before the IPO, was worth an estimated $20–$40 million, compared with newer partners like him, some of whom had worked at the firm for less than ten years and would be worth more than $50 million.

Understandably, dissatisfaction was greatest among the retired limited partners, and tension between them and the general partners (essentially, Goldman's controlling owners) became heated. As the IPO was originally structured, limited partners would have received a 25 percent premium over the book value of their equity, whereas general partners would have seen premiums of nearly 300 percent.[11] Whitehead predicted a major problem if this inequity were not resolved. Issues related to fairness and compensation were also raised by nonpartners because of Goldman's long-standing policy of not paying high salaries to the "all-important junior executives—the ones who do the grunt work—holding out instead the brass ring of partnership and its potential for eight-figure incomes."[12]

Divisions also arose between the investment bankers and the traders. While in general, investment banking partners, especially the relatively new partners, did not support the IPO because of concerns about culture change and increased risk taking, most trading-oriented partners supported it, in part, because with the additional capital they could grow their businesses larger and faster.

One investment banking partner who did support the IPO explained to me that he did so because of concerns about capital risk and liability that outweighed those about change to the culture. All his wealth from working at Goldman for more than twenty years was tied up in the firm, and the IPO offered a way to get it out. Getting out at a multiple of book value was greatly beneficial and probably sold him on the IPO, he explained (sheepishly admitting some self-interest), but he had also been genuinely worried about the risk involved in the LTCM deal and he feared massive trading losses. He felt that Corzine was willing to take bigger risks than he was, and he was worried that the big traders—many of whom he didn't know well and some of whom were not partners—were risking lots of partners' money. It spooked him. But the firm needed to grow, he said, to continue to be the best place to work, to attract the best people, and to survive. He rationalized the IPO as a necessary compromise that was a result of pressures and changes.

Key Signs of Organizational Drift

One sign of organizational drift is a change in policies and business practices associated with a firm's principles. Even before the IPO, Goldman began embracing opportunities it had once shunned out of concern for preserving its reputation for ethical conduct and to reduce conflicting interests.

When firms get into new businesses in which they lack expertise or that are at odds with the values and principles that made them successful, they become vulnerable to veering off course, adding incremental risk—financial and reputational. The pursuit of maximizing opportunities can lead to rationalizing the drift. Previous decisions made to protect the firm start to be considered too conservative or out of date. Even the fundamental business model may be challenged. Goldman was not exempt from this process. Once again, I'm not judging or evaluating the changes; I'm simply pointing them out.

Representing Hostile Raiders

Goldman had made its reputation in banking by defending companies in hostile raids or unsolicited takeovers, when a company bids for a target company despite the wishes of the target's board and management, typically when the board decides it is not in the best interests of the shareholders for the company to be sold at the price offered. A "hostile" bidder makes its offer "public," taking it directly to shareholders—implying that the board of directors and management are not acting in the best interests of the shareholders and are trying to hold on to their jobs. To the target's board and management teams, the bankers who work against the takeover to protect them and shareholders are viewed very positively. A 1982 *Wall Street Journal* headline captured this positive image: "The Pacifist: Goldman Sachs Avoids Bitter Takeover Fights but Leads in Mergers." The accompanying article praised Goldman's policy of not representing corporate raiders in hostile deals, although it included the few obligatory criticisms from competitors.[13]

Goldman had made a strategic decision not to represent companies initiating hostile bids, the only large investment banking firm to do so.[14] When questioned about the wisdom of this policy, Whitehead responded, "We have to dissuade them from going forward with this and explain to them why our experience showed that it would be unlikely that this unfriendly tender offer would turn out to be successful for them a few years later."[15] As a result, CEOs were more comfortable revealing confidential information to Goldman than to other firms, because they trusted Goldman not to use the information in representing hostile raiders against them.

This policy lost Goldman some business and restricted the profits and growth of the M&A department, but it was a sound business decision that contributed to the positive public perception of the company. It was long-term greedy, calculated to make the most money for the firm over the long term, and Goldman may well have ultimately made more money because of it. Many clients actually paid Goldman an annual retainer to be on call in case of a hostile bid. Although the policy was not strictly about integrity, it had the effect of reinforcing Goldman's reputation for integrity among clients and the public. Even a Morgan Stanley banker once said clients viewed Goldman as "less mercenary and more trustworthy than Morgan Stanley."[16] Most partners told me they felt the policy reinforced the image and culture of Goldman.

In the late 1990s, this policy was challenged, as many huge hostile deals were announced by Goldman clients and coveted potential clients. A series of internal meetings was held to discuss changing the policy. I participated in some of them.

At one meeting, the people in the room were evenly divided. I was with the group that advocated against representing hostile raiders, whether they were blue chip corporations or individuals financed by junk bonds. We felt that doing so would cause us to lose both our credibility with clients and our perceived moral high ground.

We reminded the group of Goldman's advertising slogan, "Who do you want in your corner?" and observed that Whitehead had also resisted serious challenges to the policy. John L. Weinberg had supported the policy, too, even though one of his largest clients had requested Goldman represent it in a hostile raid.

Those arguing in favor of representing hostile raiders claimed that very good clients of the firm were asking for our help. By working with them, we could try to reduce the "hostility," implying that other advisers would not have as much tactical or moral sway with clients. They also said that they feared clients would not hire us to advise them on buy-side transactions because we weren't willing to advise them on a hostile approach.

We countered that in the past, Goldman had stepped aside and other firms had stepped in, to which the others replied that this was disruptive and did not serve the client well. We pointed out that in these very large deals, it was not unusual to have co-advisers anyway, so we would simply recuse ourselves, and the client would not have to get someone up to speed from scratch.

In the end, senior partners decided that Goldman would work on hostile raids "rarely and reluctantly." We developed a series of questions, essentially a test, to determine whether we would advise a hostile raider. At the same time, we did get a minor victory in that there seemed to be a gentleman's agreement not to do it in the United States, where Goldman's market share and association with the policy were particularly strong. In hindsight, this compromise is a clear case of an incremental shift, and the compromise provisions imply that at least subconsciously we were aware that there could be adverse consequences of this change in policy.

The manner of the arguments also reflected a drift from the Goldman principles. Never did anyone say in the meetings that the policy should be changed to maximize opportunities for growth, market share, profits, or a potential IPO. Instead, people argued the need to stick with clients, make clients happy, add "another tool in the tool chest" to help clients. Ironically (or paradoxically), these arguments invoke the first business principle of keeping our clients' interests first. But for the first time I began to hear the rationalization, "If we don't, someone else will," and the rationale was not dismissed outright. "This time is different," people asserted; the world had changed and was more competitive than when the two Johns ran the firm.

One could certainly argue that the real reason for making the change was that Goldman needed to maximize revenue growth opportunities in anticipation of an eventual IPO. Goldman already had the lion's share of the raid defense business, so the only way to acquire a greater M&A market share was by tapping the other side of the equation. But the decision cannot be attributed solely to the looming IPO. The trigger was that there also had been an explosion of large, hostile transactions. One concern was surely that hostile M&A deals were very large, and if Goldman were not involved, its leading M&A market position could be threatened.

I later found out that Goldman's co-leaders at the time disagreed about changing the policy. What surprised me was that Paulson supported the change and Corzine did not. It was later reported in the press that Paulson thought the "no hostiles" tradition was costing Goldman huge fees it could have received from "advising large, ambitious, serial-aggressor corporations on takeovers," whereas Corzine was concerned about the damage to Goldman's image as "corporate management's most reliable friend."[17]

The firm's entry into this aspect of investment banking was incremental and started outside its core US market in the mid- to late 1990s with hostile acquisitions of non-US companies, outside the United States, by other non-US companies.[18] The first announced hostile M&A deal for which Goldman advised in North America was in 1999, and that was in Canada.[19]

To many of the Goldman partners I interviewed (who acknowledged change), in hindsight, there could hardly have been a more dramatic business policy decision to signal that the Goldman culture was changing.

Renewed Involvement in Asset Management

Goldman had steered clear of asset management since the Great Depression. In 1928 the firm created Goldman Sachs Trading Corporation (GTSC) as an investment trust, which worked much like modern mutual funds: the trust bought and managed a portfolio of securities, some of them speculative, and shares were sold to the public. According to one author, "It was essentially a trust which used debt to buy other companies, which used more debt to buy still more companies—in other words, a ticking time bomb of debt."[20]

GTSC itself bought many shares of the trusts it managed. The idea was that Goldman would profit enormously from the original underwriting fee, from the appreciation of shares Goldman held in the trust, and from investment banking and securities trading on behalf of companies whose stock was held by the trust. By 1928, with only \$20 million in partnership capital and either sole or joint control over funds worth \$500 million, this created a devastating level of exposure on the eve of the October 1929 stock market crash. John Kenneth Galbraith used phrases such as "gargantuan insanity" and "madness . . . on a heroic scale" to describe GTSC's strategy.[21] When the crash came, GTSC shares fell from their high of \$326 to less than \$2 per share. The ensuing debacle and damage to Goldman's reputation, leadership, and clients caused Goldman to stay away from the asset management business.

This attitude changed in the late 1980s, when, lured by the consistent profits its competitors were earning in asset management, Goldman established Goldman Sachs Asset Management (GSAM) to serve institutional and individual investors worldwide.[22] Goldman struggled to determine whether it should manage money for high-net-worth individuals or institutions, in the end doing both. According to the interviews, there was strong sentiment from many partners that Goldman should not be perceived as competing with clients, but one of the key rationales was that Goldman's competitors were doing it.

Beginning in the mid-1990s, GSAM experienced explosive growth, and Goldman now points out that it is one of the largest asset managers in the world, and yet many of the largest asset managers are still Goldman's clients.

GSAM became a strategic priority, in part, because it was not as capital intensive as proprietary trading and it offered consistent fees, which were a percentage of assets under management. When Goldman went public, establishing the asset management business proved to have been a wise strategic decision for this reason. Institutional investors buying the stocks of investment banks, and research analysts covering investment banks, liked the consistency of earnings and gave a higher valuation to the earnings from asset management divisions than to trading earnings.[23] The growth of asset management, and the strategic opportunities and strategy of the business, are cited in most research reports regarding Goldman's IPO. GSAM also is mentioned as one of the key areas of potential growth in Goldman's IPO prospectus.

The changes in Goldman's business mix in the 1990s, before the IPO, were not lost on the financial press: "Goldman intends to build up its asset management business . . . If it does not, it cannot expect to be valued as highly as Merrill and Morgan Stanley in the grim as well as the great times of the cyclical securities industry."[24]

However, some of GSAM's funds have consistently underperformed Goldman's proprietary traders, an outcome that has led some investors to suggest that the best investors and traders at Goldman went into proprietary trading to manage Goldman's money and not that of clients—claiming that this is a classic example of Goldman putting its interests ahead of its clients'. Such criticism is not entirely fair, because Goldman partners' personally invest in the funds, as well as often coinvesting the firm's capital with clients' money, and the funds have specific mandates. But on the other hand, Goldman is receiving valuable recurring revenue fees from the outside investors in the funds so the risks and rewards are not exactly the same as those for outside clients.

Advising Companies in the Gambling Industry

Goldman had also traditionally declined to do business with companies involved in the gambling industry, for reputational reasons. The firm changed this policy in 2000. Its first foray was to represent Mirage Resorts and Steve Wynn. Mirage was sold to MGM Grand Inc. for $6.6 billion ($21 a share) in June 2000. Although the gambling industry was starting to be regarded as increasingly professional and mainstream, one could argue that Goldman made this change simply because it saw a huge financial opportunity. To raise its profile in the industry and in junk bonds, Goldman hosted a lavish conference in Las Vegas, with entertainment by Cirque du Soleil and Jay Leno, which was attended by eight hundred people.

As William Cohan wrote in *Money and Power,* "One portfolio manager who attended the three-day conference said that it was something he expected from [Donaldson, Lufkin & Jenrette], not Goldman. Marc Rowland, CFO of oil and gas producer Chesapeake Energy of Oklahoma City, had previously issued $730 million in junk bonds through Bear Stearns. Rowland remarked that prior to the conference, he never would have thought of approaching Goldman to handle junk bonds."[25] Of course, one could also argue that Goldman was shrewdly capitalizing on a market opportunity and that it was true that the industry's reputation had changed.

Partners I interviewed pointed to two key examples of pushing the client envelope in terms of the questionable nature of clients taken on. Interestingly, they were both outside the US market. One was London's Robert Maxwell, whom Goldman acquired at the very end of John L. Weinberg's watch, when it was still trying to establish itself in London—and well before the IPO. The other recent example was Libya. In early 2008, Libya's sovereign-wealth fund controlled by Col. Moammar Gadhafi gave $1.3 billion to Goldman to sink into a currency bet and other complicated trades. At one time, the investments lost 98 percent of their value. Also, according to reports, afterward Goldman had to arrange for security to protect its employees dealing with Libya. Many current and former partners questioned the firm's dealing with a client like Libya—even though the United States had lifted sanctions in 2004—where employees would need security protection. Retired and current partners felt that Maxwell and Libya being clients showed a deviation from the standards of the 1980s, and were due in part to the pressure to grow.

Changing Underwriting Standards

When I joined Goldman, strict underwriting guidelines were in place for taking a company public. The process required the team to write an extensive memo for the commitments committee by a certain day and time to be considered in the following week's meeting. The committee was responsible for the standards that governed which companies Goldman would finance, take public, and be associated with. The memo had to follow a specific format and address standard questions. Mistakes in the memo or unanswered questions usually resulted in a severe dressing down at the meeting. The committee was notoriously tough.

Typically, Goldman would not take a company public if it had not been in business for three years, and it had to show profitability. But then came the technology and internet boom, and suddenly companies with little track record and no profits started being taken public by competitors. The requirement at Goldman was reduced to two years of profitability, then to one year, and then to one quarter, until finally the firm was not even requiring profitability in the foreseeable future.

Goldman has denied that it changed its underwriting standards during the internet years, but as Matt Taibbi pointed out in a *Rolling Stone* article, "its own statistics belie the claim."

> *After [Goldman] took a little-known company with weak financials*
> *called Yahoo! public in 1996, once the tech boom had already begun,*
> *Goldman quickly became the IPO king of the Internet era. Of the*
> *24 companies it took public in 1997, a third were losing money at the*

time of the IPO. In 1999, at the height of the boom, it took 47 companies public, including stillborns like Webvan and eToys, investment offerings that were in many ways the modern equivalents of Blue Ridge and Shenandoah. The following year, it underwrote 18 companies in the first four months, 14 of which were money losers at the time.[26]

In addition, Goldman's behavior in managing IPOs was questioned. As Taibbi noted, Goldman took eToys public in 1999. On the first day of trading, eToys, which was originally priced at $20 per share, opened at $79 per share, rose as high as $85, and closed at $76.56. By the end of the year, the shares had declined to $25. In 2001, eToys filed for Chapter 11 protection in bankruptcy court. Later, the eToys creditors committee filed a lawsuit alleging that eToys relied on Goldman for its expertise as to the pricing of its IPO and that Goldman gave advice to eToys without disclosing that it had "a conflict of interest," allegedly an arrangement with Goldman's customers to receive a kickback of a portion of any profits they made from the sale of eToys shares after the IPO. In addition, the complaint alleged that Goldman had an incentive to underprice the IPO because an initial lower price would result in higher profits to its customers and therefore a higher payment to Goldman.[27]

The case was dismissed in court on the grounds that there was "no fiduciary relationship" between eToys and Goldman: "[W]e find no issue of fact as to whether Goldman Sachs assumed a fiduciary duty to advise eToys with respect to its IPO price," Justice DeGrasse wrote. "We therefore need not consider whether such a duty was breached. Were we to consider the issue, we would find that Goldman Sachs met its burden of establishing that there was no breach."[28]

The Rise of Stars and "Super League" Clients

In 1970, long before he drafted Goldman's business principles, Whitehead had written a set of statements to guide internal investment banking (IBS) business development, including, "Important people like to deal with other important people. Are you one?"[29] One partner told me Whitehead's original statement had been reinterpreted and repeated verbally over the years as, "You can't run with the big dogs if you pee with the puppies." By the mid-1990s the slogan, meant to remind bankers to cultivate contacts and relationships with corporate CEOs and decision makers, was reinterpreted further and socialized to mean cultivating only the most important companies and most important people. This shift represented the preference given in partner elections to those who had relationships with important CEOs and important companies, because they had a higher value to the firm than did bankers who covered middle-market companies. Formerly, partners who covered many of these middle-market companies had been considered culture carriers and their role was deemed important, but that view had faded.

This change was dramatically represented by John Thornton when he spoke in the late 1990s at the annual internal investment banking conference held in New York each December. In his book *The Accidental Investment Banker,* Jonathan Knee describes the conference. Instead of employing the usual elaborate PowerPoint presentation, Thornton conveyed his message with a plain black marker, drawing a few dots that he said represented the "important people in the world," of whom, he conceded, there were not many. He added circles representing the orbits of these important people and said, "Pretty much everything important that happens in the world, happens in these circles." He then marked the point where the greatest number of circles intersected and said, "This is where I want to be. This is our strategy. Thank you."[30]

Few of the people in the room dealt with Goldman's most important clients or had access to the world's most important people. The Goldman culture had always prevented stars from emerging and eclipsing their peers. Thornton's new strategy singled people out, and it was accepted—a clear signal that the "no stars" policy had changed. When discussing "stars" and in explaining how much the policy continued to change, one retired partner pointed out that CEO Lloyd Blankfein was allegedly seen attending a pre-Oscars party in Los Angeles in 2013, and the partner said he guessed that it must have been a first for the head of Goldman.

This shift coincided with a new practice of designating "star clients." Clients were categorized and prioritized to help Goldman prioritize and allocate resources, and the largest clients that offered the most revenue opportunities and that had influence or influential CEOs were classified as "Super League."[31] Super League clients received increased attention from management committee members, and Goldman systematically tracked the firm's relationship and progress with these clients. Employees were also held strictly accountable for these relationships. Many bankers wanted to work on Super League clients' business, resulting in fights for clients and internal politics.

The prioritization and metric-measuring culture rose in the firm during my time. For example, senior people asked me to develop lists of the top one hundred people in business and determine who at the firm had relationships with them so that Goldman could identify any gaps. Goldman executives were assigned to make sure they personally called and met with these influential people regularly, conveyed proprietary information or views or "out of the box" ideas, and connected them to other important people. When I was in Hong Kong as an analyst, I was given a list of about ten clients and told to focus primarily on them. I was told these people made all the important decisions and that we wanted to focus all our attention and resources on them—and, if possible, coinvest with them, because that was the closest relationship the firm could have with a client. I was told that if people called me about any other clients to refer them to my bosses.

Partners pointed out that, starting in the mid-1990s, Goldman introduced time sheets (records of how much time was being spent on Super League clients and on which transactions and products) and revenue scorecards. That led to increasing contention about who got credit for what, with implications for compensation and promotion. In describing this change over time, some partners said it had brought a "FICC or trading subculture" to the banking side, a mark-to-market mentality. Before this increased emphasis on quantification and accountability, people were willing to make more time for each other and help think through issues. Bankers didn't worry about filling out time sheets or taking credit. They worried instead more about giving clients better advice.

This practice clearly signaled a shift of emphasis, and it changed the firm's culture, but it also seems to have had positive financial results, at least in the short to medium term. Conceding that Goldman is run more efficiently and with more accountability now than in the past, one partner told me that the client metrics have perhaps gone too far in measuring investment banking clients as if they were trading clients, and investment bankers as if they were traders. The prioritization has made people more accountable and productive and has improved Goldman's management, but he wondered whether it was really good for the clients—and in the firm's best long-term interest.

Rehiring People and Making Counteroffers

When I started at Goldman, departing employees were persona non grata. While I was an analyst in the M&A department, someone spoke to one of the department heads about being approached by another firm and admitted to thinking about the offer. The senior partner told him to hold on for a minute, picked up the phone, and called security to escort the offender off the floor, telling security to retrieve his suit jacket from his cubicle. Naturally, then, rehiring someone who had left the company was unthinkable.

This policy changed slowly in the mid- to late 1990s as talented people left for tech firms or hedge funds and, later, regretting the move, wanted to return. Goldman was desperate for talented people, and in many instances made a "bid to match or top" the offer from competitors to keep them. By the time I left banking, there had been several exceptions to the "no rehire" rule. One of the more visible cases was Michael Sherwood, known internally as Woody, currently vice chairman and co-CEO of Goldman Sachs International. He left for a few weeks in 1994 before quickly changing his mind and returning to the firm.

As one partner explained, in the 1990s the bids to keep people were another example in the changing culture. Some employees had come to believe they needed to produce an offer from a competitor and have Goldman match or top it; otherwise, they would be lost in a crowd of many talented people. Those who were good soldiers—formerly viewed as important role models (because they didn't complain, worked hard, didn't politick or lobby for promotions or compensation)—were now considered either naive or not desirable enough to get another offer.

An example of the change was John Thornton, who was quoted in the *New York Times* as saying he would consider going to work at Lazard, a competitor, but "only for the top job." At the time, a Goldman banker being singled out or quoted in the press was highly unusual, possibly a reason for getting fired, much less what was generally interpreted as public negotiation for a promotion. But surprisingly, there were no visible repercussions, and, in fact, Thornton would become copresident, which signaled that something had changed.[32]

Changing Compensation and Promotion Practices

When I started at Goldman, compensation and promotion were handled by class, according to the year one graduated from business school and started at Goldman. The vast majority of a class (I would guess 90 percent) was paid within a tight range. Associates in banking got bonuses that increased by about $100,000 per year; the range was less than 10 percent to 25 percent when I started. As competitive pressure to retain people increased and there were large differences in backgrounds, the ranges expanded. According to interviews, the original 90 percent had dropped to 75 percent, and the range was more like 25 percent to 100 percent. The goal was to retain and reward people, but the changing ranges also reflected the fact that the quality of the talent, which was very consistent across a class when I started, now varied more widely as more people were hired.

The way the partners were compensated also changed. I was told that in the 1980s partners were generally paid by class, according to the year they were elected. If two people were elected partner—one in M&A and the other in IT or operations—I was told they generally made the same amount at least in the first few years, because the attitude was that everyone worked hard and contributed, and, to succeed in IT or operations, a person had to be truly exceptional. But this changed over time. Steve Friedman and Bob Rubin tied partner compensation more closely to performance in the early 1990s. Also, to strengthen the link, to extend the policy to other employees, and to create a new source of developmental feedback, Goldman instituted 360-degree performance reviews in the early 1990s.

Promotions to partner typically were made a certain number of years after business school; usually it took eight to ten years after business school before someone was up for partner. Exceptions had often been made in trading. The rationale was that traders made enormous sums of money for the firm and possessed a specialized skill that was transferable to any firm (a hedge fund or another bank). Not so for bankers, whose only choice upon leaving Goldman would be to work for a competing firm, which would be a step down in social prestige. Traders did not care as much about prestige and could work at hedge funds or start their own, so exceptional traders began to make partner early. (One of the most notable exceptions was Eric Mindich, who ran equity arbitrage proprietary trading and made partner at the age of twenty-eight.)

The new attitude began to seep into other areas and then into banking. The idea that Goldman had stars and had to promote them earlier or compensate them differently set into motion a different dynamic. Some partners told me there was a deliberate effort to make exceptions and make a few people partners early, thereby creating more incentive, demonstrate a meritocratic culture, and drive people harder.

I see now that the changes—in compensation and in promotion—represent a fundamental shift in the 1980s' practices of the firm.

Lateral Partner Hires from Other Banks

When I started at Goldman, it was unusual for the M&A department to hire senior bankers from other firms laterally, because, as I was told at the time, their deal experience, training, habits, and sacrifices would not be on par with those of their Goldman peers. When I was an analyst in the early 1990s, I remember a department meeting to discuss hiring an exceptional associate from another firm—a meeting of the entire department about one associate lateral hire. In contrast, by the time of the IPO, when the firm hired three outside senior M&A professionals as partners there was no department meeting to discuss it, even though Goldman probably had fewer than a dozen M&A partners worldwide.

As the firm grew, it needed more partners. It also needed to replace pre-IPO partners who wanted to "take the money and run—I mean, retire," in the paraphrased words of one partner I interviewed. Goldman especially needed partners in FICC and in proprietary investing areas where it seemed there was tremendous growth, but a disproportionate percentage of partners retired and sought to start their own investing businesses. The IPO provided the currency to attract people from competitors. Goldman had hired laterally before, as it did with a few trading partners from Salomon Brothers in 1986, but this was a deviation from the norm.

The lateral partner hiring accelerated after the IPO. When I was in FICC, I noticed that several lateral partners were brought in at senior positions to replace departing pre-IPO partners.

Turnover Increases

In the early 1980s, Goldman's staff grew at an annual rate of approximately 8 percent. Over 90 percent of the new growth came from entry-level hires, such as analysts from college and young associates out of business school.[33] During the 1980s, annual turnover averaged only about 5 percent compared to typical turnover rates in the industry of approximately 20 percent. In the mid-1990s, however, Goldman's annual turnover rate rose to between 20 and 25 percent.[34] From 1994 to 2000, the firm's staff grew from about 9,000 people to close to 22,000, an annual growth rate of over 20 percent. At the time, it was estimated that the majority of employees had been with the firm for less than three years. Most of the partners I interviewed said that this issue was often discussed at the senior level. However, growth was viewed as imperative to the survival of the firm, and the increased turnover impacted culture and morale, and most of the partners I interviewed said this issue was discussed at the senior level. But the argument was that the increase was primarily due to the growing allure of hedge funds, private equity firms, and technology companies—not as much about Goldman itself. Goldman adjusted its practices and hired more people to compensate for losing more people.

Recruiting and Hiring

Many partners with whom I spoke thought Goldman has been much better than most firms in terms of senior commitment to recruiting. They also pointed out that Blankfein and Cohn have been very active in recruiting at all levels. When I interviewed executives at other firms, most agreed that it was less common for one of their managing directors to attend a recruiting event on a college campus, while at Goldman it is more common. Executives at competitors felt it didn't impact their promotion or pay, they explained, and their behavior reflected that lack of incentive. Managing directors were expected to produce revenues, and that was what drove their performance evaluations. A few who worked at larger investment banks that participated in industry consolidation also explained that they were unsure of the value proposition they were presenting and didn't want to sell something they didn't believe in. Before the mergers and consolidations, they felt as if their firms had distinct reputations and cultures; today, they think their reputations and cultures are muddled.

Despite Goldman's typically stronger commitment to recruiting, the quick pace of growth leading up to the IPO did result in more lenient hiring policies and less mentoring due to the larger number of new employees. When I was sent to Hong Kong to help build the M&A department, I was told I was chosen in part because of my technical skills and entrepreneurial spirit. What I quickly found out was that they should have sent someone with a human resources background. I spent half of my time interviewing people. We hired and grew at such a pace that it was challenging to keep up. Many of the people we hired would probably not have been hired at that level in New York.[35] But there was fierce competition for candidates who had language skills combined with top American MBAs.

One time I played a practical joke on an associate in Hong Kong who was originally from the New York office. We were interviewing a candidate who had grown up in China and had just graduated from an Ivy League school. Her family had made enormous sacrifices for her education, and she was an excellent candidate. The associate left on vacation, and while he was gone, we wound up hiring her. She was ensconced in a cubicle with a nameplate on the outside. (Analysts and associates worked in cubicles and vice presidents and partners had offices.) The morning the associate was due to come back from vacation, I took the new analyst's name plate off the cubicle wall and put it on the door of an empty vice president's office. When he walked in, he noticed the nameplate and asked what it was doing on a vice president's office. I explained that, although she had never worked before, there was tremendous competition for her and Morgan Stanley had offered her a VP position, so HR agreed to match their offer. The associate went nuts and started to march down to the head partner's office to complain before I stopped him and confessed. But we were so desperate for talent, my practical joke was believable. The increased demands for talent and increasing competition for the best talent available raised further cultural issues regarding hiring standards and to what extent a value fit was considered in the selection process.[36]

All of the new hiring further taxed the social network of trust. One investment banking partner explained that once he had his stock, he did not care as much if the traders wanted to bring in "rainmakers" from "second rate" firms, even if they didn't fit the culture. During the mid- to late 1990s, he explained, the firm gave up on making sure each lateral hire was a perfect cultural fit and a confirmed success, even in banking. Many of the new people would eventually adapt to the culture, add new ideas, add new businesses, add new relationships, and make significant contributions, but some would fail miserably. The "dilution" in culture and quality of people, as he called it, was just the "cost of the pace of growth."

Socialization of New Employees in International Offices

When I started at Goldman in the early 1990s, there was an unwritten policy that to grow internationally the firm would generally hire foreign students at top American business and law schools, require them to stay in New York for a year to get socialized to the culture of Goldman, and train them to go to a foreign office. At the same time, American vice presidents (even those lacking foreign language skills) who had been at the firm for a decade and were considered culture carriers were often sent to international offices along with junior employees for a rotational period, with the goal of maintaining a cohesive network and continuing the socialization process.

But international growth accelerated, and regulatory, competitive, organizational, and technological changes put pressure on the policy. For example, in Europe, economic unity and the use of a common currency allowed massive consolidation of banks, which thereby became more competitive with Goldman across Europe. European banks also began setting up large presences in the United States. So the training and socialization period was changed from one year to six months, and then to a few weeks, and finally to none; new hires would finish their training and immediately be sent abroad. Over time, the visiting American partners, who were there to help in part with the socialization process, were resented for taking partnership slots and Super League clients from locals. According to interviews, many of them, seen as out of touch with local customs and values, were marginalized, and, with no opportunities back in New York, many of them left.

Staple Financing

Staple financing is a prearranged financing package offered by investment banks to potential bidders during an acquisition. Financing terms are literally stapled to a deal's term sheet in the context of a structured deal. Essentially, a firm advises a company on its sale and also provides financing to the buyers. So the firm plays two roles. Typically banks argue that staple financing creates for sellers a convenient negotiation floor.

Goldman has used staple financing successfully, but the practice raises ethical issues. Clearly, the practice carries the potential for conflict by casting the investment bank in dual roles, on opposite sides of the table.[37] (In fact, it was one of the practices identified by the business standards committee in 2011 for review.)

One case that focused critical attention on staple financing involved the 2005 acquisition of Toys "R" Us by a club of private equity sponsors. Credit Suisse First Boston (CSFB) advised the group of buyers, led by Kohlberg Kravis Roberts (KKR). When CSFB first raised the possibility of offering a staple financing package to the KKR-led group and other potential bidders, the Toys "R" Us board objected and insisted that the bank not discuss potential financing until a merger agreement was in place. Once there was an approved merger agreement between Toys "R" Us and the KKR-led buyers, CSFB again asked permission to finance the buyers, and Toys "R" Us agreed. Consequently, CSFB earned $10 million in financing fees in addition to its $7 million sell-side advisory fee.[38]

The public stockholders of Toys "R" Us made the staple financing an issue when they challenged the proposed acquisition. The Delaware court that heard the matter did not find any impropriety but commented on the "possible perception that CSFB's advice to the seller throughout the auction process was tainted by a desire on the part of CSFB to obtain additional fees from financing the successful bidder."[39] Although the court did not find that CSFB acted improperly, it cautioned, "[I]t is advisable that investment banks representing sellers not create the appearance that they desire buy-side work, especially when it might be that they are more likely to be selected by some buyers for that lucrative role than by others."[40] Goldman also was the sell-side adviser in another deal involving staple financing—the sale of Neiman Marcus in 2005—that became the subject of a *Harvard Negotiation Law Review* case.[41]

Goldman's decision to accept the practice is yet more evidence of its shifting culture resulting from various pressures, even though it did so "carefully and reluctantly and with the right disclosures," according to a partner I interviewed. A business standards committee report in 2011 stated, "Goldman Sachs will carefully review requests to provide staple financing when IBD is selling a public company. This review will occur as part of the firm's customary staple financing approval process."[42]

Changes in the Business Mix

In its quest for growth and profits, Goldman also began to adjust its business mix. The prioritized opportunities for growth required more capital: trading, proprietary trading, merchant banking/principal investing, and international. Trading and principal investments grew 20 percent annually from 1996 to 2009, whereas investment banking grew 7 percent.

The changing business mix at Goldman, with so much more revenue beginning to come from trading in particular both reflected and contributed to organizational drift. The balance between banking and trading was changing. Also, international growth started to become a challenge.

Trading Becomes a Dominant Percentage of Revenues

Goldman already had leading market share in M&A and most areas of high-value-added investment banking, so the tremendous opportunities for growth, profits, and returns were in trading. For this reason, Bob Rubin and Steve Friedman initiated a greater push into trading, well before the IPO, and trading became a much larger percentage of Goldman's revenues. In 1996, trading and principal investing represented about the same percentage of revenues as investment banking (about 40 percent), but from 2005 to 2007, trading and principal investing accounted for about 70 percent of revenues, and investment banking had plunged to 15 percent.[43]

Banking gave Goldman access to key CEOs and information—maybe not directly to the traders, but at the very top, where people set risk limits and oversaw all the risks. It began to become clearer to me, though, that there were different values and approaches among traders and bankers and that trading made the money and would come to dominate the thinking and culture.

The new emphasis on trading caused a cultural shift not only at Goldman but on Wall Street generally. Rob Kaplan explained: "As trading came to be a bigger part of Wall Street, I noticed that the vision changed. The leaders were saying the same words, but they started to change incentives away from the value-added vision and tilt more to making money first. If making money is your vision, to what lengths will you not go?"[44] The shift may also have contributed to turnover. For example, according to Kaplan,

Wall Street was historically more balanced between trading business and client business. I ran investment banking and oversaw investment management. But as the trading business got bigger and bigger, the client side made up less of the firm's overall work. This was going on at every single firm, not just at Goldman Sachs. I began to believe I could add more value in the world by doing something else. It was a difficult decision. However, I realized I had lost some passion for what we were doing, and that's when I talked to the CEO, Hank Paulson, about leaving. It was traumatic, but I felt like I had to make a change.[45]

Trading entailed a different view and definition of "clients," and that difference became more significant at Goldman as its trading activities intensified. Blankfein explained the difference in an interview with *Fortune*: "We didn't have the word 'client' or 'customer' at the old J. Aron [the metals trading division where he worked with Gary Cohn for years]. We had counterparties—and that's because we didn't know how to spell the word 'adversary.'"[46] Former Bear Stearns asset management CEO Richard Marin described a Goldman executive's attitude as arrogance and said that it was at "the root of the problem" at Goldman: "When you become arrogant, in a trading sense, you begin to think that everybody's a counterparty, not a customer, not a client . . . [and] as a counterparty, you're allowed to rip their face off."[47] A counterparty is the person on the other side of a transaction or trade—not someone you are advising. So Goldman may see its role, as the firm has said, as a market maker (see chapter 1), and that is fine. But Goldman can get into issues when the client believes Goldman is acting as an adviser and proclaims that "our clients' interests always come first."

According to the clients I interviewed, Goldman has conveniently, for its own purposes, shifted its roles as principal and agent/market-maker back and forth—and has even added a few more potential roles on the same deal. This is an issue Goldman identifies, in its report of the business standards committee, that it needs to make clearer to clients.

Some people have argued that Lloyd Blankfein is largely responsible for this shift, but trading was already becoming a larger percentage and majority of the revenues before Blankfein became CEO. The firm also played multiple roles, including proprietary investing and investing with clients, before he became CEO. His rise in the firm reflected the pressures and changes.

Proprietary Trading Becomes a Larger Percentage of Revenues

When one looks at the business principles that John Whitehead wrote in 1979, it is a particular challenge to reconcile the goals of proprietary trading with putting clients' interests first, or the goal of being the leading adviser. Proprietary trading has one client: Goldman. As proprietary traders, we were walled off from client activity. We were not there to provide liquidity to clients, manage funds for clients, or advise clients. From time to time, we were asked by banking to tell them or their clients how hedge funds would evaluate a situation. From time to time, we were also approached by banking or trading to help finance a transaction or buy something from a client or coinvest with a client—actions that, most of the time, raised all types of potential conflicts and died because we were too busy to have long conference calls to discuss it. But generally we were in our own silo.

Proprietary trading at Goldman did not start in the 1990s. Bob Rubin joined the risk arbitrage proprietary trading area in the equities division in 1966, and by the 1980s it was considered one of the most profitable and powerful areas in the firm. When Rubin and Steve Friedman took over as senior partners in the 1990s, Goldman accelerated its additional role of risking its own capital versus being a mere "market maker." It was the size of the losses from proprietary trading in 1994 that caused many observers to think the firm would not survive.

How big and important are proprietary trading and principal investing activities at Goldman? Glenn Schorr, a Nomura Securities equity research analyst covering Goldman stock, estimated that the Volcker Rule, which is intended to restrict proprietary trading and principal investing at investment banks, would impact 48 percent of Goldman's total consolidated revenue. To put this into context, he estimated the impact at 27 percent, 9 percent, and 8 percent of total consolidated revenues of Morgan Stanley, Bank of America, and J.P. Morgan, respectively.

Certain Goldman client-oriented sales and trading desks had "proprietary trading" operations. They got to see client order flow, but theoretically they existed to provide liquidity or "facilitate client trades." This was prevalent in less liquid, more opaque products and desks, especially fixed-income securities like high-yield bonds, where it may not have been easy to immediately match a buyer and a seller. It was also prevalent in relatively lightly regulated markets such as foreign exchange. Generally, proprietary trading on client-oriented sales and trading desks was less frequent in highly transparent and highly regulated areas such as equities.

Merchant Banking and Private Equity Become a Larger Percentage of Revenues

GS Capital Partners was started in 1992 with about $1 billion in assets and grew to $1.75 billion by 1995 and $2.75 billion by 1998. Ten years later, in 2007, GS Capital Partners had $20 billion in assets, making it one of the largest private equity firms. Goldman's Whitehall Real Estate Fund also grew to have multiple billions of assets under management.[48] Although separate, the funds do leverage Goldman banking and other relationships. When I was at Goldman we were often reminded how much more money Goldman could make investing the deal versus advising on it. Goldman was competing against clients in making acquisitions of companies and real estate properties. Goldman also had internal funds for managing Goldman's own money and trying to buy assets. (The corporate and Whitehall funds raised money from external sources with Goldman's coinvestment.)

The private equity business had many synergies with other parts of the bank and wielded a lot of clout as a profit center. For example, the private equity group could take its companies public, the executives whom it backed could become private banking clients, and the companies that it controlled could use Goldman to hedge its risks or finance its debt. The private equity group was careful to maintain relationships with all the Wall Street firms (similar to an unaffiliated private equity firm), but there was no question it also was aware of its primary affiliation—and disclosed potential conflicts in its documents for investors in the funds.

An executive of a major real estate firm told me the story of a property his company was trying to buy in the 1990s. Goldman had always been the company's primary banker, and it had paid Goldman millions in fees over the years. The executive told his Goldman banker about the deal. A short time later, Goldman's Whitehall Fund purchased the property. He was furious (although he hadn't hired Goldman to advise him). He asked the banker to arrange a meeting with a senior Goldman executive. According to the client, at the meeting were senior people of the Goldman Whitehall Real Estate Fund. The corporate executive explained what had happened and expressed his frustration as a client. Goldman's senior executive assured him that there were Chinese walls so that Goldman Whitehall would not know what he had told his banker. The Whitehall executives swore that they did not know about the client's interest in the property. Goldman's CEO said that merchant banking and Whitehall were very important to Goldman and that the firm had a fiduciary responsibility to do good deals for the clients they raised money from.

Skeptical, the corporate executive told me that since that meeting, he had done business with Goldman only if he had to.

He doubted Goldman's ability to manage conflicts, its various roles, and confidential information.

Steve Friedman, however, expressed confidence that Goldman could manage any conflicts arising from the firm's new ventures: "The culture was transformed with a new strategic dynamism; and the principal investment business was well launched—although the old guard continued to worry and fret over conflicts with clients even though we explained to them that there are always conflicts, but you could manage the conflicts."[49]

International Business Becomes a Larger Percentage of Revenues

In 1984 Goldman was primarily an American firm, with one partner outside the United States: an American based in London. After the 1986 partnership meeting, the consensus was to grow the firm globally to better serve clients. Consequently, international revenues increased as a percentage of total revenues, growing at a faster rate than did the US revenues, and a rate much faster than did the rest of the business. At the time of the IPO vote in 1998, 39 of the firm's 190 partners were based in London, compared to 1 partner in the early 1980s. In 2011, 48 percent of Goldman employees were outside the United States (compared with 35 percent in 1996), and international net revenues grew 30 percent faster than US revenues from 1996 to 2011. One of the challenges Goldman faced with the increase in international business was maintaining its culture and principles outside New York, because many organizational issues arise in dealing with such rapid internationalization and global expansion, including training, socialization into culture and values, communication, local cultural nuances, and more.

When I arrived in Hong Kong in 1993, Goldman's office was small, employing fewer than two hundred people. The cultural and legal barriers, as well as low deal volumes and the existence of entrenched local competitors, were major challenges. At the time, Hong Kong was a high-risk posting for a seasoned banker. It offered an advantage to advance more quickly but had the disadvantage that as locals became socialized and trained, they would ultimately have more value than an expatriate. And it was difficult to transfer back home.

Sometimes, when a senior banker was transferred to an international office, the reality was that the banker had lost a struggle back home or had to agree to the move to make partner.[50] However, sometimes a foreign posting was intended to train a professional for a larger role. No matter how much Goldman wanted to portray itself as globally important, at the time all major decisions were made in New York.

Although the office furniture, office sizes, and set-up of cubicles were the same, the culture at Goldman in Hong Kong was different from what I experienced in New York. The Hong Kong office operated in a separate world. At the time, very few senior bankers from New York came for an extended period of time. Senior partners would jet in and jet out. Because Goldman was concerned about quality of execution, any deal of meaningful importance typically had a New York or London banker assigned to it.[51]

Because of the cost of supporting international offices like Hong Kong and because of Goldman's lack of relationships with important local people at the time, the firm realized that merchant banking and proprietary investments were much more profitable there than were advisory businesses. A team of four or five bankers would work on a deal and get paid a one-time fee of millions, and then the team would look for another deal to work on. Investing with clients, in contrast, was viewed as a way to build closer relationships with them. Once an investment was made, hopefully it would make money each year as it produced returns. Eventually, the investment would need to be sold or financed, and Goldman was in a good position to work on the deal and collect a fee (typically at a rate comparable to those charged in Europe or the United States, and not comparable to fees in Asia, which were notoriously low). The Goldman bankers' close relationship would also provide an easier entrée for private banking. All of this required teamwork and collaboration, supported by a social network of trust among the few partners in Asia and their financial interdependence with the other partners around the world. These partners also had to trust that it was for the greater good to have Americans and British flying in and out all of the time.

Proprietary trading internationally was simpler, and it was seen as a high-margin business, because it was easily scalable—it took the same time for a trader to research an opportunity large or small. The markets in Europe and Asia tended to be less liquid and efficient, creating many opportunities. As Goldman established contacts and access, there were even more opportunities in which it perceived it held an informational advantage. Interestingly, Goldman preferred that its international offices follow the New York model as closely as possible—from people having the same titles (each person would be head of something and have one employee reporting to him, whereas the counterpart in New York with the same title would have hundreds of reports) to the same style of office furniture—all to make the firm feel united and cohesive. But although similar, the local hires typically had one approach, and the New York expatriates had another, and, to add complexity, the London expatriates that came stood somewhere in the middle. Often, junior people like me were caught in between.

The internationalization of the firm also had consequences for the acculturation of new employees, which traditionally had occurred through an oral tradition. With the overseas expansion, this method of passing down the cultural legacy was more challenging.

———————

Though the partners had strongly indicated at the time of the IPO that they didn't want to undermine the firm's core values, the changes in business practices and policies, as well as in the business mix, clearly illustrate Goldman's organizational drift.

The daily grind of competition, and the success these changes led to encouraged those at the firm, including the partners, to overlook or discount them, or sometimes purposely ignore them, in the interests of rapid growth, which was seen as vital to the firm's success and survival. This pressure for growth significantly intensified after the IPO, which also brought a new set of changes to the firm.

Part Three

ACCELERATION OF DRIFT

Chapter 6

The Consequences
of Going Public

WHILE THE IPO ACCELERATED MANY CHANGES ALREADY
taking place at Goldman, it also brought about new
ones. The newly public Goldman faced the challenges
of a change in ownership and financial interdependence among the
partners, the elimination of capital and growth constraints, and the
need to take into account outsiders' perceptions of the firm—all had
distinct cultural consequences.

A fundamental change made because of the IPO was the addition
of the new principle expressing a commitment to providing superior returns to shareholders. Many observers point to this as the biggest change over time at Goldman because the firm could no longer
privately make decisions in its best long-term interests in its relationships with clients, but instead had to focus on the public market investors' shorter-term interests. They argue that this written addition was
the "smoking gun" that muddled up always putting clients' interests
first. Though as demonstrated in this book, organizational drift had

begun before this, there is no question that this change introduced its own considerable effects, as did the new structure of ownership.

Shared Ownership

When Goldman went public it awarded shares to almost every employee (including assistants), with some portion being awarded according to a formula and some by the discretion of one's manager. The formulaic part was calculated on compensation and years of service. Generally, the discretionary part was largely determined by seniority and previous years' compensation. There was a feeling among some senior nonpartner employees (those who were within a few years of partner) that part of the IPO grant should offset the lower income that the employee had gotten versus peers at other firms, now that the firm was going public and it was unclear if the partnership was going to be considered less prestigious and be less lucrative. The IPO shares were restricted to vest over years 3, 4, and 5 after the IPO (one-third each year) to ensure that everyone focused on the future and that potential outside investors knew that employees would not sell shares overnight. Compensation at Goldman had typically been in all cash versus most of its peers, which were public and generally paid bonuses both in cash and in stock that vested over time. The stock awards were also meant to "align incentives" and give employees "a sense of ownership." It sounded good, and everyone I spoke to was grateful to receive stock (although some questioned the fairness of the allocation process). I remember how proud I was to receive a thick envelope with information about my stock, complete with bar graphs of what it was worth at different prices. But over time I learned that wide stock ownership would not necessarily fully meet its objectives, and it also caused some unanticipated issues.

About a year after the IPO, Goldman stock rose to around $100 a share (from the $53 offering price) and the partners got approvals to sell shares "in order to improve trading liquidity for shareholders." That increased public ownership to 27 percent.[1] To sell, the partners needed special approval from the board (the majority of which were insiders) and the shareholder's committee (the majority of which were insiders). None of the three most senior executives sold shares, but about 160 former partners did, selling over $2 million on average, while eleven sold more than $20 million. No nonpartner employees were allowed to sell shares before the first vesting period, three years after the IPO.[2] I remember a partner sheepishly telling me he decided to sell the maximum he was allowed to in the special offering for "diversification reasons," almost seeking or expecting some sort of understanding or reassurance that it was ok. At the time a group of my peers discussed that the partners who retired before the IPO did not have the "diversification" option and that the current employees did not have the option to sell after one year. And based on conversations with those more senior to me at the time, some of my peers were certainly not the only ones who were questioning the timing of the sales. One interviewee mentioned to me that it was eerily similar to the 1994 partners "bailing out." (I am paraphrasing as always in interviewee quotes.)

A few years after the IPO stock grants, the tech bubble burst. The stock declined to the $70s and the firm laid off lots of employees. The information that quickly spread like wild fire was that in the fine print of the IPO stock grant was a stipulation that in order to cash out your stock when it vested, you still had to be employed by the firm. For those that were being laid off, the firm was "allowing" people to keep their 2002 stock "as a bonus" even though it had not vested (in some instances getting no cash bonus/severance), but they would lose the amounts for 2003 and 2004. I remember the shock and outrage not just from those laid off but from some of those who remained. There was a feeling by some that the firm had "handcuffed" employees with the large grants but then took them away because this helped the firm reduce the number of shares outstanding and therefore helped the firm's reported earnings per share to investors, which would help the stock price. To make matters even worse, some felt that the firm paid people less than peers during the tech crash because it knew that it had the "handcuffs" from the IPO shares that had not vested and that managers included the value of the shares that were to vest in the employee compensation calculations. These actions had consequences for how certain employees viewed the firm.

Many people didn't look at the grants as a sharing of ownership; they saw stock being used as a way to make it more expensive for competitors to recruit Goldman people. I remember thinking it was odd that the firm had all of these restrictions, in part to keep people and align incentives, because the firm used to pay nonpartners all cash in the early 1990s and did not seem to have a hard time retaining people then, or thinking they worked in alignment with the partners. The attrition rates were lower then than industry standards. Many employees just discounted the value of the shares—and many didn't count it at all in their equation of compensation. I remember a few people sometimes quietly questioning if Goldman's stock price abnormally moved up in the month of November before the grants because of Goldman manipulating the price through buybacks or talking to analysts and investors to lower the number of shares they needed to give to employees. (For this study, I analyzed this in depth and found nothing.[3])

During my time at the firm, I do not remember ever hearing a nonpartner employee mention to me that they felt "aligned" with either the partners or the shareholders. Many seemed more concerned about the fine print of what they could sell and when they could sell it—especially the traders when I was in FICC, as they saw the risks inherent in their compensation tied to the markets, the value of their apartments/homes in the New York metropolitan area tied to the markets, and the value of their retirement plans tied to the markets. The most senior executives and partners have more restrictions regarding their stock than the rest of the firm, but obviously this is much different than not being able to receive all of your capital until you retire, and even then over many years. A partner mentioned to me that he also thought a cultural shift occurred in part due to the way the firm treated people in the tech crash. Job security seemed more ephemeral. And he believes the result was an attitude that one should take more risk to make money fast or spend a lot more time politicking and taking credit for revenues.

Changes in Financial Interdependence

Unlike many of its investment banking peers that went public, Goldman tried to remain a "partnership," even if the partners didn't fully recognize or understand its intended and unintended benefits. For example, Goldman created the Partnership Compensation Plan (PCP). The program retained biennial public partnership elections and gave the elected partners (internally referred to as PMDs, or part ner managing directors) financial and social prestige preferences over nonpartner managing directors (MD-lites). In the original idea of the PCP, PMDs were to receive a meaningful part of their compensation as a percentage of the profits of the entire firm, as with a private part-nership. That was a sign of the thoughtfulness and concern about what the partnership meant. According to interviews, the PCP was intended to combat the consequences of the IPO. A partner explained that, in the initial 1998 vote, he voted against an IPO because "I was worried that the fabric and culture of the firm would change if it were no longer a partnership." But in the second vote, he backed the IPO because "the thing that convinced me in the end, though, was the idea of maintain-ing the partnership concept and structure within a public company."[4] Many partners told me that they were concerned about how quickly the culture of Morgan Stanley changed after its IPO. However, very quickly after the IPO even the PCP changed as a result of pressures.

Soon after the IPO, more factors than a partner's share of the profits of the "partner pool set aside for partners" began to impact their overall compensation. In addition, shares used in compensa-tion would vest typically over a few years and could then be sold, as compared with partners' having to wait until retirement to get to their capital. According to interviews, generally PMDs looked at their compensation as an annual bonus comparable to those of their peers at other firms, not as a percentage of the shared profits of a partnership.

According to interviews, over time, and in incremental steps, the percentage of the overall compensation of a PMD as a percentage of the firm's profits has shrunk further, and the percentage of the "discretionary amount" paid (similar to a discretionary bonus) has become increasingly larger. This policy—in another departure from the "long-term greedy" mentality—signaled a change from the days when each partner in an elected class got the same percentage. Even the top executives were paid on a relative basis in comparison with their peers (executives at other banks), and not purely on a percentage basis.[5] The proxy statement sent to shareholders discusses how, in determining the compensation of the CEO, Goldman looks at what other CEOs at comparable firms make—a much different approach from a partnership percentage and the financial interdependence related to the collective skills, values, and judgment of the partners.

At the time of the IPO, Goldman partners and employees owned about 50 percent of the firm. Over time, the percentage has changed dramatically. In 2011, Goldman partners owned approximately 10 percent. And keep in mind that stock is a significant part of compensation after the IPO, meaning that the sales of the original partnership shares from insiders have been even more dramatic. For example, according to research conducted by the *New York Times'* senior reporter Theo Francis and published in January 2011, Blankfein has sold a total of $94 million in shares since 1999 and Goldman's 860 current and former partners have sold more than $20 billion in Goldman stock. Overall for the partnership, the stock sales average $24 million for each partner since the IPO. This analysis does not include the billions of dollars Goldman has paid in cash salaries and bonuses to the partners.[6]

Not having a meaningful ownership stake at risk represents a significant change from the financial interdependence and attitude toward risk that formerly characterized the partnership.

Risk slowly shifted away from partners to public shareholders. Although the partners' stake in the firm now had liquidity and the risk to their personal assets had been eliminated, the loss of owner-ship and the elimination of personal liability for losses suffered by the firm eventually had unintended and far-reaching consequences to the organization's culture.

Though paying in stock was meant to align their interests closely with those of investors and discourage excessive risk taking, exec-utives can defeat the alignment effort by using complex invest-ment transactions to limit their downside when the stock goes down. According to the *New York Times*, more than one-quarter of Goldman's partners used hedging strategies from July 2007 through November 2010.[7]

Others' Capital at Risk

When Goldman was private, partners' finances were interconnected. At partnership meetings, partners from any area could question traders. A banking partner had every right to ask a trading partner about risk, because it was his or her capital at risk. An executive at a competing investment bank explained to me that at other banks, it was unheard of for an investment banking MD to challenge a trad-ing MD, and the idea of collaborating—sharing ideas or information and challenging each other—would be entirely foreign. Although the performance of an MD at Goldman can have an impact on the per-formance of the entire firm, it is not the MD's entire capital at risk or his personal liability, though he can be held accountable for behavior resulting in fines.

Furthermore, several current Goldman partners explained to me that in the absence of financial interdependence after the IPO, MDs had little motivation to question traders about matters outside their own areas of expertise. The increasing size of the firm and resulting specialization and functional silos, combined with the lack of finan-cial interdependence after the IPO, changed the social network of trust and reduced the opportunities for debate. One partner told me that he heard a story from one of his fellow senior partners about when he decided to retire that speaks to how siloed the firm became. He was in an elevator, and in trying to be friendly he introduced himself to the other person in the elevator and politely asked him what he did. The person replied that they had met before because he too was a partner. He then said he ran what the senior partner called a relatively important business, and yet he hadn't remembered meeting before. By the time the senior partner got off the elevator, he had made up his mind it was time to get out and retire.

Working with other people's money also coincided with changing attitudes toward risk management. With the change to a bonus culture, there was more incentive to take risks, and because the partners were no longer personally liable for covering losses, the constraints on risk-taking (not just financial but also reputational) were loosened. Those in areas such as proprietary trading had the opportunity to make more money than banking partners if they made the firm significant amounts of money. The incentive was to ask for and to invest as much capital as possible, because the more money you were given, the more you could potentially make with your trades. Traders could argue that if they worked at a hedge fund they would receive 10 to 20 percent of the profits they generated and if they didn't get paid correspondingly by Goldman, they could leave. And with so many more hedge funds cropping up, if the trades didn't work out and you got fired, you could be almost sure you'd get a job at another bank or a hedge fund. The attitude of many was that the Goldman pedigree would get you another job somewhere for sure.[8]

One might ask how the change in the attitude toward risk was evaluated by the board of directors. After 2002, when the Sarbanes–Oxley Act became law, Goldman's board was composed largely of independent directors, most of them prominent in business and academia. However, according to interviews, none of them had ever focused on trading for a living. None would probably have been classified as an expert in risk management by most trading experts. The directors owned very little Goldman stock (less than 0.1 percent of the total company), and what they owned generally was not significant to their net worth. An interviewee speculated that the fact that Goldman's traders were making enormous sums of money for the firm and themselves also made it unlikely the board would question that success.

In fact, it could have created the opposite effect. One partner I interviewed said that the directors were not likely to question people who made tens of millions of dollars and whose returns on equity and profits exceeded those of their peers. Another partner speculated that as trading became more important after the IPO and risk management was more critical, the board relied on Lloyd Blankfein and his number two, Gary Cohn, from trading, instead of Hank Paulson, and that may have contributed to Paulson's decision to leave to become secretary of the Treasury.

When I was in proprietary trading, one of the partners received a voicemail from Paulson, CEO at the time, on which I was copied. It related to risk. The partner forwarded the message to Blankfein, answering the question and asking Blankfein to deal with it. I asked the partner why he had not responded directly to Paulson. He seemed more than a little annoyed at my curiosity, saying essentially that Paulson knew a lot about clients but little about trading risk, and he did not have the time to explain it to Paulson. Whether or not Paulson understood trading risk, the fact that a partner did not want to deal with the CEO was surprising to me. This was in stark contrast to when I was an analyst in the early 1990s, when the senior partner was held with the deepest respect. I remember being told that when one goes to see the senior partner of the firm, one must wear a suit jacket to show respect. In hindsight, I think I intuitively felt that Hank would probably not be around for much longer if traders didn't have the time for him, and I privately questioned if a banker would ever again be head of Goldman. But I don't remember giving it that much thought. I just went back to my daily routine.

Misaligned Incentives

Goldman's incentive structure, like those of other banks, also evolved in response to the changing nature of the firm's business mix. Rob Kaplan, former vice chairman of Goldman, said that banks' visions changed as they placed emphasis on trading (see chapter 5). It became more about making money than about "the value-added vision."[9]

More Cultural Stress: Envy, Self-Interest, and Greed

One of the basic principles of the financial system is that risk is rewarded. Exactly how well Goldman partners were rewarded—what they earned or owned—had been a closely guarded secret, but it became public information in the filings for the IPO. Some might even say that it was in everyone's face. When I joined Goldman as an analyst, a list was published by a finance magazine of the one hundred most highly paid people on Wall Street, and it was passed around among the junior people in great secrecy. I was told that I would be in deep trouble if a partner caught me with it. The list contained so many Goldman partner names that, except for a few top partners, the names were listed at the bottom of the page, with no bio or background, unlike the non-Goldman partners, each of whom got a short description.

The general reaction of the public disclosure of wealth within the firm was envy stoked by self-interest, and that, when coupled with freedom from personal liability, translated into greed and lack of restraint. (Bear in mind that this was during the dot-com and equity market booms, when many people were becoming extremely wealthy. And even some of the partners would privately question why people who they didn't feel were nearly as smart or hardworking or as committed to the long term were making more money than they were.)

I cannot emphasize strongly enough the impact on the organization of the resentment stemming from knowing who was gaining how much at the IPO; there was a reason many partners did not like Goldman's financial information being disclosed, and Jimmy Weinberg argued in 1986 that this was one of the reasons the firm should not go public.[10] The average partner received around $63 million at the IPO price, an amount that became $84 million after the first day of trading. In the class of 2000, of those who just missed making partner before the IPO, some received a fraction of that amount. The discrepancy was enough to cause a great deal of resentment, especially among those who were hired at the same time as members of the class of 1998 but were not nominated for partnership until after the IPO.[11] (See appendix D for a table showing percentages, shares, and value of partners' shares at the IPO.)

I remember working with an MD-life who had just missed making partner before the IPO. Upon finding out the difference between her payout and that of those who were elected in 1998, she did not come to the office or return calls or voicemail for days. It was like a "mini strike," and it worked: the shares she received were increased. It sent a strong message about how one needed to act to get what one believed was promised, fair, and/or justifiable.

Some of the tensions were eerily similar to many of those who were around in 1994, when so many partners retired, when the prevailing sentiment was that the retirees were "sellouts," leaving to save themselves. After 1999, MD-lites and VPs, like the partners who remained in 1994, wondered whether they had been sold "motherhood and apple pie" or principles of brotherhood, only to realize that there was a limit to the values and the bond. I was also surprised that some nonpartners mentioned they felt that the retirees who stayed in 1994 but left before the IPO, and even those who really built the firm but had retired, were being treated unfairly.

Weinberg and Whitehead's ideas about being custodians of the firm for future generations of partners seemed to be less of a priority. For those who believe that greed was always prevalent at Goldman, imagine that if the earlier partners had decided to go public sooner— they would have received multiples on their capital instead of book value when they retired. In particular, interviewees estimated that John L. Weinberg and Whitehead each owned about 5 percent of the firm, which would represent billions of dollars today.[12]

As a Goldman partner explained to me in an interview, Goldman was slowly losing its allure: the prestige of partnership, the mystique that had always marked the difference between Goldman and its competitors.[13] At the time of the IPO, no one knew that Goldman would (or would have to, as explained in some interviews with partners) become the highest-paying firm on Wall Street. It had traditionally paid less than its peers, except for partners, a business practice Whitehead felt reflected long-term greedy and attracted the right people who had this perspective. Before the IPO, Goldman partners made outsized returns, in part by pocketing the difference in lower compensation for the nonpartners. One partner with whom I spoke said that what made Goldman unique was that it found really smart and dedicated people with certain values to "drink the Kool-Aid" and buy into the culture instead of taking more money. He felt, over time, people didn't value the "Kool-Aid" or buy into the culture enough anymore, and Goldman raised the compensation level to be competitive—another signal of the drift at the firm. Goldman was not special enough, its culture not distinct enough, the value of the partnership not high enough for people to be "long-term greedy" and accept lower pay for a long period of time.

In addition, Goldman faced heated new competition for talent from other firms as well as other opportunities. The firm reacted by significantly increasing compensation, becoming the highest-paying firm on Wall Street. Also, compensation per employee increased with the profits from proprietary trading and growth—and the changes. For example, in 2004 the average compensation per employee at Goldman was $445,390, compared with $279,755 and $199,230 at J.P. Morgan and Lazard, respectively. In 2007, the numbers were $661,490, $311,827, and $466,003 for Goldman, J.P. Morgan, and Lazard.[14] According to interviews, before Goldman went public, it typically paid its nonpartners less than its peers paid their nonpartners.

The idea of making partner, and its social meaning and identity, had been taken down a notch—or at least there was a market price for it. Before the IPO it was highly unusual for retired Goldman partners to work at other firms, but after the IPO this phenomenon increased. Many partners who had just made their fortunes in the IPO were primed to retire, and when they left, they took not only their money but also their expertise and their knowledge and respect for the firm's history and traditions. Of 221 total partners at the IPO in 1999, only 39 (16 percent) remained as of 2011.[15]

Changes in the Social Network of Trust

The net $2.6 billion in proceeds raised by the IPO allowed Goldman to expand rapidly, and the partnership pool grew to meet the demands created by rapid growth, changing what had once been a close social network. The firm had started selectively hiring more lateral senior people in the mid-1980s, and this accelerated in the 1990s as the firm grew. But after the announced and expected retirements after the IPO, hiring outsiders as partners became a necessity. Within five years of the IPO, almost 60 percent of the original partners were gone. Goldman did not have the luxury of time to build product and geographic expertise from within.

According to the partners I interviewed, the priority of recruiting, training, and mentoring changed. The process of identifying and nurturing partner candidates was pushed aside in favor of those who could show immediate results—metrics, revenue production, and Super League relationships—and measurable results such as a trading P&L. And if the firm did not have the right people, the feeling was that it could hire them from other firms by using the valuable currency of Goldman stock. The firm's executives did not want to wait and slowly develop people internally for partnership positions. It would constrain growth. According to my interviews, candidates for partner or lateral hires at the partnership level were not vetted as thoroughly for the match between their personal values and the firm's business principles and culture—a consequence in part of the drop in financial interdependence and the greater emphasis on the financial contribution. Some partners I interviewed believed that this coincided with an increasing shift of balance in considering people for partner to more weight being given to a person's ability to contribute commercially and less to other considerations, like values and culture.

The Effects of Wall Street Models

A distinct change as the result of going public was the deep effect of Wall Street investors and analysts on the firm. A partner who voted for the IPO, whom I interviewed, said that the firm way underestimated the scrutiny it would receive as a public company. He said at the time of the IPO the firm had a handful of employees in public relations who essentially said "No comment" when the press asked about its business. Today, he estimated that over a dozen people were involved in public relations, talking to the press, investors, and analysts and preparing information for them.

The new scrutiny came from many camps. Each of these groups used different tools, including the firm's valuation, to assess Goldman as an investment opportunity. Now having to compete in this way with other firms for investors' cash and positive analyst assessments, Goldman became concerned with how it appeared when assessed by models, and therefore it instituted some new practices that made it more similar to its competitors. In a process that is described by academics as *performativity*, the models used by Wall Street to assess the firm had a reflexive effect on how the firm chose to perform.[16]

Formerly, Goldman had generally held itself apart from the crowd, to a separate standard of its own devising. A colleague once explained to me in the mid-1990s during a late-night pizza break in a conference room, which Goldman regularly paid for in order to promote bonding, that at Goldman, people never spoke badly about other firms. (Goldman principle number 13 states, "Never denigrate other firms.") According to him, Goldman employees didn't really care what the other firms did, or that other firms badmouthed Goldman or told people they were better than Goldman. He said that Goldman was "the Harvard of investment banking." I asked what he meant, and he elaborated by saying, "You know how people at very good colleges wear t-shirts saying things like 'XYZ college, the Harvard of the Midwest? It's like a subconscious insecurity about where they actually did go, or an acknowledgment that they wanted to go to Harvard instead." He then asked rhetorically, "Have you ever seen anyone at Harvard wearing a shirt with the name of another college on it?" I thought the example was a little absurd, and in part to be a smart-aleck I asked him, "So do you think people at Morgan Stanley are wearing t-shirts saying, 'Morgan Stanley, the Goldman Sachs of Midtown?'" Annoyed, he got up and walked away, and I couldn't stop myself as I called out after him, "I am going to copyright that."

While those at Goldman might still have thought of the firm as the Harvard of Wall Street after the IPO, they started to care a great deal about how the other firms were doing. According to interviews, after the IPO, both Goldman's investors and its employees constantly compared its performance to that of other firms. In addition, partners' and CEO compensation was compared to peers'. Before the IPO, Goldman was not required to report its earnings—and chose not to do so. Earnings, compensation, and similar information were closely guarded secrets and helped to add to the Goldman mystique. The prevailing sentiment was that the firm's record of success meant it did not have to care how others were managing their business, the ratios they looked at, their margins, or their return on equity. Goldman might choose to compare itself to these models and benchmarks, but it did not have to manage to them to appease outsiders. The partners reported only to themselves and could choose to measure risk or performance however they saw fit. They did not have to explain their decisions to outside board members, and, because they did not have to answer to the outside world (the previous outside private investors had no say in management), the partners could make the decisions that were best for the partnership in the long term. This ability to protect confidential information was one of the arguments used for remaining a private partnership. "Are you ready to lose the flexibility we now have in reporting up and down earnings?" Whitehead and Weinberg wrote in a letter to Corzine and Paulson.[17]

As a public company, in contrast, Goldman had to comply with the demands and requirements of the capital markets. Among these is the preference for all companies to have common measures, so Goldman was expected to employ the financial models used by the street and capital markets, including the desired measures of risk and performance. Ellis notes, "The persistent demand to meet or beat both internal and external expectations of excellence [is one of the] penalties of industry leadership."[18]

Traditionally, firms want to meet or exceed expectations, believing it demonstrates how well they are run. I analyzed Bear Stearns, Goldman, Lehman, Merrill Lynch, and Morgan Stanley's ability to meet or beat analyst EPS and revenue published expectations from 1999 (when Goldman went public) to 2008 (the credit crisis). There was a statistically significant difference between the firms. Bear Stearns and Lehman more consistently met or exceeded analyst expectations and showed the highest correlations, implying that they were "managing to analyst models." Obviously those two firms failed. Goldman showed a correlation to meeting or exceeding expectations (demonstrating the effect of analyst models) but actually had the least correlation among the firms; it was the worst, implying that it was willing to accept losses or deviate from the analysts more than the other firms. This may reflect cultural characteristics and possibly elements that helped Goldman do relatively better in the credit crisis (discussed later).

Source of Revenues

At the time of the IPO, analysts and investors wanted to see Goldman increase its asset management revenues because of the resulting more-consistent fees. They also discussed Goldman's international growth and placed a premium on it, because Goldman had market share opportunities internationally. International growth had already been a priority, a benchmark by which the firm measured itself. Whitehead knew that if Goldman could not take care of its clients' banking needs anywhere in the world, it risked losing them to firms that could. Rubin and Friedman pushed for more international growth and executed the vision. Corzine and Paulson had pushed even further. But still Wall Street wanted more, according to interviews from analyst investors at the time.

Analysts did not place a high value on the sales and trading revenues and revenues from private equity, even though they were highly profitable and important for Goldman, because of their volatility and inconsistency. Goldman made a larger percentage of its profits related to trading than its peers in 1998. Largely for this reason, the firm's revenue mix became a topic of avid discussion among analysts and investors in the months leading up to the IPO, because the revenue mix was more volatile than that of firms that were less reliant on trading. The greater stability of asset management revenues can provide a cushion against market volatility, but in the mid- to late 1990s, the firm lagged behind its rivals in building its asset management business.

Only a few short years later, however, Goldman's asset management business was strong enough to attract more of the firm's top talent to move over from other areas of the firm, as well as some "outside honchos [brought in with] the promise that they [would] become partners (which is rarely done at Goldman)."[19]

Thus, growth was particularly strong in both asset management and international expansion. Asset management grew faster than banking over time, and international growth was higher than domestic. Goldman even said so in its prospectus: "We pursue our strategy to grow our core business through an emphasis on: expanding high value-added businesses . . . increasing the stability of our earnings . . . pursuing international opportunities . . . [and]

leveraging the franchise."[20] When discussing "increasing the stability of our earnings," Goldman said it would emphasize "growth in investment banking and asset management." Goldman's investment banking revenues, however, actually declined as a percentage over time. Growing banking was a good story for analysts and investors (though not necessarily a representation of reality), especially in light of potential investors worrying about the impact of trading. Analysts I interviewed said it was probably better to have Paulson, from a banking background, lead the firm during the IPO instead of Corzine, because it made Goldman's story of emphasis on advisory businesses more believable, although some had their doubts.

What really happened in the following years, though, was that trading became an increasingly dominant part of Goldman's business, and this had a significant impact on drift.

Chapter 7

From Principles to
a Legal Standard

APPLYING A LEGAL STANDARD TO DEFINE WHAT IS RIGHT AND wrong, rather than an ethical standard higher than the law, helps managers maximize business opportunities, because the law allows for certain practices that a high ethical standard, in particular regarding clients' interests, would preclude. Any standard above the law restricts opportunities.

At Goldman, my interviews and research made clear, over time, the interpretation of what the "clients' interests first" principle meant changed from applying a higher ethical standard than that required by law to simply meeting those requirements. The standard changed to as long as one properly disclosed the risks to clients and followed all the legal rules and regulations, then one was ethically, morally, and responsibly adhering to the primary business principle. The "ethics" drifted closer to the legal definition over years, and the fundamental reasons were that the firm was seeking to maximize opportunities for rapid growth, which was an organizational goal.

What I concluded from my discussions and research was that many at Goldman don't think they're doing anything wrong, and that adherence to the first principle hasn't changed.[1] Most of the current partners I interviewed said that they were abiding not only by the firm's business principles, including the first principle related to clients' interests, but also by the law. My interviews made it clear that the two had become one in the same in their minds. When I asked them about accusations that the firm has behaved immorally and unethically, most countered that the definitions of those terms are highly subjective.

This is a far way from how John S. Weinberg described his father's orientation to the question of morality and ethics: "He saw right and wrong clearly, with no shades of gray." Those I interviewed also pointed to the many systems in place at Goldman that were implemented specifically to protect against misconduct, by which they meant illegal or criminal behavior, which they said Goldman takes very seriously. In addition, some of the partners I interviewed made the point that considering the large number of daily transactions and communications with clients by tens of thousands of Goldman people located in different countries with different legal jurisdictions, it is relatively rare that Goldman gets in legal trouble or is fined, in part because of the care the firm takes in dealing with clients. They said that misconduct or failure, when it happens, is more often a mistake than criminally intended: something was overlooked, some scenario was not considered, or someone was not consulted, because the person was not aware of the need to do so; something in a complex system that is designed to protect the firm and clients somehow failed.[2]

Most of the partners I interviewed said that, given Goldman's volume of business, the depth of its client network, its leading market shares, and its various business activities, *something* is bound to happen. Most seemed to be implying that such errors are a cost of doing business. And my calculations indicate that it is a cost the firm can bear, in terms of finances. From reviewing publicly available documents, I estimate that Goldman has paid less than $1 billion in fines since 2003, compared with some $58 billion in net income over the same time period. The very year (2010) Goldman paid the largest fine in SEC history at the time ($550 million), the firm made almost $8 billion. Fines are almost like an expense that Goldman attempts to minimize but cannot avoid.[3]

However, many current partners also did generally admit that "mistakes" seem to be happening with greater frequency. Some suggested this might be attributed not to a change in behavior but to changes in the laws and in enforcement; that there may be no greater incidence of mistakes, it's only that the authorities are more focused on them. But based on my interviews and a review of congressional testimony, changes in regulation have in general been more biased about the investment banks having more self-regulation. Regarding enforcement, the SEC has publicly stated that SEC staff levels have not kept pace with industry growth; in fact, with increased funding in 2009 and 2010, SEC staff levels are only returning to 2005 levels. Next, we'll consider a number of the criticisms made against Goldman and several of the cases brought against them for alleged misconduct and Goldman's general views about them.

Chinese Walls

Maintaining client confidentiality is crucial to any investment banking firm; it is one of Goldman's stated principles. Client confidentiality is the principle that an institution or individual should not reveal information about clients to a third party (in a bank that can be another area within the firm) without the consent of the client or a clear legal reason. When firms are providing a wide range of services, clients must be able to trust that their information will not be used by other areas of the firm that do not need to know and exploited for the benefit of other clients or of the firm, which may have different interests. For this reason, banks say that they have erected so-called Chinese walls between departments, such as between investment advisors and traders.[4] Given all of the Wall Street scandals in recent years, however, some people doubt the effectiveness of those Chinese walls, and even with effective barriers, how and when and what information may have been transferred from one part of a bank to another is difficult to follow and monitor, and even to understand, both for banks' compliance departments and for regulators.

This makes enforcing the legal requirements difficult. From my interviews with regulators and corporate lawyers, it is not as simple as a bank asking a client to sign a waiver; rather, it is a matter of explaining to a client exactly how and when and what information Goldman learns is used and who knows it. As an easy and straightforward example, if Goldman was about to receive confidential information from a publicly traded company that was interested in potentially selling itself, then the team would have to check with a conflicts and compliance group to see if it is okay to receive such information. Technically there is a Chinese wall between banking and trading, so trading may not legally need to be restricted from trading the stock of the public company, because both sides should not know what the other is doing. The firm may place its own restrictions on trades of the stock or bonds of the company, however, from a proprietary basis for its own account.

Let's now complicate the situation. Goldman's private equity area may have at some time in the past talked to another client about jointly buying the company, and that should be logged into the system. But in order to see where those conversations are or went, the conflicts and compliance area needs to ask someone in the private equity group. The simple fact of asking could tip someone in the private equity group that banking may have a client interested in buying the company, or that the company may be looking to sell or doing something strategic. Who in private equity knows, and when, and then what they do in checking, is ambiguous. They may need to ask the team leader, also potentially tipping people off. So how you ask, when you ask, what you ask, and whom you ask is very subjective, and each request, while ensuring that private equity has no conflict, also adds to the risk that certain information may be passed on to someone the client might not want to know.

The banking team themselves may not know who knows what and when. What is legal or what or where the Chinese wall should be in this instance is very ambiguous. If, for instance, Goldman decides that because of prior conversations, the firm cannot work for the public company because its private equity group had verbally committed to work with a potential buyer, and then by coincidence a few months later Goldman's potential coinvestment client calls the company saying it is interested in buying the company—the public company that spoke to Goldman about the idea may question whether Goldman shared confidential information. It could look bad, even if the Chinese wall was in place and no confidential information was shared with the Goldman client.

The fact that it's so difficult to adhere to the legal line makes maintaining a high ethical standard, and having a business mix that potentially reduces conflicts, all the more important if a bank wants to be sure not to violate the interests of its clients. But the sharing of information and teamwork are also operating principles at Goldman, and one of the firm's biggest legal or compliance issues is that it shares information among different areas—something that clients love when it helps Goldman provide liquidity or improve execution for the client. Indeed, information sharing among different areas of specialty within the firm is one of the things clients value about Goldman and believe differentiates the firm (when the client believes it's benefiting). But, paradoxically, that same information sharing can sometimes seems to place the client at a disadvantage.

This has made the ethical line also difficult to draw for Goldman. Clients and the public, and even some employees, seem genuinely confused about the firm's relationships and responsibilities as an adviser, fiduciary, underwriter/structurer, and market participant.[5] This is in part because Goldman has characterized its relationship to clients and its responsibilities to them differently in different circumstances. For example, in the congressional hearings investigating Goldman's role in selling mortgage securities to clients, Goldman argued that its role was simply that of a market maker, toeing the legal line, which only requires that in such sales, the bank or broker inform the clients of the risks. But Goldman executives couldn't really answer to some senators' satisfaction why the executives instructed traders to "cause maximum pain" and "demoralize" market participants if they were simply matching buyers and sellers.[6] Goldman also often touts the role it plays as a coinvestor with clients in certain deals, and how it will use its own money to facilitate certain transactions, and in those cases is acting as a principal in the deals. This has led some clients and regulators to make the point that the firm will point to whichever definition of its role, and associated responsibilities, allows it to justify, excuse, or rationalize whichever behavior it's engaged in that is being questioned.

A recent example of Goldman's allegedly inappropriate handling of information happened in April 2012. Civil charges were filed against Goldman arising from company procedures that allegedly created a risk that select clients would receive market-sensitive information, such as changes to Goldman's recommendation lists of what clients should buy and sell and its ratings of stocks. Goldman ultimately paid $22 million to settle the charges, which the SEC and the Financial Industry Regulatory Authority (FINRA) said stemmed from Goldman's weekly "huddles"—meetings set up for analysts to present their best ideas to the firm's traders.[7] Although the SEC claimed that the traders relayed those tips to a select group of Goldman's best clients, Goldman was not charged with insider trading. The settlement with FINRA stated that Goldman sometimes did not monitor the huddle conversations to determine whether the analysts revealed or discussed any impending research changes regarding buy and sell recommendations. For example, FINRA stated that in late 2008, an analyst who had received approval to add a company to a Goldman list of best investment ideas told the huddle the next day that the company remained a "favorite idea." One day later, Goldman published a report adding the stock to its "conviction buy list," which is a list of recommendations about which Goldman has a stronger opinion than a recommendation.[8] It was estimated in the press that Goldman could bring in enough money to pay for the sanction in about seven hours of trading and investing, highlighting the "fines as a cost of doing business" aspect of the mistake.

Goldman's policy required that market-sensitive information from analysts be broadly distributed but did not apply to certain internal messages regarding general trading issues or market color. Regulators said that Goldman failed to clearly define the exceptions. One report quotes Robert Khuzami, the SEC's enforcement director, as saying, "[H]igher-risk trading and business strategies require higher-order controls" and that "Goldman failed to implement policies and procedures that adequately controlled the risk that research analysts could preview upcoming ratings changes with select traders and clients." Goldman agreed to pay the penalty, split between the SEC and FINRA, and to revise its policies.[9]

There are older examples as well. One is of allegations that Goldman mishandled information related to the Long-Term Capital Management (LTCM) books when Goldman was analyzing how it could potentially bail out LTCM in 1998. Roger Lowenstein writes in his account of the collapse of LTCM, *When Genius Failed*:

> *In Greenwich, Goldman's sleuths, who had the run of the office, left no stone unturned . . . A key member of the Goldman team . . . [who] appeared to be downloading Long-Term's positions, which the fund had so zealously guarded, from Long-Term's own computers directly into an oversized laptop (a detail that Goldman later denied). Meanwhile, Goldman's traders in New York sold some of the very same positions. At the end of one day, when the fund's positions were worth a good deal less, some Goldman traders in Long-Term's offices sauntered up to the trading desk and offered to buy them. Some questioned if, how and when and who had what information and how it was being used. Brazenly playing both sides of the street, Goldman represented investment banking at its mercenary ugliest . . . Goldman was raping Long-Term in front of their very eyes.[10]*

In other words, the accusation was that Goldman was exploiting its privileged position of trust and confidentiality to identify exactly what LTCM would need to dump, thereby affecting the market price.[11] As

Lowenstein portrays it, when Rubin and Friedman took over in 1990, Goldman started getting over its previous inhibitions against using confidential information for proprietary trading. In effect, clients hadn't fully realized that the public image of higher ethics was changing at the firm, and the firm slowly and covertly taking advantage of it.

Goldman's Research Alignment Process

In 2003, the SEC announced that it had settled charges against Goldman, as well as nine other banks, arising from an investigation of research analyst conflicts of interest. As part of the settlement, Goldman agreed to pay a total of $110 million in fines. The settlement was related to the passage of the Sarbanes–Oxley Act in 2002, which was intended to restrict communication and influence between banking and research. The SEC acknowledged that Goldman strategically aligned its investment banking division, the equities division, and the research division to foster collaboration;[12] the court acknowledged that Goldman's research alignment process fostered collaboration among divisions "to insure a strategic alignment of [Goldman Sachs'] business."[13] So Goldman's research alignment program was consistent with the firm's teamwork approach, because it required different divisions to work together. But the SEC concluded that it violated securities laws requiring the firm to protect clients, even if there was an alignment that followed the principles of Goldman. To executives and board members, because Goldman had leading market share in IPOs and equity offerings, the collaboration seemed to be working effectively—it was an example of teamwork. One would have to believe that the lawyers in each division were also aware of the collaboration. Yet Goldman's research alignment resulted in a fine. And not just for Goldman, but for nine other firms, totaling $1.435 billion. It shows the ambiguity in the law and people's ability to rationalize and potentially abuse an interpretation of it.

In fact, in the findings included in the consent order, one of the pressures facing Goldman goes beyond its own self-interest: pressure from clients. In a section titled: "Influences of investment banking personnel on research and the timing of research coverage," it stated that in early 2000, a Goldman investment banking client, Ask Jeeves, expressed concern that Goldman had yet to initiate research coverage. Typically a bank initiates research coverage as soon as it is legally able to do so after it participates in an equity offering. Ask Jeeves e-mailed its Goldman investment banker, saying its stock was "dropping like a rock," and stating, "our hopes were that a buy coverage from our lead banker might help stabilize the stock."[14]

While reviewing the findings, I discovered a reference to something I personally worked on. I was the only nonpartner on the firmwide marketing committee, which included some of the most respected partners. One of the initiatives of the committee was described: "Goldman Sachs introduced a new program in June 2000 to strengthen 'firm-wide marketing . . . including how we leverage our brand, advertise, and in particular, cross-sell . . .'" Strengthening cross-selling efforts was defined as a "top strategic priority for 2000." A $50,000 award was created "to recognize individuals across all divisions of the firm who 'cross-sell or help deliver a significant mandate to another business unit or division.'"[15]

As the point person on the initiative, I can assure you that all the partners signed off on it. People in the legal department were aware of the initiative. The award was even named after John C. Whitehead.[16] Because we thought that the award exemplified the concept of teamwork between one area and another, the only debate concerned the idea of a financial award to people for doing what many thought should be a natural part of their jobs, making it feel like a "brokerage commission." The nominations themselves were helpful to Goldman in understanding and tracking the teamwork and collaboration that were happening.

I was part of a team that discussed the award and the committee's initiatives with the management committee. I would have described the committee's work as successful. As the firm expanded, it was more difficult for people to collaborate; people did not know each other as well as before, because there was a division of labor and specialization. These were all challenges of the firm's organization and culture struggling with growth.[17] At that point, the award was a way to get people to talk about collaborating. No one intended it to be an incentive for unethical behavior, nor did we consider that it could be perceived that way or could lead to unethical or illegal behavior.

In hindsight, I see that it might have encouraged a research analyst, for example, to suggest a transaction to Goldman bankers and then tout the idea in a written research piece to investing clients, impacting the stock price, or to write positive things about the company in order to make the company more receptive to Goldman's bankers' suggestions. There is a lot less room for conflicts when research analysts simply analyze companies and make buy or sell recommendations for the firm's investing clients. It is also a lot cleaner if analysts' interactions with banking personnel are monitored by compliance officials so the analysts can't be influenced or pressured by banking personnel. The potential conflict introduced by offering the analyst an award is an example of an unintended consequence of a complex system.

Conflicts of Interest

In investment banking, a *conflict* means that the bank could have an incentive to act in a way contrary to the best interests, needs, or concerns of a client. *Perceived conflict* is defined as a situation in which one could argue it was possible that an investment bank had a conflict. Such conflicts, perceived or actual, are inevitable in large, global investment banks; it is the nature of the beast. Goldman and other banks regulate themselves internally, through processes such as conflict clearance, to avoid not only actual conflicts that could result in fines and penalties but also even the appearance of conflict, which can cause reputational loss (translating, of course, into other kinds of losses). As discussed earlier, actions can look bad to clients even if the firm does nothing legally wrong.[18] For these reasons, the management of conflicts of interest is an important part of Goldman's business model.

One can come up with an endless number of potential conflicts in all types of extremely hypothetical scenarios because there are so many different scenarios and possibilities as to what may happen in the future and so many different ways in which the parties may react. Because the possible scenarios are endless, and because investment banking is so complex, with numerous products, departments, divisions, and geographic regions, the timing or sequence of events and their consequences are challenging to completely evaluate and predict. No foolproof system can be designed to keep track of every potential conflict, and conflict management can never become a formula-driven science.[19]

As a result, Goldman, and all banks, must rely on judgment calls about when it might be crossing the line into a conflict, and those judgments are susceptible to pressure because of the strong incentives to always be making as much money for the firm and clients as possible. If the firm were to err on the side of being too cautious, it could risk missing opportunities and possibly alienating clients who want to work with it. If it were to err on the side of being too reckless, the firm could risk alienating its clients and hurting its reputation. Over time at Goldman, this is a key factor in the firm moving to the legal standard for making these judgment calls (and relying on "big boy" letters). The law is the standard that allows Goldman to maximize its business opportunities.

Consider a hypothetical example of a conflict and its resolution. A bank owns a position in company X through its private equity arm, and another client, company Y, now asks the bank to help it buy company X. The bank is in a potentially conflicted position. Its client, company Y, wants to pay the lowest price for company X. The bank's private equity business manages money for itself and other clients; it has a fiduciary responsibility to clients from whom it takes money to get the highest price for company X.

This dilemma could be resolved if the bank turned down the opportunity to work with company Y and simply worked with company X to get the highest price. There would still be a small conflict in that the private equity arm would have to negotiate an appropriate fee with its own M&A department. However, the bank has a strong incentive to work with Company Y, because it might need financing (a lucrative fee opportunity) to fund the purchase price. How can the bank represent both? It can draft a legal letter explaining all the potential conflicts and risks and have both companies agree to indemnify Goldman if there is an issue. If the two clients sign big boy letters, then Goldman could argue that it had put the clients' interests first—it told them about all the potential risks and conflicts and disclosed everything. This would fulfill its legal obligation.

Some might counter that the perception of conflict, regardless of the law, was so bad that the bank must work only for company X. In both cases, the bank will have done nothing illegal, and herein lies the problem: trying to maximize opportunities and shareholder returns in the short term may well be in conflict with the firm's higher ethical principles. The interpretation of what is right and wrong can also change over time as the situation and facts evolve. And making things trickier is that shareholder returns are easily quantified, whereas the issue of putting clients' interests first is more subjective, harder to measure. While measuring market share and superior returns is easy, judging what is right and wrong—gauging if you put your clients' interests first—is tough. When a conflict situation has not been managed properly, any decision Goldman made may seem obviously inappropriate with the benefit of hindsight, but those decisions are much more difficult in the moment. Here's an actual example.

"Hello, Doug, it's been a long time since we have had the chance to visit," say the notes Blankfein prepared for his call with

Douglas L. Foshee, chief executive of El Paso Energy Corporation, a big energy company that was in talks in 2011 to be sold to Kinder Morgan.[20] "I was very pleased you reached out to us on this most recent matter," the script goes, and Blankfein went on to thank Foshee for using Goldman as El Paso's adviser in the transaction. Blankfein added that he knew Foshee was aware of Goldman's investment in Kinder Morgan "and that we are very sensitive to the appearance of conflict."

Goldman's private equity arm owned a 19.1 percent stake (worth about $4 billion) in Kinder Morgan, and had two seats on the Kinder Morgan board, making the situation of advising the buyer not only awkward but also full of at least perceived conflicts. The Goldman banker advising El Paso also owned $340,000 worth of Kinder Morgan stock (a fact that was not raised or disclosed in the call, and it's unclear whether and when Goldman knew about the personal investment). The two Goldman board members recused themselves to reduce the perception of a conflict, and El Paso hired a second adviser, Morgan Stanley. Kinder Morgan soon announced it was about to acquire El Paso for $21.1 billion in cash and stock. Goldman, in its role as matchmaker for El Paso, received a $20 million fee.

When the matter ended up in court as a result of a shareholder lawsuit—alleging, among other things, that the merger was the product of breaches of fiduciary duty by the board of directors of El Paso, aided and abetted by Kinder Morgan and by El Paso's financial adviser, Goldman—the judge made it clear that Goldman's conflicts were not only a matter of appearance. For example, rather than walk away from the deal and lose its fee, Goldman recommended another adviser so that El Paso would receive impartial advice. But the judge, Chancellor Leo E. Strine Jr., of Delaware's Court of Chancery, disagreed:

> *When a second investment bank was brought in to address Goldman's economic incentive for a deal with, and on terms that favored, Kinder Morgan, Goldman continued to intervene and advise El Paso on*

strategic alternatives, and with its friends in El Paso management,
was able to achieve a remarkable feat: giving the new investment
bank an incentive to favor the merger by making sure that this bank
got paid only if El Paso adopted the strategic option of selling to
Kinder Morgan . . . In other words, the conflict-cleansing bank got
paid only if the option Goldman's financial incentives gave it a reason
to prefer was the one chosen.[21]

Foshee also received the brunt of Strine's judicial irritation
because Foshee had, as it turns out, used a "velvet glove negotiating
strategy . . . influenced by an improper motive" to get the deal he
wanted, planning to later buy El Paso's exploration and production
unit from Kinder Morgan.

In the press, Goldman's conduct in the El Paso deal was portrayed
as brazen, incestuous, and shameless. It was particularly shocking
in that it occurred soon after Goldman issued its business standards
report, a recommitment to its values and principles.[22] It indicated that
in some ways the organizational drift continued.

After Strine's opinion was read, Goldman continued to claim that
it had been completely transparent with El Paso regarding Goldman's
conflicts, and El Paso chose to continue to work with Goldman. Once
again, Goldman claimed it completely fulfilled its legal responsibilities. Many observers found it hard to believe that Goldman would
even get involved in the deal, with its $4 billion investment in Kinder
Morgan on one side of the negotiating table, and a $20 million fee
on the other, especially considering the scrutiny Goldman had been
under since the congressional hearings.[23]

Lloyd Blankfein had clearly defined Goldman's position on conflicts in an interview years before:

The crucial differentiating advantage of Goldman Sachs would
be one that outsiders might find surprising: Its complex variety of
many businesses was sure to have lots of conflicts. Goldman Sachs,
Blankfein said, should embrace the challenge of those conflicts.

Like market risk, the risk of conflicts would keep most competitors away—but by engaging actively with clients, Goldman Sachs would understand these conflicts better and could manage them better. Blankfein (who spends a significant part of his time managing real or perceived conflicts) said, "If major clients—governments, institutional investors, corporations, and wealthy families—believe they can trust our judgment, we can invite them to partner with us and share in their success."[24]

Blankfein's concept of the relationship between an adviser (that is also an investor for itself and with clients) and its clients (that are not coinvesting) can be at very least confusing and have unintended consequences. The competitive, organizational, technological, and regulatory pressures are there to maximize opportunities in this confusion and ambiguity.[25] And so the organization drifts, accepting a legal standard as its ethical base.

Conflict Clearance

In my role as business unit manager of Goldman's global M&A department in the late 1990s, I addressed strategy, business processes, organizational policy, business selection, and conflict clearance issues. Before Goldman could accept work with a client, it needed approval (clearance) from me or the people with whom I worked.

This position was both an honor and a curse. Keep in mind that I did this job in the late 1990s, when there was a boom in investment banking, stock market, and tech industry activity and the firm was growing at a rapid pace internationally and in proprietary trading.

I had two voicemail boxes that could accept some seventy to one hundred voicemails each. I regularly went home at 2 or 3 a.m. and woke up at 7 a.m.—and both message boxes would be full. It is hard to imagine, but e-mail was just starting to catch on and there were concerns about security and potential legal implications. More and more issues arose with Goldman's growth as conflicts were becoming more complex and global.

My predecessors in the job typically had to worry about issues such as, If two clients wanted to buy the same company, whom would we represent, and why? (Typically, we would represent the first to have raised the idea, particularly when we had done previous work for the client.) But now, the first question typically was, Have we worked in the past with another company analyzing the transaction, or have we advised the target company? We might have made commitments and possess confidential information, both of which could preclude us from working on the deal or would complicate our potential involvement. To determine whether we had worked on it or for the target previously, we consulted a huge Yellow Pages phone book in which we catalogued and cross-referenced each assignment by the target's name and the acquirer's name, so that if someone asked, we could look it up. Generally, senior partners had a good institutional memory and could help identify potential issues. But so many companies were merging and their names and legal structures changed, and the book could not necessarily keep up.

Suddenly, companies were being bought, reincorporated, and renamed at an amazing pace. In addition, when Goldman worked on an assignment, a confidentiality agreement usually had to be signed. We filed those and made sure the companies involved were listed in the book, which was getting larger by the day. We had the added issues of international names and entities, and the regional offices sometimes were less forthcoming in sharing the information, concerned about who learned what information and about protecting their clients' confidentiality. With all that was going on, and with the money being invested in systems for managing trading risk, we still had an essentially manual process. The complexity was far outpacing our methods.

We began to push for more automation. We even developed a factory floor diagram, breaking the M&A and other advisory processes into parts, so that we could track the process as it moved down a virtual conveyer belt. In hindsight, our system had flaws, but we were reacting to the challenges we faced as investment bankers who had to process as much information as possible to facilitate deals or opportunities. We were neither compliance experts nor systems experts, and we did not understand all the possible consequences of our approaches. There was no way we could know whether every conversation that might have divulged confidential information had been entered into the system. We kept trying to hire more people to help us. We brought people in from compliance to help. One of them was so overwhelmed and overworked that, sadly, he had a clinical breakdown and had to take time off.

The pressures were enormous, because everyone wanted to work for his own clients and lobbied for clearance—as well as for a speedy resolution, because a delay could be interpreted by the client as a problem and the client might start speaking to other firms. If we said no, some people took their views (and anger at us) to a higher court—meaning someone on the management committee. And, in the end, if we disagreed and thought there was a potential or perceived conflict, there was always the possibility of getting the client to agree to sign a big boy letter that indemnified us and represented that the client understood the situation and the risks.

Some clients strongly wanted Goldman to work on the deal despite a conflict, actual or perceived, because they anticipated a reward that outweighed the risk. Then the issue became, Who are we to tell a smart, sophisticated CEO with her own advisers that she is not smart enough to agree to such a thing? We felt the pressure of our competitors doing it, and we felt that if any firm would hold itself to a higher standard, it would be Goldman. The internal thinking was, We are *different* from the other firms; we have higher standards and principles. As discussed later, it was this rationalization—a sense of higher purpose supported by Goldman's public and community service and folklore—that in part helped create the unintended consequence of a blind spot.

In my position, something else began to come up more often: the issue of our having a proprietary equity position in the publicly traded target or owning its bonds. The questions were becoming more frequent, just as in the El Paso case. The decision I found the most difficult, and one I did not like, was advising multiple private equity firms on a transaction. Traditionally, Goldman would only work with one private equity firm in a potential acquisition. In the early 1990s, there were not very many leverage buyout (LBO) firms. If a bank aligned with only one, it would risk missing out on advising the winner, but it was accepted practice to work with one. But by the late 1990s several private equity firms would come to us to help finance the same leveraged buyout transaction and the commercial banks adopted the practice of having separate teams within the bank work for separate private equity firms. The rationale was that there were only so many banks, so if each bank committed to only one firm, then one could argue that it would limit the number of buyers, which would hurt the seller. So in the end we changed our policy and we set up separate teams. At first we preferred they were physically on separate floors, but then there were not enough floors. This policy change was another signal of business practices changing.

Even more concerning to me was the policy change to allow our internal funds to bid for a company while providing financing advice to competing private equity firms. There is a real possibility in that situation that a client will lose to Goldman and will perceive that the firm misused information, such as the knowledge of what the client was going to pay. Even if all information is in fact completely protected, if Goldman wins the bidding in such a case, the perception may be bad. I'm not alone in my concern. In its 2011 business standards committee report, Goldman mentions that to "strengthen client relationships and reputational excellence . . . Goldman will carefully review requests to provide financing to competing bidders when a MBD [Goldman's Merchant Banking Division] fund or other firm-managed private fund is pursuing an acquisition as a bidder."

The report states that when Goldman has "multiple roles in a particular transaction . . . the firm may be able to address potential conflicts by providing disclosure to its clients, obtaining appropriate consents, relying on Information Barriers, carefully defining its role and/or requesting that the client engage a co-advisor." When I discussed this with a legal expert, he said that this policy basically covers most imaginable scenarios and would technically allow the firm to play multiple roles and follow different legal standards in serving clients, from the highest, that of having a fiduciary responsibility to them, to the lowest, that of being a market maker.

More often, we had clients sign big boy letters. The phrase itself is telling. It neutralized what we were doing; it implied the client was sophisticated and that it was OK. If we were not convinced about a company—typically a smaller company that might be less sophisticated—we would not allow the banker to get a big boy letter from the client. Which clients qualified as big boys was subjective. Usually, it was an easy discussion, because we could determine that a smaller company with a smaller potential fee was not a big boy and therefore not worth the banker's appeal to the management committee.

All these decisions were highly vetted and discussed with senior management, appropriate committees, and the legal and compliance departments. We had whiteboard sessions trying to figure out what might be a problem or what might look bad. During the time of my role in the late 1990s, the gold standard for determining the proper behavior expected at Goldman was to imagine how we would feel if our actions were disclosed in the *Wall Street Journal*. This test was constantly drilled into our heads. In fact, if it was a decision that would even make the *Wall Street Journal*, we tried to err toward caution. But we couldn't imagine all scenarios.

Slowly, even during my years, the world incrementally changed from more "one off" instances—"No, we can't do that; it could look bad"—to, "If both clients agree, or if the sophisticated client signs a big boy letter, then it is okay." Because of Goldman's market share and proprietary trading, and because Goldman's growth coincided with a booming market, issues came up often. Eventually, the key senior person who reviewed conflicts and was seen as "more administrative or compliance-oriented" rose all the way to the management committee because of the importance of the job. No other firm had (or has) such a person at such a high level. It is a critical job, because it involves not only figuring out how to get to yes, how to please clients, and how to maximize revenue opportunities, but also ensuring that the firm is protected and following a process that will stand up in court. This is what Goldman refers to as "managing conflicts." During our interview, one partner compared the chief conflict management person with the chief risk officer for the firm.

Goldman still has its leading market share, in part because it effectively manages conflicts to its advantage—and it also faces reputational and legal questions and consequences, because conflict management is art and not science. If Goldman had not managed conflicts, its ability to grow and maintain market share would have been challenged. The management of conflicts maximizes opportunities to access scarce resources. The diligence and effort and thoughtfulness and angst that go into managing conflicts are immense, and it is inevitable that something will not be considered or given the proper weight as a possibility. And when that happens, Goldman most likely will be sued, and it will be on the front pages, with its reputation questioned. Such questions are the consequence of Goldman doing business and maximizing opportunities as well as the consequence of the limitations of human thought, processes, and systems.

About the time of the IPO, a partner told me that there was a limit to the number of transactions, of capital flows, in the world. What Goldman was good at was getting involved in those transactions or discussions because of its relationships, smarts, and information. What Goldman was better at than any other bank was working to maximize the revenue from the transaction or flow—finding and managing "multiple roles in a particular transaction." For example, if it were a cross-border M&A deal, then Goldman would provide M&A advice as well as involve its foreign exchange desk to handle the currency exchange for the purchase price. If Goldman missed the deal—meaning our bankers were not involved—then proprietary trading might possibly be involved in merger arbitrage (oftentimes, Goldman would make more money in proprietary merger arbitrage than if it had been hired to advise on the deal). Goldman ensured that we looked at each transaction and each flow and had some way to make money from it. The more roles we played in a transaction, the more opportunities we had to make money on a cost base that was essentially fixed, and thus the transaction would be much more profitable for us than if we had played only one role.

Managing conflicts maximizes that opportunity. Because of this recognition, the firm has invested many more resources into conflict management.[26] This is one of the keys to Goldman's higher returns on equity compared with those of its peers. But it also relies heavily on an organizational culture, a "residual partnership mentality," the partner told me, that emphasizes sharing information to maximize opportunity.

Goldman has the same conflicts as most other Wall Street firms. However, unlike other firms, according to William Cohan, "Goldman has taken the decision that it is in the business of managing conflicts and the joke around Goldman was 'If you have a conflict, we have an interest.' While that has led to tremendous success it is also the firm's Achilles heel—because of its unfailing belief that it can manage conflicts it gets itself into positions where other firms will just say no."[27]

When I raised this issue with a Goldman partner, his comment was that the other firms do not just say no. He implied that this argument was based on the premise that the other firms had some sort of higher values, which, he said, based on his experience working against and alongside them for decades, he believes is wrong. He said they most likely wished they had Goldman's network of relationships (a network with leading market shares), which means Goldman must deal with these conflicts. It is easy not to have client conflicts, he stated, when you have fewer trusted clients and so many clients asking you to advise on or provide liquidity in so many situations. I pointed out that it's not really the number of clients but rather Goldman's various roles or proprietary investing businesses causing the conflicts.

Management Committee Composition

The changes in the membership of Goldman Sachs' management committee corroborate the idea of a shifting emphasis toward the legal standard of compliance and away from the original interpretation of the first principle, as well as reflecting the increasing complexity of Goldman's business. In 1999 the firm had twenty-two management committee members, two of whom were in legal functions (around 9 percent). In 2009, the management committee had grown to twenty-nine members. There are two members related to legal functions plus one individual who is known for political connections, one individual responsible for compliance, and one person responsible for conflicts (representing 17 percent of the committee). At the IPO, banking and trading/PIA members represented around one-third of the members each. In 2009, banking was around 20 percent and trading/PIA/markets-oriented backgrounds represent close to half the committee.[28] So there has been a shift at the management committee level as illustrated by an increase in legal and in trading/PIA/markets-oriented people. Remember, Sidney Weinberg had sought balance with a trader running the firm and banking having a large presence on the committee.

The balance of composition between banking and trading in leadership has been an important organizational element (as was the balance between newer and older partners). Sidney Weinberg sought this balance when he selected Gus Levy, a trader, to become senior partner, but he created the management committee with a majority of banking partners to instill some balance. There's been a shift in the management committee composition as well as at the very top, with the top two having trading backgrounds.

Outside Board of Directors

Some have argued that boards of directors of the banks must take more responsibility for oversight of conflicts, so it's important to consider the role of the Goldman board here briefly.

The Sarbanes–Oxley Act, which became law in 2002, sought to improve the oversight of boards by requiring the appointment of more outside directors. In 1999, Goldman's board of directors had seven members, including four executives of the firm; two outside, independent directors; and John L. Weinberg. In 2001, Goldman's board of directors had eight members: four executives at Goldman and four outside directors (John L. had decided not to seek reelection to the board after his initial three-year term at the IPO). After Sarbanes–Oxley passed, and in compliance with new requirements of the NYSE, Goldman added two outside directors. Thus, the majority of its board (60 percent) was comprised of outside, independent directors.

While a board's legal and fiduciary responsibilities are typically explained by legal counsel at board meetings for board members, according to those I interviewed, understanding, interpreting, and protecting Goldman's principles, values, and ethics, and determining whether practices are consistent with them, would be very difficult for outside board members. Many of the partners whom I interviewed generally agreed that it is reasonable to conclude that the outside board members' understanding of the firm's principles, values, and ethics most likely differs from that of Whitehead and John L. Weinberg because the organizational and regulatory structures and legal liabilities the firm is subject to have changed since their time. At the same time, most of the Goldman "insiders" (executives) on the board have a trading background, and some partners suggested that this may mean that they are less sensitive to issues regarding managing client relationships than Whitehead and Weinberg were.

A Change of Meaning

While some at Goldman told me that the firm continues to abide by its first principle, I believe the evidence shows that that can only be considered true if the interpretation of the principle has changed. I believe the process of this change was one of social normalization, or rationalization, which was gradual, and this in part explains why they do not see it. This kind of rationalization happens because the pressures are so strong to grow and change, which can result in client conflicts. It is vital in evaluating how an organization's culture has drifted to recognize that organizations generally must adapt to new competitive demands and other external pressures, and Goldman's change to applying a legal standard in regard to serving clients' interests is a good case in point. While the differences may now look to outsiders like a clear change of standards, discerning drift that is detrimental from healthy adaptation in the moment is a very difficult judgment for those inside an organization to make. That was all the more true for Goldman due to its increasing complexity and size. Also, this has contributed to making conflicts much more complicated to manage.

Part Four

GOLDMAN'S
PERFORMANCE

Chapter 8

Nagging Questions: Leadership, Crisis, and Clients

THE MERE FACT THAT GOLDMAN SURVIVED AS AN INDEPENDENT company in 2008 during the financial crisis when many of its peers did not can be considered a success, at least in a relative sense, but it is a precarious one at best. Goldman wrote in its proxy statement, "In 2008, we outperformed our core competitors due, in part, to the outstanding performance of our Named Executive Officers (NEOs)."[1] Goldman had a return on equity of 4.9 percent versus −5.0 percent for its peers in 2008, and 22.5 percent versus −1.8 percent, in 2009.

Whether Goldman would have survived without government intervention is debatable.[2] In fact, in the days immediately following the collapse of Lehman, it became apparent that both Goldman and Morgan Stanley could have shared the same fate as Lehman.[3]

I focus here first on the aspects of Goldman's culture that helped it relatively outperform its peers during the credit crisis. Then I'll explore the accusations of wrongdoing leading up to and during the financial crisis that were made against Goldman and how the firm has responded. The nature of the accusations, and Goldman's responses, offer much food for thought about the change in culture and the potential future risks that Goldman, and the whole banking system, face. Organizational drift doesn't necessarily involve a total abandonment of prior values and principles. Elements of the culture may be retained, or retained in part, and that is true of Goldman. For simplicity I will use the word *residual* in front of a word describing an element of the culture that has changed but not enough that it is gone or unrecognizable.[4] In fact, the residual elements help obscure the changes and add to the process of organizational drift.

One of the most important elements of Goldman's culture that has changed but is still recognizable is what I'll call its residual dissonance. As discussed, *dissonance* is the term used by Columbia University sociologist David Stark to describe the ability of those in an organization to challenge one another, to ask questions and explain their own views. Dissonance of this type leads to more scrutiny of decisions as well as greater innovation and performance. The financial interdependence of partners during Goldman's partnership days, as well as the social network of trust among them and the less hierarchical structure, encouraged this, and though the new organizational and incentive structure of the company has limited this residual dissonance, a strong enough social network among executives at the firm still exists that these were key factors that differentiated Goldman during the credit crisis. They helped to break through structural secrecy, and that, combined with more expertise at the top of the firm in trading and risk assessment, enabled Goldman to do a better job of perceiving and managing the risk that led to losses. Blankfein was an expert in trading, and David Viniar, Goldman's chief financial officer, had vast experience outside traditional CFO responsibilities. The combination of expertise and residual dissonance at the top enabled Goldman to overcome structural secrecy.

Based on my interviews with executives at competitors, these cultural elements did not exist at other firms in the same way or intensity as they did at Goldman during the credit crisis. While discussing Goldman's success with me, a widely respected consultant, who has experience working with many firms, explained that Goldman is exceptionally good at looking at overall risk and firmwide risk and understanding the aggregate size of the risk and correlations across the firm. He believes that Goldman had so many different proprietary desks in so many different asset classes with so many different correlations that it benefits from a diversification effect. When the corporate credit or equities businesses are doing poorly, then foreign exchange or interest rate businesses may be doing well. No other bank had invested as much in sophisticated, computer-driven quantitative systems to reveal the signals. And several senior people had the expertise to read the signals, ask the right questions, and then react.[5] Goldman was the only firm that had so many risk experts in the highest levels of management. As mentioned earlier, Goldman had learned from its 1994 experience.

Value at Risk, Models, and Risk Management

Models are widely used in risk management to synthesize risk and help analysts, investors, and company boards determine acceptable trading parameters under different scenarios. Value at risk (VaR) is a widely used measure of the risk of loss on a specific portfolio of financial assets, expressed in terms of a probability of losing a given percentage of the value of a portfolio—in mark-to-market value— over a certain time. For example, if a portfolio of stocks has a one-day 5 percent VaR of $1 million, there is a 0.05 probability that the portfolio will fall in value by more than $1 million over a one-day period. Informally, a loss of $1 million or more on this portfolio is expected on one day in twenty. Typically, banks report the VaR by risk type (e.g., interest rates, equity prices, currency rates, and commodity prices).

VaR may be an unsatisfactory risk metric, but it has become an industry standard. Wall Street equity analysts expect banks to provide risk (VaR) calculations quarterly, and they talk about risk increasing, or decreasing, depending on the output of the models. The models and VaR calculations, however, make numerous assumptions, some of which proved over time to be invalid, making it dangerous to rely on or extrapolate too much on VaR. Analysts and investors (and boards of directors) overrely on VAR as a measurement of risk, and therefore management teams do also, one of the external influences of being a public company. Yet the overreliance on VaR, one of the key measures employed in risk management, is controversial. Some of the claims made about it include that it "[ignores] 2,500 years of experience in favor of untested models built by non-traders; was char-latanism because it claimed to estimate the risks of rare events, which is impossible; gave false confidence; would be exploited by traders."[6] Comparing VaR to "an airbag that works all the time, except when you have a car accident," David Einhorn, the hedge fund manager who profited from shorting Lehman stock, charged that VaR also led to excessive risk-taking and leverage at financial institutions before the crisis and is "potentially catastrophic when its use creates a false sense of security among senior executives and watchdogs."[7]

Leading up to the crisis most of Wall Street essentially used the same models and metrics for risk management, particularly VaR (an effect of being public—analysts and investors compare VaR between firms in analyzing performance). But Goldman did not rely as heavily on it. Interviews confirmed the level of dissonance at Goldman, even as a publicly traded firm, in discussing and understanding that the output of the models was and is unique to Goldman, which meant the firm was not as dependent on the models as were other firms, and that, combined with what sociologists call a "heterarchical struc-ture" (less hierarchy in the chain of command than in many firms) and the trading experience of its top executives, gave Goldman an edge.[8] The more intense scrutiny of the models and risk factors led Goldman's top executives to pick up on market signals that other firms' executives missed.[9] As Emanuel Derman, the former head of the quantitative risk strategies group at Goldman and now a professor at Columbia, wrote, at Goldman, "Even if you insist on representing risk with a single number, VaR isn't the best one . . . As a result, though we [Goldman] used VaR, we didn't make it our religion."[10] (Meanwhile, at other firms, measures like "VaR [value at risk] . . . became institutionalized," as the *New York Times'* Joe Nocera put it. "Corporate chieftains like Stanley O'Neal at Merrill Lynch and Charles Prince at Citigroup pushed their divisions to take more risk because they were being left behind in the race for trading profits. All over Wall Street, VaR numbers increased."[11])

Even though VaR has flaws, it is the only relatively consistent risk data that is publicly reported from the various banks, which is why I analyzed it. When analyzing the publicly reported data from 2000 to 2010 for Goldman and its peers, what stands out is that Goldman's standard deviation of VaR is higher (meaning that the level of the total VaR was more varied) than most other firms, implying that Goldman more dynamically managed risk than its peers over the time period.

Goldman also had the organizational structure and environment to complement and support risk management systems and procedures. During an interview for this book, an executive at a competing firm (who had earlier worked at Goldman) explained that his firm simply did not give the same attention to risk management. He did not think his firm had the capability to aggregate risk at a level similar to Goldman and said the top executives neither had the capability nor dedicated the time to interpret, discuss, and debate risk. He said that Goldman's focus on proprietary trading and its profits had caused the firm to invest in systems and groom future leaders who understand it. He explained that Goldman's biggest advantage was that its top people were real traders and risk takers or had access to and dialogue with such traders, as well as the culture to support investment in the systems and the dialogue. He explained that this was why he hadn't been surprised when Hank Paulson and the board had bypassed John Thornton and John Thain (to whom

Paulson allegedly had verbally promised the CEO position) and picked Blankfein to succeed him as CEO. Thornton and Thain did not have as much real time and extensive expertise in trading and risk. The firm gained trading expertise at its top with Blankfein, and that helped it navigate the credit crisis.[12]

One executive at a competitor speculated that although his firm had people running around doing lots of things related to risk, including analyzing lots of models, no one knew how it all added up and, more important, what it meant. He questioned whether it was even possible to understand risk management in such large, complex organizations. But he said if one firm could, it was probably Goldman, which seemed to prioritize risk management because of its dependence on proprietary trading and because it had the cultural heritage of teamwork, as well as its near-death experience in 1994.

While some analysts of the crisis have pointed to the failure of the boards of directors at the banks to question risk-taking, most of the people I interviewed said that those on the boards of the banks had limited trading and risk expertise and that it would be almost impossible, anyway, for an outside, independent director who has an important full-time job and attends monthly or quarterly meetings to be able to take the time to understand and question such complex risks.[13] That made having executives at the top of the firm with trading and risk management experience all the more important, especially when there wasn't a mechanism like financial interdependence of a partnership.

Communicating the Signals

Goldman's relatively flat organizational structure and the relative strength of its social network are exemplified in a series of e-mails and memos from as early as the end of 2006 that were sent to top Goldman executives by traders. They discussed the firm's exposure to mortgages and the top executives' ability to understand the issues, concluding that Goldman should reduce risk as quickly as possible. There are e-mails from Blankfein and Viniar giving direct guidance related to risk.[14]

In one e-mail, CFO Viniar wrote, "Let's be aggressive distributing things because there will be very good opportunities as the markets [go] into what is likely to be even greater distress, and we want to be in a position to take advantage of them." Blankfein wrote in one e-mail, "Could/should we have cleaned up these books before . . . and are we doing enough right now to sell off cats and dogs in other books throughout the division?" The communications show how involved the leaders were. (They also raise serious questions and concerns about what Goldman leaders knew, did, and instructed others to do, and the impact of these actions on the firm's culture.)

Meanwhile, even as Goldman reversed course and tried to reduce risk in mortgages—and even allegedly shorted the market—its competitors were adding risk. For example, Chuck Prince at Citi was, as described and paraphrased in an interview, "dancing with elephants."[15] A former Citi executive I talked to at the time expressed doubt that Prince (whose professional background was more legal and administrative in nature) had the same sort of direct communication, knowledge, and discussion that Viniar and Blankfein were having or the expertise to do so. One could argue that, at the time, Citi's structure may have been more hierarchical and more complex than Goldman's (Citi had more than 300,000 people in more than one hundred countries), making it harder for information to get to the top. Other elements, such as dissonance, may also have been missing, adding to structural secrecy and restricting information flow.

Goldman, by contrast, encourages the discussion and disagreement needed to arrive at the best answer. For example, when I was in proprietary trading in the early 2000s, I participated in meetings wherein the portfolio managers of proprietary trading groups presented their ideas and strategies to other proprietary portfolio managers in other groups. Once, a manager presented a trade that appeared to be a good investment based on models, but the other proprietary traders quickly ferreted out a weakness in the model: it was not properly accounting for the illiquidity and the severe downside that would happen in selected, albeit low-probability, scenarios. It is hard to believe that a risk management department or accountant expected to value the investment would be able to identify all the issues raised in that room of traders.

Taking Action, Continuous Adjustment: Risk Management Systems

Before the heavy trading losses Goldman experienced in 1994, the firm's risk management system was informal; traders made their own decisions with little intervention from management, and risk was often assessed "with a series of phone calls and a quick tally on a scratch pad."[16] By 1995, it had implemented an "interdisciplinary, firm-wide risk management system, a risk committee that [met] weekly, and a loss limit on every trading seat."[17] Current risks became instantaneously visible through the new computer-based system, which enabled managers to "aggregate the firm's market and credit risks across the entire organization [despite any organizational silos] at any point during the day."[18]

One Goldman partner I talked to pointed out that most of the heads of the other firms had not gone through what happened to Goldman in 1994 when so much of the capital of the firm and of Blankfein, Viniar, and other partners was put at serious risk. The other heads had been working in organizations that had worked with other people's capital with different incentives for a longer time. So, the partner told me, Goldman was much more aggressive with regard to building risk management systems.

The computer system was only one aspect of the overall risk management system. Traders no longer operated with little oversight. A risk committee, composed of partners from around the world, met by teleconference to examine "all of the firm's major exposures, including the risks related to the market, individual operations, credit, new products and businesses, and the firm's reputation."[19] The committee members had the expertise to question and challenge each other and the organizational structure and culture to support the dissonance.

The traders were not always happy about being subjected to more oversight: "There was, in fact, a vigorous debate within Goldman about the right level, just as there was over the firm's overall risk levels," William Cohan writes. "Angry at being reined in by its powerful risk managers, traders dubbed them the 'VaR Police.'"[20]

Crisis Leadership

Often, leaders get too much credit or blame, with too little emphasis on the organizational elements that leaders inherit or are a product of. Lloyd Blankfein has been blamed for a "J Aron/FICC takeover" of the firm, which has resulted in a change in culture.[21] Yet, he also is credited with saving the firm in the crisis. The role of the organizational elements received a lot less consideration or publicity.

Blankfein's career took off as a sales trader and a manager of traders. He has been described as having "a sixth sense about when to push them to take more risk and when to take their collective feet off the accelerator."[22] According to interviews, Blankfein thought the best traders were quick adjusters, a trait he, too, possessed. He was not a trader per se, although many people have the impression that he was, and yet he gained credibility with his traders by managing a small trading account that could be monitored. A former partner of Blankfein's said that Blankfein knew he could lose credibility if he lost money, but he thought "even if he lost money he would get credibility because the credibility of being right isn't so important. The credibility of knowing what a trader experiences when they lose might even be more valuable, so maybe he figured out that either way it was good to show that he was learning."[23] An executive at a competitor that I interviewed pointed out, this is precisely what out-side boards of directors at banks typically lack.

Blankfein's background in trading made him a wholehearted sup-porter of a strategic move toward proprietary trading. He acknowl-edged the challenges of balancing agency business with a growing proprietary business but viewed the move as not only a "momentous strategic opportunity" but also a necessity that had been deferred to maximize profits and should be deferred no longer.[24] Blankfein did not propose making the proprietary (or principal) investing business dominant but rather talked about combining the two busi-nesses, agency and principal, in an "unbeatable whole."[25] He actively promoted this theme as he gained authority and reputation within the organization, even though clients continued to express concern about whether, in any given situation, Goldman was acting as their agent or as a competitor.[26] Blankfein's argument raises questions about Goldman executives' argument that in certain trades the firm was simply acting as a market maker.

Blankfein gained professional respect from peers and senior part-ners for his ability to evaluate possible ramifications of alternative courses of action. He has been described as "original in his percep-tions and analysis . . . accessible to others" and as having "a detached rationality."[27] His personal style and actions reflected and modeled for others some of the best aspects of the firm's partnership culture as it had been at its strongest. He asked many questions of the very smart people with whom he surrounded himself, until he was satis-fied that he had gotten the right answer. He tapped in to the expertise and vast experience of retired partners, who many times (and in my experience) had been treated almost as outsiders after they became inactive. He used his extensive global social network to promote the firm's goals, something that became critical to the firm's survival during the credit crisis.

Any discussion of Goldman's leadership during the crisis must also acknowledge the role of David Viniar, Goldman's chief finan-cial officer from 1999 to January 2013, a man who, many of my interviewees said, was the key person responsible for the firm's survival. A former investment banker working specifically in structured finance, Viniar worked on several credit and risk committees before becoming CFO. He understood structured products, which were at the heart of the crisis. He had the expertise to question traders or have a dialogue with them; he had their respect, unlike most CFOs, who would not have worked directly in structuring such complex products. Viniar also took advantage of a culture in which an element of dissonance was still alive, one that supported playing devil's advocate, collecting and channeling information that challenged taken-for-granted assumptions in the organization, when it came to trading risk.

Viniar's rotation through various assignments was crucial to his ability to help guide Goldman through the crisis. These rotations were the result of an organizational design that served to improve understanding and strengthen social networks.[28] One Goldman partner told me something to this effect (I am paraphrasing): "You can't BS David. He has a lot of experience and knows more than you. He may not be smarter than you in your area of expertise, but he knows more about risk than you do because of his training and experiences. What makes him particularly effective is his ability to check out what you tell him. He and his group have the contacts and know the people—internally and externally."[29]

A Goldman partner credited Blankfein with retaining Viniar when Blankfein became CEO and not replacing him with those he considered loyal to him, as the partner said Blankfein did in many other important areas. He elaborated that for Goldman's board, Blankfein, Viniar, and Gary Cohn were not only the top three from a reporting perspective but also the top three authorities on risk; no other firm had that much talent and expertise in their top three working so closely together during the crisis. However, in many ways their active involvement in risk management—supported by the remarkable number of e-mails and other communication, and knowing what they knew and directing people to reduce risk—put them closer to the actions and behavior of those at Goldman prior to and during the financial crisis. This, therefore, raises the issue of their personal role in, at the very least, the change of meaning of putting the clients' interest first.

A Goldman spokesperson told *Rolling Stone* that "its behavior throughout the period covered in the Levin report was consistent with responsible business practice, and that its machinations in the mortgage market were simply an attempt to manage risk."[30] The question here is whether its behavior is consistent with the original meaning of the business principles, not if these were responsible business practices. In my interviews, most of the current and former partners who believe there has been a change in culture strongly stated that in this instance the behavior was not consistent with those principles. In my interviews with clients, I asked them what they think when Goldman tells them about the business principles, even today, based on what they have learned about its behavior. Most told me Goldman's behavior does not reflect how clients interpret the principles, which is based in part on how Goldman itself portrays them externally. However, most people I interviewed said that does not necessarily make the firm's behavior criminal or illegal.

More Concentration of Trading Experience at the Top

David Viniar retired in January 2013 and was replaced with Harvey Schwartz. Like Viniar, Schwartz worked in various areas of the firm, including banking for a short time, which should give him a more nuanced view and access to more information. But Schwartz got his start in the J. Aron area at Goldman, similar to Cohn and Blankfein, as well as the person who is head of human resources (the head of human resources would typically interact with the board on matters like compensation and performance). Many current and former banking partners that I spoke to pointed to this J. Aron concentration at the top. From a sociological perspective, it does raise the risk of changing the element of dissonance and increasing structural secrecy.

Some partners also raised the concern that Blankfein has put people loyal to him in key positions throughout the firm and/or lateral hires who may not have as good an understanding of the original meaning of the principles. Once again, this is interesting from a sociological perspective in terms of raising the risk of a change in dissonance and increase in structural secrecy. Some current and former banking partners speculated that they believe that Blankfein learned from Paulson's coup of Corzine and wanted to consolidate power. From an organizational perspective, the fact that this could happen reflects the changes. The fact that a board would allow this also reflects the changes. And with the passage of time and Blankfein and Goldman's many successes, who is to question it?

Does Outperformance Signal a Shift from Principles?

The tricky issue about the residual dissonance that represents a degree of preservation of Goldman's culture at the time the principles were codified is that Goldman does not consider that, in some instances, it has an obligation to share the benefit of this wisdom with its clients. In late 2006, Goldman recognized the need to de-risk and moved swiftly to do so without warning clients or the government. This is one of the things about Goldman that spurred the vitriol of Matt Taibbi and many others. After a period of mounting concern about Goldman's overexposure to mortgages, in late 2006 Viniar and a group of executives drafted a memo describing their course of action for reducing that exposure. Goldman's critics are quick to point to this statement: "Distribute as much as possible on bonds created from new loan securitizations and clean previous positions."[31] Taibbi translates this to, "Find suckers to buy as much of [the] risky inventory as possible." Taibbi then provides an apt analogy: "Goldman was like a car dealership that realized it had a whole lot full of cars with faulty brakes. Instead of announcing a recall, it surged ahead with a two-fold plan to make a fortune: first, by dumping the dangerous products on other people, and second, by taking out life insurance against the fools who bought the deadly cars."[32] According to Taibbi, within two months of the memo, Goldman had gone "from betting $6 billion on mortgages to betting $10 billion *against* them—a shift of $16 billion."

As a public company, Goldman has a fiduciary responsibility to its shareholders, which confers the highest standard of legal care and loyalty.[33] Therefore, if Goldman thought that it was in the best interests of shareholders to de-risk immediately, it had a duty to do so. But to de-risk, Goldman sold the risk to clients. Many current partners at Goldman whom I interviewed (corroborated by congressional testimony by Goldman executives) pointed out that the "sophisticated, institutional clients" wanted the risk, and Goldman sourced it for them. The partners argue Goldman did not defraud its clients. However, the SEC charged Goldman and an employee with fraud on a specific deal for its role as an underwriter (which has different legal obligations than those of a market marker). Goldman settled the charges for $550 million, and the employee is fighting the civil case.

Legal experts I interviewed explained that Goldman has no legal fiduciary responsibility to clients when it is acting as a broker on their behalf. Investment banks are not held to a "fiduciary standard" in their dealing with these clients, but rather a "suitability standard," which is less stringent.[34] Under a suitability standard, Goldman is not required to put the client's interests first and is not obligated to disclose its own proprietary views or positions. A suitability standard instead requires the firm to ask whether the product is suitable for the client (for example, whether it meets the investment objectives) and to disclose the risks.[35]

The impression of Blankfein's testimony at the Levin hearings, in response to accusations of not putting customers' interests first in the mortgage trades, is that Goldman, or at least its executives, did not think the firm did anything wrong.[36] Their argument, as articulated by Blankfein on numerous occasions, hinges on the firm's claim that when Goldman sold the mortgage securities, it was not acting as an adviser to the clients, it was acting as a broker, and its role was simply to sell sophisticated institutional clients whatever they wanted to buy. As such, it completely fulfilled its legal duties when it acted as a market maker or broker with counterparties. Goldman maintains that it was essentially only making markets (making a bid and an offer for securities) and used responsible business practices in fulfilling all of its legal obligations.[37] The firm had a legal obligation to ensure that its clients are provided the proper disclosures, but that is as far as Goldman's legal obligation goes: caveat emptor, or "buyer beware."[38]

Goldman argues that it was acting as a broker, not an advisor, in selling mortgage securities. Maybe that's true legally, but there's another question about their role. Can Goldman, or any bank, really so cleanly delineate when they are acting as a broker and when as an adviser? An executive at a competitor believed that Goldman's characterization as simply acting as a broker was like Goldman suggesting a client called them to ask it to buy shares in IBM and the firm did so. He explained that this is not the case with complicated, fixed income securities that are not traded on an exchange. First, the bank typically maintains inventory to sell because the market is not as liquid. This does not mean the bank is not acting as a broker, but it certainly complicates the relationship. Second, banks are calling up with ideas and suggestions (unlike in stocks, which are more regulated and liquid) and the client does need some explanation of what the securities are and advice on how it meets what they are looking for. He felt that Goldman was disingenuous in saying it was merely acting as a broker when executing transactions in complicated securities.

A client elaborated that there are times when he calls Goldman and expects them only to simply execute and actually pays a higher commission than going to another bank that would do it cheaper in order to pay Goldman back for its ideas, research, and advice. But he also gets calls from Goldman making recommendations and suggestions, which he would characterize as advising him, to buy certain complicated securities that generally meet what he is looking for, some of which Goldman provides what could be called research and analysis on. He said that Goldman has an unbelievable ability to source and develop these investment opportunities. But many of them require a dialogue, an explanation, analysis, and expertise. He said it was unclear to him in many instances when Goldman was acting as a broker/agent or principal, even when giving "advice." But he clarified Goldman was doing nothing that the other banks were not doing too; it is just that Goldman's principal investing is much larger so it does raise more questions. And he felt the ultimate responsibility was his if he were to buy or not buy. But, it seemed to him that Goldman was being a little disingenuous in its characterization of its role. He pointed out that he thought Goldman's objective was to be the adviser of choice, not the broker of choice.

"The investors that we're dealing with on the long side, or on the short side, know what they want to acquire," Blankfein said. "I don't think our clients care, or that they should care," what Goldman's opinion is, he said. The rationalization was that Goldman's clients were sophisticated investors, after all, and asked for the risk, which Goldman provided to them.[39]

As mentioned earlier, according to my interviews with several Goldman partners, the general attitude at the firm was that the clients were "big boys." Goldman was not selling products to "widows and orphans." They insisted that the firm used legally responsible business practices. Some partners explained that, for all the Goldman partners knew, they could have been wrong and the clients could have been right—and no one would have wept for Goldman. Some clients I interviewed said they understood this argument, but in this case they believed the size of Goldman's short (or hedge, as Goldman describes it) of the securities showed a great deal of confidence in its view and that the firm understood the catastrophe that could happen if it did nothing. They argued that, given the size of the short and direct communication amongst executives, and that Goldman clearly perceived clients could suffer, the firm did have an ethical obligation to warn them (especially considering its first business principle). Some partners I interviewed countered that they were just doing what they thought was right from an organizational perspective and right for their shareholders—and right for the survival of the firm. They told me they did not think they were breaking any legal rules or regulations or violating a business principle.

But the behavior was certainly in sharp contrast to John L. Weinberg's insistence on making good on the BP loss even though Goldman had no legal obligation to the British government, as discussed in chapter 1. Nor was it in keeping with Paulson's sitting on the other side of the table in the Sara Lee meeting.

I don't believe that the Goldman executives understood all the unintended consequences, the magnitude of the consequences, or the way their actions would be interpreted and processed externally and internally. If Goldman had understood the magnitude of the potential problems, it would have been even more aggressive in its actions, effecting even larger shorts, deleveraging faster, and raising more equity sooner. Based on my interviews and their actions, I don't believe that the Goldman leaders realized they were so close to being swept away in a financial tsunami. In addition, I don't believe that they truly understood how their actions would be interpreted by employees and how much that would most likely exacerbate the organizational drift.

Finding a balance between duty to clients and duty to shareholders is a long-standing issue. Most clients I interviewed argued that Goldman formerly believed that putting the clients first would benefit the owners over the long term, thereby serving shareholder interests. They generally did not interpret Goldman's actions, such as selling the mortgage securities, as consistent with the business principles they expected from Goldman. They did not see it as illegal; they saw it as Goldman acting like the rest of Wall Street, but maybe a little worse, because Goldman waved its principles in front of clients and said it acted more ethically than others on Wall Street.

I asked some executives who were Goldman's competitors about this dilemma—duty to clients versus duty to shareholders—and they, too, explained that Goldman was generally behaving as the industry does. The industry generally has moved to a legal standard in determining its duties. It was unclear to them when or how or why the legal standard became the industry standard. They believe no one really focused on it because, with a few exceptions, people were making so much money on Wall Street for such a long time as financial institutions generally grew—clients, employees, shareholders, even the public—that no one thought about it or cared. Many said the financial crisis should be a wakeup call to how cultures and incentives have changed, how the environment has changed, and how large and interconnected everything is. Many executives at competitors also said that in their opinion Goldman was living off the brand or reputation for trustworthiness that it had created in the 1980s (some questioned if it were even true at that time). They said that Goldman got away with it for so long because the firm was crafty in always playing up its "good guy" image, aura of public service, and powerful network.

Several current Goldman partners told me that since the Senate committee hearings, Goldman has been trying to take its business principles more seriously (and client anecdotes about this surfaced in my interviews). The partners also mentioned that the firm is educating its employees about the proper use of e-mails (including not using bad language) and about the firm's various roles and legal obligations. The comments about e-mail training reminded me of an exchange between Viniar and Levin during the Senate hearings about both e-mails and behavior:

> LEVIN: And when you heard that your employees, in these e-mails, when looking at these deals said, God, what a shitty deal, God what a piece of crap—when you hear your own employees or read about those in the e-mails, do you feel anything?

VINIAR: I think that's very unfortunate to have on e-mail.

(The gallery bursts out laughing.)

LEVIN: On an e-mail?

VINIAR: Please don't take that the wrong way. I think it's very unfortunate for anyone to have said that in any form.

LEVIN: How about to believe that and sell them?

VINIAR: I think that's unfortunate as well.

LEVIN: That's what you should have started with.

The responses in the committee hearings are signals to the employees as to what is appropriate behavior. They also reflect a cultural change at Goldman.

Is Goldman Likely to Recognize the Change?

The perception of Goldman changed virtually overnight in 2008. I analyzed 345 selected articles in the *New York Times* from 1980 to 2012 and categorized them as positive or negative based on tone. From 1980 to 2007, no matter how I cut the data by time period, the number of positive articles was always higher than the number of negative articles (the total was 288 positive articles to 118 negative, for a ratio of 2.4 times as many positive). Using the same criteria, from 2008 to 2012 there were 103 negative articles to 57 positive articles, for a ratio of 0.6 times as many. I divided the articles into topic categories, and the two most common negative article topics were Goldman's conflicts with clients and its connections to the government.[40]

When Goldman announced it would review its business practices, Blankfein explained that there was "a disconnect between how we as a firm view ourselves and how the broader public perceives our role and activities in the market."[41] Goldman was concerned not only about public perception but also about client perception. The firm's business standards committee commissioned an independent study conducted by a prestigious consulting company to interview two hundred clients to explore their concerns about whether the firm still lived up to its core values and business principles after the rapid growth and shift in Goldman's business mix toward proprietary trading.

Management had been enthusiastic about the proprietary trading business since the early 1990s but approached it carefully, with top talent and "attentive management," and, financially, it was an "unqualified success."[42] Still, the study revealed that clients believed Goldman was placing too much emphasis on its own interests and not enough on those of its clients. The report stated, "Clients raised concerns about whether the firm has remained true to its traditional values and business principles given changes to the firm's size, business mix and perception about the role of proprietary trading. Clients said that, in some circumstances, the firm weighs its interests and short-term incentives too heavily."[43]

Clearly, Goldman knows that it has a serious public relations problem. The business standards report expresses Goldman's recommitment to the core values that once made the firm the most respected of Wall Street institutions. However, some clients I interviewed said that Goldman's response has been more to increase its investment in public relations and public service, and to reassure clients and the public that Goldman has not lost its customer focus, and less to make substantive changes such as spinning-off or closing businesses, as the firm had done with the Water Street Fund when clients complained. The clients are not surprised because Goldman is in a much more powerful position than it was then.

The lead in the *Wall Street Journal*'s sneak peek at highlights of the business standards committee's report attributes a defensive motive to Goldman's imminent release of the report: "Goldman Sachs seeking to beat back criticism that it abused its muscle and trading savvy to put its own interests ahead of clients, agreed to release details on how and where the Wall Street giant makes its money."[44] The report was released "to great fanfare" but was not received by the outside world with much enthusiasm.[45] Its primary purpose seemed to be "a more aggressive defense of Goldman's image, not a deep restructuring of its business model."[46] Or it sought "to reassure Goldman's clients, to placate regulators, and to direct employee activity."[47] More bluntly, the report was described as "an exercise in misdirection."[48]

The starting point for evaluating the report must be the assumption that Goldman is not very likely to shift away from trading, because "at least as Goldman has pursued it . . . [trading] can make money in good markets and bad" and because it cannot return to its earlier self: "smaller and a partnership that defined itself as an adviser or intermediary."[49]

The media's treatment of the report implied that it avoided the real issues, including Goldman's "size, complexity and the role of shareholders and employees."[50] What some found most notable was that the report did not include "mention of any issues that are of first order importance regarding how Goldman (and other banks of its size and with its leverage) can have big negative effects on the overall economy, [even though] one of Goldman's business principles is 'we consider our size an asset that we try hard to preserve.'"[51] Consequently, another critic claimed that the report read "more like a consultant's brief—banal, crowd-pleasing, and recommending organizational changes. It will, for this reason, be little read and less heeded."[52]

In May 2013, Goldman released a thirty-page report on its business standards that followed up on its January 2011 report. Goldman stated that by February 2013, all thirty-nine recommendations had been fully implemented. The report's opening line is "Our clients' interests always come first." The report's standards address relationships with clients and conflicts of interests, with an emphasis on client understanding, transparency, and disclosure. The media reaction was that "ambitions like these are frequently aspired to in public policy statements, but are difficult to effectively implement . . . in the profit-led and bonus-driven culture of Wall Street that led up to the financial crisis. Such a culture is most prevalent among traders and front-office staff, but it can also influence compliance and control functions."[53]

Hiring Lawyers

On August 22, 2011, shares of Goldman tumbled nearly 5 percent, knocking $2.7 billion off the firm's market value, after a report that Blankfein had hired a prominent criminal defense lawyer. Goldman portrayed it as routine, given the several government investigations faced by the firm. But the sharp reaction in the stock price showed the fragile nerves of investors, who were worried that potential legal liability could damage the firm and its earning power.[54]

Goldman executives were expected to be interviewed by the Justice Department. The agency was conducting an inquiry that resulted from a 650-page report produced earlier in 2011 by the Senate Permanent Subcommittee on Investigations. That report said that Goldman generally had misled clients about its practices related to mortgage-linked securities.

Some partners told me that Blankfein's action was interpreted and processed by Goldman employees. However, some of the partners also saw it as a reflection of a change in culture and the environment. They said that now if an employee is unhappy with a bonus or feels he or she was unfairly passed over for a promotion, he or she will consider consulting a lawyer or speak to human resources (or both). They said partners privately complain about such behavior as a change in culture and rationalize it as a "sign of the times." They said employees were following the lead of the executives, who had resorted to legalese defensive language in the hearings by executives. In any case, some conceded Blankfein's actions had the unintended consequence of supporting behavior that would not have occurred otherwise.

Identity and Identification

The most recent glaring criticism of Goldman's reputation came from Greg Smith, an employee who had worked at Goldman for twelve years. Smith delivered his resignation in an op-ed piece published in March 2012 in the *New York Times:* "Why I Am Leaving Goldman Sachs."

In the op-ed, Smith attributed his resignation to the drastic changes in Goldman's culture in the past decade or so: "The firm has veered so far from the place I joined right out of college that I can no longer in good conscience say that I identify with what it stands for."[55] He pointed out specific symptoms of the current "toxic and destructive" environment, such as referring to clients as "Muppets."

More significantly, Smith pointed out the lack of focus on clients, which had been crowded out by a "how much did we make off the client?" attitude. Smith saw Goldman's cultural ills as the result of leadership style—specifically charging that Blankfein and Cohn had "lost hold of the firm's culture on their watch" because of a sea change in the way the firm thought about leadership. Smith claimed that there were now three quick ways to become a leader at Goldman: persuading clients to invest in the things Goldman wanted to get rid of because they were not sufficiently profitable; hunting elephants—that is, getting clients to buy things that may be wrong for them but have the highest profit potential for Goldman; and finding yourself "sitting in a seat where your job is to trade any illiquid, opaque product with a three-letter acronym."

Goldman's formal internal response to Smith's op-ed piece, issued over the signatures of Blankfein and Cohn, characterized Smith as "disgruntled" and expressed disappointment that an individual opinion spoke louder than the "regular, detailed and intensive feedback" from the 89 percent of employees who believed Goldman served its clients well.[56] Citing both internal and external surveys, Blankfein and Cohn maintained that Smith's assertions did not "reflect [Goldman's] values . . . culture and how the vast majority of people at Goldman Sachs think about the firm and the work it does on behalf of our clients."[57]

Though Goldman aggressively dismissed both Smith and his accusations, some current and former employees say that there is "a sizable, yet silent contingent within the investment bank, a group of people who are increasingly frustrated with what they see as a shift in recent years to a profit-above-all mentality."[58] Therefore the normalization process doesn't impact everyone in the same way and at the same time. While many partners I interviewed thought that the culture had not changed, there were a few that would admit it and could see it. Two partners I interviewed admitted that they may be in the minority in seeing or admitting the culture has changed. I asked why they did not leave. They explained that they heard the culture is much worse at other firms. Also, they know of others leaving and being bored, unimpressed, and disappointed with their new employers. They said there are many things they like about Goldman, such as individual friends/relationships, the intelligence and drive of the people, the social status (which they said had taken a hit, but they believed most people still think it is the best and most prestigious firm with the best people), the network internally and externally one builds at the firm, and the good work that the firm and its people do. They talked about how much good the firm and its employees do that gets no real press. They said the firm is better run operationally today than it ever has been, but admitted that its operational efficiency does not mean the culture has not changed.

Goldman performed an exhaustive investigation of Smith's allegations, including combing through e-mails looking for the word "Muppet," and claimed it found nothing material. However, it was unclear to a partner I interviewed if the goal was to prove Smith wrong, to identify badly behaving people and punish them, to show that Goldman is taking the charges seriously, to frighten staff into being more discreet in what they write in corporate e-mails—or all of the above.

Goldman aggressively went after Smith personally. But one partner I interviewed explained with reflection that in the end it didn't matter whether Smith was disgruntled or not, too junior or not, in enough strategically important areas of the firm or not, motivated by money or not, and it didn't even matter whether he got the reasons right; at a high level, his letter was making a basic claim: that the culture of Goldman had changed from when he started, and for the worse. That statement could not easily be dismissed, because after the hearings, the fines, the negative articles, and the investigations, and the executives' responses to them, many people were taking a minute out of their busy lives and daily routines and looking around and starting to wonder whether the culture itself had indeed changed. But for whatever reason, most people went back to their jobs, and maybe the silent group would slowly leave not just Goldman, but the industry.

Another partner compared what Smith had done to an employee who had been elected partner in 1994 and whose name had been listed publicly as being elected. But then he turned down partnership and left the firm to join a private equity firm with a reputation of values in its industry. The partner explained it was hard for the firm to dismiss him, considering he was elected a partner just weeks prior, but as if it were standard operating organizational response, rationalization rumors of why he didn't accept were whispered. But when the event happened, whether or not intentional, it sent a signal questioning what was going on at the firm in 1994 that someone would turn down what so many were looking to become, and maybe people thought about what it meant and then went back to their daily routine. I remember it was only discussed very privately because it was a very sensitive topic. Maybe it was a data point for those already wondering about the firm, and then they just quietly left. Maybe, the people who stayed processed it and it impacted their future behavior. Based on my interviews and my own personal experience, upon reflection it had some impact, but what or how much is unclear.

Why Do Clients Stay?

Despite public outcry and even disappointment among clients, Goldman doesn't lack for business. Its brand is still highly rated, and Goldman offers a unique value proposition to clients for several reasons, primarily related to access, information, risk management, and people.[59] Goldman has the best network of connections globally and attracts the best and brightest people. For the Vault Banking Survey in 2012, some thirty-five hundred investment banking professionals were interviewed. For the thirteenth straight year, banking professionals named Goldman the most prestigious bank to work for in North America. Professionals also ranked Goldman first in Europe.

Goldman is in the center of a large information flow that it gathers from clients. Goldman uses its risk management capabilities and its culture of teamwork to gain insights and then packages the insights and information, makes timely introductions, and executes smart trades. According to client interviews, the firm will continue to excel and dominate, because, relative to its competitors, it generally provides better advice, information, access, and liquidity. However, there are signs that Goldman's culture continues to drift, and therefore Goldman runs the risk of becoming less ethically distinguishable than its competitors in the long term (if it isn't already). Many competitors and clients believe that ethically Goldman is already where the rest of Wall Street is—but smarter about it. However, they generally agreed that its ability to execute and take advantage of the information and network and use it for itself and its clients is unparalleled. And so until there is a system failure of such massive proportions from unintended consequences or significant regulatory changes, it is difficult to imagine that Goldman will not continue its leadership position.

Why do people continue to do business with Goldman? The simplest answer is that they need to, although that does not necessarily mean they are always happy about it. Some profess to a love-hate relationship.[60] For example, a senior executive at a large European industrial company claims not to be very concerned about Goldman's image problems: "We hated Goldman as a matter of policy. You kept your hands in your pockets when you dealt with them . . . They are indeed very aggressive and you better not turn your back on them . . . They are also highly competent. It is like everywhere else: high risk equals high return. If you deal with Goldman you always have to keep that in mind and then you can't complain if the more intelligent guys are sitting on the other side of the table."[61] Referencing Taibbi's *Rolling Stone* article, a client I interviewed said Goldman is everywhere; it is the most powerful investment bank. When I rhetorically asked if it is "a great vampire squid wrapped around the face of humanity, relentlessly jamming its blood funnel into anything that smells like money," he said not exactly, but then he explained that Goldman is everywhere, knows everyone, and is wherever there is a market in which to make money.[62] And to make money as an investor, he needs to deal with them and get along with them.

Moving into the credit crisis, with trading and principal investing contributing 68 percent of the company's 2007 revenue, compared with 9 percent from advisory fees, some clients questioned whether they could count on Goldman to provide unbiased advice:

> *"We always need to worry a little about Goldman because we need them more than they need us, and the firm is run by traders,"* Todd Baker, then-executive vice president for corporate strategy and development at Washington Mutual Inc., wrote in an October 2007 e-mail to Kerry Killinger, CEO at the time. Killinger, in considering whether to hire Goldman Sachs for advice on transferring credit risk off of WaMu's balance sheet, wrote back, *"I don't trust Goldy on this . . ."*
>
> *"There was an underlying suspicion that Goldman did play in the gray areas [of the law], and I've spoken to a number of clients who finally did leave Goldman or refuse to do business with Goldman because of that concern,"* [Charles Peabody, an analyst at Portales Partners LLC in New York] said, declining to name any.[63]

It may be that *Guardian* financial editor Nils Pratley is right when he says that "the clients (or most of them) know they are at risk of being treated as Muppets" and even profess to hate Goldman, but choose to continue doing business with the firm because as an investment bank it enjoys "an extraordinarily privileged position in being trading houses, market-makers and advisers to companies[, making] them both impossible to avoid and riddled with conflicts of inter-est."[64] Dealing with Goldman simply makes good business sense, but it carries a sense of caveat emptor these days.

Joe Nocera, a *New York Times* columnist, agrees: "The [client] calculus at Goldman has always been, 'There's no one smarter out there. I actually can get the best advice from Goldman Sachs and they will often bring me the best deals, but I also know that I can't trust them, that ultimately, their motives aren't necessarily aligned with my motives.'"[65] Perhaps this lack of trust is less important in trading, where competition is based more on price and liquidity, but it should be of concern in investment banking, where clients must be able to trust that Goldman will not use the client's information against the client's best interests.

But the Goldman response to Smith's letter hangs over its client relationships. One client, the very large Dutch investment adviser APG, said it took Goldman more than a day to contact APG with reassurances about Smith's allegations: "We would have expected that a company that faces such a big media backlash over some-thing so core to their business such as client trust would have instantly reached out to those clients to say something."[66] The cli-ent's real objection was having to explain to its own clients why it was doing business with Goldman, and having to explain about Goldman's culture.[67] Ultimately, however, another client said, "For us it's about what these banks bring to the table. I think Goldman has the intellectual capital; they've got the know-how to do these transactions. There are other banks out there, but Goldman is still the preeminent investment bank and they give solid advice."[68]

As a client, I had a chance to see how different Goldman's value-added proposition was. I had a potential investment idea, but it required the coordination and collaboration of several parts of a bank to execute the transaction. I took the idea to several banks, but I never got past the first meeting with any of them. The groups within the same bank couldn't agree on who would get what credit or revenues, something that would impact their bonuses (they never said this out loud, and I am reading between the lines of politically correct bankerspeak). So instead of executing a trade for a client, the banks did nothing.

I had a meeting with Goldman, and the partners understood that overall the firm would make money, even though each area might not be happy with its individual credit or revenues. The partners saw an overall opportunity, spoke among themselves, came to an agreement, and agreed to do the transaction (my personal relationship with them probably also helped). This teamwork in execution is a tremendous advantage for Goldman and shows that a residual social network and partnership culture still exists.

As the deal progressed, Goldman better understood what I was doing and thought it was a great investment idea. Later, Goldman said it wanted to coinvest in the deal. This is an example of the powerful strategy Goldman claims of combining advisory work with coinvesting. Goldman, to its credit, was the only bank smart enough to figure out how to get the deal done and recognize it was a good deal. Goldman's coinvestment helped execute the deal for us at attractive terms.

I was very happy with Goldman's advice and execution. However, a few months later I heard a rumor from a competitor that Goldman had done a similar deal with another client—much larger than we were—implying that Goldman took information about the deal and showed it to another client. I do not know whether this is true. So even though I had good feelings about Goldman getting the deal done for me, recognizing I never would have gotten it done without Goldman's approach and ability to execute, I was slightly annoyed that, allegedly, Goldman used information to benefit itself with a larger client.

When I heard the rumor (again, only a rumor), it kept me on my guard. I didn't say anything. I didn't want to upset Goldman, because it is a very important player in the marketplace. I kept doing business with Goldman (and later I was involved in hiring Goldman to sell my firm). In my opinion, its people were responsive, well prepared, thoughtful, and connected. However, I did not feel as if all the people at

Goldman could be trusted completely all the time. This should not be a shocking revelation in hindsight, but it was for someone who started at Goldman in the early 1990s. And the point I am making is the change.

What makes Goldman a tough competitor is its depth of talent and its systematic approach to providing high-quality client service (including getting senior partners to connect with clients). As an outsider, one can appreciate that, relatively speaking, Goldman is stacked with talent. The bench is deep, and the quality of the talent is relatively consistent. The firm's expertise is phenomenal, again benefiting by pulling information from various people, geographies, and areas.

In my interviews with clients, many said the quality of talent on Wall Street had declined overall, Goldman included, perhaps because many clients themselves have become specialized in their knowledge and technology has commoditized information and the business in many ways. There is also strong competition for the best talent. Many talented individuals interested in finance go to private equity firms and hedge funds, which offer attractive opportunities.[69] Many smart people are going into technology or other fields. But clients felt that Goldman would probably be considered the best alternative generally, not necessarily in every area of specialization, if one is interested in banking or wants training and credentials.

Clients I interviewed said that other firms have equal (if not better) talent in selected people or specialties, but it is not nearly as broad, consistent, and deep, nor as coordinated, as it is at Goldman. A Goldman banker or employee will speak to multiple people to get their views and then present a firm view. At many other banks, clients explained they typically get the talent of only one person of high quality that they trust. They elaborated that one individual has a tough task competing against Goldman even if the one person is more trustworthy. The organizational elements that support coordination set Goldman apart, and this is one reason clients still use the firm. This differentiator has been and will be challenging to maintain. Some partners I interviewed said that the volume of deals, geographic dispersion, information overload, technology changes, new regulations, and client expectations have changed the dynamics of collaboration and that they are more rushed and have less time to help others than they had in the early 1990s, for example. However, they pointed out that their peers have the same challenges and were confident that Goldman has the ability to adapt.

Many clients pointed out that not just at Goldman but at its peers, even if they trust their one key adviser, they are always skeptical of the organizational pressures. Their adviser may have the client's best interests at heart, but at the same time the adviser has internal pressures to sell products or do things in order to get paid or keep his job or get promoted. Therefore, the quality of execution, the ability to provide liquidity or find a buyer that no one else thought of or find a creative solution often trumps trust on deciding which firm to hire because clients are skeptical anyway.

Goldman still attracts a staggering amount of business. If clients were sick of alleged abuses, they would go to another competitor. Every time clients choose to do business with Goldman, essentially they are subconsciously performing a cost–benefit analysis, and they are making the unpopular (even if financially prudent) decision of giving their business to Goldman. Even though Goldman's market shares seem to be fine after the crisis, I did find one interesting fact, that the premium fees that it charged clients above its competitors dissipated in at least one key area.[70] Perhaps this is a coincidence or there are not enough data points, but it is interesting to see if changes in Goldman's fees in the future will be a barometer of what clients think beyond just market share.

Justice Department Declines to Prosecute Goldman

The Justice Department began an investigation of Goldman in 2011 after the Senate's Permanent Subcommittee on Investigations issued a report highlighting questionable conduct by Goldman and other banks. The Justice Department focused on Goldman's practices in selling pools of subprime mortgage securities to clients while simultaneously betting on a decline in the housing market. The report essentially alleged that Goldman had profited by betting against the very mortgage investments that it sold to clients. In addition, the report insinuated that Blankfein might have misled lawmakers when testifying about the mortgage deals. Blankfein testified that the bank never bet against its clients for its own profit. In April 2011, Senator Carl Levin, chairman of the subcommittee, referred Goldman's case to the Justice Department for a criminal investigation.

In August 2012, the Justice Department took the unusual action of publicly announcing that its investigation into Goldman was closed and it would not bring a case: "[B]ased on the law and evidence as they exist at this time, there is not a viable basis to bring criminal prosecution."[71] The statement continued, "The department and its investigative partners conducted an exhaustive review of the report and its exhibits, independently gathered and scrutinized a large volume of other documents, and tenaciously pursued potential evidentiary leads, including conducting numerous witness interviews."

According to news reports, this action came as a result of pushing by Goldman's lawyers.[72] Senator Levin responded, "Whether the decision by the Department of Justice is the product of weak laws or weak enforcement, Goldman Sachs' actions were deceptive and immoral."[73] In addition, separately, Goldman soon afterward disclosed that the SEC would not pursue any further claims against the bank related to a $1.3 billion mortgage bond deal.

Goldman seemingly focuses on its legal exoneration, although it does not claim to be free of all wrongdoing. At an investor conference in 2009, Blankfein said, "We participated in things that were clearly wrong and we have reasons to regret and apologize for."[74] But as a current partner pointed out to me, upon further reflection, legal exoneration does not mean that the original principles have been upheld or that the ethical standards are the same as they were ten or twenty or thirty years ago. He said he doubted Goldman would ever publicly admit to that.

Chapter 9

Why Doesn't Goldman See the Change?

DESPITE GOLDMAN'S ADMISSION IN 2011 THAT IT NEEDED TO "strengthen the firm's culture in an increasingly complex environment," its name keeps popping up in the news. For example, Goldman's actions while underwriting a closely watched private financing deal for Facebook raised serious ethical questions.[1] Goldman sold its own Facebook shares by bundling them under one name and selling them to favored clients, circumventing SEC reporting requirements. As Jon Stewart quipped on Comedy Central's *The Daily Show*, "Oh, Goldman, is there any regulation's intent you can't subvert?"[2]

Even when Goldman thinks it is doing something good, its actions sometimes have negative consequences. Goldman's procurement of doses of the swine flu vaccine for its employees when the drug was being rationed to hospitals and schools had consequences. People wanted to know why Goldman got as many doses for its bankers as a local hospital got, while people at much greater risk had to wait. "Can you not read how mad people are at you?" demanded Amy Poehler on a *Saturday Night Live* skit poking fun at Goldman. She added, "When people saw the headline, 'Goldman Sachs Gets Swine Flu Vaccine' they were super happy—until they saw the word 'vaccine.'"[3]

Clearly, there is a gap between the way Goldman views itself and the way some people outside the firm view it, particularly regarding its government connections and the ethics surrounding its business practices.[4] What are the organizational elements that prevent Goldman from noticing, or acknowledging, its changes or their consequences? We've considered many reasons that Goldman has trouble recognizing its organizational drift—including the incremental nature of the changes and the social normalization process. Here we'll focus on an important additional factor in the rationalization: the firm's sense of higher purpose, which is driven by its commitment to public service.

A Sense of Higher Purpose

My argument is that Goldman employees are socialized to believe their work is fulfilling a higher social purpose, and that this contributes to their justification, or rationalization, of what others view as ethically (and some have claimed legally) inappropriate behavior. As covered earlier, public service is deeply embedded in the culture. (See appendix E, which is from Goldman's governance report. No other bank has disclosed as much about its commitment and history of commitment to public service in its public documents.) Many of Goldman's leaders have gone into public service, and the firm also regularly recruits people from public service. The firm also makes substantial philanthropic contributions and encourages its employees to volunteer. While those at the firm may no longer be so modest in their lifestyles and demeanor as was true back in my early days there, the ethic of doing public service has remained strong, though the emphasis of the reasons of why it's encouraged may have changed.

Based on my interviews with employees, the sense of serving a higher purpose that pervades the firm leads to the rationalization that they must strive to be the best (and that they deserve to be paid the most) because they are serving a more important master than just the drive for money.[5] This leads them to believe that Goldman should be given the benefit of the doubt about its dealings.

Many at Goldman subscribe to the notion that because the firm serves a higher purpose, they are more driven to excellence and are more dedicated than their peers at other firms. The pursuit of profit is portrayed as virtuous, and hard work is viewed as a kind of, for lack of a better phrase, religious duty. The idea of a corporate culture having the characteristics of religious belief only works as a kind of general parallel. And my use of religious terms or phrases should be understood only as analogy, to help explain the ethos.

Employees at Goldman do even often use religious terms to describe the nature of the firm's work, and there is the element of something like blind allegiance, or faith, in the devotion of employees to the firm. A religious-like work ethic is an important force behind Goldman's relentless pursuit of excellence and its people's devotion. Goldman's atmosphere is one in which the pursuit of excellence is seen as the good and right thing to do, and its success (including economic gain) is well deserved. The feeling is augmented by the belief that a higher judge (or partnership committee) "elects" people who are destined for something greater and whose good favor is reflected in successes. Continuing with the religious parallel, the business principles can be seen as a form of Goldman's own Ten Commandments, and the election to partnership as a sort of ascension to heaven. This organizational aura or overtone is such a part of the culture and identity of the people at Goldman that an attack on the firm tends to be perceived psychologically as almost a "holy war" (the wording is paraphrasing from an interview of an executive at a competitor). This helps explain why the firm is so aggressively defensive, and why it is blinded by the sense of higher purpose. It is difficult for someone who has been socialized through training and has rationalized and made sense of what he or she is doing in this way, who has become, for lack of a better word, a zealot, to question behavior or instructions.

This belief in the good of the firm seems to contribute to the commitment to hard work and outperformance, which has benefited the firm, but it has slowly and incrementally changed to also be used as a rationalization for behavior that may not be consistent with the original meaning of the firm's principles. The sense of higher purpose explains why Goldman brushes off cases of bad behavior as "one-offs" or "exceptions," why its employees should get swine flu vaccinations ahead of others, and why the firm believes that while its peers may not be able to handle situations where conflicts need to be managed through ethical behavior, Goldman can.

I'm not saying that Goldman doesn't expect its employees to do good in the world, or that they don't do so. The firm and its employees have given hundreds of millions of dollars to charity (keep in mind, though, that they have also made tens of billions). Goldman runs many community and public service initiatives, including pledging $500 million to help develop ten thousand small businesses and dedicating resources to develop the business and management skills of ten thousand women in the developing world.

Two of the most visible examples of Goldman's philanthropy are the Goldman Sachs Foundation, created at the time of the IPO with $200 million, and Goldman Sachs Relief Fund and Outreach, created in response to the attacks of September 11, 2001. Charles Ellis writes, "[N]o other organization spawns so many trustees of colleges and universities, art museums, foundations, libraries and hospitals" and states that at Goldman, "service and serious giving are expected, and leaders are expected to set the pace."[6] There is also a serious expectation that Goldman employees will participate in the firm's philanthropic and charitable activities. According to a Goldman's website section called "Citizenship," in 2012, more than twenty-five thousand Goldman Sachs employees from forty-eight offices partnered with 950 nonprofit organizations. When I worked at Goldman, almost everyone I worked with gave time to Community Teamworks, one of the very few acceptable excuses for delaying a meeting, call, or deadline. This still holds true. For an employee not to participate would be frowned upon.

But the firm's corporate citizenship, well intended and generous as it may be, serves a dual purpose. Goldman promotes and leverages the positive publicity that attends its and its current and former employees' public service, and the firm's reputation and network of external connections both benefit from it.

"God's Work"

CEO Lloyd Blankfein has spent a lot of time explaining Goldman's actions since the credit crisis. On one occasion, he defended Goldman's profits and bonuses with a nod to the firm's fiduciary responsibility to its shareholders and a further claim that "preserving the franchise" for them is "also for the good of America . . . I think a strong Goldman Sachs is good for America."[7] More notoriously, he was quoted in London's *Sunday Times* as saying, "We have a social purpose." in referring to the banking industry and further explained, "I'm doing *God's work*." The media response was overwhelmingly derisive. Jon Stewart joked that when Blankfein said he was doing God's work, he most likely meant "earthquakes and hurricanes."[8] Stephen Colbert pointed out that Blankfein never specified which God, and speculated that it perhaps was "Shiva, Lord of Destruction."[9] Blankfein quickly apologized for his remarks. In fact, he later remarked that he had learned his lesson about joking around with reporters and no longer even says "God bless you" when someone sneezes.[10]

It is not the first time Goldman and religion have been associated. For example, when discussing the management committee in an interview, then senior partner Steve Friedman said, "Our management committee is like a college of cardinals. They're very talented people, and in the College of Cardinals, a substantial number of them have a reasonable, legitimate belief that they should be elevated."[11] What's more, at Goldman a mentor, or someone who was supportive of your career, was often referred to as a "rabbi." According to my interviews, without a rabbi it would be difficult to be elected a partner.

In a discussion about morality and markets at St. Paul's Cathedral in London in 2009, Goldman international vice chairman Brian Griffiths, a former adviser to Margaret Thatcher, described giant paychecks for bankers as an economic necessity: "We have to tolerate the inequality as a way to achieve greater prosperity and opportunity for all."[12] Again, there is an allusion to individual sacrifice for a higher purpose—in this case, the common good. Dedication to a higher purpose can also account for what William Cohan describes as "the mystery of Goldman's steadfast, zealous belief in its ability to manage its multitude of internal and external conflicts."[13]

One of the problems with zeal, religious or otherwise, is that it can blind zealots to considerations not directly associated with their higher purpose, and that blindness might be, at least in part, behind Blankfein's subconscious choice of words in referring to the firm doing "God's work," as well as Goldman's failure to see the larger picture (including believing that its network in public service is a disadvantage), and its inability to immediately grasp the public outrage at its conduct during the financial crisis. The belief in serving a higher purpose is implicit in the way Goldman defines itself, not only as an elite firm, smarter and better than the others, but as something *more*. This is not a new phenomenon, because "there has always been a whiff of sanctimony about the firm. It not only wants to make money; it wants to be seen as a force for good."[14]

The need to endure years of grueling work to be elected partner was offset not only by money but also, more importantly, by the "psychic rewards" found in a sense of affiliation, of "belonging to a select group with a hallowed history and a common purpose."[15] Rob Kaplan, who spent his entire career at Goldman and ultimately rose to vice chairman, attributes this sense to the need of humans, as social animals, to "be part of an organization that has meaning . . . [which] helps give their lives meaning," noting that the reason people are willing to work hard for relatively low compensation is that they "aspire to something that is bigger and more meaningful than financial reward. People want to be proud of what they do.

Yes, they want to be rewarded, but they typically need other reasons to 'join up' and stay with an organization. Otherwise, they'll treat it as a convenient stopping point on the way to something more meaningful."[16]

"Government Sachs"

The sense of higher purpose is reinforced by the relationship between Goldman and the government. The White House has often looked to Wall Street experts for advice, and Goldman partners have advised several presidents and cabinet members, leading to an incestuous web between government and Goldman—hence the nickname Government Sachs. Goldman also realized the wisdom of hiring former senior government officials. At the highest levels within Goldman, there was, and is, a conscious effort to build and maintain relationships with important people. The emphasis on this network accelerated when Goldman began to expand. The firm benefited greatly and was able to increase its network when John Rogers, former Undersecretary of State for Management, and Gerald Corrigan, former president of the Federal Reserve Bank of New York, both joined Goldman in 1994. Today, they serve very senior and important roles at the firm. The web of connections between Goldman and government adds to the firm's mystique and promotes the sense of higher purpose felt by many Goldman employees. However, internally the sense of higher purpose obscures the dual purpose of public service. To many at Goldman, the only reason Blankfein visits government officials so often is that he is performing a civic duty as an expert. Many do not concede any possible truth in the accusations of undue influence or advantageous access.

Over the years, the extent of Goldman's network of government connections has been viewed externally as a great competitive asset or as a way to gain an unfair advantage, depending on the viewer's perspective, the prevailing economic scenarios, and the competitive environment.[17] One admirer is impressed by the "phenomenal number of people rotating out of the firm at an early age, looking to do something good for their country."[18] Another, speculating about "what [it is] about Goldman that makes it such a popular feeding ground for Democratic and Republican administrations alike," says that "many insiders attribute the firm's stature in Washington largely to a Goldman culture that values teamwork over individual self-gratification."[19]

Others have taken a more cynical view, implying a self-serving motivation behind Goldman's predilection for public service and for hiring former government officials. James Grant, years before the credit crisis, commented, "It is probably no accident, as the Marxists used to say, that the ex-president of the Federal Reserve Bank of New York, Gerald Corrigan, is today a managing director of Goldman. Mr. Corrigan would be just the right man to have on the premises in case the firm should trade itself into the kind of financial crisis from which only the Federal Reserve could help to extricate it."[20] Also, there has been criticism that public officials give Goldman better treatment because they are hoping that when they finish their political careers, they can return to or work at or lobby for Goldman. Stephen Colbert joked, "Why are government employees filing a civil suit against Goldman Sachs? That's just going to be embarrassing in a few years when they all go back to work at Goldman Sachs."

Many non-Goldman people I interviewed said that Goldman exploits its good works and sense of higher purpose to help rationalize or explain why it is uniquely able to manage potential client conflicts ("because we are Goldman"). From my interviews of non-Goldman employees, the consensus is that Goldman shrewdly uses its government contacts and its good guy image to benefit the firm in increasing its opportunities. As long ago as 1992, for example, Goldman's successful bids for deals with the Russian government were attributed in large part to the firm's Washington connections.[21]

Such concerns led CBS News to analyze the "revolving door between Goldman and government."[22] Good press or bad, by being associated with the most important people, Goldman spun the image to its advantage, prior to being questioned about it during the crisis.

The fact that Goldman partners did so much good for humanity did serve for many years to help distinguish the firm in the eyes of the public and added to the Goldman mystique. It still helps the firm attract and retain employees, as well as motivate them.

Whitehead, Rubin, and Friedman were seen as having used government positions to apply their skills to do good for the nation, as well as satisfy any personal ambition. As role models, they inspired Goldman employees to think about public service, and the firm leveraged that sense of social responsibility to further the perception of Goldman's sense of higher purpose as well as for other purposes that help differentiate the firm.

Public Service Rationalizing Behavior

Of course, the sense that one is doing God's work or serving a higher purpose can easily transmute into a holier-than-thou attitude and an excuse for any behavior, until the ends begin to justify the means. Believing that Goldman was different—doing good for others, better than any other firm at managing conflicts, viewed as a source of important expertise by the government—became an excuse for questionable behavior, as though Goldman's good guy status exempted individual behavior from close scrutiny. The consequence was the development of the sort of arrogance that comes with believing one's actions are beyond question because of the rarefied atmosphere within which one operates. On the flip side, it must also be said that there have been some positive organizational consequences of the sense of higher purpose. In addition to the public good done, it has also encouraged employees to work harder than one might think possible, at least in part because it imparted a sense of greater meaning to that work. It also makes it more difficult for employees to leave once they are socialized into the beliefs.

Concerns are increasingly raised about Goldman's influence, its connections to government, and the potential for impropriety. Bloomberg News columnist Matthew Lynn put it this way: "While no one would dispute that New York-based Goldman Sachs is a money-making machine full of alpha-brains, it isn't healthy for so many decision-makers to be drawn from one source . . . It is hard to ignore the trend for appointing Goldman employees to big government-appointed jobs. In the information technology business, they used to say, 'No one ever got fired for buying IBM.' In politics right now, the motto seems to be, 'No one ever got fired for hiring Goldman Sachs.'"[23]

There is certainly a long list of Goldman alumni in government and government alumni at Goldman (see appendix C for a summary). At the time of the financial crisis, Hank Paulson, former Goldman CEO, was secretary of the Treasury and had many Goldman alumni working for or advising him.[24] Meanwhile, the chairman of the New York Fed at the time was Steve Friedman, who was on the Goldman board of directors.

Undoubtedly Goldman, its employees, and its alumni have made many valuable contributions in their public service. Obviously this should be commended and appreciated. The danger, though, for Goldman and for the public, is that this strong commitment to public service is a contributing factor in the firm's cultural change, not seeing the change and justification of behavior that increasingly pushes up against—some have argued crosses—the line of legality.

Conclusion

Lessons

CERTAIN RESIDUAL ELEMENTS OF GOLDMAN'S CULTURE WILL continue to fight organizational drift. But the drift will likely continue, and possibly will accelerate, given the continuing competitive, organizational, technological, and regulatory pressures the firm faces. Goldman's response to these pressures will most likely continue to be the pursuit of growth. In that pursuit, Goldman will be challenged by the law of large numbers. It most likely will continue to occasionally cross regulatory or legal lines as it negotiates what its principles mean and what is legal. As the firm gets closer to this line, at the very least its ethics will continually be questioned in part because of how the firm portrays itself and its principles. It will most likely continue to be blinded by both social normalization as well as by rationalization, reinforced by the strength of its conviction that the firm has a higher purpose and its many successes.[1] And therefore, we should expect that Goldman's organizational response to any criticism will be defensive and aggressive.

In the short to medium term, Goldman's residual cultural elements will allow it to maintain its informational and teamwork advantage, which will continue to support its client franchise, market position, and superior financial returns. That will help its reputation and attract and retain the best people, giving it a relative advantage. But this can change quickly because it will face challenges from various pressures, such as new competitors utilizing new technologies and new regulations; the landscape is dynamic and continually changing.

Although this book focuses on the Goldman case, the story has much broader implications. The organizational drift Goldman has experienced—is experiencing—can affect any organization, regardless of its many successes. And leaders of the organization may not be able to see that it is happening until there is a public blowup or failure, or until an insider calls it out. The signs may indicate that there aren't changes—signs such as leading market share, returns to shareholders, brand and attractiveness as an employer—but slowly the organization is losing touch with the original meaning of its principles and values as it responds to various pressures and its environment.

A Victim or a Perpetrator?

The leaders of Goldman have certainly wanted to make money for themselves and their shareholders throughout its history. The original Goldman business principles were written in 1979 to help regulate behavior and acted as a balance between short-term greedy and long-term greedy when dealing with clients as the firm grew. In addition, the organization had many elements besides the principles that impacted behavior, from financial interdependence, to the social network of trust, to constraints on capital and dissonance. The Goldman leaders knew the values and principles, but various pressures left them with the conviction that the firm needed to grow rapidly and often caused them to make incremental decisions that were not consistent with the original meaning of the principles and values, moving the firm increasingly further from the original meaning. With conflicting organizational goals and scarce resources, the interpretation of the principles had to change and the culture had to change. This process was enabled by social normalization and structural secrecy. Complicating this drift was the sense of higher purpose that employees felt Goldman, and they themselves, served (including public service contributions), which contributed to rationalization about the deviations.

Goldman most likely will continue to pursue and maximize opportunities and undergo organizational drift, until the business is severely negatively impacted or the fines and other consequences are too high, and then perhaps the firm will readjust. It did so in the aftermath of its near bankruptcy in the stock market crash in the late 1920s, for example, getting out of the asset management business. However, the public and regulators should be concerned—not only about Goldman but also about all of the systemically important financial institutions that pose a risk to the economic system. They may be doing what is in their own and their shareholders' best interests as they respond to pressures, incentives, and environment, but it may not be in the public's best interests. And when the public must pay for their failures (which, as we have seen, can be breakdowns on a massive scale), they should be focused on the consequences of the organizational drift that has, is, and mostly will continue happening.

A concerning issue about the organizational drift toward a legal definition of ethics is that Goldman and the other banks have a significant influence or role in determining the legal line. For example, Goldman has reportedly spent over $15 million in lobbying related to Dodd–Frank and less than two-thirds of the regulations have been implemented.[2] Securities and investment firms spent more than $101 million lobbying regulators in 2011, according to the Center for Responsive Politics, a nonpartisan research group. That is on top of $103 million spent lobbying lawmakers and regulators in 2010.[3] If the pressure is to maximize the opportunities, especially as banks get larger, then the legal line will be pressured to change accordingly, and not just by Goldman, but by all of the banks. And the larger the banks and the bigger the challenges of the law of large numbers, the more pressure there will be to impact the legal line.

In the 1990s I received a letter from senior executive asking me to donate money to Goldman's political action committee (PAC). The letter explained that participation was completely discretionary and that non-participation wouldn't negatively affect me, but many people I spoke to about it were skeptical that our bosses didn't review the list. According to some, Goldman's PAC and its employees have donated more than $20 million to federal political campaigns from 1999 to 2009.[4]

Can Organizational Drift Be Constrained or Managed?

Organizations must adapt to compete and be successful in achieving their organizational goals, which is what Goldman has done and will surely continue to do. At the same time the competitive, regulatory, technological, and organizational pressures that have affected the culture and the firm's behavior will continue. Therefore, I believe ongoing drift is inevitable.

Are all organizations doomed to failure in the long run because of organizational drift combined with organizational and environmental complexity, and therefore, is Goldman also ultimately doomed? A very good question, for which I don't have a good answer, except that, as John Maynard Keynes famously remarked, "In the long run, we are all dead."[5]

Perhaps it is naive or idealistic or nostalgic to believe that organizations can implement ways to manage or constrain organizational drift. For an organization that is already drifting, there are many questions. What will be the catalyst for the self-evaluation? A massive failure, congressional investigation, public outcry, shareholder activism, stock price performance, or an independent chairman of the board? Why would a firm do a self-evaluation if it is widely viewed as successful by its shareholders? Who would even do the evaluation? Is such an investigation better done by an external party or internally?

All are very good questions. And ones that deserve consideration and study, though unfortunately they do not seem to get as much attention as they deserve, not just for banking but organizations generally. However, some good ideas have been shared about addressing the banks specifically as a result of the financial crisis.

For example, Peter Weinberg, who is the grandson of senior partner Sidney Weinberg and nephew of senior partner John L. Weinberg, and is a former Goldman partner, made a proposal in a September 2009 *Wall Street Journal* op-ed that focused on incentives. He proposed a "10/20/30/40" compensation plan under which "junior employees would receive regular competitive pay, but senior employees would be paid as follows: 10 percent of annual compensation in cash now; 20 percent of annual compensation in cash later; 30 percent of annual compensation in stock now (with a required holding period); and 40 percent of annual compensation in stock later." *Now* means immediately at the end of a compensation period. *Later* means after a period during which a cycle can be evaluated and the award maintained or adjusted accordingly. The other main aspect of his plan was that the people who manage trading or asset management businesses should have some of their own capital at risk in the business. Weinberg's proposal is based on the premise that success should be viewed in hindsight and wealth creation should occur on the back end, to ensure that "through-the-cycle compensation [is] linked to through-the-cycle value creation. Requiring those who manage a business or fund to have some of their own money invested in it would "better align the pocketbooks of Wall Street with the pocketbooks of financial markets and our economy."[6]

Assuming that the banks won't be broken up or forced back to private partnerships, I would suggest examining ideas on locking up capital for longer similar to Peter Weinberg's, but perhaps complementing them with a greater emphasis on organizational elements. I would examine some sort of quasi partnership-partner compensation plan with an election for banks.

A partnership compensation plan could offer a degree of financial interdependence if it had a greater emphasis on fixed percentages of profits versus discretionary compensation for those in the partnership plan. That might lead the partners to place a greater emphasis on the whole enterprise than on themselves or their group. Financial interdependence and personal liability—forcing those in the partnership to disproportionately share in fines, settlements, compliance or risk management failures, or certain losses with shareholders—might make risk management and ethical standards a higher priority and reemphasize a social network of trust while creating an environment for dissonance.[7]

In discussing the ramifications of the personal liability of executives having been limited, a retired Goldman partner rhetorically questioned, why is it that when one person or a handful of senior persons at the firm does something bad that costs the shareholders and possibly puts the public at risk, that one person gets fired (maybe with some clawbacks of compensation) but the managing directors of the entire firm don't have their compensation significantly affected? Another person I interviewed suggested that if Goldman partners collectively had to disproportionately pay the $550 million settlement with the SEC out of their bonus pool, or if J.P. Morgan had a partnership structure and the partners together had to disproportionately pay the losses from the "London whale," perhaps they collectively would take stronger action to prevent such behavior. He pointed out that when Goldman paid settlements related to Robert Maxwell, all the partners paid, not just the one responsible for the relationship, and the firm went back retroactively to those who were partners at the time for payments. Enacting individual clawbacks that hold one person accountable has taken away the emphasis on organizational elements of financial interdependence and social networks of trust by which the executives could be holding each other accountable and self-regulating.

Some critics of the banks have suggested that bankers who do not like the idea of increasing their personal liability or risk "should look at the portraits on the wall of their predecessors who, as partners of the very same firms, worked and prospered under such a personal liability rule every day of their lives."[8]

The regulatory focus on the banks has been on quantifiable and measureable factors like minimal capital requirements and certain business restrictions. These are important; however, they alone will not address the issues of the banks, including Goldman. This may be in part because these regulations typically have some ambiguity and motivated organizations with a certain culture can seek to circumvent the spirit of the regulations.

As I mentioned before, this study is much more than a case study on Goldman, or even systemically important, publicly traded banks. It has much broader implications for organizations generally. This sociological study opened my eyes to the organizational elements as they relate to a culture and the importance of understanding them as they relate to organizational, competitive, technological, and regulatory pressures. The organizational elements help form the culture, the incentives and behavior—they can help a firm be "long-term greedy." In addition, organizational elements can help constrain or manage organizational drift.

Lessons Learned

As I consider what I've learned about Goldman, and the sociological theory that supports my analysis and conclusions, I am mindful that this book has implications that resonate beyond Goldman. The following summary should help leaders and managers think about the organizational drift that has, is, and will be happening at their own organizations.

- Shared values, whether codified or uncodified, tie an organization together. A firm should determine its own basic set of nonnegotiable values, the minimal constraints. Leaders, not just boards of directors, should look to the meaning of a firm's principles to define corporate ethics and guide employees' actions, and try to determine objective ways in which to check deviations from the original meaning (for example, attrition rates, independent client interviews, independent exit interviews with departing employees).[9]

- Social networks can create competitive advantages and improve performance. An organization should consider creating some sort of partnership or sharing that is bound by financial or other interdependence and focus on improving the trust among the group members through socialization. The election or promotion into a leadership group should put a greater emphasis on culture-carrying qualities in the process.[10] Leaders and board members should also monitor changes in the nature of the members of the group, cognizant that they can have an impact on the social network.

- Financial interdependence is important as a self regulator. Leaders' compensation should be based more on collectively generated profits and culture carrying. Leaders should disproportionately and jointly share in fines, settlements, and other negative consequences out of their compensation plan or their stock. Meaningful restrictions on leaders' ability to sell or hedge shares should be imposed, which can lead to better self regulating and longer-term thinking.

- Public disclosure supports an organization's values and strengthens the organization itself. An organization should consider making personnel decisions more public. When people are dismissed or specifically not promoted because of bad behavior, it should be more public. There is a value to having public signals when behavior is not acceptable. Conversely, culture carriers, those that represent the values, even if they may not be the firm's biggest revenue producers, must be promoted as a signal of what's important.[11]

- Generating dissonance or perplexing situations that provoke innovative inquiry can create competitive advantages and improve performance. Having some sort of interdependence should help create an environment that supports discussion and debate. Complementing this debate is balance between groups. Getting the input of leaders from different areas or regions, who have worked together and have good working relationships, is also important in encouraging dissonance. At the board level, in many situations, an independent lead director or independent chairman can add to dissonance.

- A sense of higher purpose, beyond making money in a materialistic society, can help people make sense of their roles. A firm needs to give employees a clear understanding of its values, its social purpose, and its sense of responsibility. However, leaders need to be conscious of not using the good works of their employees or of the firm to rationalize behavior that is inconsistent with its principles.

- An organization's culture is transmitted from one generation to the next as new group members become acculturated or socialized. It is crucial to recruit people who have the same values and socialize them into the firm's culture. Even if this restricts growth in the short run, it is important not to undervalue recruiting, interviewing, training, mentoring, and socializing. This is also very important in international expansion.

- Organizational exceptions may address short-term issues but may cause long-term ones. Early promotions and outsized compensation can indicate that a firm is a meritocracy, but they can also encourage behavior inconsistent with principles. Leaders need to be cognizant that sometimes letting top performers go, if they do not have a long-term perspective and buy into the system, may be better for the overall organization in the future.

- The ability to make rational decisions is limited, or bounded, by the extent of people's information. To broaden employees' understanding, a firm should promote a tradition of teamwork and interdependence and develop future leaders by rotating them among work assignments in different departments and geographic locations. In order to reduce structural secrecy, there may be short-term opportunity costs, but the long-term benefits are significant.[12]

- Firms must think about long-term greed and what it means. Through actions and training, leaders must explain the pressures on short-term thinking and how the firm resolves the conflicts of short- and long-term goals. Potentially conflicting or confusing organizational goals, such as putting clients first while also having a duty to shareholders, require strong signals from leadership as to what is acceptable and unacceptable behavior. These nuances cannot be left to statements of principles; they must be modeled by leaders' actions each day.

- Leaders must understand that external influences can shape the culture. For example, there are competitive, technological, and regulatory pressures. Responses to them can have unintended consequences, including drifting from principles. This can increase the probability of an organizational failure.

- An organization needs to understand to what extent models impact behavior, decisions made by business leaders, and organizational culture. For example, boards of directors of public companies should ask questions if earnings per share (EPS) estimates are too consistent with analysts' estimates. They should ask whether the firm is managing to models or to what is in the best long-term interests of the firm.

- Leaders get too much credit and too much blame. Leaders need to uphold the firm's shared values—and that is a key component to leadership.[13] But too little emphasis is given to the organizational elements that shape behavior or provide an environment for leadership or change.

- An organization's structure, incentives, and values last longer and have more impact than those of individual leaders. Usually when there is a change or loss or failure there is a tendency to blame one thing or one person, when typically there are complex organizational cultural reasons. It is the duty of leaders and board members to examine what is responsible, not who is responsible.

One of the most difficult issues in guarding against organizational drift is that adaptation is critical to the survival of an organization, and the difference between healthy adaptation and organizational drift is very, very difficult to discern. And when a business appears to be successfully reaching its organizational goals, it is especially challenging, and most likely unpopular, to start questioning whether the culture has drifted. What is the incentive to do so? But it may be precisely at this time that changes may be occurring that are setting a firm up for failure. Leadership requires a "curiosity that borders on skepticism" and that "questions are answered with action."[14] Examining your own organization will be messy, but I hope the observations from sociological analysis outlined in this book will provide useful guidelines and inspire the risk taking required to tackle the challenges.

Goldman and
Organizational Drift

Ship captains set out an intended course and use sophisticated tools for navigation to constantly revise their speed and direction based on an analysis of the external conditions under which they're sailing. They know that otherwise, no matter how carefully they aim the prow of the ship when they leave port, the cumulative effect of ocean currents and other external factors over long periods will cause the ship to veer off course.

Organizational drift is akin to that deviation from an intended course; it's the slow, steady uncoupling of practice from original procedures, principles, processes, and standards or protocols that can lead to disasters like the space shuttle *Challenger* explosion or the Black Hawk shoot-down incident in northern Iraq. As Harvard Business School professor Scott Snook argues, detecting organizational drift requires a sensitivity to the passage of time; single snapshots won't do.[1]

To understand what's happened to Goldman since the writing of the business principles in 1979, then, we have to look back to its performance over time, how its interpretation of the principles has changed, and the conditions in which it operates. But before we get to that analysis, it's worth developing a deeper understanding of organizational drift and its implications.

Drift into Failure

Sidney Dekker, a professor who specializes in understanding human error and safety, has used complexity theory and systems thinking to better understand how complex systems "drift into failure" over an extended period of time. His theories are worth exploring because they, and the ideas of other researchers, provide us with a clear understanding of how systems interact and drift away from intended goals. In some cases, this can end in disaster. In the case of Goldman, it means that there's a distinct gap between the principles by which the firm purports to steer itself and what it's actually doing in the world.

Earlier theories, Dekker argues, have been tripped up by their tendency to explain instances of failure in complex environments by blaming flawed components rather than the workings of the organizational system as a whole.[2] Dekker concludes, by contrast, that failure emerges opportunistically, nonrandomly, from the very webs of relationships that breed success and that are supposed to protect organizations from disaster. Dekker also observes that systems tend to drift in the direction of failure, gradually reducing the safety margin and taking on more risk, because of pressures to optimize the system in order to be more efficient and competitive.

We are able to build complex things—deep-sea oil rigs, spaceships, collateralized debt obligations—all of whose properties we can understand in isolation. But with complex systems in competitive, regulated societies—like most organizations—failure is often primarily due to unanticipated interactions and interdependencies of components and factors or forces outside the system, rather than failure of the components themselves. The interactions are unanticipated, and the signals are missed. Dekker points out that empirical studies show that reliable organizations with low failure rates tend to have a distinct set of traits: safety objectives and a safety culture promoted by leadership, appropriate internal diversity to enable looking at things from multiple perspectives and deploying a variety of responses to disturbances, redundancy in physical and human components, decentralization of safety decision making to enable quick responses by people close to the action, and the ability to continually and systematically learn from experience and adapt. The attitudes in such a safety culture include a preoccupation with avoiding failure, reluctance to simplify, deference to expertise (while recognizing the limits of expertise), sensitivity to operations (with vigilant monitoring to detect problems early), and suspicion of quiet periods. Last, Dekker recommends that when investigating why a failure occurred, we need to remember that what appears clearly wrong in hindsight appeared normal, or at least reasonable, at the time, and that abnormal data can be rationalized away by participants. As investigators of system failure we need to put ourselves in the shoes of the people who were involved.

Dekker argues that drift is marked by small steps. He puts it like this: "Constant organizational and operational adaptation around goal conflicts, competitive pressure, and resource scarcity produces small, step-wise normalization. Each next step is only a small deviation from the previously accepted norm, and continued operational success is relied upon as a guarantee of future safety."[3] Of course, not all small steps are bad. They allow complex systems to adapt to their environment, producing new interpretations and behaviors. It's important to remember, too, that the steps are small. "Calling on people to reflect on smaller steps probably does not generate as much defensive posturing as challenging their momentous decision."[4]

Dekker explains that organizations also drift due to uncertainty and competition in their environments. Organizations adapt because of a need to balance resource scarcity and cost pressure with safety. Resources to achieve organizational goals can be scarce because their nature limits supply, because of the activities of regulators and competitors, and because others make them scarce.[5]

What about the protective infrastructure that is designed to ensure against failure? Dekker warns, "Complex systems, because of the constant transaction with their environment (which is essential for their adaption and survival), draw on the protective structure that is supposed to prevent them from failing. This is often the regulator, or the risk assessor, or the rating agency. The protective structure (even those inside an organization itself) that is set up and maintained to ensure safety is subject to its interactions and interdependencies with the operation it is supposed to control and protect."[6]

Interestingly, the protective infrastructure, with uncertain and incomplete knowledge, constraints, and deadlines, can contribute to drift—as well as failing to function when it should.[7] Its functioning or lack thereof is legitimized.

Practical Drift

You can see exactly this kind of drift in complex systems in Scott Snook's analysis of the accidental shoot-down of two US Army Black Hawk helicopters over northern Iraq in 1994 by US Air Force F-15 fighters. All twenty-six UN peacekeepers onboard were killed. With almost twenty years in uniform and a PhD in organizational behavior, Lieutenant Colonel Snook, now a Harvard Business School professor, uses sociological analysis to thoroughly examine individual, group, and organizational accounts of the accident. Using his practical experience, combined with his academic training, he concludes that what happened was what he calls "practical drift"— the slow, steady uncoupling of practice from written procedure.[8]

Snook describes the potential pitfalls of organizational complacency that every executive should take to heart. He insightfully applies several key sociological theories of organizational behavior, structure, and change to analyze how bad things can happen to good organizations. His resultant theory of practical drift provides dramatic insight into how such seemingly impossible events can be expected to occur in complex organizations. He describes how a practical drift of local adaptations and procedures can lead to a widening gap between safety regulations and practical operations. Individually, the adaptations can be inconsequential. But over a longer period, the accumulated drift results in a vulnerable system. Snook uses the word *practical* because he is looking at everyday practices. Culture and practice are interrelated. Also, Snook examines local practices and how a subunit changes and creates practices to adhere to its own norms but doesn't necessarily coordinate with the dominant practices of the units they must connect with. So the expected coordinated action is not coordinated. The Black Hawk accident happened because, or perhaps in spite of, everyone behaving just the way we would expect them to behave, just the way rational theory would predict. Snook also points out that, depending on one's perspective, the slow, steady uncoupling can seem random and dangerous in hindsight.[9]

Social Normalization

Why don't those involved in organizational drift see what's going on and correct for it? When norms for behavior shift within an organization, members of that organization can become so accustomed to deviant behavior that they don't consider it abnormal, despite the fact that it strays far from their own codified rules or principles. The firm's mission, its reason for existence, is assumed to be implicit in its business principles; it is those principles, together with the firm's strategic decisions, that drive the actions of employees. Eventually, the execution of the strategy adapts to match incremental changes in the interpretation and meaning of the principles, but the perception remains one of business as usual. It is a complex process with a certain level of organizational acceptance: the people outside recognize the change, whereas the people inside get accustomed to it and do not. And new members accept it as standard practice.

A number of sociologists have offered explanations as to why organizations drift: scarce resources, misaligned incentives, system complexity, multiple goal conflicts, and more. There rarely is a single moment or event that one can point to as that moment when change occurs, or a single individual that one can point to as the responsible party. Rather, multiple small steps occur over an extended period of time. Therefore, the effects go unnoticed, and norms are continuously and subtly redefined; a "new normal" is established with each incremental step. This is how a succession of small, everyday decisions can produce breakdowns that can be massive in scale.

Man-Made Disasters, by Barry Turner, originally published in 1978, suggested the possibility of systematically analyzing the causes of a wide range of disasters. The working subtitle of the book was *The Failure of Foresight*, and in it, Turner gives a very good description of the successive stages that lead to failure, particularly what he calls the "incubation period," during which the preconditions for disaster develop but go unnoticed."[10] The sequence of events is as follows: (1) A notionally normal starting point where culturally accepted beliefs about the world and its hazards are regulated by precautionary norms set out in rules and codes of practice; (2) An incubation period where the accumulation of an unnoticed set of events is at odds with accepted beliefs about norms; (3) Precipitating events bring attention to themselves and transform general perceptions of the incubation period; (4) The immediate consequence of the collapse of cultural elements becomes evident; (5) The change is recognized, and there is an ad hoc rescue and salvage mission to make adjustments; and (6) Real cultural readjustment occurs, where a serious inquiry and assessment is carried out and cultural elements are adjusted.[11]

Lisa Redfield Peattie, a now-retired anthropology professor at MIT, uses the extreme example of the Nazi death camps to describe normalization. (And, no, I'm not comparing Goldman to the Nazis in any way.) The two key mechanisms through which normalization occurs, she states, are "division of labor, which separates, in understanding and potential for collective organization, what it makes interdependent in functioning" and "the structure of rewards and incentives which makes it to individuals' personal and familiar to undermine daily, in countless small steps, the basis of common existence."[12] Peattie describes how work and daily routines, right down to scrubbing the cobblestones in the crematorium yard, were normalized for long-term prisoners and personnel alike by the division of labor, affording a degree of distance from personal responsibility for the atrocities being committed. People were simply doing their normal jobs and carrying out the normal routines established by those in charge; they had lost sight of all aspects of the big picture.

Edward S. Herman, a retired professor of finance at the Wharton School who specialized in regulation, borrowed the term "normalizing the unthinkable" from Peattie to describe how once unthinkable acts become routine. Herman explains, "Normalization of the unthinkable comes easily when money, status, power, and jobs are at stake. Companies and workers can always be found to manufacture poison gases, napalm, or instruments of torture, and intellectuals will be dredged up to justify their production and use."[13]

Obviously these are extreme examples, but they are reminders that complicity, obscured by the routines of the work, the division of labor, and distance from the results, is possible even in the most egregious of acts. Herman goes on, "The rationalizations are hoary with age: government knows best; ours is a strictly defensive effort; or, if it wasn't me, somebody else would do it. There is also the retreat to ignorance—real, cultivated, or feigned. Consumer ignorance of process is important."[14]

Diane Vaughan's now classic investigation of the decision making that led to the launch of the space shuttle *Challenger* in 1986 focuses on organizational factors. Vaughan learned that work groups typically develop a concept of "acceptable risk" that becomes part of the culture.[15] Managers pay attention to only a few parameters and do not develop a formal, systematic definition of what is acceptable risk for the organization. More troublesome, it is difficult for them to see the full implications of their actions. Deviance from the norm starts to become institutionalized, resulting in "an incremental descent into poor judgment."[16] The acceptance of risk sets a precedent, and it is repeated and becomes the norm. This process mushrooms as the organization becomes larger and more complex. To the outside world, what is going on in the organization may look deviant, but to the work group everything is normal, and people believe they are adhering to what the organization expects of them. Once produced, deviant interpretations are reinforced and maintained by what Vaughan describes as an "institutionalized belief system that shapes interpretation, meaning, and action at the local level."[17]

Initially, the regrettable decision to launch the *Challenger* and the ensuing tragedy appeared to be a case of individuals—NASA managers—who, under competitive pressure, violated rules in order to meet the launch schedule. But what at first appeared to be a clear case of misconduct proved to be something entirely different: Vaughan discovered that the managers had not violated rules at all, but had actually conformed to all NASA requirements. Her work revealed, however, that they were also conforming to NASA's need to meet schedules, which ended up affecting engineering rules about what constituted acceptable risks in space flight technologies and the decisions that were made regarding those risks. She discovered that NASA managers could set up rules that conformed to the basic engineering principles yet allowed them to accept more and more risk. A social normalization of that deviance occurred, meaning that once they accepted the first technical anomaly, they continued to accept more and more with each launch, because to do so was not deviant to them. In their view, they were conforming to engineering and organizational principles. As with practical drift, the normalization of deviance concerns practices.[18]

Thus, the first time the O-rings were found to be damaged, the engineers found a solution and decided the shuttle could fly with acceptable risk. The second time that damage occurred, they thought the trouble came from something else. Believing that they had fixed the newest problem, they again defined it as an acceptable risk and just kept monitoring the situation. As they observed the problem recurring with no consequences, they got to the point that flying with the flaw was normal and acceptable. Of course, after the accident, they were horrified.

Something similar happened at Goldman. There was a social normalization of the change as the culture slowly shifted; the changes were so subtle that everything seemed normal. On a virtually day-to-day basis, normal was redefined. Once the partners normalized a given deviation—a shift in policies related to recruiting, promotion, compensation, underwriting, client relations, risk management—the deviation became compounded. Goldman was experiencing the norm shift described by Diane Vaughan: "When the achievement of the desired goals receives strong cultural emphasis, while much less emphasis is placed on the norms regulating the means, these norms will tend to lose their power to regulate behavior."[19]

Vaughan explains why people within organizations do not pick up on the fact that drift has occurred: "Secrecy is built into the very structure of organizations. As organizations grow large, actions that occur in one part of the organization are, for the most part, not observable in others. Divisions of labor between subunits, hierarchy, and geographic dispersion segregate knowledge about tasks and goals. Distance—both physical and social—interferes with the efforts of those at the top to 'know' the behavior of others in the organization, and vice versa. Specialized knowledge further inhibits knowing. The language associated with a different task, even within the same organization, can conceal rather than reveal."[20]

She explains how "structural secrecy" develops within organizations, defining it as "the way that patterns of information, organizational structure, processes, and transactions and the structure of regulatory relations systematically undermine the attempt to know [the extent of the danger]" and the ability of people to make decisions on the basis of that knowledge to manage risk.[21] Structural secrecy helps explain how people failed to notice the signs of impending disaster that were present during the incubation period first described by Turner, and it supports Peattie's and Herman's ideas regarding the normalization of the unthinkable. Vaughan explains that in the *Challenger* case, information was filtered as it moved up the chain of command, so people at the higher levels were largely unaware of events that may have been dealt with as "acceptable risk."[22] The managers missed signals because some signals were mixed, some were weak, and some seemed routine. Vaughan concludes that deep-rooted structural factors were responsible for the tragic decision to launch the *Challenger*. It is important to note that in the case of the *Challenger* disaster, the cause Vaughn identifies is not deviance from rules and norms, but conformity with them. In the case of Goldman, I have identified organizational drift from the principles, with some signals of that drift having been missed as people conformed to the incremental changes and rationalized their behavior.

A Framework to Analyze Goldman and Organizational Drift

Diane Vaughan's work on the *Challenger* disaster offers a framework for examining the influences that cause organizations to deviate from "both formal design goals and normative standards or expectations . . . producing a 'suboptimal outcome.'"[23] Her framework is grounded in her observation that organizational deviation is systematically produced by the impact of the elements of environment and organization.[24] Recognizing the commonalities found in organizations, Vaughan examines the interactions between an organization's structure and processes, influences of the environment within which this system operates, and how both shape individual choice. It is this combination of competitive pressures, organizational characteristics, and regulatory factors, this "dynamic of competition and scarce resources, together with the unclear norms regulating business behavior," that Vaughan believes "exerts structural pressures on organizations toward misconduct."[25]

To Vaughan's framework of regulatory, organizational, and competitive pressures, I add technological pressure.[26] Appendix B illustrates my adaptation of Vaughan's causal framework for my analysis of Goldman.[27] It highlights the interaction of the causative factors and pressures with key developments affecting Goldman and Wall Street over the past few decades. This appendix can be considered in tandem with the timeline in appendix G, which also identifies selected pressures (competitive, regulatory, technological, and organizational) associated with particular events. The result of the two is a clearer picture of the organizational changes and pressures as they developed over time. In addition, it supports my conclusion that the pressures and changes were happening before the IPO and before Blankfein became CEO.

While the frameworks set forth by the authors discussed in this appendix offer valuable insights into the process of the drift at Goldman and constitute a promising starting point for analysis, their studies are primarily focused on analyzing organizational failure in retrospect from a specific event. This is different from the Goldman case, because what has happened and is happening is messy and, depending on one's point of view, could be labeled a variety of things; but more importantly the outcome is unknown. To their analyses, I have added consideration of the role played by residual elements of the organization's culture and structure that have made the organization successful; these elements may mitigate drift or regulate or impact the various processes. My analysis of Goldman encompasses a period of more than three decades because it is important to evaluate organizational elements and regulatory, technological, and competitive factors dynamically over time and to appreciate how change happens at different paces and with different emphases. My analysis illustrates that the process of change is not as simple as identifying an independent variable that affects a dependent variable in a direct chain of events. Examining the changes over time helps to illuminate how many factors interact in producing the change.

Analytical Framework
Applied to Goldman

Diane Vaughan's analytical causal framework examines three main pressures—environmental and organizational (for simplicity, "organizational"); regulatory; and competitive—to analyze change over time.[1] In order to analyze Goldman, I utilize Vaughan's framework and add technological pressure.

When the framework is applied to Goldman, as shown in Table B-1, the result illuminates changes more clearly over time. Even though the changes are presented in temporal sequence from 1979, when the firm's business principles were written by John Whitehead, to today and are divided by who ran the firm or oversaw major changes, this is only for simplicity of presentation. The changes are related to each other, impact each other, and compound each other and have varying degrees of importance and significance. I selected 1979 because that is when the principles were written; 1990 because that year was when John L. Weinberg retired as senior partner (Whitehead had left in 1984); 1996 because it marked the legal structural change to a limited liability corporation; 1999 because it was the year of the IPO; and 2012 because it is the current year as this is written.

To help the reader understand the chart, I will give at least one example illuminated for each pressure.

Organizational pressure: Goldman's legal structure changed from a private partnership with full personal liability and illiquidity until retirement, to a limited liability private company with liability capped at the capital in the firm, and finally to a public company at the IPO with the liability capped at the capital in the firm, but with liquidity for shareholders. The firm changed from being completely privately held, to taking outside private capital, to taking outside public capital. The ownership changed from 100 percent Goldman partners to around 10 percent Goldman partners.

Regulatory pressure: Goldman operated under Glass–Steagall before the law was repealed in 1999 through the Gramm–Leach–Bliley Act. In 1970, the NYSE changed a rule allowing investment banks to become public.

Competitive pressure: The tech boom, the alternatives (hedge fund and private equity) boom, foreign competitors entering the US market, and US commercial banks were all factors that increased the search for talent. This impacted Goldman's ability to attract and retain not only the best people but also people with the same values. The firm added a new level of executives, known as managing directors, in part to offer people a comparable title. The firm changed certain business practices in order to maintain and grow market share (e.g., no hostile raids, underwriting standards requiring at least three years of profits, and no gambling clients).

Technological pressure: Technology made information more of a commodity, impacting the ability for people to add value to clients. Technology added transparency to markets, lowering profitability margins and emphasizing scale.

Under the time frames, I provide some data to illustrate the changes in business mix. It's important to keep in mind that before 1999, Goldman was a private firm and therefore not required to make certain information public.

TABLE B-1

Analytical framework of Goldman Sachs

	1979	1990	1996	1999	2012
Head of firm (background)/#2*	Weinberg (banker)	Friedman (banker)	Corzine (trader)	Paulson (banker)	Blankfein (trader)
	Whitehead (banker)	Rubin (trader)	Paulson (banker)*	Thain/ Thornton (banker/ multi)*	Cohn (trader)*
Organizational characteristics					
Private/public structure	Private partner- ship	Private partnership	Private LLC	Public corpora- tion	Public corporation
Investment bank (IB)/ Bank	IB	IB	IB	IB	Bank
Liability	Personal	Personal	Limited	Limited	Limited
Ownership	100% partners	87.5% part- ners, 12.5% Sumitomo	82.5% part- ners, 12.5% Sumitomo, 5% Bishops	48% partners, 12% public, 40% other	11.5% partners, 8% Berkshire, 80% public/other
Compensation **Partners/ Nonpartners**	Fixed % cash	Fixed % cash	Fixed % cash	Fixed % plus dis- cretionary Cash and stock	Discretionary plus fixed % Cash and stock
Partner liquidity	Starting at retirement	Starting at retirement	Starting at retirement	Public market with vesting	Public market with vesting
Partner election	Every 2 years	Every 2 years	Every 2 years	Every 2 years	Every 2 years
Partner titles	Partner	Partner	MD	MD	MD
Departnering process	Public	Public	Public	Not public	Not public

(continued)

TABLE B-1

Analytical framework of Goldman Sachs (*continued*)

	1979	1990	1996	1999	2012
Partner compensation philosophy	% based on tenure	% based on tenure and performance	% based on tenure and performance	% based on tenure/ performance and comparables	Discretionary and % based on tenure/ performance and comparables
Employee compensation average	Below peers	Below peers	Below peers	At peers	Above peers
Regulation					
Number of business principles	12	12	12	14	14
Clients' interests first	Yes	Yes	Yes	Yes	Yes
Shareholder returns	No	No	No	Yes	Yes
Board	100% partners	100% partners	100% partners	Majority "insiders"	Majority "outsiders"
Banking activities	Glass– Steagall	Glass– Steagall	Glass– Steagall	Glass– Steagall repealed	Dodd–Frank
Competition					
Employees	US IBs	US IBs	US IBs	US IBs, banks, foreign banks, tech firms, hedge funds, privateequity firms	US IBs, banks, foreign banks, tech firms, hedge funds, private-equity firms
Turnover	~5%	~5%–10%	~20%–25%	~20%– 25%	~20%–25%
Capital	GS private (competitors public)	GS private (competitors public)	GS private (competitors public)	GS private (competitors public)	GS private (competitors public)

	1979	1990	1996	1999	2012
Clients					
No-hostile policy	Yes	Yes	No	No	No
International	Limited	~20%	~30%	~40%	40%–50%
HF dedicated group	No	No	No	No	Yes
PE dedicated group	No	No	No	Yes	Yes
GSAM	No	Yes	Yes	Yes	Yes
Average tenure of CEO	~8 years	~7 years	~6 years	~6 years	~5 years
Returns					
IB % revenues	>50%	~50%	~30%–35%	~30%–35%	~10%–15%
Prop % revenues	<10%	<10%–20%	~20%–30%	~60%–70%	~50%
Technology					
Voice mail	No	Limited	Yes	Yes	Yes
e-mail	No	No	Limited	Yes	Yes
Credit derivatives	No	No	Limited	Yes	Yes

Note: This table is based on publicly filed information and general consensus of estimates from interviews. Much of the information has not been reported by Goldman, especially prior to Goldman; is subjective; and requires various assumptions and interpretations.

Appendix C

Selected Goldman Employees and Lobbyists with Government Positions (Before or After Goldman)

JOSHUA BOLTEN

> *Government:* President George W. Bush's chief of staff, 2006–2009; director of Office of Management and Budget, 2003–2006; White House deputy chief of staff, January 20, 2001–June 2003
>
> *Goldman:* Executive director of legal affairs for Goldman based in London (the bank's chief lobbyist to the EU), 1994–1999

KENNETH D. BRODY

> *Government:* President and chairman of the Export-Import Bank of the United States, 1993–1996
>
> *Goldman:* Former adviser and board member of the management committee at Goldman, where he worked from 1971 to 1991

KATHLEEN BROWN

Government: Former California state treasurer

Goldman: Senior adviser responsible for public finance, western region

MARK CARNEY

Government: Governor of the Bank of Canada since 2008

Goldman: Thirteen-year career with Goldman; left in 1995

ROBERT COGORNO

Government: Former aide to Richard Gephardt (D.-Mo.) and one-time floor director for Steny Hoyer (D-Md.), the number two House Democrat

Goldman: Works for [Steve] Elmendorf Strategies, which lobbies for Goldman

KENNETH CONNOLLY

Government: Staff director of the Senate Environment and Public Works Committee, 2001–2006

Goldman: Vice president at Goldman from June 2008 to present

E. GERALD CORRIGAN

Government: President of the New York Fed, 1985–1993

Goldman: Joined Goldman in 1994, currently a partner and managing director; also appointed chairman of GS Bank USA, the firm's holding company, in September 2008

JON CORZINE

Government: Governor of New Jersey, 2006–2010; US Senator, 2001–2006, where he served on the Banking and Budget committees

Goldman: Former Goldman CEO; worked at Goldman from 1975 to 1998

GREGORY CRAIG

Government: White House Counsel in Obama administration

Goldman: Took position as Goldman's chief lawyer to defend against an SEC suit

GAVYN DAVIES

Government: Former chairman of the BBC, 2001–2004

Goldman: Chief economist at Goldman, where he worked from 1986 to 2001

PAUL DIGHTON

Government: Chief executive of the London Operating Committee of the Olympic Games (LOCOG)

Goldman: Worked at Goldman for twenty-two years beginning in 1983

MARIO DRAGHI

Government: Governor of the Bank of Italy since January 2006; since 2011, President of the European Central Bank

Goldman: Vice chairman and managing director of Goldman Sachs International; member of the firmwide management committee, 2002–2005

WILLIAM DUDLEY

Government: President, Federal Reserve Bank of New York, 2009 to present

Goldman: Partner and managing director; worked at Goldman from 1986 to 2007

STEVEN ELMENDORF

Government: Senior adviser to then–House minority leader Richard Gephardt

Goldman: Runs his own lobbying firm; Goldman is a client

DINA FARRELL

Government: Deputy director, National Economic Council, Obama administration, since January 2009

Goldman: Financial analyst at Goldman, 1987–1989

EDWARD C. FORST

Government: Adviser to Treasury Secretary Henry Paulson in 2008

Goldman: Former global head, investment management division at Goldman, where he worked from 1994 to 2008

RANDALL M. FORT

Government: Assistant secretary of state for intelligence and research, November 2006–January 2009

Goldman: Director of global security, 1996–2006

HENRY H. FOWLER

Government: Secretary of the Treasury, 1965–1968

Goldman: After leaving the Treasury Department, joined Goldman in New York as a partner

STEPHEN FRIEDMAN

Government: Chairman, President's Foreign Intelligence Advisory Board and of the Intelligence Oversight Board; chairman, Federal Reserve Bank of New York, 2008–2009; former director of National Economic Council under George W. Bush; economic adviser to Bush, 2002–2004

Goldman: Joined Goldman in 1966; former cochairman; left in 1994; was board member until April 2013

GARY GENSLER

Government: Chairman of the US Commodity Futures Trading Commission since 2009; undersecretary of the Treasury, 1999–2001; assistant secretary of the Treasury, 1997–1999

Goldman: Former co-head of finance worldwide; worked at Goldman from 1979 to 1997

RICHARD GEPHARDT

Government: US Representative, 1977–2005

Goldman: President and CEO, Gephardt Government Affairs (since 2007); represents Goldman interests on issues related to TARP

JUDD GREGG

Government: Three-term New Hampshire senator; ranking Republican on the Appropriations, Banking, Housing and Urban Affairs Committee and on the Health Education Labor and Pensions Committee

Goldman: International adviser

LORD BRIAN GRIFFITHS

Government: Head of the prime minister's policy unit, 1985–1990

Goldman: International adviser since 1991

THOMAS HEALEY

Government: Assistant Secretary of Treasury for Domestic Finance in Reagan administration

Goldman: Started at Goldman in 1985; founded the Pension Services Group in 1990

JIM HIMES

Government: Congressman from Connecticut (on Committee on Financial Services) since 2009

Goldman: Began working at Goldman in 1995, eventually promoted to vice president

ROBERT D. HORMATS

Government: Under secretary of state for economic, energy and agricultural affairs-designate since July 2009; assistant secretary of state for economic and business affairs, 1981–1982

Goldman: Vice chairman of Goldman Sachs International; worked at Goldman from 1982 to 2009

OTTMAR ISSING

Government: Bundesbank board member and ex-chief economist of the European Central Bank

Goldman: Senior adviser

CHRIS JAVENS

Government: Ex-tax policy adviser to Senator Chuck Grassley (R.-Iowa)

Goldman: Lobbies for Goldman

REUBEN JEFFERY III

Government: Under secretary of state for economic, business, and agricultural affairs, 2007–2009; chairman of the Commodity Futures Trading Commission, 2005–2007

Goldman: Former head of the Goldman Paris office; worked at Goldman from 1983 to 2001

DAN JESTER

Government: Former Treasury adviser

Goldman: Former Goldman vice president and deputy chief financial officer

JAMES JOHNSON

Government: Selected to serve on Obama's vice presidential section committee but stepped down

Goldman: On board of directors since May 1999

NEEL KASHKARI

Government: Interim head, Treasury's Office of Financial Stability, October 2008–May 2009; assistant secretary for international economics (confirmed 2008); special assistant to Treasury Secretary Henry Paulson, 2006–2008

Goldman: Vice president, 2002–2006

LORI E. LAUDIEN

Government: Former counsel for the Senate Finance Committee, 1996–1997

Goldman: Lobbyist since 2005

ARTHUR LEVITT

Government: Chairman, SEC, 1993–2001

Goldman: Adviser, June 2009 to present

MARIO MONTI

Government: Prime minister of Italy

Goldman: International adviser, 2005 until his nomination to lead the Italian government; also worked closely with Goldman to reduce the apparent size of Italian government debt

PHILIP MURPHY

Government: US ambassador to Germany since 2009

Goldman: Former partner of Goldman, where he worked from 1983 to 2006

MICHAEL PAESE

Government: Top staffer to House Financial Services Committee Chairman Barney Frank

Goldman: Director of government affairs/lobbyist, 2009

MARK PATTERSON

Government: Treasury Department chief of staff since February 2009

Goldman: Lobbyist, 2003–2008

HENRY "HANK" PAULSON

Government: Secretary of the Treasury, March 2006–January 2009; White House Domestic Council, serving as staff assistant to the president, 1972–1973; staff assistant to the assistant secretary of defense at the Pentagon, 1970–1972

Goldman: Former CEO; worked at Goldman from 1974 to 2006

ROMANO PRODI

Government: Two-time prime minister of Italy

Goldman: From March 1990 to May 1993 and when not in public office, acted as a consultant to Goldman Sachs

RICHARD Y. ROBERTS

Government: Former SEC commissioner, 1990–1995

Goldman: Principal at RR&G LLC; retained by Goldman to lobby on TARP

John F. W. Rogers

Government: Served as undersecretary of state for management at the US Department of State, 1991–1993

Goldman: Executive vice president since April 2011; chief of staff and secretary to board of directors since November 2001; joined in 1994 in the fixed income division and served in various positions, 1994–2001

Robert Rubin

Government: Treasury secretary, 1995–1999; chairman, National Economic Council, 1993–1995

Goldman: Former co-senior partner at Goldman, where he worked from 1966 to 1992

Steve Shafran

Government: Adviser to Treasury Secretary Henry Paulson

Goldman: Worked at Goldman from 1993 to 2000

Sonal Shah

Government: Director, Office of Social Innovation and Civic Participation (April 2009); advisory board member, Obama-Biden Transition Project; variety of positions in the Treasury Department, 1995–2002

Goldman: Vice president, 2004–2007

Faryar Shirzad

Government: Served on the staff of the National Security Council at the White House, March 2003–August 2006; assistant secretary for import administration at US Department of Commerce in the Bush administration

Goldman: Global head of government affairs (lobbyist) since 2006

GENE SPERLING

Government: Director of the National Economic Council in Obama administration

Goldman: Consultant to Goldman in 2008

ROBERT K. STEEL

Government: Under secretary for domestic finance, Treasury, 2006–2008

Goldman: Former vice chairman of Goldman, where he worked from 1976 to 2004

ADAM STORCH

Government: Managing Executive of the SEC's enforcement division, October 2009 to present

Goldman: Former vice president at Goldman, where he worked from 2004 to 2009

MARTI THOMAS

Government: Assistant secretary in legal affairs and public policy, 2000; deputy assistant secretary for tax and budget, Treasury Department, 1998–1999; executive floor assistant to Richard Gephardt, 1989–1998

Goldman: Joined Goldman as federal legislative affairs leader, 2007–2009

MASSIMO TONONI

Government: Italian deputy Treasury chief, 2006–2008

Goldman: Former partner, 2004–2006

MALCOLM TURNBULL

Government: Member of the Australian House of Representatives since 2004

Goldman: Chairman and managing director, Goldman Sachs Australia, 1997–2001

SIDNEY WEINBERG

Government: Vice-Chair, War Production Board, during World War II

Goldman: Worked at Goldman from 1907 to 1969

JOHN WHITEHEAD

Government: Under secretary of state from 1985 to 1989; former Chairman of the Board of the Federal Reserve of New York

Goldman: Worked at Goldman from 1947 to 1984. Was co-senior partner with John L. Weinberg

KENDRICK WILSON

Government: Adviser to Treasury Secretary Henry Paulson

Goldman: Senior investment banker at Goldman, where he worked from 1998 to 2008

ROBERT ZOELLICK

Government: President, World Bank, since 2007

Goldman: Vice chairman, Goldman Sachs International; managing director and chairman, Board of International Advisors, 2006–2007

A reminder: I am not judging the involvement of these individuals— good or bad. This is merely to present a selected group as data.[1] A spokesman of Goldman stated: "We're proud of our alumni, but frankly, when they work in the public sector, their presence is more of a negative than a positive for us in terms of winning business. There is no mileage for them in giving Goldman Sachs the corporate equivalent of most-favored-nation status."[2]

Appendix D

Value of Partners' Shares at IPO

A list of Goldman partners at the time of the IPO is shown in table D-1. The names, percentages of shares, shares outstanding, values at IPO, and values at close are all provided. This analysis is based on reported percentages from the *New York Times*.

TABLE D-1

Percentages, shares, and value of partners' shares at the IPO and first closing prices

Name	Percentage	Implied shares outstanding	Value at IPO price ($53)	First closing price ($70.38)
Henry M. Paulson Jr.	1.100%	2,915,210	$154,506,120	$205,172,466
Jon S. Corzine	1.100%	2,915,210	154,506,120	205,172,466
Robert J. Hurst	1.100%	2,915,210	154,506,120	205,172,466
John A. Thain	1.050%	2,782,700	147,483,114	195,846,445
John L. Thornton	1.050%	2,782,700	147,483,114	195,846,445
Daniel M. Neidich	0.900%	2,385,172	126,414,098	167,868,381

(continued)

TABLE D-1

Percentages, shares, and value of partners' shares at the IPO and first closing prices (*continued*)

Name	Percentage	Implied shares outstanding	Value at IPO price ($53)	First closing price ($70.38)
John P. McNulty	0.900%	2,385,172	126,414,098	167,868,381
Lloyd C. Blankfein	0.900%	2,385,172	126,414,098	167,868,381
Michael P. Mortara	0.900%	2,385,172	126,414,098	167,868,381
Richard A. Friedman	0.900%	2,385,172	126,414,098	167,868,381
Robert K. Steel	0.900%	2,385,172	126,414,098	167,868,381
Jacob D. Goldfield	0.825%	2,186,407	115,879,590	153,879,349
Jon Winkelried	0.825%	2,186,407	115,879,590	153,879,349
Mark Schwartz	0.825%	2,186,407	115,879,590	153,879,349
Patrick J. Ward	0.825%	2,186,407	115,879,590	153,879,349
Peter A. Weinberg	0.825%	2,186,407	115,879,590	153,879,349
Philip D. Murphy	0.825%	2,186,407	115,879,590	153,879,349
Robert S. Kaplan	0.825%	2,186,407	115,879,590	153,879,349
Steven M. Heller	0.825%	2,186,407	115,879,590	153,879,349
W. Mark Evans	0.825%	2,186,407	115,879,590	153,879,349
David B. Ford	0.725%	1,921,388	101,833,579	135,227,307
Gavyn Davies	0.725%	1,921,388	101,833,579	135,227,307
Gene T. Sykes	0.725%	1,921,388	101,833,579	135,227,307
J. David Rogers	0.725%	1,921,388	101,833,579	135,227,307
John S. Weinberg	0.725%	1,921,388	101,833,579	135,227,307
Robert B. Morris III	0.725%	1,921,388	101,833,579	135,227,307
Robert E. Higgins	0.725%	1,921,388	101,833,579	135,227,307
Robert J. Katz	0.725%	1,921,388	101,833,579	135,227,307
Thomas E. Tuft	0.725%	1,921,388	101,833,579	135,227,307
Barry L. Zubrow	0.650%	1,722,624	91,299,071	121,238,275
David A. Viniar	0.650%	1,722,624	91,299,071	121,238,275

Name	Percentage	Implied shares outstanding	Value at IPO price ($53)	First closing price ($70.38)
Eff W. Martin	0.650%	1,722,624	91,299,071	121,238,275
James P. Riley Jr.	0.650%	1,722,624	91,299,071	121,238,275
Kevin W. Kennedy	0.650%	1,722,624	91,299,071	121,238,275
Lee G. Vance	0.650%	1,722,624	91,299,071	121,238,275
Leslie C. Tortora	0.650%	1,722,624	91,299,071	121,238,275
Richard A. Sapp	0.650%	1,722,624	91,299,071	121,238,275
Richard E. Witten	0.650%	1,722,624	91,299,071	121,238,275
Robin Chemers Neustein	0.650%	1,722,624	91,299,071	121,238,275
Sharmin Mossavar-Rahmani	0.650%	1,722,624	91,299,071	121,238,275
Terence M. O'Toole	0.650%	1,722,624	91,299,071	121,238,275
Thomas B. Walker III	0.650%	1,722,624	91,299,071	121,238,275
Barry S. Volpert	0.600%	1,590,114	84,276,065	111,912,254
Christopher A. Cole	0.600%	1,590,114	84,276,065	111,912,254
David W. Blood	0.600%	1,590,114	84,276,065	111,912,254
Donald C. Opatrny Jr.	0.600%	1,590,114	84,276,065	111,912,254
Eric M. Mindich	0.600%	1,590,114	84,276,065	111,912,254
Eric S. Schwartz	0.600%	1,590,114	84,276,065	111,912,254
Gary D. Cohn	0.600%	1,590,114	84,276,065	111,912,254
Gregory K. Palm	0.600%	1,590,114	84,276,065	111,912,254
J. Michael Evans	0.600%	1,590,114	84,276,065	111,912,254
Joseph H. Gleberman	0.600%	1,590,114	84,276,065	111,912,254
Masanori Mochida	0.600%	1,590,114	84,276,065	111,912,254
Paul M. Achleitner	0.600%	1,590,114	84,276,065	111,912,254
Peter C. Gerhard	0.600%	1,590,114	84,276,065	111,912,254
Peter S. Kraus	0.600%	1,590,114	84,276,065	111,912,254

(continued)

TABLE D-1

Percentages, shares, and value of partners' shares at the IPO and first closing prices (*continued*)

Name	Percentage	Implied shares outstanding	Value at IPO price ($53)	First closing price ($70.38)
Robert J. O'Shea	0.600%	1,590,114	84,276,065	111,912,254
Scott B. Kapnick	0.600%	1,590,114	84,276,065	111,912,254
Scott M. Pinkus	0.600%	1,590,114	84,276,065	111,912,254
Steven T. Mnuchin	0.600%	1,590,114	84,276,065	111,912,254
Sylvain M. Hefes	0.600%	1,590,114	84,276,065	111,912,254
Thomas K. Montag	0.600%	1,590,114	84,276,065	111,912,254
Wiet H. Pot	0.600%	1,590,114	84,276,065	111,912,254
Byron D. Trott	0.550%	1,457,605	77,253,060	102,586,233
George W. Wellde Jr.	0.550%	1,457,605	77,253,060	102,586,233
Jim O'Neill	0.550%	1,457,605	77,253,060	102,586,233
John J. Powers	0.550%	1,457,605	77,253,060	102,586,233
Michael S. Sherwood	0.550%	1,457,605	77,253,060	102,586,233
Richard S. Sharp	0.550%	1,457,605	77,253,060	102,586,233
Andrew M. Alper	0.525%	1,391,350	73,741,557	97,923,222
Carlos A. Cordeiro	0.525%	1,391,350	73,741,557	97,923,222
Charles B. Seelig Jr.	0.525%	1,391,350	73,741,557	97,923,222
Daniel W. Stanton	0.525%	1,391,350	73,741,557	97,923,222
E. Gerald Corrigan	0.525%	1,391,350	73,741,557	97,923,222
E. Scott Mead	0.525%	1,391,350	73,741,557	97,923,222
John L. Townsend III	0.525%	1,391,350	73,741,557	97,923,222
John O. Downing	0.525%	1,391,350	73,741,557	97,923,222
Jonathan R. Aisbitt	0.525%	1,391,350	73,741,557	97,923,222
Joseph R. Zimmel	0.525%	1,391,350	73,741,557	97,923,222
Kendrick R. Wilson III	0.525%	1,391,350	73,741,557	97,923,222
Lawrence H. Linden	0.525%	1,391,350	73,741,557	97,923,222

Name	Percentage	Implied shares outstanding	Value at IPO price ($53)	First closing price ($70.38)
Michael J. Zamkow	0.525%	1,391,350	73,741,557	97,923,222
Michael R. Lynch	0.525%	1,391,350	73,741,557	97,923,222
Reuben Jeffery III	0.525%	1,391,350	73,741,557	97,923,222
Simon M. Robertson	0.525%	1,391,350	73,741,557	97,923,222
Sir Peter D. Sutherland	0.525%	1,391,350	73,741,557	97,923,222
Suzanne M. Nora Johnson	0.525%	1,391,350	73,741,557	97,923,222
Timothy J. O'Neill	0.525%	1,391,350	73,741,557	97,923,222
Anthony G. Williams	0.475%	1,258,841	66,718,552	88,597,201
Armen A. Avanessians	0.475%	1,258,841	66,718,552	88,597,201
Arthur J. Reimers	0.475%	1,258,841	66,718,552	88,597,201
Edward A. Mulé	0.475%	1,258,841	66,718,552	88,597,201
Frank L. Coulson Jr.	0.475%	1,258,841	66,718,552	88,597,201
Henry Cornell	0.475%	1,258,841	66,718,552	88,597,201
Howard A. Silverstein	0.475%	1,258,841	66,718,552	88,597,201
Joseph D. Gatto	0.475%	1,258,841	66,718,552	88,597,201
Joseph Della Rosa	0.475%	1,258,841	66,718,552	88,597,201
Lawton W. Fitt	0.475%	1,258,841	66,718,552	88,597,201
Peter G.C. Mallinson	0.475%	1,258,841	66,718,552	88,597,201
Richard G. Sherlund	0.475%	1,258,841	66,718,552	88,597,201
Robert Litterman	0.475%	1,258,841	66,718,552	88,597,201
Robert V. Delaney	0.475%	1,258,841	66,718,552	88,597,201
Tracy R. Wolstencroft	0.475%	1,258,841	66,718,552	88,597,201
Connie K. Duckworth	0.425%	1,126,331	59,695,546	79,271,180
Danny O. Yee	0.425%	1,126,331	59,695,546	79,271,180

(continued)

TABLE D-1

Percentages, shares, and value of partners' shares at the IPO and first closing prices (*continued*)

Name	Percentage	Implied shares outstanding	Value at IPO price ($53)	First closing price ($70.38)
David L. Henle	0.425%	1,126,331	59,695,546	79,271,180
Esta E. Stecher	0.425%	1,126,331	59,695,546	79,271,180
Gary W. Williams	0.425%	1,126,331	59,695,546	79,271,180
Michael G. Rantz	0.425%	1,126,331	59,695,546	79,271,180
Peter D. Kiernan III	0.425%	1,126,331	59,695,546	79,271,180
Thomas J. Healey	0.425%	1,126,331	59,695,546	79,271,180
Ann F. Kaplan	0.400%	1,060,076	56,184,043	74,608,169
Cody J. Smith	0.400%	1,060,076	56,184,043	74,608,169
Donald F. Textor	0.400%	1,060,076	56,184,043	74,608,169
Fredric E. Steck	0.400%	1,060,076	56,184,043	74,608,169
Jonathan M. Lopatin	0.400%	1,060,076	56,184,043	74,608,169
Joseph Sassoon	0.400%	1,060,076	56,184,043	74,608,169
Mark A. Zurack	0.400%	1,060,076	56,184,043	74,608,169
Nomi P. Ghez	0.400%	1,060,076	56,184,043	74,608,169
Stephen D. Quinn	0.400%	1,060,076	56,184,043	74,608,169
T. Willem Mesdag	0.400%	1,060,076	56,184,043	74,608,169
Zachariah Cobrinik	0.400%	1,060,076	56,184,043	74,608,169
Bradford C. Koenig	0.375%	993,822	52,672,541	69,945,159
David B. Heller	0.375%	993,822	52,672,541	69,945,159
Howard B. Schiller	0.375%	993,822	52,672,541	69,945,159
Mark R. Tercek	0.375%	993,822	52,672,541	69,945,159
Milton R. Berlinski	0.375%	993,822	52,672,541	69,945,159
Peter L. Briger Jr.	0.375%	993,822	52,672,541	69,945,159
Robert S. Harrison	0.375%	993,822	52,672,541	69,945,159
Ron E. Beller	0.375%	993,822	52,672,541	69,945,159

Name	Percentage	Implied shares outstanding	Value at IPO price ($53)	First closing price ($70.38)
Stuart M. Rothenberg	0.375%	993,822	52,672,541	69,945,159
Alok Oberoi	0.325%	861,312	45,649,535	60,619,138
Barry A. Kaplan	0.325%	861,312	45,649,535	60,619,138
C. Steven Duncker	0.325%	861,312	45,649,535	60,619,138
Douglas W. Kimmelman	0.325%	861,312	45,649,535	60,619,138
Eric P. Grubman	0.325%	861,312	45,649,535	60,619,138
Erland S. Karlsson	0.325%	861,312	45,649,535	60,619,138
Francis J. Ingrassia	0.325%	861,312	45,649,535	60,619,138
Geoffrey T. Grant	0.325%	861,312	45,649,535	60,619,138
Glenn P. Earle	0.325%	861,312	45,649,535	60,619,138
Gregory H. Zehner	0.325%	861,312	45,649,535	60,619,138
James M. Sheridan	0.325%	861,312	45,649,535	60,619,138
Jido J. Zeitlin	0.325%	861,312	45,649,535	60,619,138
John C. "Jack" Ryan	0.325%	861,312	45,649,535	60,619,138
John R. Tormondsen	0.325%	861,312	45,649,535	60,619,100
Jonathan L. Kolatch	0.325%	861,312	45,649,535	60,619,138
Joseph D. Gutman	0.325%	861,312	45,649,535	60,619,138
Karsten N. Moller	0.325%	861,312	45,649,535	60,619,138
Kipp M. Nelson	0.325%	861,312	45,649,535	60,619,138
Lawrence R. Buchalter	0.325%	861,312	45,649,535	60,619,138
Marc A. Spilker	0.325%	861,312	45,649,535	60,619,138
Mary C. Henry	0.325%	861,312	45,649,535	60,619,138
Muneer A. Satter	0.325%	861,312	45,649,535	60,619,138
Paul C. Deighton	0.325%	861,312	45,649,535	60,619,138
Peter Savitz	0.325%	861,312	45,649,535	60,619,138
Randolph L. Cowen	0.325%	861,312	45,649,535	60,619,138

(continued)

TABLE D-1

Percentages, shares, and value of partners' shares at the IPO and first closing prices (*continued*)

Name	Percentage	Implied shares outstanding	Value at IPO price ($53)	First closing price ($70.38)
Ronald G. Marks	0.325%	861,312	45,649,535	60,619,138
Steven J. Wisch	0.325%	861,312	45,649,535	60,619,138
Timothy C. Plaut	0.325%	861,312	45,649,535	60,619,138
Timothy D. Dattels	0.325%	861,312	45,649,535	60,619,138
David G. Lambert	0.250%	662,548	35,115,027	46,630,106
Girish V. Reddy	0.250%	662,548	35,115,027	46,630,106
Jacquelyn M. Hoffman-Zehner	0.250%	662,548	35,115,027	46,630,106
Steven M. Shafran	0.250%	662,548	35,115,027	46,630,106
Abby Joseph Cohen	0.200%	530,038	28,092,022	37,304,085
Alexander C. Dibelius	0.200%	530,038	28,092,022	37,304,085
Amy O. Goodfriend	0.200%	530,038	28,092,022	37,304,085
Andrew A. Chisholm	0.200%	530,038	28,092,022	37,304,085
Andrew M. Gordon	0.200%	530,038	28,092,022	37,304,085
Anthony D. Lauto	0.200%	530,038	28,092,022	37,304,085
Antoine Schwartz	0.200%	530,038	28,092,022	37,304,085
Avi M. Nash	0.200%	530,038	28,092,022	37,304,085
Bradley I. Abelow	0.200%	530,038	28,092,022	37,304,085
Chansoo Joung	0.200%	530,038	28,092,022	37,304,085
Christian J. Siva-Jothy	0.200%	530,038	28,092,022	37,304,085
Christopher G. French	0.200%	530,038	28,092,022	37,304,085
Christopher J. Carrera	0.200%	530,038	28,092,022	37,304,085
Claudio Costamagna	0.200%	530,038	28,092,022	37,304,085
David A. Dechman	0.200%	530,038	28,092,022	37,304,085

Name	Percentage	Implied shares outstanding	Value at IPO price ($53)	First closing price ($70.38)
David J. Mastrocola	0.200%	530,038	28,092,022	37,304,085
David M. Baum	0.200%	530,038	28,092,022	37,304,085
Dinakar Singh	0.200%	530,038	28,092,022	37,304,085
Edward C. Forst	0.200%	530,038	28,092,022	37,304,085
Emmanuel Roman	0.200%	530,038	28,092,022	37,304,085
George H. Walker	0.200%	530,038	28,092,022	37,304,085
Greg M. Ostroff	0.200%	530,038	28,092,022	37,304,085
Hsueh J. Sung	0.200%	530,038	28,092,022	37,304,085
Jeffrey B. Goldenberg	0.200%	530,038	28,092,022	37,304,085
John E. Urban	0.200%	530,038	28,092,022	37,304,085
Jonathan S. Savitz	0.200%	530,038	28,092,022	37,304,085
Jonathan S. Sobel	0.200%	530,038	28,092,022	37,304,085
M. Roch Hillenbrand	0.200%	530,038	28,002,022	37,304,085
Malcolm B. Turnbull	0.200%	530,038	28,092,022	37,304,085
Mary Ann Casati	0.200%	530,038	28,092,022	37,304,085
Matthew G. L'Heureux	0.200%	530,038	28,092,022	37,304,085
Michael A. Price	0.200%	530,038	28,092,022	37,304,085
Michael D. Ryan	0.200%	530,038	28,092,022	37,304,085
Michael E. Novogratz	0.200%	530,038	28,092,022	37,304,085
Michael J. Carr	0.200%	530,038	28,092,022	37,304,085
Gordon Dyal	0.200%	530,038	28,092,022	37,304,085
Michael S. Rubinoff	0.200%	530,038	28,092,022	37,304,085
Paul S. Efron	0.200%	530,038	28,092,022	37,304,085
Philip M. Darivoff	0.200%	530,038	28,092,022	37,304,085
Pieter Maarten Feenstra	0.200%	530,038	28,092,022	37,304,085
Ralph F. Rosenberg	0.200%	530,038	28,092,022	37,304,085
Richard J. Bronks	0.200%	530,038	28,092,022	37,304,085

(continued)

TABLE D-1

Percentages, shares, and value of partners' shares at the IPO and first closing prices (*continued*)

Name	Percentage	Implied shares outstanding	Value at IPO price ($53)	First closing price ($70.38)
Richard J. Gnodde	0.200%	530,038	28,092,022	37,304,085
Richard M. Ruzika	0.200%	530,038	28,092,022	37,304,085
Robert B. Tudor III	0.200%	530,038	28,092,022	37,304,085
Robert H. Litzenberger	0.200%	530,038	28,092,022	37,304,085
Robert J. Pace	0.200%	530,038	28,092,022	37,304,085
Sanjeev K. Mehra	0.200%	530,038	28,092,022	37,304,085
Scott S. Prince	0.200%	530,038	28,092,022	37,304,085
Stefan J. Jentzsch	0.200%	530,038	28,092,022	37,304,085
Thomas D. Lasersohn	0.200%	530,038	28,092,022	37,304,085
Thomas S. Murphy Jr.	0.200%	530,038	28,092,022	37,304,085
Timothy J. Ingrassia	0.200%	530,038	28,092,022	37,304,085
Tsutomu Sato	0.200%	530,038	28,092,022	37,304,085
Wayne L. Moore	0.200%	530,038	28,092,022	37,304,085
Yasuyo Yamazaki	0.200%	530,038	28,092,022	37,304,085
Yoel Zaoui	0.200%	530,038	28,092,022	37,304,085
Total	99.20%	262,898,920	$13,933,642,782	$18,502,826,019
Average per partner		1,189,588	$63,048,157	$83,723,195

Note: The percentages came from a *New York Times* article; see http://dealbook.nytimes.com/2011/05/16/the-goldman-sachs-diaspora/. It notes that the information was based on the most recent available data for the partnership class at Goldman's IPO. The shares were calculated by taking the total shares owned by the partners—265,019,073—as disclosed on page 30 of Goldman's IPO prospectus. In the article Gordon Dyal's percentage was "not available;" his percentage was based on interviews. The implied shares for Paulson, Corzine, Hurst, Thain, and Thornton are different than the shares disclosed in the IPO prospectus. The values were calculated by multiplying the IPO price of $53.00 per share and the closing price on the first day of $70.38 per share. The total of the percentages provided in the *New York Times* article is 99.2%, and it appears one partner is missing because the list has 220 names. The analysis indicates an IPO total of $13.9 billion, or an average of $63 million per partner. Reported average estimates in the press have been from $52 million to $75 million per partner.

Goldman's History of Commitment to Public Service

Figures E-1 and E-2 highlight key milestones demonstrating Goldman's long-standing commitment to public service and corporate citizenship.[1]

FIGURE E-1

Goldman document listing its commitment to public service

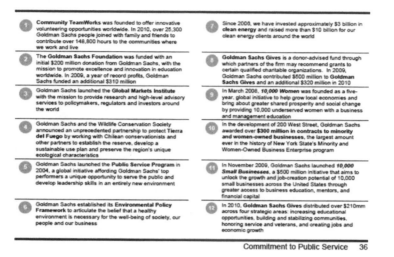

A History of Commitment to Public Service
Key Milestones

1. **Community TeamWorks** was founded to offer innovative volunteering opportunities worldwide. In 2010, over 25,300 Goldman Sachs people joined with family and friends to contribute over 148,800 hours to the communities where we work and live

2. The **Goldman Sachs Foundation** was funded with an initial $200 million donation from Goldman Sachs, with the mission to promote excellence and innovation in education worldwide. In 2009, a year of record profits, Goldman Sachs funded an additional $310 million

3. Goldman Sachs launched the **Global Markets Institute** with the mission to provide research and high-level advisory services to policymakers, regulators and investors around the world

4. Goldman Sachs and the Wildlife Conservation Society announced an unprecedented partnership to protect **Tierra del Fuego** by working with Chilean conservationists and other partners to establish the reserve, develop a sustainable use plan and preserve the region's unique ecological characteristics

5. Goldman Sachs launched the **Public Service Program** in 2004, a global initiative affording Goldman Sachs' top performers a unique opportunity to serve the public and develop leadership skills in an entirely new environment

6. Goldman Sachs established its **Environmental Policy Framework** to articulate the belief that a healthy environment is necessary for the well-being of society, our people and our business

7. Since 2006, we have invested approximately $3 billion in clean energy and raised more than $10 billion for our clean energy clients around the world

8. **Goldman Sachs Gives** is a donor-advised fund through which partners of the firm may recommend grants to certain qualified charitable organizations. In 2009, Goldman Sachs contributed $500 million to **Goldman Sachs Gives** and an additional $320 million in 2010

9. In March 2008, *10,000 Women* was founded as a five-year, global initiative to help grow local economies and bring about greater shared prosperity and social change by providing 10,000 underserved women with a business and management education

10. In the development of 200 West Street, Goldman Sachs awarded over **$300 million in contracts to minority and women-owned businesses**, the largest amount ever in the history of New York State's Minority and Women-Owned Business Enterprise program

11. In November 2009, Goldman Sachs launched *10,000 Small Businesses*, a $500 million initiative that aims to unlock the growth and job-creation potential of 10,000 small businesses across the United States through greater access to business education, mentors, and financial capital

12. In 2010, **Goldman Sachs Gives** distributed over $210mm across four strategic areas: increasing educational opportunities, building and stabilizing communities, honoring service and veterans, and creating jobs and economic growth

Commitment to Public Service   36

Source: Goldman Sachs, www.goldmansachs.com/investor-relations/corporate-governance/corporate-governance-documents/culture.pdf.

FIGURE E-2

Goldman document showing a timeline of public service projects

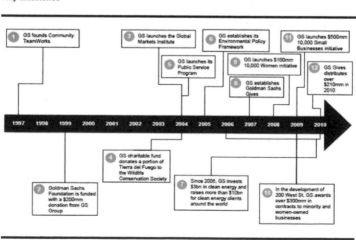

A History of Commitment to Public Service
Key Milestones

Commitment to Public Service   35

Source: Goldman Sachs, www.goldmansachs.com/investor-relations/corporate-governance/corporate-governance-documents/culture.pdf.

Key Goldman People

Following is a list of key Goldman people who are mentioned in this book: the Weinbergs and others who formerly ran the firm, those currently running the firm, and other former executives. Individuals are categorized by role or position and alphabetized within those categories.

The Weinbergs

John L. Weinberg, with John C. Whitehead, was co-senior partner from 1976 to 1984 and continued to lead the firm after Whitehead retired in 1984, until Weinberg's own retirement in 1990, capping a forty-year career at the bank. "John L.," as he was known (to distinguish him from John Whitehead), also served briefly on Goldman's board of directors following the public offering in 1999. John L. was part of a family dynasty that has been at the firm since 1907. His father was Sidney Weinberg. Jimmy Weinberg was his brother, John S. Weinberg is his son, and Peter Weinberg is his nephew.

John L. Weinberg graduated from Deerfield Academy, Princeton University, and Harvard Business School. During his senior year at Deerfield, he joined the Marines and led troops in the Pacific while still a teenager. After beginning at Goldman, he returned to duty during the Korean War and was promoted to captain before returning to Goldman. He died in 2006.

John S. Weinberg has been vice chairman of Goldman since June 2006 and has been co-head of Goldman's investment banking division since December 2002. From January 2002 to December 2002, he was co-head of the investment banking division in the Americas. Before that, he served as co-head of the investment banking services department, beginning in 1997. He was elected partner in 1994. John S. Weinberg graduated from Princeton University, where he was on the tennis team, and from Harvard Business School. His father was John L. Weinberg, and Sidney Weinberg was his grandfather. Jimmy Weinberg was his uncle, and Peter Weinberg is his first cousin.

Peter Weinberg is a partner in Perella Weinberg Partners LP. Before joining the firm, Peter Weinberg held a number of senior management positions at Goldman, where he was elected partner in 1992. For the last six years of his career there, Weinberg was CEO of Goldman Sachs International. Peter Weinberg spent time at Morgan Stanley before joining Goldman. He received a bachelor's degree from Claremont McKenna College and an MBA from Harvard Business School. His father was Jimmy Weinberg, and Sidney Weinberg was his grandfather. John L. Weinberg was his uncle, and John S. Weinberg is his first cousin.

Sidney J. Weinberg led Goldman from 1930 to 1969 and in many ways defined the art of relationship banking on Wall Street. Starting as a janitor's assistant, Weinberg became partner in 1927 and became head of the firm in 1930, saving it from bankruptcy, and held that position until his death in 1969. He organized the Business and Advisory Council for President Franklin D. Roosevelt. In 1942, he took a leave of absence and entered government service as assistant to the chairman of the War Production Board. John L. Weinberg and Jimmy Weinberg were his sons; John S. Weinberg and Peter Weinberg are his grandsons.

Sidney James (Jimmy) Weinberg, Jr., joined Goldman's investment banking department in 1965. He worked as a vice president of the textile division at Owens Corning before joining Goldman. From 1978 to 1988, he ran the firm's investment banking services department, a unit created by former Goldman co-chairman John C. Whitehead to help manage client relationships and win business. Jimmy Weinberg retired from the general partnership in 1988, when he turned sixty-five. He remained a limited partner until the firm went public and then became a senior director. Jimmy Weinberg graduated from Princeton University and Harvard Business School. He served in the Philippines as a first lieutenant in the US Army during World War II. His father was Sidney Weinberg, and John L. Weinberg was his brother. Peter Weinberg is his son, and John S. Weinberg is his nephew.

Senior Partners (Excluding Weinbergs)

Lloyd Blankfein joined Goldman's commodities trading arm, J. Aron & Co., in 1981, as a precious metals salesman in its London office. He has been chairman and CEO of Goldman since June 2006, when Hank Paulson left to become secretary of the Treasury. Blankfein has served as president and COO of Goldman since January 2004. From April 2002 to January 2004, he was a vice chairman of Goldman, with management responsibility for Goldman Sachs's FICC and equities divisions. He served as co-head of the FICC division after its formation in 1997. From 1994 to 1997, he headed or co-headed the currency and commodities division. The *Financial Times* named Blankfein its 2009 Person of the Year. In January 2010, Blankfein testified before the Financial Crisis Inquiry Commission. He testified before Congress in April 2010 at a hearing of the Senate Permanent Subcommittee on Investigations, denying any wrongdoing by Goldman. His father was a clerk with the US Postal Service; his mother was a receptionist. As a boy, Blankfein worked as a concession vendor at Yankee Stadium.

He graduated from Harvard College and Harvard University Law School.

Jon Corzine joined Goldman in 1975 to become a bond trader. Corzine took over the firm after Steve Friedman suddenly resigned over health concerns and after Goldman had suffered significant trading losses. Corzine was chairman and CEO of Goldman from 1994 to 1999 and oversaw the conversion of Goldman from a private partnership to a publicly traded corporation. In 1999, having lost a power struggle with Hank Paulson, Corzine left the firm to run for the US Senate, representing New Jersey. He served as senator from 2001 to 2005, when he was elected New Jersey governor, serving from 2006 to 2010. In March 2010, Corzine was named chairman and CEO of MF Global, a financial services firm specializing in futures brokerage. The company filed for bankruptcy protection in October 2011, and Corzine resigned in November 2011. Corzine was subpoenaed to appear before a House committee in December 2011 to answer questions regarding money missing from MF Global client accounts. In school, Corzine had been football quarterback and basketball captain. While in college, he enlisted in the US Marine Corps Reserve and served from 1969 to 1975, attaining the rank of sergeant. He graduated from the University of Illinois and University of Chicago Business School.

Stephen (Steve) Friedman joined Goldman in 1966, helped start the M&A department within investment banking, and became a partner in 1973. In 1984, he ran the fixed income division, together with Bob Rubin. Friedman was vice chairman and co-COO from 1987 to November 1990 with Bob Rubin, and co-senior partner and chairman or senior partner and chairman from 1990 to 1994. Friedman suddenly resigned in 1994 due to health concerns and after Goldman had suffered significant trading losses. He currently serves as chairman of Stone Point Capital. From 1998 to 2002, he served as a senior principal of March & McLennan Capital, an investment arm of the professional services and insurance brokerage firm. From 2002 to 2005, Friedman was assistant to the president for economic policy under

President George W. Bush; from 2002 to 2004, he served as director of the National Economic Council. Friedman was on the board of directors of Goldman but resigned in April 2013 when he reached the age limit of 75 years old. In 2009, Friedman resigned as chairman of the Federal Reserve Bank of New York while under criticism for his December 2008 purchase of $3 million in Goldman stock. He graduated from Cornell University, where he was on the wrestling team, and Columbia University Law School.

Gus Levy joined Goldman in 1933 to head the then one-man trading department. Between 1933 and 1969, Levy headed Goldman's trading department and pioneered new trading strategies. He was senior partner from 1969, succeeding Sidney Weinberg, until his death in 1976. It was thought that, because he was from the trading department, Levy was not naturally banking oriented. According to stories, when he was about to retire in 1969, the highly banking-oriented Sidney Weinberg had reservations about leaving Levy in charge. Ultimately, he appointed Levy as senior partner but also introduced an eight man management committee composed of seven older, experienced senior banking partners to "supervise" Levy. Gus Levy is credited with coining the phrase "long-term greedy" to describe Goldman's philosophy.

Henry (Hank) Paulson Jr., joined Goldman in 1974, working in the firm's Chicago office, after having worked in the Nixon White House. Paulson became a partner in 1982. From 1983 until 1988, Paulson led the investment-banking group for the Midwest region and became managing partner of the Chicago office in 1988. From 1990 to November 1994, he was co-head of investment banking, then served as COO from December 1994 to June 1998, and eventually succeeded Jon Corzine as chairman and CEO. Paulson pushed Goldman's growth into Asia and into principal investing activities. In 2006, Paulson resigned from Goldman to become secretary of the Treasury for President George W. Bush. *Time* magazine named Paulson runner-up for its 2008 Person of the Year. After leaving his role as Treasury secretary, Paulson spent a year at the Paul H. Nitze School of Advanced International Studies at Johns Hopkins as a distinguished visiting fellow. He is a senior fellow at the University of Chicago's Harris School of Public Policy. In school Paulson was on the wrestling and football teams. He graduated from Dartmouth College and Harvard Business School. He is author of *On the Brink: Inside the Race to Stop the Collapse of the Global Financial System* (2010).

Robert (Bob) Rubin joined Goldman in 1966 as an associate in the risk arbitrage department in the equities division, a proprietary investing area. He became a general partner in 1971 and joined the management committee in 1980. Rubin ran the J. Aron commodities trading business in the early 1980s. He ran the fixed income division with Steve Friedman in 1984. Rubin was vice chairman and co-COO with Steve Friedman from 1987 to 1990. From the end of 1990 to 1992, Rubin served as co-chairman and co-senior partner along with Steve Friedman. Then Rubin resigned to serve in the White House as assistant to the president for economic policy under President Clinton. Rubin served as secretary of the Treasury during the first and second Clinton administrations. In 1999, he became a director on the board, chairman of the executive committee, senior adviser, and member of the office of the chairman of Citigroup, where he performed advisory and representational roles for the firm. In 2009, he left Citigroup while under criticism that he should have recognized and acted on the extreme circumstances faced by the financial system and Citigroup. Rubin is currently engaged actively as a founder of The Hamilton Project, an economic policy think tank that produces research and proposals for creating a growing economy that benefits more Americans. He is co-chairman of the Council on Foreign Relations and sits on the board of the Harvard Corporation, Harvard University's executive board. He was a member of Boy Scout Troop 35, sponsored by the American Legion, and received the rank of Eagle Scout. In 1960, Rubin graduated from Harvard College and Yale Law School. He is coauthor, with Jacob Weisberg, of *In an Uncertain World: Tough Choices from Wall Street to Washington* (2003).

John C. Whitehead joined Goldman in 1947. He was co-senior partner with John L. Weinberg from 1976 to 1984, succeeding Gus Levy after Levy died. Whitehead codified Goldman's principles in 1979. He also set up the investment banking services department to help manage client relationships, win business, and reduce the firm's reliance on any one individual. Both were innovations for Wall Street. He helped focus the firm on international growth. He retired in 1984 to serve as deputy secretary of state, under George Shultz, in the Ronald Reagan administration, from 1985 to 1989. Whitehead is currently a board member of the World Trade Center Memorial Foundation and, until his resignation in May 2006, was chairman of the Lower Manhattan Development Corporation. Whitehead graduated from Haverford College and Harvard Business School and is author of *A Life in Leadership: From D-Day to Ground Zero: An Autobiography* (2005).

Selected Current/Recently Retired Executives

Gary Cohn has been president and COO (or co-COO) and on the board of directors of Goldman since June 2006. From December 2003 to June 2006, he was co-head of global securities businesses, having been co-head of FICC since September 2002. Before that, he served as co COO of FICC after having been responsible for commodities and a number of other FICC businesses from 1999 to 2002. Cohn was head of commodities from 1996 to 1999. In 1990, Cohn was hired by Goldman Sachs's J. Aron & Co. unit as a metals trader which traded commodities and currencies; he traded silver. Lloyd Blankfein became co-head of J. Aron in 1994, and two years later he tapped Cohn as global head of the commodities businesses. Cohn graduated from American University.

J. Michael Evans has been global head of growth markets since January 2011, a vice chairman of Goldman since February 2008, and chairman of Goldman Sachs Asia Pacific since 2004. Before becoming a vice chairman, he had served as global co-head of Goldman's securities business since 2003. Previously, he had been co-head of the equities division. Evans joined Goldman in 1993, from Salomon Brothers, as head of equity capital markets in London. He was named a Goldman partner in 1994, and he became head of the business standards committee. Evans was part of the Canadian Olympic team in 1984 and won a gold medal in eight-man rowing crew. Evans graduated from Princeton in 1981 and attended Oxford University from 1982 to 1984 for his graduate studies.

Harvey M. Schwartz has been the chief financial officer of Goldman since January 2013. From 2008 to 2013, he was global co-head of the securities division. From 2005 to 2008 he was involved in executive sales positions in the securities division. From 2004 to 2005, he was co-head of the Americas Financing Group. He started at Goldman's J. Aron & Co. unit in 1997 as a gold salesman. Prior to Goldman, he worked at J.B. Hanauer & Co, First Interregional Equity Corp., and Citicorp. He graduated from Rutgers in 1987 and Columbia University Business School in 1996.

David A. Viniar had been the chief financial officer of Goldman from 1999 until January 2013. Viniar was also head of the operations, technology, finance, and services division. He was a member of the management, firmwide risk, finance, firmwide capital, and principal investment committees. From 1998 until 1999, Viniar was deputy CFO. He assumed responsibility for the firm's financing activities in the treasury department in 1992 and for the controllers department in 1994. Before that, he was a member of the structured finance department of the investment banking division. He joined Goldman's investment banking area in 1980 and became a partner in 1992. He graduated from Union College, where he played basketball, and from Harvard Business School.

Selected Former Partners Mentioned

Rob Kaplan served as vice chairman of Goldman, with oversight responsibility for the investment banking and investment management divisions. He was also a member of the firm's management committee and served as co-chairman of the firm's partnership committee and chairman of the Goldman Sachs Pine Street Leadership

Development Initiative. During his career at the firm, Kaplan served in various other capacities, including global co-head of the investment banking division (1999–2002), head of the corporate finance department (1994–1999), and head of Asia-Pacific investment banking (1990–1994). He became a partner in 1990. Since 2005, Kaplan has taught at Harvard Business School. Kaplan graduated from the University of Kansas and Harvard Business School. He is the author of *What to Ask the Person in the Mirror: Critical Questions for Becoming a More Effective Leader and Reaching Your Potential* (2011) and *What You're Really Meant to Do: A Road Map for Reaching Your Unique Potential* (2013).

John Thain was president and COO of Goldman from 1999 to 2005. He was co-president and co-COO with John Thornton from 1999 to 2003. During his Goldman career, Thain also served as chief financial officer and head of operations, technology, and finance. He was co-head of European operations from 1995 to 1997 and was head of the mortgage group from 1985 to 1990. After leaving Goldman, Thain served as chairman and CEO of the New York Stock Exchange and then Merrill Lynch, before it merged with Bank of America. Currently, he is chairman and CEO of CIT Group. He was considered a protégé of Corzine's, although the relationship suffered when Thain supported Paulson's taking over the firm. Thain and John Thornton were widely expected to co-run Goldman. Thain graduated from MIT and Harvard Business School.

John Thornton served as co-president and co-COO of Goldman from 1999 to 2003. He retired in 2003 after more than twenty years at the firm. Thornton served as co-CEO of Goldman Sachs International, Goldman's business in Europe, the Middle East, and Africa. From 1998 to 1999, he held oversight responsibility for international operations. From 1995 to 1997, he served as a co-CEO for European operations and was chairman of Goldman Asia from 1996 to 1998. Thornton joined Goldman in 1980 and was elected partner in 1988. He set up Goldman's M&A department in London in the early 1980s. He imported hard-nosed US investment banking techniques into what had been a conservative and traditional M&A

environment in London. Thornton helped drive Goldman's growth into Europe and Asia and was the first non-Chinese full professor at Tsinghua since the Communist revolution. He is chairman of the board of the Brookings Institution and co-chairman of Barrick Gold. Thornton graduated from Harvard College, where he played tennis. He holds bachelor's and master's degrees in jurisprudence from Oxford University and a master's degree in public and private management from the Yale School of Management.

Goldman Timeline
of Selected Events

Following is a timeline summarizing selected key events for Goldman and its industry. Although the timeline covers events starting in 1869, the book starts its analysis from 1979, when the business principles were codified. The timeline goes through most of 2012. In order to help demonstrate that pressures started impacting the firm before its IPO in 1999 and before Blankfein took over as CEO, the events are categorized in terms of the analytical framework used for the analysis in the book.[1]

As discussed in appendix B, the framework categorizes four main pressures (or responses to those pressures) that impact an organization: organizational (O), regulatory (R), technological (T), and competitive (C). Although many events may apply or occur in response to multiple pressures, for simplicity in this timeline I use "O," "R," "T," or "C" to indicate what I believe was the primary set of factors at work. It is challenging to precisely characterize each event. Also, I may inadvertently have missed selected events.

1869: Marcus Goldman moves to New York and starts selling promissory notes (early commercial paper) from a one-room office on Pine Street.

1882: Samuel Sachs, Goldman's son-in-law, joins the business.

1885: The firm becomes a general partnership, Goldman Sachs & Company.

1896: The company joins the New York Stock Exchange.

1900: Goldman's first branch office opens in Chicago.

1904: The firm's capital reaches $1 million.

1906: Goldman co-manages its first IPO for one of its clients, United Cigar Manufacturers. The same year, Goldman handles the initial equity sales for Sears, Roebuck, pioneering the IPO business.

1907: Walter Sachs (grandson of Marcus Goldman) joins the firm as a commercial paper salesman. Sidney Weinberg is hired as assistant janitor.

1909: Marcus Goldman dies, and Henry Goldman leads the firm.

1910: Goldman now has a few partners, all members of the Goldman or Sachs families.

1917: Henry Goldman's pro-German stance causes a rift between the Goldman and Sachs families. Henry Goldman retires and withdraws his capital. Sidney Weinberg leaves to serve in the US Navy during World War I.

1920: Sidney Weinberg returns to Goldman as a bond trader.

1925: Weinberg buys a seat on the NYSE with money from his own earnings, not from trading.

1927: Weinberg becomes only the second partner from outside the Goldman and Sachs families.

1929: Waddill Catchings, who joined the firm eleven years earlier to head up underwriting, holds the largest single percentage in the partnership and takes over leadership. He pushes for the creation of Goldman Sachs Trading Corporation, a collection of highly leveraged investment trusts. When the stock market collapses, Goldman Sachs Trading Corporation suffers heavy losses, and Goldman's reputation is severely damaged.

1930: After devastating trading losses, Catchings is forced to resign. The Sachs brothers name Sidney Weinberg senior partner. Weinberg takes over leadership of Goldman and builds its investment banking operation. The Sachs family covers the partners' losses. Goldman will not reenter the asset management business again for nearly forty years.

1933: Weinberg organizes the Business and Advisory Council for President Franklin D. Roosevelt, creating a bridge between business and government during the New Deal. Congress passes the Securities Act of 1933, creating the Securities and Exchange Commission. The Banking Act of 1933, known as the Glass–Steagall Act, is passed, prohibiting commercial banks from engaging in investment activities.

1937: Sidney Weinberg's percentage of the partnership has tripled since 1927 and stands at 30 percent.

1942: Weinberg takes a leave from the firm and enters government service as assistant to the chairman of the War Production Board, forming relationships with America's top executives, many of whom will later become Goldman clients.

1945: At the end of the war, Weinberg resigns from government service.

1947: John C. Whitehead joins Goldman from Harvard Business School.

1948: The Justice Department files an antitrust suit (*U.S. v. Morgan* [Stanley] *et al.*) against nineteen investment banking firms. Goldman had only 1.4 percent of the underwriting market and was last on the list of defendants. Goldman would not be included in a 1950 list of the top seventeen underwriters. Sixty years later, of the nineteen firms named in the suit, only Goldman and Morgan Stanley remain as independent firms.

1950: John L. Weinberg, Sidney's son, joins Goldman. A list of the top seventeen underwriters does not include Goldman.

1956: Goldman leads the underwriting of Ford Motor Co.'s IPO, building the firm's reputation in investment banking. Whitehead and John L. Weinberg become partners. Goldman's capital stands at $10 million.

1969: Upon retiring, banking-oriented Sidney Weinberg has reservations about leaving Gus Levy, a trader, as senior partner, so he introduces an eight-man management committee with seven older banking partners to supervise Levy. Sidney Weinberg dies. Gus Levy, now senior partner, takes charge of Goldman and rebuilds its trading business. Because of the potential for direct conflicts with its large block-trading clients and because of the Goldman Sachs Trading Corporation debacle, Goldman steers clear of asset management until Gus Levy creates the investment management services (IMS) unit.

1970: The NYSE amends its rules to admit publicly traded members, prompting investment banks to consider abandoning their partnership structures and offering shares for sale to the public.

Credit ratings are created for every issuer of commercial paper after the Penn Central Transportation Company goes bankrupt with more than $80 million in commercial paper outstanding, much of it issued by Goldman. The ensuing litigation threatens the firm's existence. Goldman opens its first international office in London.

1971: Merrill Lynch goes public.

1972: Goldman starts a private wealth division and a fixed income division. Goldman pioneers a "white knight" strategy, defending Electric Storage Battery against a hostile take-over bid from International Nickel and Goldman rival Morgan Stanley.

1973: Fischer Black and Myron Scholes first describe their Black-Scholes model to price options.

1975: May 1 marks the end of fixed trading commissions in the stock market, forcing investment banks to compete in negotiations over transaction fees.

1976: After Gus Levy's death, John L. Weinberg (Sidney's son) and John Whitehead take over as senior partners and continue to build Goldman's investment banking business. This is the beginning of Goldman's tradition of having co-heads, setting a Wall Street precedent. The firm sets a record for pre-tax profits of $40 million.

1979: John Whitehead drafts a set of business principles that codifies Goldman's core values, setting a Wall Street precedent (O).

1980: Goldman's capital stands at $200 million.

1981: Salomon Brothers goes public (C). Goldman diversifies by absorbing the commodities trading company J. Aron & Co. Lloyd Blankfein, who worked at J. Aron before the merger, joins Goldman. J. Aron becomes Goldman's currency and commodities trading division (C). In 1997, it is merged with the fixed income division.

1982: Goldman makes its first international acquisition, London-based First Dallas, Ltd., later renamed Goldman, Sachs, Ltd (C). Stocks in the late 1970s and early 1980s are in a bear market. The Dow Jones Industrial Average bottoms at 777 on August 12, 1982. But a steady decline in interest rates—with yields on thirteen-week treasuries having eased to 8.6 percent from nearly 13 percent in the previous month and a half—finally gets stock moving. On August 17, the Dow leaps a then-record 38.81, or 4.9 percent, to 831.24, and the equity market begins a long bull run, with some bumps. Massive wealth creation over the course of the next twenty-five years, the likes of which the United States and the world had never seen, would follow.

1983: The firm's capital has grown to $750 million, some $500 million from the active partners themselves. In 1983, John L. Thornton co-founds Goldman's European M & A business in London (O).

1984: Continental Illinois National Bank and Trust becomes the largest-ever bank failure in US history. Continental was at one time the seventh-largest bank in the United States as measured by deposits, with approximately $40 billion in assets. Because of the size of Continental Illinois, regulators are not willing to let it fail (R). The term "too big to fail" becomes popularized.

1985: Bear Stearns goes public (C). Whitehead leaves Goldman after thirty-eight years and later becomes deputy secretary of state to George Schultz, serving until 1989 (O). Steve Friedman, a former M&A banker, and Bob Rubin, a former equities proprietary trader, co-head Goldman's fixed income division (O).

1986: Goldman's capital has grown to $1 billion, almost entirely through retained earnings. Morgan Stanley, Goldman's primary competitor, goes public (C). Goldman's growing trading business is capital intensive (C). The management committee conducts a study, led by Steve Friedman and Bob Rubin, and recommends taking Goldman public (O, C). John L. Weinberg and Jimmy Weinberg do not support the idea, and it is not brought to a vote (O). To raise capital, Goldman accepts a $500 million private equity investment from Sumitomo Bank, as a silent partner, in exchange for 12.5 percent of Goldman's annual profits and appreciation in equity value (O, C). One of Goldman's largest partner classes is voted in (twice as large as any previous class), including three partners from other firms who have never worked at Goldman, as well as Goldman's first female partner and first African American partner (O, C). Goldman takes Microsoft public and joins the London and Tokyo stock exchanges (C).

1987: In October, the Dow Jones Industrial Average drops 508 points, a stunning 22.6 percent, on "Black Monday," raising fears that the US economy is headed for a severe recession. The Federal Reserve acts quickly to cut interest rates and pump cash into the banking system, helping end the threat. The October market crash, in part, causes Goldman to reduce overhead; several hundred employees are laid off by the end of the decade (O). It is the first time in recent memory that Goldman lays people off. Robert Freeman, Goldman's head of arbitrage, receives a prison sentence for insider trading. As a result of the crash, Value at Risk models receive more emphasis (R, T, O). Wall Street begins to increasingly focus on hiring academically trained and quantitatively oriented traders and risk managers and increase spending on financial innovation (T, O).

1988: Leon Cooperman, head of equity research, assumes responsibilities for building the investment management business, and a new division is launched: Goldman Sachs asset management (GSAM) (O, C). Hundreds of savings and loans (S & Ls) are shut down, at a total cost of more than the reserves in the federal insurance fund. US taxpayers make up the difference.

1989: As an alternative to going public to raise capital, Goldman forms a ten-year consortium with seven insurance companies, bringing in $225 million in new capital to expand Goldman's merchant-banking capabilities. The insurance companies receive a fixed return on their investment but do not share in profits or management and have no voting rights (O, C). The firm also creates a holding company, Goldman Sachs Group (technically not subject to NYSE capital requirements), and spins off several subsidiaries (R, C). The Berlin wall falls, igniting global expansion for American businesses (C, O).

1990: Bob Rubin and Steve Friedman take charge as co-senior partners and co-chairs of the management committee, expanding global operations and seeking other opportunities for growth, including proprietary trading (O, C). They make partners' compensation more dependent on performance than on tenure, and they initiate the firm's first lateral hiring initiatives (O, C). High-yield bond investors threaten to boycott Goldman after accusations that GSAM and Goldman improperly used proprietary information gained in its underwriting role (O, C); Cooperman is forced to change GSAM's strategy to focus on mutual fund sales to individual investors rather than institutional clients. Drexel Burnham Lambert, once the fifth-largest US investment bank, is forced into bankruptcy in February.

1991: Goldman's management committee again studies the option of going public but drops the idea before the proposal can be put before the partnership (C, O). Warren Buffett helps save Salomon Brothers from bankruptcy (C). Goldman shuts down debt investing fund Water Street (O). Goldman creates GSCI, a benchmark for investment performance in the commodities markets (T).

1992: Bob Rubin leaves Goldman to become assistant to the president on economic policy (O). The move adds to the

Goldman mystique but is unusual in that Rubin's is one of the shortest tenures as senior partner. A Hawaiian educational trust, the Kamehameha Schools/Bishop Estate, invests $250 million in Goldman and receives a stake of more than 5 percent in the firm. It is a passive investment; the trust has no voting privileges but will participate in Goldman's profits and losses. In an effort to further link pay to performance, and to create a new source of developmental feedback, Goldman institutes 360-degree performance reviews (meaning that even junior staff reviews senior staff). New offices are opened in Frankfurt, Milan, and Seoul (O, C).

1993: Goldman is one of the most profitable firms in the world with record profits and experiences rapid growth and global expansion. A federal appeals court rules against Goldman and prohibits investment banking firms from advising corporate clients with which they had a business relationship in bankruptcy proceedings (R, O). This limits money-making opportunities for Goldman and other investment banks (R). Goldman conducts another formal study of the possibility of taking the firm public (O). There are now approximately 160 partners. Goldman advises business tycoon Li Ka-shing and his family in selling a majority stake to Rupert Murdoch's News Corp (C, O). Goldman's involvement in such a high-profile deal with two major business tycoons in Asia puts Goldman on the map in Asia. It also highlights Goldman's strategy of focusing on very important people. Credit derivatives are pioneered at J.P. Morgan (C, T). By 1996, credit derivatives would be a $40 billion market and by 2008 it would be measured in the trillions of dollars.

1994: Lehman Brothers goes public (C). Goldman suffers large losses in the bond market as interest rates rise (C, O). Goldman settles suits brought by a number of pension funds related to its involvement with media mogul Robert Maxwell after it was alleged that Maxwell stole money from Maxwell company pension plans by hiring Goldman to broker a trade between various Maxwell-controlled entities. Goldman pays out $253 million in settlements, allocated to the people who were general partners in Goldman between 1989 and 1991. A significant number of partners leave the firm (many times more than normal) to protect their capital, taking their capital with them (C, O). Steve Friedman, senior partner for only four years, retires (O). Many of the partners who stay at the firm have some resentment toward those who left, and they question the culture. Goldman names 58 new general partners (one and a half times as many as usual), the firm's largest partner class ever (O, C). The unprecedented amount of change at the partnership level impacts the partnership network. One M&A banker who is elected partner turns down the opportunity, something exceptional in the history of the firm (O). In a power struggle after Steve Friedman's announced retirement, Jon Corzine (from trading) becomes sole senior partner, never having rotated through other areas such as investment banking (O). Hank Paulson is named COO (O), never having co-headed a division with Corzine (O). Some partners are convinced, in part, to stay because of the possibility of an IPO (O). The partners who stay form a unique bond, supporting each other through tough times, determined to make Goldman a success, but they also see firsthand the risks of a private partnership. Goldman starts implementing risk management systems (T). Corzine and Paulson immediately reduce employee head count and costs by slashing pay and bonuses. Some people still remember the large layoffs in the late 1980s, affecting how employees think about the firm as a place to work, and it was now happening so soon again (O, C). Despite issues, the firm is still ranked first in US and foreign common stock offerings, IPOs, worldwide completed mergers and acquisitions, investment-grade debt, and US equity research. J.P. Morgan pioneers the concept of the modern credit default swap, which will play a major role in the credit crisis. Eric Mindich, who ran the equities arbitrage department that invested the firm's own capital, becomes, at age twenty-seven, the youngest partner in the firm's history, signaling the importance of proprietary trading (O, C). Restrictions are put on the withdrawal of partners' capital (O). Goldman opens a Beijing office (O).

1995: Corzine replaces the twelve-member management committee with a six-member executive committee (O). Goldman opens offices in Shanghai and Mexico City and creates joint ventures in India and Indonesia (O, C). Treasury provides aid to Mexico during the peso crisis, an action that helps save Lehman Brothers, which had made a big, mistaken bet without hedging. Global Alpha, one of the earliest "quant vehicles" was founded in GSAM and would spawn a new wave of quant funds (C, T).

1996: Goldman is back on track and profits are restored to 1993 levels. Corzine and Paulson push for business diversification, increasing international, investing, and asset management business. There are media rumors of a Goldman IPO. There is a push for a partnership vote on an IPO, but it is withdrawn in the face of overwhelming opposition. An independent compensation firm concludes that the top five to ten partners would increase their compensation if Goldman were a public company but that most would be worse off. Also discussed were issues such as impact to culture, moral obligations to earlier and future generations, and the attractiveness of the business model. The most commonly stated reason for the opposition is the potential unknown impact on Goldman's culture in losing the partnership structure. A new class of "junior partners" is created (called "partnership extension") in an effort to prevent further defections and retirements. Partners as well as nonpartners are now referred to as "managing directors," although internally, partners are known as "partner managing directors" (PMDs) and nonpartner managing directors are referred to as "MD-lites." To the outside world, it is difficult to distinguish who is a partner and who is not. The title of managing director (versus partner) is the same at competitors like Morgan Stanley (C, O). Goldman also adopts a limited liability structure, limiting personal risk (R). Goldman helps take Yahoo! public, triggering the internet IPO boom. Goldman experiments with e-mail (C).

1997: Paulson says Goldman's policy of not advising on hostile takeovers is no longer in the firm's interest, but Corzine resists any change that might damage Goldman's image. They compromise on an experiment with a test case outside the United States, and Goldman advises Krupp in a successful hostile take-over of Thyssen (O, C). J.P. Morgan develops a proprietary product that helps banks clean up their balance sheets using credit default swaps—the first synthetic collateralized debt obligations (CDOs) (T, C). Morgan Stanley merges with Dean Witter Reynolds, the financial services business of Sears that serves retail clients (C). The acquisition extends Morgan Stanley's ability to sell stock offerings and makes Morgan Stanley larger. Travelers Group, run by Sandy Weill, purchases Salomon Brothers, a major bond dealer and investment bank, for $9 billion (C). Bankers Trust purchases Alex Brown for $2.1 billion (C). The Asian debt crisis presents a large opportunity for Goldman to invest its own capital in the region (O, C). Goldman's GSAM acquires Commodities Corporation (CC) for an undisclosed amount, estimated to be more than $100 million (C). At the time of its acquisition, CC had approximately $2 billion in assets under management, primarily as a fund of hedge funds: a fund investing in a variety of hedge funds to diversify risk. It was part of GSAM's continued push into higher-margin, more-sophisticated products for its clients. The firm merges J. Aron with fixed income to create the division known as FICC, to be run by Blankfein (O, C).

1998: Long-Term Capital Management (LTCM), a hedge fund, is about to fail. Wall Street fears that LTCM is so big that its failure would cause a chain reaction in numerous markets, causing significant losses throughout the financial system. Goldman, AIG, and Berkshire Hathaway offer to buy out the fund's partners for $250 million, to inject $3.75 billion, and to operate LTCM within Goldman's own trading division. Many of the partners worry about the risk they would assume (O). A deal is not worked out, and the Federal Reserve Bank of New York organizes a bailout (R). The Goldman executive committee discovers that Corzine has been holding talks with the CEO of Mellon Bank about merging the firms. In what some describe as a coup d'etat, Corzine is told to focus on and leave after an IPO of the firm (O). After being made co-CEO, Paulson supports the IPO (some believe it was a quid pro quo). After significant debate and letters from both John Weinberg and John Whitehead advising against it, Goldman decides to go public (C, O, R). Thain and Thornton are allegedly promised to become co-CEOs in two years for supporting Paulson. The IPO, originally planned for September, is postponed because of instability in the global markets. The Russian financial crisis begins. Deutsche Bank agrees to purchase Bankers Trust for $10.1 billion (C), signaling that foreign competition is coming to the United States. Citicorp and Travelers Group merge, creating a $140 billion firm with assets of almost $700 billion (C). The deal enables Travelers to market mutual funds and insurance to Citicorp's retail customers while giving the banking divisions access to an expanded client base of investors and insurance buyers. The remaining provisions of the Glass–Steagall Act—enacted following the Great Depression—forbid banks to merge with insurance underwriters, and this means that Citigroup has two to five years to divest any prohibited assets. However, Weill states at the time of the merger that he believes that the legislation will change over time. (On CNBC's "Squawk Box" in July 2012,

Weill calls for a return of the Glass–Steagall Act.) Under pressure from competitors taking companies public that have no revenues or profits, Goldman starts to take companies like eToys and NetZero public, which have limited operating history and little to no profits (O, C).

1999: In January, Jon Corzine leaves Goldman to run for US Senate from New Jersey, leaving Paulson as sole chairman and CEO (O). Goldman advises on its first hostile deal in North America (O). Goldman adds a new business principle—most significantly, a commitment to provide superior returns to shareholders (C, O). In May, Goldman goes public and changes its name to The Goldman Sachs Group, Inc. The firm is valued at $33 billion at the time of the IPO. The IPO is one of the largest events in the firm's history. The decision to go public was debated for decades. In the end, Goldman offers only a small portion of the company to the public, with some 48 percent still held by the partners, 22 percent of the company held by nonpartner employees, and 18 percent held by retired Goldman partners and two longtime investors: Bank Ltd. and Hawaii's Kamehameha Activities Association (the investing arm of Kamehameha Schools). This leaves approximately 12 percent of Goldman held by the public. In November, portions of the Glass–Steagall Act of 1933 (prohibiting a bank holding company from owning other financial companies) are repealed, opening the door to financial services conglomerates offering a mix of commercial banking, investment banking, insurance underwriting, and brokerage (R). Even with Goldman's success, it is still valued less than many internet or dot-com companies. Some of the best and brightest are now more interested in working at a technology company than at Goldman (C). Other firms, such as Donaldson, Lufkin & Jenrette, start to offer significantly higher compensation than Goldman, especially at the entry-level positions (C). Goldman acquires Hull Trading Company, a leading technology-driven algorithmic trading firm and electronic market maker, for $531 million (C, T). Technology-driven trading is starting to dominate (T). In November, Goldman establishes the Pine Street Leadership Development Initiative, in part, to help socialize larger numbers of managers (O). The Euro becomes an accounting currency and was scheduled to enter circulation in 2002, helping to accelerate pan-European banking consolidation.

2000: The Commodity Futures Modernization Act determines that credit default swaps are neither futures nor securities and therefore are not subject to regulation by the Securities and Exchange Commission or the Commodities Futures Trading Commission (CFTC) (R, T). The CFTC changes a rule called Regulation 1.25 to permit futures brokers to take money from their customers' accounts and invest it in an expanded number of approved securities (some people think this contributed to the issues related to MF Global) (R). The NASDAQ Composite, reflecting the dot-com bubble, hits an all time high. Credit Suisse acquires Donaldson, Lufkin & Jenrette for $11.5 billion (C). Goldman purchases Spear, Leeds & Kellogg, one of the largest specialist firms on the New York Stock Exchange, for $6.3 billion, strengthening Goldman's ability to market directly to the growing ranks of retail investors and to gain market information (C, T). Selected Spear, Leeds & Kellogg partners became Goldman PMDs.

2001: Goldman disbands its M&A department and places its M&A bankers in groups focused on specific industries (C, O, T). Goldman is the top global M&A adviser and underwriter of all IPOs and common stock offerings. The September 11 terrorist attacks have significant economic impacts. The Fed reduced the federal funds rate to 1 percent from 2001 to 2002, leading to a surge in home sales and refinancing. Goldman issues a report on the emerging BRIC (Brazil, Russia, India, and China) economies.

2002: In a faltering economy, with the high degree of consolidation of banks after the repeal of the Glass–Steagall Act, there is media speculation that Goldman could be forced into a merger to remain viable against large competing banks having assets double or triple those of Goldman. Paulson announces Goldman's strategy for becoming the leading global investment bank, securities, and investment management firm (C). Goldman gives special stock offerings to executives in twenty-one companies that it took public, including Yahoo! cofounder Jerry Yang, Tyco's Dennis Kozlowski, and Enron's Ken Lay, to win new investment banking business. Goldman pays $110 million to settle an investigation by New York state regulators into manipulations (C, R). The Sarbanes–Oxley Act is signed into law, setting specific reporting and auditing requirements intended to protect investors. It specifically establishes tight accountability standards for the boards of US public companies, management companies, and public accounting firms (R). IPO volume goes down, creating pressure for banks to find other ways to meet earnings growth and return on equity targets. Various investment banks offer complex financial products with which European governments can push part of their liabilities into the future (C). Greece's debt managers agree to a transaction with Goldman. The structure disguises the debt so that it does not show up in the Greek debt statistics for the euro convergence criteria.

2003: In January 2003, Paulson is criticized for saying that about 15 percent to 20 percent of Goldman employees add 80 percent of the value and that even significant staff cuts would leave the firm well positioned for the upturn (O). He later issues an apology to all of the company's employees via voicemail. The SEC charges Goldman with conflicts of interest among its research analysts, charges that the firm eventually settles for $110 million. Goldman pays $9 million in sanctions to settle a separate SEC case involving allegations that it failed to maintain policies to prevent the firm from misusing material, nonpublic information obtained from outside consultants about US Treasury thirty-year bonds.

A former Goldman economist pleads guilty to insider trading. In October, in a move to eliminate a potential source of criticism and conflicts of interest, Goldman tells its MDs that they may no longer serve on the boards of public companies.

2004: The alternatives (hedge fund and private equity) boom begins after investors see that alternatives performed well during the bear market and dot-com bust (C). Goldman proprietary traders begin leaving and forming their own firms. The proliferation of hedge funds and private equity firms makes it difficult to recruit and retain the best and brightest. This trend is aggravated by the end of the five-year vesting period for those given restricted stock in the IPO. Now employees can sell all their IPO stock. The stock vested in years 3, 4, and 5 after the IPO, 33 percent each year. At the request of Goldman and other major Wall Street firms, the SEC agrees to release them from the net capital rule, which required that investment firms hold a certain amount of capital to limit their leverage and provide a cushion of liquid assets to ensure payment of the firm's obligations to its clients (R). The SEC establishes a risk management office to monitor the industry for signs of potential problems, but it is soon dismantled (R). Goldman settles with the SEC for $10 million over charges it improperly promoted a stock sale involving PetroChina (R).

2005: Lloyd Blankfein argues that principal investing represents a momentous strategic opportunity for Goldman (C). Goldman represents both sides in the $9 billion merger between the NYSE and Archipelago holdings, earning a $100 million fee. Goldman promotes the person responsible for business selection and conflict clearance to the management committee. No other firm has someone this senior serving in this kind of position.

The SEC fines Goldman $40 million for allegedly trying to pump up the prices of IPOs. Goldman pays the fine without admitting or denying wrongdoing. Peter Weinberg, son of Jimmy Weinberg and nephew of John L. Weinberg, leaves Goldman and cofounds a competing firm the next year. In a push to pool knowledge across asset classes, Goldman merges its corporate bond and credit area with its equity counterparts (O). Goldman reportedly changes its compensation policy in sales and trading areas to be more quantitative and transparent (O, C).

2006: Invited, along with four other investment banks, to make a pitch to defend BAA against a possible take-over, Goldman proposes buying a chunk of BAA itself, in what sounds to BAA like another take-over bid. After Goldman pursues a few other unsolicited bids, it receives a "spank from Hank," as it is dubbed in the press—a rebuke from Paulson reminding bankers that they should not be pursuing unsolicited or unfriendly bids for listed companies, acknowledging the thin line between an unsolicited approach and a hostile take-over (O, C). Paulson leaves to become secretary of the Treasury in the Bush administration (O). Blankfein becomes Goldman's chairman and CEO. Goldman is the only Wall Street firm to make *Fortune*'s list of America's most admired companies (ranking eighteenth). Two former Goldman employees are charged with having run an international insider trading ring during their years at Goldman. Both men are eventually convicted and jailed. Goldman's Alternative Mortgage Products (GSAMP), its mortgage bond division, issues eighty-three home-loan-backed bonds, valued at $44.5 billion. The *Washington Post* states that one of Goldman's 2006 mortgage deals, the GSAMP Trust 2006-S3, may actually be "the worst deal . . . floated by a top-tier firm."[2] (One in every six of the 8,274 mortgages bundled in GSAMP Trust 2006-S3 would be in default eighteen months later. People who bought the S3 bonds either had to take a 100 percent loss or sell it at a heavy discount.)

In December, anticipating a housing crisis, Goldman takes a negative stance on the mortgage market but does not announce this publicly. Head of the Special Situations proprietary trading area in FICC, who reportedly was paid a $70 million bonus (larger than the CEO's reported $53 million), leaves Goldman —supposedly because he was frustrated by the bureaucracy at Goldman and because the group was not compensated like a hedge fund or private equity firm for the reported $4 billion in profits the group generated (O). John L. Weinberg passes away.

2007: The credit and housing booms help Goldman post a profit of $11.6 billion on $45.99 billion in revenues, setting a firm record. Goldman's 31.6 percent return on equity is exceptional on Wall Street. The top five Goldman executives split $322 million in compensation, a Wall Street record. An article reports that Goldman is hedging its mortgage exposure by building short positions to offset "long" positions elsewhere in the bank and thereby profit from the collapse in subprime mortgage bonds in the summer.[3] Media reports ask how Goldman fared so well in avoiding the mistakes made by other Wall Street firms that lost money from mortgages.

It is rumored that Goldman is not quite as careful with its clients' money as with its own; GSAM's Global Alpha hedge fund, which at one time had more than $10 billion in assets from clients, tumbles significantly, as do similar hedge funds. Half of the members of the Principal Strategies proprietary trading team in the equities division create a fund called GSIP in GSAM. Blackstone, an alternative asset manager and financial advisory firm, goes public, adding to the pressure for talent. Other alternative asset managers follow (C). A Goldman subsidiary settles with the SEC for $2 million over allegations that faulty oversight allowed customers to make illegal trades (R).

2008: Goldman becomes a bank holding company, giving it greater government protection as the nation's financial crisis worsens. (Morgan Stanley, the only other remaining independent investment bank, takes the same step.) Just before Thanksgiving, Goldman stock reaches an all-time low of $47.41 per share after trading at about $165 per share in early September. The Federal Reserve Bank of New York agrees to pay Goldman 100 cents on the dollar for its trading position with American International Group (AIG). Warren Buffet invests $5 billion in Goldman, roughly a 10 percent stake, an action that gives a vote of confidence in the firm. Through the Troubled Asset Relief Program (TARP), the US government buys $10 billion in preferred shares from Goldman. Goldman is questioned about paying 953 employees bonuses over $1 million each after taking TARP funds. CEO Lloyd Blankfein and six other senior executives opted to forgo bonuses. It is later reported that Goldman was the company from which Obama raised the most money in 2008 and that its CEO Lloyd Blankfein had visited the White House ten times.

2009: A Senate panel, led by Senator Carl Levin (D.-Mich.) and Senator Tom Coburn (R.-Okla.), convenes under the auspices of the Permanent Subcommittee on Investigations to investigate the causes of the credit crisis. The investigation will continue for the next two years. By October, Goldman's stock price has more than fully recovered, selling at about $194 per share. In June 2009, Goldman Sachs repaid the US Treasury's TARP investment, with 23% interest (in the form of $318 million preferred dividend payments and $1.418 billion in warrant redemptions). Blankfein sends letter to Financial Services Committee members of the US House of Representatives thanking the government for its extraordinary efforts and the taxpayers' patience; stating that it regrets that it participated in the market euphoria and didn't raise a responsible voice; and stating that it has obligations to the public interest. Lloyd Blankfein is named CEO of the Year by *Directorship* magazine. Matt Taibbi publishes a scathing article on Goldman in *Rolling Stone*, which includes the often-quoted "vampire squid" analogy.[4] A Goldman subsidiary settles with the SEC for $1.2 million over improper proprietary trading by employees. The SEC charges a former Goldman trader and his brother with insider trading based on information the trader obtained while at Goldman (R). The Massachusetts attorney general announces a $60 million settlement with Goldman over the alleged role the investment bank played in the subprime mortgage crisis (R). Goldman, among others, created a credit default swap index to cover the high risk of Greece's national debt. The firm is reported to have systematically helped the Greek government disguise the true facts concerning its national debt between 1998 and 2009.

2010: Goldman reports a record profit of $13.39 billion for 2009. The SEC charges Goldman with deception for selling clients mortgage securities secretly designed by a hedge fund being run by John Paulson. A number of civil lawsuits are filed against the firm. Blankfein and other Goldman employees are called to testify before the Levin–Coburn panel about the financial crisis. Rumors about Goldman's behavior abound. Warren Buffet, Goldman's largest individual shareholder, and other major clients defend Goldman's ethical character and behavior. The Dodd–Frank Wall Street Reform and Consumer Protection Act is signed, implementing broad changes to the regulation of the US financial system. After several months of studying Goldman's business standards and practices, the internal business standards committee issues its report, calling for a recommitment to the firm's business principles. Goldman agrees to pay $553 million, the largest fine ever paid to the SEC, to settle fraud claims related to disclosure about the design of the mortgage security called Abacus 2007-AC1. Fabrice Tourre, an employee at Goldman, who is also charged, is not included in the settlement and categorically denies the charges against him, seeking dismissal of the case. Tourre and Goldman acknowledge that the marketing for the Abacus deal contained incomplete information and that it was a mistake not to inform investors that a prominent hedge fund manager had helped design the deal. Tourre says that he and Goldman did not have a duty to give investors details that the SEC says they should have disclosed and that the SEC did not show that he acted with the intention of defrauding investors. Goldman starts to shut down several proprietary trading groups, and many proprietary traders begin to leave as the SEC fines Goldman $225,000 for violating a rule aimed at regulating short selling (R). The Financial Industry Regulatory Authority (FINRA) says it is fining Goldman $650,000 for failing to disclose that the government was investigating two of its brokers. One of the brokers was Goldman vice president Fabrice Tourre. FINRA says Goldman did not have the proper procedures in place to make sure that this disclosure was made (R).

2011: In March, former Goldman board member Rajat Gupta is charged by the SEC with insider trading for passing information to the hedge fund Galleon Group that he learned in his capacity as a board member. Six months later he is arrested on criminal charges, soon after the SEC charges another Goldman employee with insider trading. In April, Senator Carl Levin (D.-Mich.) releases the 650-page report of the Senate investigation into the credit crisis (R). It concludes that Goldman misled clients and Congress about the collateralized debt obligations that helped cause the financial crisis. The report urges regulators to identify any violations of law in the activities of Goldman leading up to the financial crisis. The report asserts that conflicts of interest led Goldman to place its financial interests before those of its clients. The report is the result of a two-year probe by the Permanent Subcommittee on Investigations. In May, the report is referred to the Department of Justice and the SEC. In early June, Goldman begins fighting back against the Senate report, emphasizing inconsistencies in it. Blankfein hires a high-profile Washington defense attorney to represent him personally as the Department of Justice continues to investigate the bank (O). Goldman is the top-ranked M&A adviser worldwide based on total value of deals announced, according to Thomson Reuters.[5] KKR, a private equity firm, starts to get into the capital markets and lending businesses, competing with the investment banks (C). The SEC charges a Goldman employee and his father with insider trading based on information the employee gained in his position at Goldman (R). Goldman pays state regulators in Massachusetts a $10 million fine to resolve the allegations of "research huddles" (R).

2012: The SEC notifies Goldman that it may face charges related to mortgage-backed securities. In February, the board agrees to appoint an independent board member as lead director to avoid a shareholder vote on splitting Blankfein's chairman and CEO roles. As a reaction, the American Federation of State, County & Municipal Employees Pension Fund withdraws its shareholder resolution for investors to vote on at the annual shareholder meeting. Greg Smith, a London-based Goldman employee, delivers his resignation in a *New York Times* op-ed piece.[6] He attributes his resignation to the negative changes in Goldman's culture in the past decade or so, decrying the lack of focus on client interests. The op-ed sparks a flurry of responses in the media (O). The Volcker Rule, a section of the Dodd–Frank Wall Street Reform and Consumer Protection Act, is slated to go into effect in August (R). It mandates proprietary trading restrictions, with the goal of preventing US banks from exposing customers to excessive risk through speculative investments. The rule would bar banks from trading for their own accounts and from market making and places limits on how much banks can invest in hedge funds and private equity funds. Within weeks of its approval, Goldman decides to shut down the principal strategies group, which managed about $11 billion. As of this writing, Goldman and other firms are lobbying to delay implementation of the Volcker Rule pending further revision. A Delaware judge rules in a suit brought by the shareholders of El Paso Energy Corporation contesting Kinder Morgan's purchase of the company and sharply criticizes Goldman for conflict of interest in advising El Paso, because Goldman owned 19 percent of Kinder Morgan and controlled two seats on Kinder Morgan's board (R). El Paso was aware that there was a conflict of interest but asked Goldman's advice anyway when Kinder Morgan launched its take-over attempt. A Goldman banker on the deal allegedly owned shares in one of the companies and did not disclose it. In response, Goldman launches a review of conflict management, and many competitors and law firms do the same. Goldman agrees to pay $22 million to settle civil charges arising from company procedures that created the risk that select clients would receive market-sensitive information, such as changes to Goldman's recommendation lists and its ratings of stocks (R). The SEC says that the settlement includes violations of the same law that was at issue in the 2003 Treasury bond settlement. Blackrock, the world's largest money manager, announces that it is setting up an electronic bond-trading platform that will allow it to make transactions directly with other investors and bypass investment banks (C). In August, the Justice Department announces that its investigation is closed and that it will not seek criminal charges against Goldman. Goldman eliminates most two-year contracts programs for most analysts hired out of college (C). CFO David Viniar announces that he will retire in January 2013. Goldman named 70 employees to its partnership, which are down from 110 in 2010 and 94 in 2008 (C, O). Around 14 percent of the new partners in 2012 are women (the highest percentage since at least 2006), and 59 percent are based in the Americas. The total partners represent 1.7 percent of the total employees.

Appendix H

Goldman's Culture and Governance Structure

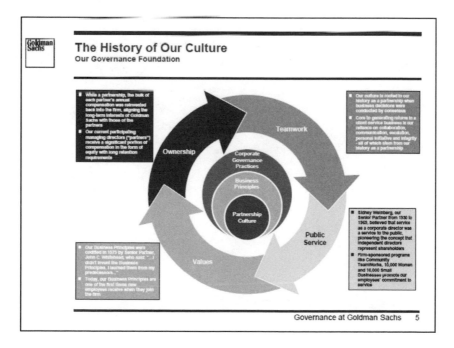

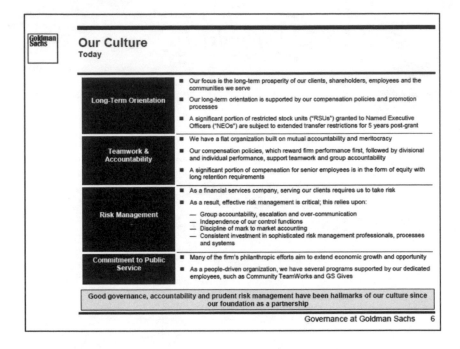

Our Culture
Today

Long-Term Orientation	■ Our focus is the long-term prosperity of our clients, shareholders, employees and the communities we serve ■ Our long-term orientation is supported by our compensation policies and promotion processes ■ A significant portion of restricted stock units ("RSUs") granted to Named Executive Officers ("NEOs") are subject to extended transfer restrictions for 5 years post-grant
Teamwork & Accountability	■ We have a flat organization built on mutual accountability and meritocracy ■ Our compensation policies, which reward firm performance first, followed by divisional and individual performance, support teamwork and group accountability ■ A significant portion of compensation for senior employees is in the form of equity with long retention requirements

Risk Management	■ As a financial services company, serving our clients requires us to take risk
	■ As a result, effective risk management is critical; this relies upon:
	  — Group accountability, escalation and over-communication
	  — Independence of our control functions
	  — Discipline of mark to market accounting
	  — Consistent investment in sophisticated risk management professionals, processes and systems

Commitment to Public Service	■ Many of the firm's philanthropic efforts aim to extend economic growth and opportunity ■ As a people-driven organization, we have several programs supported by our dedicated employees, such as Community TeamWorks and GS Gives

Good governance, accountability and prudent risk management have been hallmarks of our culture since our foundation as a partnership

Governance at Goldman Sachs   6

Notes

Prologue

1. C. D. Ellis, *The Partnership—The Making of Goldman Sachs* (New York: Penguin Press, 2008), 539.

2. See http://www.nytimes.com/2006/11/02/business/02welch.html and http://www.nysun.com/obituaries/remembering-john-weinberg-of-goldman-sachs/40311/.

Chapter 1

1. http://money.cnn.com/magazines/fortune/fortune_archive/2007/02/05/8399175/.

2. M. Taibbi, "The Great American Bubble Machine," *Rolling Stone*, April 5, 2009, http://www.rollingstone.com/politics/news/the-great-american-bubble-machine-20100405.

3. B. Montopoli, "Levin Repeatedly References 'Sh**ty Deal' at Goldman Hearing," *CBS News*, April 27, 2010, http://www.cbsnews.com/8 301-503544_162-20003526-503544.html.

4. B. Groysberg, S. Snook, and D. Lane, "The Pine Street Initiative at Goldman Sachs," Case 9-406-002 (Boston: Harvard Business School, 2006).

5. When one examines Goldman's history over time, there are examples of Goldman putting its interests ahead of clients, especially Penn Central Transportation Company in 1970 and Goldman Sachs Trading Corp in 1928. However, both of these examples are before Whitehead codified the business principles in the late 1970s. So we cannot be sure as to what Goldman said to its clients before that time. I could only analyze from the principles being written. See http://article.washingtonpost.com/2012-03-16/opinions/35447344_1_goldman-sachs-commercial-paper-younkers.

6. http://money.cnn.es/magazines/fortune/mostadmired/2010/.

7. http://money.cnn.com/galleries/2012/pf/jobs/1205/gallery.top-MBA-employers/index.html.

8. http://hereisthecity.com/2013/01/07/mergers-acquisitions-review-financial-advisors-worldwide-ranking/.

9. http://www.goldmansachs.com/investor-relations/financials/archived/other-information/ipo-prospectus-gs-pdf-file.pdf.

10. http://www.huffingtonpost.com/2009/06/02/government-sachs-goldmans_n_210561.html.

11. Ibid.

12. Organizational drift as I describe it is neither precisely Sidney Dekker's "cultural drift" nor Scott Snook's "practical drift" nor Diane Vaughan's "normalization of deviance." Although I draw upon many elements from each, there are not only slight

differences in their work but in mine as well. Also, rightly or wrongly, their concepts of drift are often associated with organizational "failure" when examining a specific event. Organizational drift does not necessarily always lead to a recognizable event of failure.

13. Paraphrased from http://www.ohsbok.org.au/downloads/chapters/5_Global_Safety.pdf.

14. Jack and Suzy Welch, "Goldman Sachs and a Culture-Killing Lesson Being Ignored," CNNMoney, April 12, 2012, http://management.fortune.cnn.com/2012/04/12/goldman-sachs-culture-values/.

15. Lisa Endlich, *Goldman Sachs—The Culture of Success* (New York: Simon & Schuster, 2000), 18.

16. There are some notable exceptions, including the scandal surrounding the bankruptcy of Penn Central, a client of Goldman's, in 1970.

17. See William Cohan, *Money and Power: How Goldman Sachs Came to Rule the World* (New York: Doubleday, 2012).

18. The number of partners more than doubled from 75 in 1991 to 190 in 1998. In 1999, when Goldman went public, it had 221 partners. Some additional facts: The number of total employees has grown from 3,600 people in 1984 to around 30,000, representing a growth rate of around 8 percent per year. Out of 221 total partners at the IPO, less than 10 to 15 percent of the pre-IPO partners remain today, making up less than 0.1 percent of current GS employees. Earnings before tax (EBT) has grown from $50 million in 1977 to over $6 billion in 2001, which is a compounded annual growth rate of about 15 percent—while staffing was growing at 8 percent, EBT was growing at almost two times that.

19. Goldman Sachs Group, "Letter to Shareholders," *Annual Report*, 1999, http://www.goldmansachs.com/investor-relations/financials/archived/annual-reports/attachments/1999-annual-report.pdf.

20. http://levin.senate.gov.

21. When Goldman faced criticism about reserving over $16 billion for its employee compensation, just a year after it received $10 billion from the government, Blankfein said at a conference: "We participated in things that were clearly wrong and have reason to regret . . . we apologize" (see http://dealbook.nytimes.com/2009/11/17/blankfein-sorry-for-goldmans-role-in-crisis/). Shortly after, the firm said it would spend $500 million to help small business growth (see http://business.time.com/2009/11/18/goldman-sachs-tries-to-make-ammends/). Blankfein also wrote a letter to Congress stating, "While we regret that we participated in the market euphoria and failed to raise a responsible voice, we are proud of the way our firm managed the risk it assumed . . . " (see http://dealbook.nytimes.com/2009/06/16/goldman-regrets-market-euphoria-that-led-to-crisis/.)

22. http://money.cnn.com/2010/04/27/news/companies/goldman_sachs_hearing/index.htm.

23. Goldman Sachs Group, *Report of the Business Standards Committee*, n.d., www.GoldmanSachs.com/Business Standards.

24. See http://www.nytimes.com/2010/05/19/business/19goldmanquestions.html?pagewanted=all&_r=0. The full question and the full answer are: "3. On the topic of putting clients first, Goldman's Mortgage Compliance Training Manual from 2007 notes that putting clients first is 'not always straightforward' because the firm is a market maker for a wide variety of companies, and because the firm's traders are in a position to gather and use information from a variety of sources— a mosaic constructed of all of the pieces of data received, is how the manual describes it. How does the firm, in practice, address this nuance? And what does Goldman mean by 'not always straightforward'?" Goldman's response: "We strive to provide all our sales and trading clients with excellent

execution. This manual recognizes that like many businesses, and certainly all our competitors, we serve multiple clients. In the process of serving multiple clients we receive information from multiple sources. This policy and the excerpt cited from the training manual simply reflects the fact that we have a diverse client base and gives our sales people and traders appropriate guidance."

25. Greg Smith, "Why I Am Leaving Goldman Sachs," *New York Times*, March 14, 2012, http://www.nytimes.com/2012/03/14/opinion/why-i-am-leaving-goldman-sachs. html?pagewanted=all.

26. Edgar Schein writes, "Where incongruities exist between espoused values and basic assumptions, scandal and myth explosion become primary mechanisms of culture change. Nothing will change until the consequences of the actual operating assumptions create a public and visible scandal that cannot be hidden, avoided, or denied . . . [I]t is usually discovered that the assumption by which the organization was operating had drifted toward what was practical to get the job done, and those practices came to be in varying degrees different from what the official ideology claimed." See Edgar Schein, *Organizational Culture and Leadership*, 4th ed. (San Francisco: Jossey-Bass, 2010), 291.

27. http://www.cnbc.com/id/49368892.

28. Securities and Exchange Commission, "Alternative Asset Management Acquisition Corp, EX-99.2," 2008, http://www.secinfo.com/dr66r.t1Fx.b.htm.

29. The Institutional Clients Group—which includes global banking, global markets, global transaction services, Citi Private Bank, Citi Capital Advisors, and Citi Investment Research & Analysis—had about $35 billion in revenues in 2010. ICG is essentially what was Salomon Brothers plus Citibank's corporate and investment banking businesses; it does not include Citigroup's credit cards or the retail branch network.

30. See http://www.sec.gov/Archives/edgar/data/1393816/000089109208003155/ e3206cx99-1.htm. Ultimately the deal did not close.

31. Endlich, *Goldman Sachs*, 18.

32. This and other Levitt quotations in this paragraph are from C. Harper and E. Schatzke, "Goldman Should Stop Saying Clients Come First, Levitt Says," *Bloomberg*, March 29, 2012, http://www.bloomberg.com/news/2012-03-29/goldman-should-stop-saying-we-put-customers-first-levitt-says.html.

33. Whereas a structured interview has a formal, limited set of questions, a semistructured interview is flexible, allowing new questions to be brought up during the interview as a result of what the interviewee says. The interviewer in a semistructured interview generally has a framework of themes to be explored. I received approval from an institutional review board (IRB) at Columbia for my interview processes and procedures, interviewee consent process, and confidentiality of interviewees and study data.

34. During our discussions Whitehead did not comment on Goldman, including its culture or leadership, after 1984. I referred to public sources as they relate to Whitehead's views after 1984.

35. A first-person narrative is unusual in scholarly writing, and for good reason: some objective distance between the researcher and his subject is needed for an unbiased study. However, I use the first person and insert myself at certain points to provide unique information and perspectives. I think there are significant advantages to my being both an academically trained researcher and an insider; without this stance, it would not be possible, in my view, to conduct such an in-depth study because of the complexity of Goldman and the deep, embedded assumptions of the interviewees, assumptions that must be raised to consciousness to be analyzed. On the other hand, it brings academic issues and baggage, something that

cannot be completely avoided. Additionally, I was concerned that revisionist history might enter into the book. I wanted to make sure that my conclusions would hold true whenever this book was written. I asked myself whether, if I had conducted this study in 2006—before the financial crisis—I would have ended with the same conclusions. Therefore, I use a framework of organizational drift to help ensure consistency in the analysis. I have donated the entire advance I received from Harvard Business Review Press for this book to educational and medical charities.

36. See D. Vaughan, *The Challenger Launch Decision: Risky Technology, Culture, and Deviance at NASA* (Chicago: University of Chicago Press, 1996); and S. A. Snook, *Friendly Fire: The Accidental Shootdown of U.S. Blackhawks over Northern Iraq* (Princeton, NJ: Princeton University Press, 2002).

37. Vaughan, *The Challenger Launch Decision*, 238.

Chapter 2

1. A. Blitz, interview with John Whitehead, 2002, http://www.hbs.edu/entrepreneurs/pdf/johnwhitehead.pdf.

2. "I believe the most important thing I did was to set down in writing what Goldman Sachs stood for. I did it out of necessity. By the early 1960s, our business was expanding so rapidly that new people were coming in faster than we could fully assimilate them . . . I wondered how they would ever get inculcated with the Goldman Sachs ethic, which we old hands learned over time by osmosis. We did our best to import these values in new hires through fairly extensive training sessions, but I thought it would be helpful to identify our core values—this was long before that became a vogue term—in a short document that all employees could have to read and to remember. Values like putting the customers' interests first, emphasizing quality, and working as a team," from John C. Whitehead, *A Life in Leadership: From D-Day to Ground Zero* (New York: Basic Books, 2005), 107.

3. "In corporate management circles, *culture* is arguably one of the most pervasive buzzwords, often used to sum up 'the way we do it here'—either explicitly or implicitly—and is seen as a central piece of an organization's identity. That being said, the very term, even when used in the most general sense, has been called a 'weasel word,' devoid of academic legitimacy" (Chalmers Johnson, lecture, Goldman Sachs, Berkeley, CA, 1993). Eminent Japanologist Chalmers Johnson is not alone among scholars in dismissing it as a "weasel word," devoid of academic legitimacy, http://citation.allacademic.com/meta/p_mla_apa_research_citation/1/0/9/5/9/pages109592/p109592-4.php.

4. http://www.escholarship.org/uc/item/00v999cr.

5. Mary Douglas, "Cultural Bias," in Mary Douglas (ed.), *In the Active Voice* (London: Routledge, 1982), 183–254.

6. Ibid., 183.

7. Social anthropologist Mary Douglas defined culture as "a blank space, a highly respected, empty pigeonhole. Economists call it 'tastes' and leave it severely alone. Most philosophers ignore it—to their own loss. Marxists re-create it obliquely as ideology or superstructure. Psychologists avoid it, by concentrating on child subjects. Historians bend it any way they like. Most believe it matters, especially travel agents," from Douglas, *In the Active Voice*. When it comes to the more specific term *organizational culture*, the definitions are just as multitudinous, with anthropologists, sociologists, and scholars from other disciplines struggling to describe the "ideational superstructure of a work organization"

(G. Morgan, *Images of Organization* [Beverly Hills, CA: Sage, 1986], 139). Definitions of organizational culture address everything from common behavioral patterns to symbolic corporate values—e.g., Terrance Deal and Allan Kennedy, *Corporate Cultures: The Rites and Rituals of Corporate Life* (New York: Perseus, 1982); Thomas Peters and Robert Waterman, *In Search of Excellence: Lessons from America's Best-Run Companies* (New York: HarperCollins, 1982). Of course, it is not uncommon for researchers to deploy the same terms while adhering to different connotations, thereby clouding the relevance of research results. Generally, scholars acknowledge the socially constructed role that culture plays in promulgating appropriate, productive behavior within a company. Edgar Schein, a professor emeritus of management at MIT, with the most (more than five hundred) cited articles on organizational culture, according to Google Scholar, defined organizational culture as follows:

> *The deeper level of basic assumptions and beliefs that are learned responses to the group's problems of survival in its external environment and its problems of internal integration; are shared by members of an organization; that operate unconsciously; and that define in a basic "taken-for-granted" fashion in an organization's view of itself and its environment. They come to be taken for granted because they solve those problems repeatedly and reliably . . . culture . . . is a learned product of group experience and is, therefore, to be found only where there is a definable group with a significant history.*

From Edgar Schein, *Organizational Culture and Leadership*, 4th ed. (San Francisco: Jossey-Bass, 2010), 6–7.

8. This definition is similar to A. L. Kroeber's and Talcott Parsons's suggested definition when speaking of culture more broadly than organizations:

> *We suggest that it is useful to define the concept of culture for most usages more narrowly than has been generally the case in the American anthropological tradition, restricting its reference to transmitted and created content and patterns of values, ideas, and other symbolic-meaningful systems as factors in the shaping of human behavior and the artifacts produced through behavior.*

From A. L. Kroeber and Talcott Parsons, "The Concepts of Culture and of Social Systems," *American Sociological Review* 23 (1958): 582.

9. Typically, the definitions assume that culture concerns collective groups of people (not individuals), who, through their shared experiences day by day in the work environment, build a shared vision of what the organization is about and how it undertakes its purpose, and that this shared vision grows through learning how to behave for career survival and advancement. Typically, the definitions describe culture as behavior that is learned or taught and represents the general operating norms in the organization. Culture affects how people behave when no one is telling them what to do because of shared values, assumptions, and socialization experiences, which unite members and maintain a distinction from nonmembers. J. C. Collins and J. I. Porras (*Built to Last: Successful Habits of Visionary Companies* [New York: HarperBusiness, 1994], 253) note that the basic elements that distinguish the "visionary" companies they studied were present throughout the companies' histories, "long before they became hugely successful, premier institutions."

10. Collins and Porras, in *Built to Last*, concluded that successful companies had decentralized management combined with a strong culture.

11. To my knowledge Goldman is the only Wall Street firm that has had the same general principles for such a long time. My interviews with people from competing firms revealed that most firms that had a set of written principles have changed

them significantly or abandoned them over time, as the firms underwent mergers and consolidations. In some cases, principles were routinely revised with each change in top management. McKinsey & Company, considered by many to be a world-class professional services organization, has a similar list of principles, and they can be found framed and hanging on some partners' walls and posted on the company website. According to interviews, McKinsey's values and principles are very well understood: they are discussed, breathed, and lived every day, from the first day of employment. They include putting the client's interest ahead of the firm's, behaving as professionals, keeping client information confidential, telling the truth as McKinsey sees it, and delivering the best of the firm to every client as cost effectively as possible. Citigroup also has a list of principles posted on its website, although interviewees have never seen or heard anyone discuss them during a meeting with clients. Citi's four key principles are common purpose, responsible finance, ingenuity, and leadership.

12. Whitehead, *A Life in Leadership*, 110.

13. The firm's stance on balancing family and work responsibilities changed dramatically after the Whitehead era, as evidenced by a couple of anecdotes. An out-of-state partner who passed on his first annual partners' meeting and dinner dance to be home for his daughter's birthday received a call from Sidney Weinberg, complimenting the partner for having the right priorities; his wife received roses. When the same issue arose years later, "Friedman let the same partner know that skipping partners' meetings was not looked upon kindly." (See Lisa Endlich, *Goldman Sachs—The Culture of Success* [New York: Simon & Schuster, 2000], 121.)

14. Whitehead, *A Life in Leadership*, 110.

15. Because of the many mergers, it is difficult to identify when and whether other firms had stated business principles. However, my interviews with competitors and Goldman partners indicates that if they had them, no one took them as seriously or clung to them as much as Goldman. Most agreed: no firm has had them for as long as Goldman has.

16. When I refer to a current Goldman partner, I mean someone elected into the partnership compensation program (PCP). Goldman is no longer a private partnership, and internally those elected into the PCP are referred to as partner or PMD (partner managing director) to distinguish them versus those managing directors not in the partnership participation program.

17. I am reminded of an article I read about the UBS trading fraud not being a system failure, but rather a cultural failure. The general claim was that UBS had gone through so many mergers and had grown so quickly that it had no defining culture. I found the article insightful. In my experience it is challenging even for insiders to design foolproof systems to catch fraud, because the complexity is too great. See J. B. Stewart, "Common Sense: At UBS, It's the Culture That's Rogue," *New York Times*, September 24, 2011, www.nytimes.com/2011/09/24/business/global/at-ubs-its-the-culture-thats-rogue.html?pagewanted=all.

18. B. Groysberg and S. Snook, "Leadership Development at Goldman Sachs," Case 9-406-002 (Boston: Harvard Business School, 2007).

19. I. Ross, "How Goldman Sachs Grew and Grew, *Fortune*, July 9, 1984, 158.

20. Milton C. Regan (*Eat What You Kill: The Fall of a Wall Street Lawyer* [Ann Arbor, MI: University of Michigan Press, 2004], 86–87) provides a concise account of the short-lived Water Street Corporate Recovery Fund.

21. C. D. Ellis, *The Partnership—The Making of Goldman Sachs* (New York: Penguin, 2008), 304.

22. "As a long-time employer of choice for elite undergraduates and MBAs, Goldman was able to select from a broad array of talented applicants for the traits it preferred" (see B. Groysberg and S. Snook, "Leadership Development at Goldman Sachs").

23. In *Organizational Culture and Leadership* (4th ed. [San Francisco: Jossey-Bass, 2010], 231–232), Schein discusses the importance of culture carriers. Culture does not survive if the main culture carriers depart and if a critical mass of the members leave.

24. C. Harper and A. Choudhury, "Sidney Weinberg, Goldman Sachs Senior Director, Dies at 87," *Bloomberg*, October 6, 2010, http://www.bloomberg.com/news/2010-10-06/goldman-sachs-senior-director-sidney-j-weinberg-jr-dies.html.

25. W. D. Cohan, *Money and Power: How Goldman Sachs Came to Rule the World* (New York: Doubleday, 2011), 363.

26. Whitehead remarked in an interview that his starting salary at Goldman, in 1947, was $3,600 a year. He went on to say, "$3,600 a year, not $3,600 a month. And it wasn't $3,600 a day, as they now earn." (A. Blitz, interview with John Whitehead, 2002, http://www.hbs.edu/entrepreneurs/pdf/johnwhitehead.pdf.)

27. Endlich, *Goldman Sachs*, 20.

28. Ellis, *The Partnership*, 561.

29. Ellis, *The Partnership*, 558.

30. In *A Life in Leadership* (p. 72), Whitehead recalls his experiences as a recruit. "After meeting with the two partners in charge of investment banking at the firm, I sat down with the top brass, a rather imposing group of older men who seemed very worldly to a business neophyte like me. For much of the afternoon, they peppered me with questions that often left me tongue-tied. But I must have handled myself adequately because a few days later, I received word that I had been accepted for employment at Goldman, Sachs & Co." Looking back on his experiences recruiting others, he writes, "Even after I was a senior partner, I spent a lot of time twisting the arms of twenty-year olds, and that was very likely one of the most important things I did" (p. 110).

31. Robert Steven Kaplan, *What to Ask the Person in the Mirror: Critical Questions for Becoming a More Effective Leader and Reaching Your Potential* (Boston: Harvard Business Review Press, 2011), 60.

32. Whitehead, *A Life in Leadership*, 111.

33. Endlich, *Goldman Sachs*, 21.

34. Cohan, *Money and Power*, 231.

35. To ensure the acculturation of the teamwork and other values at Goldman, the organization "grew" its own talent by using entrenched recruitment and training programs. "Out of 1,500 applicants one year, only 30 individuals were given jobs; they were the ones with the brains, humor, motivation, confidence, maturity, and, needless to say, an inclination to play on the team." (R. D. Freedman and J. Vohr, "Goldman Sachs/Lehman Brothers," Case Studies in Finance and Economics, C49 [New York: Leonard N. Stern School of Business, 1991, rev. 1999]).

36. Cohan, *Money and Power*, 232.

37. G. Tett, *Fool's Gold: How the Bold Dream of a Small Tribe at J. P. Morgan Was Corrupted by Wall Street Greed and Unleashed a Catastrophe* (New York: Free Press, 2009), 8.

38. "John L. Weinberg," *The Telegraph*, August 11, 2006, http://www.telegraph.co.uk/news/obituaries/1526056/John-L-Weinberg.html.

39. Goldman moved into its new headquarters building, "a 43-story super-green tower of glass and steel located directly across from the World Trade Center in Battery Park" in 2009 (from Cohan, *Money and Power*, 242). It has "cool modern art, a bike path,

and a sick gym" (from "Goldman Employees Are Psyched to Move into Their Awesome New Building," *Business Insider*, December 4, 2009, http://www.businessinsider.com/ goldman-employees-are-psyched-to-move-into-their-awesome-new-building-2009-12). However, the building does not bear a vanity address, and "the name of the firm appears nowhere on the exterior, or in the lobby, or even on the uniforms of the security personnel or the badges given to visitors. Forty-three stories tall and two city blocks long, the Goldman building appears to have been designed in the hope of rendering the company invisible." Goldman's low profile preceded the firm's recent reputational and legal difficulties, so the design of its headquarters building is completely consistent with its "obsession with being extremely powerful and utterly inconspicuous" (from P. Goldberger, "Shadow Building," *The New Yorker*, May 17, 2010, http://www.newyorker.com/arts/ critics/skyline/2010/05/17/100517crsk_skyline_ goldberger#ixzz1xQltbdUd).

40. In *The Partnership*, Ellis (p. 565) relates a discussion John Whitehead led in the late 1970s on the danger of arrogance creeping into the culture. When he asked the audience for a way to prevent arrogance at Goldman, one young banker facetiously offered this advice: "Hire mediocre people." There was a certain truth to the young banker's statement. Goldman hired people who were accustomed to excelling, who had done so all their lives—in the classroom, on the playing field, in almost any endeavor they attempted. No one was used to failing.

41. Cohan, *Money and Power*, 225.

42. Ellis, *The Partnership*, 187.

43. Harper and Choudhury, "Sidney Weinberg."

44. In *Gatekeepers: The Professions and Corporate Governance* (Oxford, UK: Oxford University Press, 2006, 2, 3), John Coffee studied the role played by *gatekeepers* in corporate governance in acting as "a reputational intermediary to assure investors as to the quality of the 'signal' sent by the corporate issuer." Gatekeepers include securities analysts, auditors, attorneys, investment bankers, credit rating agencies, and so on. He describes how reputational capital "can be placed at risk by the gatekeeper's vouching for its client's assertions or projections."

45. Ellis, *The Partnership*, ix.

46. Blitz, interview with John Whitehead, 2002.

47. Harper and Choudhury, "Sidney Weinberg."

48. Blitz, interview with John Whitehead, 2002.

49. The long-term perspective associated with success in investment banking began to lose importance as the firm's business mix shifted toward trading. Reputational capital also starts to lose significance as a concept in a trading environment. In trading, one side provides a price, and the other side thinks it is either too high or too low. If it is low enough, they do business together. It is price that matters, not relationships. But in banking, it takes years to develop a relationship to the point that the client is willing to share confidential information, and a reputation for integrity matters a great deal (paraphrased from Endlich, *Goldman Sachs*, 18).

50. Today, Goldman's focus is on "the long-term prosperity of our clients, shareholders, employees, and the communities we serve." Shareholders, employees, and communities now rank alongside clients, and the long-term focus is supported by compensation policies and promotion processes, and not by values. Also, much of the restricted stock issued to named executive officers (NEOs) cannot be transferred for a five-year period; when Goldman was a partnership, the restriction was in effect until the partner retired. See N. Lindskoog, *Long-Term Greedy: The Triumph of Goldman Sachs* (Appleton, WI: McCrossen, 1998), 20.

51. Joel M. Podolny, in "A Status-Based Model of Market Competition" (*American Journal of Sociology* 98, no. 4 [1993]: 851, 839), cites industry research supporting the idea that "a higher-status firm can retain an employee of a given level of quality at a more favorable compensation arrangement for the firm." He points out that "if an employee does indeed value the status of her workplace, she should be willing to accept a lower wage or salary to work for a higher-status firm than for a lower-status one."

52. McKinsey & Company is also successful at getting recruits and employees to buy into long-term greedy while earning less as partners earn more. Diane Vaughan, in *Controlling Unlawful Organizational Behavior: Social Structure and Corporate Misconduct* (Chicago: University of Chicago Press, 1985, 70), offers a particularly descriptive simile for this phenomenon: "The luster of future financial rewards binds members to the organization like a pair of golden handcuffs securing their continued affiliation with the firm."

53. Harrison C. White's work on identity and control is relevant in explaining what, from the outside, looks like self-sacrificing ignorance of a harsh reality: "Membership in a group presumes, as the norm, lack of questioning. Character is a suitable term for what membership is to reflect." See Harrison C. White, *Identity and Control: How Social Formations Emerge* (Princeton, NJ: Princeton University Press, 2008), 45.

54. In *The Accidental Investment Banker: Inside the Decade That Transformed Wall Street* (New York: Random House, 2006, 88–89), Jonathan Knee writes, "Any moves, even in many cases a move from being just a vice president at Goldman to being a partner somewhere else—which might well include a multi-year contract providing for guaranteed compensation above what could conceivably be secured at Goldman—usually represented a step down in the social pecking order. . . . But from a brand perspective, Morgan Stanley was a reasonably close second."

55. Groysberg and Snook, "Leadership Development at Goldman Sachs," 6.

56. I may have been too junior and inexperienced to notice or see other things at that time, and, as I gained experience, I might have noticed more. Or maybe there was more. In retrospect, when thinking about the deal, I remember that we did not have to write a *fairness opinion*, which provides legal liability to Goldman for its advice. I now wonder whether this had anything to do with the approach. I discuss this issue in chapter 3.

57. In hindsight, this made me think about the influence clients have on culture and behavior. The vice president could have told the potential buyer that there was a minimum price, and, to get a deal done, it was the price that needed to be reached. I should have asked why we didn't speak to the client about approaching the buyer in that way.

58. I worked closely with partners and senior partners, and it was a relatively flat organization, so I doubt that the behavior or culture was much different at other levels. My interviews with partners, clients, and competitors, along with news articles at the time, support that view.

Chapter 3

1. http://www.goldmansachs.com/investor-relations/corporate-governance/corporate-governance-documents/culture.pdf.

2. Interdependence exists within an organization when the actors are tied together in a meaningful manner. In Goldman's case, there was financial interdependence among partners, who shared in one another's profits and losses, trading risks, and reputation risks. Each partner depended on the others to make money and to work to benefit the group as a whole. Partners also trusted that the others would not put them at personal

risk, would not place the entire group at risk by taking excessive financial risks, and would not engage in improper behavior that could have legal or other repercussions. Partners had an unlimited liability that would make them personally liable—down to their houses and their spouses' cars.

3. According to interviews, before the early 1990s, the review process was less formal, because the firm was smaller and managers felt they could easily assess their employees' performance.

4. "The key to successfully managing large numbers of highly competitive, ambitious people, it seems, is to feed their most unrealistic illusions about themselves. And the best way to keep them is to instill a subconscious belief that those illusions will be shattered when exposed to the light of the outside world. I remember particularly a leadership training course that I went to with a dozen other young vice presidents at Goldman at which we were all asked to put our heads down on the table. The facilitator asked those who believed that they were among the top one percent of their peer group to raise their hand. The bar was then lowered to the top three percent and then the top five percent. When we sat up, I discovered that I was the only member of the group who had not raised his hand. It takes a special skill to keep more than 90% of the bankers believing they are in the top five percent of their class." (See Jonathan Knee, *The Accidental Investment Banker: Inside the Decade That Transformed Wall Street* [New York: Random House, 2006], 58).

5. "The culture at Goldman emphasizes a unique 'loose-tight' management style, where the organization is rigidly controlled at the top concerning operational procedures and overhead, yet each department is allowed autonomy concerning entrepreneurship and innovation." See R. D. Freedman and J. Vohr, "Goldman Sachs/Lehman Brothers," Case Studies in Finance and Economics, C49 (New York: Leonard N. Stern School of Business, 1991, rev. 1999).

6. Laurence Zuckerman, "The Good life After Goldman, "*New York Times*, October 16, 1994, www.nytimes.com/1994/10/16/business/the-good-life-after-goldman.html?page wanted=all&src=pm.

7. P. Weinberg, "Wall Street Needs More Skin in the Game," *Wall Street Journal*, September 30, 2009, http://online.wsj.com/article/SB10001424052748704471504574435 91328265858.html.

8. The partnership committee oversees personnel development and career management issues. It focuses on such matters as recruiting, training, performance evaluation, diversity, mobility, and succession planning. Together with the management committee, it is integral in selecting and compensating partners. The partnership committee was established in 1994; before that, the management committee generally performed these functions. With the establishment of the title of managing directors, the partnership committee also included elections of nonpartner managing directors.

9. Goldman still had a partner election process after the IPO, and the partner election process continues in much the same manner as it did when the firm was a private partnership.

10. Freedman and Vohr ("Goldman Sachs/Lehman Brothers") note that "since it is their own money on the line, partners are very disciplined and profit-oriented. Nonpartner employees share this mentality because they aspire to reach partnership ranks." Truell (1996) comments on "the financial attractiveness of senior status in Goldman, Sachs. Partnership usually brings compensation of millions of dollars a year, and has been the brass ring the firm used to draw in talent and keep its ambitious employees working

long hours." See also P. Truell, "Goldman Sachs Partners Decide Not to Sell, After All," *New York Times*, January 22, 1996, http://www.nytimes.com/1996/01/22/business/goldman-sachs-partners-decide-not-to-sell-after-all.html.

11. Robert Steven Kaplan, *What to Ask the Person in the Mirror: Critical Questions for Becoming a More Effective Leader and Reaching Your Potential* (Boston: Harvard Business Review Press, 2011), 82.

12. P. Maher and R. Cooper, "Image and Reality at Goldman Sachs," *Investment Dealers' Digest*, October 4, 1993, 20.

13. In hindsight, from a sociologist's perspective, it is clear that too many partner additions or departures would have an impact on Goldman's interdependent social network of trust, but I hesitate to suggest that the partners themselves were fully aware of or concerned about all the potential consequences or rationales at the time.

14. For a discussion of closure, see R. Burt, *Brokerage and Closure: An Introduction to Social Capital* (Oxford, UK: Oxford University Press, 2007).

15. Ibid.

16. Burt's research shows that social networks create competitive advantages in and for organizations. The basic idea is that better-connected people have more social capital; as a result, they gain certain advantages. Burt's social structure theory suggests that, when there is a gap between two individuals with complementary resources or information and the two are connected through a third individual, the gap (or hole) is filled, creating an important advantage for the third individual as well as for the organization. A company's competitive advantage is a matter of access to the structural holes in the markets: obtaining information that allows it to make deals and connecting buyers and sellers, borrowers and lenders. The partnership provides that access by tying partners together financially, socially, and culturally. Trust is also important, and a partnership structure creates that foundation as a result of the partner screening and election process and the intertwining of partners' financial interests. Goldman's partnership structure provided the opportunity to connect diverse parts of an enterprise. When Goldman connected private banking with investment banking or a portfolio manager in commodities with a trader in equity derivatives, the firm played the role of the *gaudius tertius*, "the third who benefits." In *Brokerage and Closure*, Burt suggests that the *gaudius tertius* is typically an individual, but the concept can be expanded to apply to organizations as well—especially in the case of a partnership wherein the partners are financially interdependent and benefit together. The "third" party may not control the relationship but still benefits by controlling the information flow between the two parties it brings together.

17. "I've always been a team player and, by now, I'd become a fierce partisan of Goldman Sachs. I liked being a part of a storied institution that held so much promise." See John C. Whitehead, *A Life in Leadership: From D-Day to Ground Zero* (Princeton, NJ: Princeton University Press, 2005), 88.

18. C. D. Ellis, *The Partnership—The Making of Goldman Sachs* (New York: Penguin, 2008), 189.

19. A *social network* is a social structure made up of a set of actors (such as individuals or organizations) and the ties between them (such as relationships, connections, or interactions). Trust developed from the familiarity that Goldman partners had with each other by virtue of having worked together for a long time and from having undergone the same partnership election process. Trust is built up as a part of socialization and shared experiences.

20. See K. Kuwabara, "Cohesion, Cooperation, and the Value of Doing Things Together: How Economic Exchange Creates Relational Bonds" (*American Sociological Review* 76 [2011]) for an extended discussion of this type of network. He shows that integrative and two-way exchange lead to cooperation, and joint action produces or reinforces cohesion. In *Foundations of Social Theory* (Cambridge, MA: Belknap Press of Harvard University Press, 2010) J. S. Coleman discusses the cliquish nature and density of partnership networks. R. Reagans, E. Zuckerman, and B. McEvily, in "How to Make the Team: Social Networks vs. Demography as Criteria for Designing Effective Teams" (*Administrative Science Quarterly* 49 [2004]: 101–133), look at the power of networks and cohesion.

21. W. D. Cohan, *Money and Power: How Goldman Sachs Came to Rule the World* (New York: Doubleday, 2010), 474.

22. M. Graham, "Top 10 Commandments of Business Growth," *Overdrive: The Official Blog of the Entrepreneurs' Organization*, January 31, 2011, http://blog.eonetwork. org/2011/01/top-10-commandments-of-business-growth/.

23. A partner explained that cross-selling is important to Goldman's profitability and return on equity especially relative to those of its peers. There is a fixed infrastructure cost of being in business, so if banking/M&A can notify and introduce a cross-border deal to the foreign exchange desk as part of a full solution, then the customer acquisition costs to obtain the deal would be zero and the profits would flow straight to the bottom line. In addition, the company could benefit from favorable foreign exchange pricing by avoiding a public, competitive auction, because the information had to be kept confidential.

24. See Joel M. Podolny, "A Status-Based Model of Market Competition" (*American Journal of Sociology* 98, no. 4 [1993]: 839, 851), for a discussion of a status-based model of market competition.

25. Although it is often overlooked, Goldman made diversity of people, including women and minorities, a priority throughout my time at the firm. However, like most Wall Street firms, Goldman struggled to attract, develop, and retain women and minorities, and they tended to represent a smaller percentage of the senior ranks. Goldman, as in many things, continued to improve throughout my tenure, and many senior partners and others put a lot of emphasis on diversity. Although Goldman has many programs for recruiting, career development, and advancement to promote diversity, like most Wall Street firms it has been sued several times for discrimination. According to Goldman, in 2010 women constituted about 29 percent of its vice presidents, 17 percent of its managing directors, 14 percent of its partners, and about 13 percent of members of its management committee. These percentages may be among the highest on Wall Street. However, diversity of people was not nearly as strong as diversity of ideas. A little-noticed provision in the Dodd–Frank legislation tries to address those low percentages. Section 342 mandates gender and racial hiring quotas for the financial services industry.

26. "The thrust of the Goldman culture has been its indomitable team spirit. Partners and staff 'gang tackled' problems with a near mania for interdepartmental and interpersonal communication and coordination." See Freedman and Vohr, "Goldman Sachs/ Lehman Brothers."

27. Burt, *Brokerage and Closure: An Introduction to Social Capital.*

28. In Burt's work at Raytheon, his mission was to integrate several acquisitions. Managers were set up with discussion partners in other groups and should have been sharing ideas across business units. Burt found, however, that the people they cited for discussion of ideas were overwhelmingly colleagues in their existing informal discussion

network. The ideas ended up never going anywhere. Burt writes that results would have been different had the managers reached beyond their typical contacts, particularly to people having enough power to be allies but not actual supervisors. Border crossing is essential to overcoming what Burt calls "structural holes." See R. S. Burt, *Structural Holes: The Social Structure of Competition* (Cambridge, MA: Harvard University Press, 1995).

29. "Open dialogue was another principle. Part of this was posting: keeping everyone informed. Part was the deliberate flat organization structure. During the seventies, the firm initiated monthly meetings of partners. Any partner whose area was doing better or worse than anticipated would be expected to stand and explain the difference." (See Ellis, *The Partnership*, 190).

30. This was the case except for certain situations that arose in 1986, 1994, and 2000, which I touch upon later. Some people think Lehman Brothers failed because it had become too insular. It had a unique culture and cohesion, but it reached a tipping point where it offered limited ways to challenge the status quo. A systematic influx of new partners and elimination of older partners helped keep Goldman a private firm longer than most. New partners generally always wanted to be near retirement at the point when they had the maximum amount of ownership when selling their shares, so they wanted to delay such discussions. They wanted to invest in the business. In contrast, the more-senior partners had reached their highest ownership percentage and were likely incentivized to maximize the value and liquidity of their shares. Swedberg notes that in the case of Lehman (see R. Swedberg, "The Structure of Confidence and the Collapse of Lehman Brothers," in *Markets on Trial: The Economic Sociology of the U.S. Financial Crisis*, ed. M. Lounsbury and P. M. Hirsch [Bingley, UK: Emerald, 2010], 81), CEO Richard Fuld ran Lehman in an authoritarian manner, "setting his own distinct mark on the aggressive and competitive type of corporate culture that seems to be characteristic of modern investment banks." Fuld's leadership and personal styles were both in sharp contrast to what was typical at Goldman.

31. See Cohan, *Money and Power*, (388–399) for an example of productive dissonance among management committee members.

32. Kaplan, *What to Ask the Person in the Mirror*, 157. This syndrome was on display during the recent economic crisis. A lack of diversity (in the broadest sense) at the top of a number of companies contributed to monolithic thinking, insulation, and, ultimately, severe damage to (or even failure of) organizations.

33. Bill Cohan, "Meet John F. W. Rogers, Goldman's Quiet Power Player," *Business week*, September 1, 2011, www.businessweek.com/magazine/meet-john-f-w-rogers-goldmans-quiet-power-player-09012011.html.

34. Ibid.

35. A. Blitz, interview with John Whitehead, 2002, http://www.hbs.edu/entrepreneurs/pdf/johnwhitehead.pdf.

36. B. Groysberg and S. Snook, "Leadership Development at Goldman Sachs," Case 9 406 002 (Boston: Harvard Business School, 2007), 6.

37. Ibid.

38. Ibid.

39. David Stark, *The Sense of Dissonance: Accounts of Worth in Economic Life* (Princeton: Princeton University Press, 2009).

40. Stark argues that different criteria of worth are valuable in different domains. This different value may be an interesting nuance between traders and bankers. Clients depend on investment bankers to give advice. Clients may value longer-term investment and are willing to wait until trust is built. They also may value people smarter than they

are, or who have better technical expertise or better education. They look for a banker who has access and a competitive advantage that they can leverage. This is what is sold. In trading, on the other hand, clients are looking for liquidity and price. They fear that the counterparty is smarter than they are or knows more than they do or has a different competitive advantage. Clients don't care whether the trading counterparty went to an elite business school or has a pedigree. If clients believe a firm's insights are being shared with them and are advantageous, they value them, but they wonder whether the counterparty is on the other side of the deal, talking up its own book.

41. Beunza and Stark, in Stark's *Sense of Dissonance*, develop this theory in the context of traders' use of models "to translate stock prices into estimates of what their rivals think." I discuss this point in greater detail in chapter 6 in the context of performativity.

42. S. McGee, *Chasing Goldman Sachs: How the Masters of the Universe Melted Wall Street Down—and Why They'll Take Us to the Brink Again* (New York: Crown, 2010).

43. Stark, *The Sense of Dissonance*, 15.

44. Stark, *The Sense of Dissonance*, 21.

45. "Interview with John Whitehead, MBA 1947," www.hbs.edu/entrepreneurs/pdf/johnwhitehead.pdf.

46. Once Goldman became a public company, the partners had liquidity. They no longer had to wait until retirement to pull out their capital. At any time they could sell their Goldman shares—those shares that were not restricted or in a restricted time period—and they were also compensated as employees. Goldman now has five-year restrictions on selected stock grants to certain executives, a situation that clearly is much better for partners than having their equity tied up until they retire. I discuss this later.

47. Capital is usually thought of in monetary terms alone, but in the Goldman partnership, the personal capital contributed by the partners included something intangible but of great value: reputation. Reputation was so important that it was mentioned in Goldman's second business principle:

> *Our assets are our people, capital and reputation. If any of these is ever diminished, the last is the most difficult to restore. We are dedicated to complying fully with the letter and spirit of the laws, rules and ethical principles that govern us. Our continued success depends upon unswerving adherence to this standard.*

Partners not only were paid from the same pool of profits generated by the overall firm but also depended on each other for managing both reputational and capital risk.

48. It is, however, noted in the current description.

49. Peter Weinberg, "Wall Street Needs More Skin in the Game," *Wall Street Journal*, September 30, 2009, http://online.wsj.com/article/SB1000142405274870447150457444359 1328265858.html.

Chapter 4

1. L. Endlich, *Goldman Sachs—The Culture of Success* (New York: Simon & Schuster, 2000), 124.

2. Pub L. 73-66, 48 Stat. 162 was enacted on June 16, 1933. The law established the Federal Deposit Insurance Corporation (FDIC) and introduced banking reforms, some of which were designed to control speculation. The term "Glass–Steagall Act," however, is most often used to refer to four provisions that limited commercial bank securities activities as well as affiliations between commercial banks and securities firms. Provisions that prohibit a bank holding company from owning other financial companies were repealed on November 12, 1999, by the Gramm–Leach–Bliley Act (GLBA). Many commentators

have stated that the repeal of the affiliation restrictions was an important cause of the 2007–2008 financial crisis by allowing banks to become "too big to fail."

3. In the 1990s, a number of investment banks claimed that some commercial banks had coerced customers into hiring their Section 20 (securities) affiliates to underwrite securities in order to receive loans from the bank, in violation of the "anti-tying" provisions of the Bank Holding Company Act. Investment banks continued to make claims of illegal tying after the GLBA became law. Many Wall Street experts expected that investment banks would change their legal structures to become bank holding companies so that they could compete with securities firms affiliated with commercial banks, but no major investment bank took that route until 2008, when they did so to gain a measure of federal protection during the credit crisis.

4. Morgan Stanley was formed by J.P. Morgan partners Henry S. Morgan (grandson of J. P. Morgan), Harold Stanley, and others, on September 16, 1935, in response to provisions of the Glass–Steagall Act that required the splitting of commercial and investment banking businesses.

5. The Securities and Exchange Commission (SEC) was established by Franklin D. Roosevelt in 1934 to address issues arising from the Great Depression. The SEC is a federal agency with primary responsibility for enforcing the federal securities laws and regulating the US securities industry, including the stock and options exchanges and other electronic securities markets. It also licenses and regulates the companies whose securities are traded on US exchanges as well as the brokers and dealers who conduct the trading.

6. Lazard went public in 2005. Although it is a very prestigious firm, it was not a "capital-intensive," full-service investment bank. Rather, it was a boutique advisory firm with an asset management business.

7. See Alan D. Morrison and William J. Wilhelm, Jr., *Investment Banking: Institutions, Politics, and Law* (Oxford, New York: Oxford University Press, 2007), and Alan D. Morrison and William J. Wilhelm, "Partnership Firms, Reputation, and Human Capital," *American Economic Review* 94, no. 5 (2004): 1682–1692.

8. C. D. Ellis, *The Partnership—The Making of Goldman Sachs* (New York: Penguin, 2008), 394–395.

9. R. D. Freedman and J. Vohr, "Goldman Sachs/Lehman Brothers," Case Studies in Finance and Economics, C49 (New York: Leonard N. Stern School of Business, 1991, rev. 1999), 13.

10. The specific legal risks partners were exposed to were spelled out in Goldman's IPO prospectus and include: Potential liability under securities or other laws for materially false or misleading statements made in connection with securities and other transactions; potential liability for the "fairness opinions" and other advice they provide to participants in corporate transactions and disputes over the terms and conditions of complex trading arrangements; the possibility that counterparties in complex or risky trading transactions will claim that Goldman improperly failed to tell them the risks or that they were not authorized or permitted to enter into these transactions with the firm and that their obligations to Goldman are not enforceable; exposure to claims against the firm for recommending investments that are not consistent with a client's investment objectives or engaging in unauthorized or excessive trading; claims arising from disputes with employees for alleged discrimination or harassment, among other things. See www.goldmansachs.com/investor-relations/financials/archived/other-information/ipo/prospectus-gs-pdf-file.pdf.

11. H. Sender, "Too Big for Their Own Good," *Institutional Investor*, February 1987, 63.

12. Ibid.

13. A few partners told me they asked or considered asking John L. Weinberg to come out of retirement as chairman or in another senior role.

14. W. D. Cohan, "The Rage over Goldman Sachs," *Time*, August 31, 2009, http//www.time.com.

15. Ibid.

16. Ellis, *The Partnership*, 539.

17. W. D. Cohan, *Money and Power: How Goldman Sachs Came to Rule the World* (New York: Doubleday, 2010).

18. Cohan, "The Rage over Goldman Sachs."

19. It was alleged that Maxwell stole money from Maxwell company pension plans by hiring Goldman to broker a trade between various Maxwell-controlled entities. See Endlich (*Goldman Sachs*, 137–160) for a detailed account of the relationship between Goldman and Robert Maxwell.

20. Endlich (*Goldman Sachs*, 197) notes, however, that management had "over-reserved in anticipation of such a financial charge" and was eager to put the case behind it.

21. According to A. Raghavan ("Goldman Sticks to Plan on Allocating Settlement Costs," *Wall Street Journal*, April 13, 1995), "eighty-four of the more than 164 partners who will wind up footing the settlement are now 'limited' partners, or retired from active duty at the firm." The firm's management committee allocated "80 percent of the settlement cost to those who were general partners in 1991, 15 percent to those of 1990, and 5 percent to those of 1989." Endlich (*Goldman Sachs*, 197) describes the "stunned" reaction of the limited partners, many of whom "were told simply to take out their checkbooks."

22. Freedman and Vohr, "Goldman Sachs/Lehman Brothers."

23. "New Round of Layoffs at Goldman, Sachs," *New York Times*, January 25, 1995, http://www.nytimes.com/1995/01/25/business/new-round-of-job-cuts-at-goldman-sachs.html.

24. Among Corzine and Paulson's early official acts was to announce layoffs, and they were now doing it again, but "barely a month before bankers would be entitled to their annual bonuses (which represented their annual compensation). They apologized for the timing and manner of the layoffs but promised they would never do it again. When they then [announced] another round in January 1995, many at the firm felt betrayed." See J. A. Knee, *The Accidental Investment Banker: Inside the Decade That Transformed Wall Street* (New York: Random House, 2006), xvii, 48.

25. Endlich, *Goldman Sachs*, 256. These layoffs can have an effect on both the organization and the external environment. University of Minnesota anthropology professor Karen Ho, in her book *Liquidated: An Ethnography of Wall Street* (Durham, NC: Duke University Press, 2009), investigates the experiences and ideologies of investment bankers. She describes how a highly unstable market system (e.g. job insecurity, constant downsizing, continual restructuring) is understood and justified through the experiences and practices of restructuring corporations. Bankers are recruited from "elite universities" and are socialized into a short-term world of high reward. The workplace culture and network of privilege create the perception that job insecurity results in better performance. The banker's mantra is improving "shareholder value," but the assumptions and practices often produce crises. She finds that in many ways the investment bankers and their approaches become an example of how their clients should behave. She believes Wall Street shapes not only the stock market but also how both companies and employees value each other. Wall Street's values are intertwined in many people's daily lives.

26. Carol J. Loomis, "The Goldman Standard Slips," *Fortune*, November 28, 1994, http://money.cnn.com/magazines/fortune/fortune_archive/1994/11/28/80028/.

27. W. D. Cohan, *Money and Power: How Goldman Sachs Came to Rule the World* (New York: Doubleday, 2011), 359.

28. Ibid.

29. http://www.vanityfair.com/online/daily/2011/03/william-d-cohan-on-goldman-sachs-how-secret-merger-talks-with-mellon-bank-led-to-jon-corzines-demise.

30. B. Burrough, W. D. Cohan, and B. McLean, "Jon Corzine's Riskiest Business," *Vanity Fair*, February 2012, http://www.vanityfair.com/business/2012/02/jon-corzine-201202.

31. P. Truell, "Partners Vote for Changes at Goldman," *New York Times*, May 21, 1996, http://www.nytimes.com/1996/05/21/business/partners-vote-for-changes-at-goldman.html.

32. http://articles.latimes.com/1997/oct/22/business/fi-45322.

33. There is some reason to believe, however, that this change was mainly psychological; most active partners retained upward of 90 percent of their capital with Goldman while working at the firm. See Endlich, *Goldman Sachs* (p. 237), and P. Truell, "Goldman Sachs Partners Decide Not to Sell, After All," *New York Times*, January 22, 1996, http://www.nytimes.com/1996/01/22/business/goldman-sachs-partners-decide-not-to-sell-after-all.html.

34. P. Truell, "Goldman Sachs Partners Decide Not to Sell, After All."

35. By the time Goldman became an LLC, the reporting matrices had started to add division executive committees and then geographic executive committees. Even before the 1990s, organizational changes were occurring. Capital commitments by the firm typically went to the management committee, but as the number of decisions increased, a commitments committee was established to make them.

36. In January 1999, the executive committee was dismantled and a fifteen-member management committee was restored as the firm's senior leadership group.

37. Endlich, *Goldman Sachs*, 252.

38. Freedman and Vohr, "Goldman Sachs/Lehman Brothers," 13.

39. Cohan, *Money and Power*, 392.

40. Here is a clear example of the impact of a change in the organization's legal structure. According to interviews, when Goldman was a private partnership, such a vote would have been held on a one person/one vote basis; with Goldman as an LLC, however, a majority vote by the executive committee determined the future status of the firm.

41. In a letter to the firm, Whitehead wrote, "I don't find anyone who denies that the decision of many of the partners, particularly the younger men, was based more on the dazzling amounts to be deposited in their capital accounts than on what they felt would be good for the future of Goldman Sachs." See J. Cassidy, "The Firm," *The New Yorker*, March 8, 1999, 35.

42. A. R. Sorkin, *Too Big to Fail: The Inside Story of How Wall Street and Washington Fought to Save the Financial System—and Themselves* (New York: Viking, 2009).

43. The Gramm–Leach–Bliley Act is also known as the Financial Services Modernization Act of 1999, or the Citigroup Relief Act. It repealed part of the Glass–Steagall Act of 1933, removing barriers in the market between an investment bank, a commercial bank, and an insurance company. "The government's decision . . . to allow the large commercial banks to aggressively pursue investment banking business put further pressure on the old way of doing things. The Depression-era legislation known as Glass–Steagall had long insulated

the rarified investment banking partnerships from assault by these better-capitalized institutions. Its ultimate repeals in 1999 paved the way not only for radically intensified competition but a wave of mergers that created enormous financial supermarkets with an entirely different ethos." (See Knee, *The Accidental Investment Banker*, xi.)

44. "Even with one arm tied behind their backs, these institutions [commercial banks] had been investing heavily for at least a decade in expanding their investment banking activities in anticipation of the rule's ultimate repeal. They hired high-profile investment bankers, pressed various loopholes in the existing rules, exploited their balance sheets." (See Knee, *The Accidental Investment Banker*, 24.)

45. Endlich, *Goldman Sachs*, 124.

46. "New organizations such as multibillion-dollar hedge funds and LBO [leveraged buyout] firms have begun to step in and play some of the roles once dominated by investment banks." (See Knee, *The Accidental Investment Banker*, xvi.)

47. S. Butcher, "Deconstructing Goldman's Q2 Conference Call: What Was Said, What It Means, What Comes Next," *Reuters*, July 18, 2012, http://news.reuters-gulf. efinancialcareers.com/newsandviews_item/wpNewsItemId-107560.

48. http://faculty.chicagobooth.edu/steven.kaplan/research/km.pdf and http://www. businessinsider.com/shortest-tenure-ceo-2011-5.

49. http://www.bloomberg.com/news/2013-04-04/bond-traders-club-loses-cachet-in-most-important-market.html.

50. John Whitehead pointed this out in our discussion. In *The Challenger Launch Decision: Risky Technology, Culture, and Deviance at NASA* (Chicago: University of Chicago Press, 1966), sociologist Diane Vaughan writes that all organizations share certain basic aspects of structure (hierarchy, division of labor, goals, normative standards, patterns of coming and going) and certain common processes (socialization, conflict, competition, cooperation, power and inequality, and culture) and points to the "complexity of the internal processes and structure that accompany increased size" (see page 68).

51. C. Perrow, *Normal Accidents: Living with High-Risk Technologies* (New York: Basic Books, 1984), 308.

Chapter 5

1. Goldman Sachs Group, "Letter to Shareholders," Annual Report 1999, http://www.goldmansachs.com/investor-relations/financials/archived/annual-reports/attachments/1999-annual-report.pdf.

2. W. D. Cohan, *Money and Power: How Goldman Sachs Came to Rule the World* (New York: Doubleday, 2011), 234.

3. B. McLean and A. Serwer, "Goldman Sachs: After the Fall," *Fortune*, October 23, 2011, http://features.blogs.fortune.cnn.com/2011/10/23/goldman-sachs-after-the-fall-fortune-1998/.

4. Bankers Trust, Barclays, Chase, Credit Suisse First Boston, Deutsche Bank, Goldman Sachs, Merrill Lynch, J.P. Morgan, Morgan Stanley, Salomon Smith Barney, and UBS each put up $300 million.

5. C. Chandler, "Goldman's Golden Chance: An IPO or Merger Could Reap Millions for Partners at the Wall Street Titan—But Would It Destroy What Makes Goldman Sachs Goldman Sachs?" *Washington Post*, June 7, 1998, H01.

6. McLean and Serwer, "Goldman Sachs: After the Fall."

7. It was rumored that Corzine ultimately agreed to pay out the limited partners at two times book value. (See J. A. Knee, *The Accidental Investment Banker: Inside the Decade That Transformed Wall Street* [New York: Random House, 2006], 103.) Many limited partners believed that their historical contributions to Goldman were being seriously underappreciated and undervalued. (See J. Kahn, "Goldman, Sachs Tries to Soothe Limited Partners," *New York Times*, July 30, 1998, D1.)

8. There were indications, some of them subtle, that a culture shift was already under way. In the years leading up to the IPO, adherence to Goldman's principles was less obvious. According to interviews, it was rare for the principles to be included in the front of presentations to clients as they once were, and they were certainly not as regularly hanging on anyone's office wall. The principles were still taught, but it would be difficult to argue that they held the same prominence as they once had.

9. L. Endlich, *Goldman Sachs—The Culture of Success* (New York: Simon & Schuster, 2000).

10. Ibid.

11. Until 1996, according to interviews, partners who retired and became limited partners took out half their capital at retirement but the rest remained with the firm for at least four more years. After 1996, when the firm became an LLC, that period was increased to six years.

12. McLean and Serwer, "Goldman Sachs: After the Fall."

13. T. Metz, "The Pacifist: Goldman Sachs Avoids Bitter Takeover Fights but Leads in Mergers," *Wall Street Journal*, December 3, 1982, 1.

14. Goldman also refrained from doing business with companies involved in the gambling industry.

15. Cohan, *Money and Power*, 225.

16. I. Ross, "How Goldman Sachs Grew and Grew," *Fortune*, July 9, 1984, 158.

17. C. D. Ellis, *The Partnership—The Making of Goldman Sachs* (New York: Penguin, 2008), 645.

18. According to Dealogic, Goldman advised Krupp in a 1997 hostile takeover of Thyssen in Germany for a fee of nearly $10 million. Also, internationally Goldman advised Banque Nationale de Paris (BNP) in its hostile acquisition of a majority interest in Compagnie Financiere de Paribas (Paribas) in 1997. It was a large and high-profile transaction. It also gained attention because Goldman's investment bankers had done work for Paribas. The same issue came up when Goldman advised Vodafone in its acquisition of Mannesmann in one of the largest M&A deals in history. Goldman has also represented many leading foreign companies in hostile deals, including Repsol, Air Canada, Royal Bank of Scotland, Foster's Group, and Mittal Steel (Lakshmi Mittal is on the board of Goldman). It advised Sara Lee (John Brian, the former Sara Lee CEO, is on the board of Goldman) in its hostile M&A acquisition of Courtaulds Textiles in the United Kingdom in 2000. Also in 2000, it advised Unilever in its hostile acquisition of Bestfoods. In 2005, it represented Novartis in its hostile purchase of Chiron Corp. In 2011, Goldman advised Terex Corp in its hostile acquisition of a majority interest of Demag Cranes.

19. Goldman represented Westmont Hospitality Group in buying its remaining interest in UniHost, a Canadian hotel operator.

20. B. McLean, "The Bank Job," *Vanity Fair*, March 23, 2012, http://www.vanityfair.com/business/features/2010/01/goldman-sachs-200101.

21. Endlich, *Goldman Sachs*, 45.

22. Keep in mind that this is when John L. Weinberg was still at the firm.

23. Ezra Zuckerman's work (1999, 2000, 2004) regarding analysts' impact on the behavior of Wall Street firms also has relevance here.

24. "Goldman Sachs Lex Column [MG1]," *Financial Times*, April 26, 1999, 22.

25. P. S. Cohan, *Value Leadership: The 7 Principles That Drive Corporate Value in Any Economy* (San Francisco, CA: Jossey-Bass, 2003), 196.

26. M. Taibbi, "The Great American Bubble Machine," *Rolling Stone*, April 5, 2010, http://www.rollingstone.com/politics/news/the-great-american-bubble-machine-20100405.

27. http://www.dechert.com/files/Publication/355765b1-8255-4d1c-8792-f34bf2843970/Presentation/PublicationAttachment/259fc2a6-c9fe-4448-9787-f699d9a8a5c5/FSSL_Alert_6-05.pdf.

28. Brendan Pierson, "Dismissal of Action Against Goldman Over eToys IPO Stands," *New York Law Journal*, December 9, 2011, http://www.newyorklawjournal.com/PubArticleNY.jsp?id=1202534952140&slreturn=1.

29. The full list of IBS business development commandments is as follows: "1) Don't waste your time going after business you don't really want; 2) The boss usually decides—not the assistant treasurer. Do you know the boss?; 3) It is just as easy to get a first-rate piece of business as a second-rate one; 4) You never learn anything when you're talking; 5) The client's objective is more important than yours; 6) The respect of one person is worth more than an acquaintance with 100 people; 7) When there's business to be found, go out and get it!; 8) Important people like to deal with other important people. Are you one?; 9) There's nothing worse than an unhappy client; 10) If you get the business, it's up to you to see that it's well-handled."

30. J. A. Knee, *The Accidental Investment Banker: Inside the Decade That Transformed Wall Street* (New York: Random House, 2006), 49.

31. The Super League is also mentioned in chapter 7.

32. Knee reports telling Thornton of his (Knee's) plan to leave the firm and joking, when asked by Thornton to stay on to help with the global reorganization of CME, that Thornton could hire him back when Thornton took over the firm. When Thornton reminded Knee of the "cultural taboo" against rehiring people who left Goldman, Knee retorted that if Thornton were in charge, "this would probably not be the most important cultural taboo that would have already been swept aside." (See Knee, *The Accidental Investment Banker*, 49, 93.)

33. B. Groysberg and S. Snook, "Leadership Development at Goldman Sachs," Case 9-406-002 (Boston: Harvard Business School, 2007), 4.

34. Ibid.

35. The subject of conflicts is discussed in greater detail in chapter 7.

36. Garza Baldwin and Seth Huffstetler, "Staple Financing: Proceed with Caution," *M&A Update*, July 3, 2007, www.wcsr.com/resources/pdfs/M%26AUpdate_3July2007.pdf.

37. R. Hall, "Stapled Finance Packages under Scrutiny," http://www.iflr1000.com/LegislationGuide/146/Stapled-finance-packages-under-scrutiny.html.

38. Baldwin and Huffstetler, "Staple Financing."

39. B. Klempner, D. Mathur, L. Molefe, J. Reynolds, and T. Uccellini, "Case Study: Selling Neiman Marcus," *Harvard Negotiation Law Review*, Winter 2007.

40. A business standards committee report in 2011.

41. "When combined with the toxic ecology of bonus systems that emphasize short-term revenues, banks evolved a transactional business model. Deals and profits dominated at the expense of client interests and longer term relationships, a practice known as 'scorched earth banking.'" (See S. Das, "Goldman Sachs' Flawed Model," *The Independent*, March 17, 2012, http://www.independent.co.uk/news/business/comment/satyajit-das-goldman-sachs-flawed-model-7575865.html.)

42. A. Garfinkle, "A Conversation with Robert S. Kaplan," *The American Interest*, March 15, 2012, http://www.the-american-interest.com/article.cfm?piece=1223.

43. Ibid.

44. S. Gandel, "Goldman Says It Can Profit from Europe's Bust," *Fortune*, May 31, 2012, http://finance.fortune.cnn.com/tag/gary-cohn/.

45. M. Abelson and C. Harper, "Succeeding Blankfein at Goldman May Be Hurdle Too High for Cohn," *Bloomberg*, July 24, 2011, http://www.bloomberg.com/news/2011-07-24/succeeding-blankfein-at-goldman-may-prove-hurdle-too-high-for-no-2-cohn.html.

46. This is after Water Street, which is not mentioned on Goldman's website. The funds listed are only merchant banking funds.

47. Ellis, *The Partnership*, 537.

48. Knee, *The Accidental Investment Banker*, 24–25.

49. One manager said, "Things have to be done in a very high-end way. People at Goldman Sachs are pretty intolerant of weak execution and weak quality, even of things most people might think of as trivial." (See Groysberg and Snook, "Leadership Development at Goldman Sachs.")

Chapter 6

1. http://money.cnn.com/2000/08/01/companies/goldman/.

2. http://www.economist.com/node/28791.

3. I compared the daily change in Goldman's stock price to the daily change in a couple of US financial indexes and looked to see whether the daily change increased over the month (i.e., if Goldman had manipulated the price in the period close to the fiscal year end). I tried a couple of different basic specifications to see if there was any non-linearity in this. Every way I looked, though, there was no increase in returns on Goldman's price versus the indexes as we got closer to the end of the fiscal year. So it looks like Goldman wasn't doing this.

4. http://www.efinancialnews.com/story/2012-11-12/goldman-sachs-protecting-the-partnership.

5. Compensation is described in the proxy statements filed by Goldman.

6. http://dealbook.nytimes.com/2011/01/18/study-points-to-windfall-for-goldman-partners/.

7. http://dealbook.nytimes.com/2011/02/05/stock-hedging-lets-bankers-skirt-efforts-to-overhaul-pay/.

8. *Leverage* is the ratio of debt to equity. At 33-to-1 leverage, a 3 percent drop in the value of an investment bank's assets can wipe out its equity.

9. A. Garfinkle, "A Conversation with Robert S. Kaplan," *The American Interest*, March 15, 2012, http://www.the-american-interest.com/article.cfm?piece=1223.

10. L. Endlich, *Goldman Sachs—The Culture of Success* (New York: Simon & Schuster, 2000).

11. http://dealbook.nytimes.com/2011/05/16/the-goldman-sachs-diaspora/.

12. According to interviews and publicly filed documents, however, around the time of the IPO, John L. Weinberg was put on the board and granted tens of millions of dollars in stock and a consulting agreement that paid millions of dollars.

13. "People have come to Goldman Sachs despite the promise of very long hours and possibly less compensation, because becoming a partner at Goldman Sachs was the brass ring. It was the highest accolade on Wall Street, and now that no longer exists." (See P. Viles and J. Cafferty, "Goldman Sachs' IPO," CNNfn, May 4, 1999.)

14. The sources are annual reports and the Wall Street Comps Survey. The numbers for J.P. Morgan relate only to its investment bank, without commercial banking. Morgan Stanley was excluded because it includes a large brokerage business.

15. http://dealbook.nytimes.com/2011/05/16/the-goldman-sachs-diaspora/.

16. See Donald MacKenzie, *An Engine, Not a Camera: How Financial Models Shape Markets* (Cambridge, MA: MIT Press, 2006), and his similar works.

17. B. McLean and A. Serwer, "Goldman Sachs: After the Fall," *Fortune*, October 23, 2011, http://features.blogs.fortune.cnn.com/2011/10/23/goldman-sachs-after-the-fall-fortune-1998/.

18. C. D. Ellis, *The Partnership—The Making of Goldman Sachs* (New York: Penguin, 2008), xvi. Goldman's trading position marks were shown to be more accurate than those of the other Wall Street firms. Its longstanding "mark-to-market" discipline and cultural element of dissonance may have meant it was more accurate and generated more volatility in positions.

19. McLean and Serwer, "Goldman Sachs: After the Fall."

20. The IPO prospectus can be found at http://www.goldmansachs.com/investor-relations/financials/archived/other-information/ipo-prospectus-gs-pdf-file.pdf.

Chapter 7

1. Matthew Gill explores the work of accountants and the accounting profession to find the causes of problems of trust behind scandals and the headlines. His focus is largely on the way that accountants construct knowledge, and he emphasizes the need to understand the "underlying norms according to which accountants approach the rules, rather than the rules themselves." The uncertainty resulting from the subjectivity inherent in this situation can easily lead to moral ambiguity. See M. Gill, *Accountants' Truth: Knowledge and Ethics in the Financial World* (Oxford, UK: Oxford University Press, 2009), 8.

2. They pointed to the data supporting this; it is rare for an employee of Goldman to be criminally convicted. However, that can be said for many firms and may be more of a statement on the law or enforcement, as pointed out by Senator Carl Levin (D-Mich.) when the Department of Justice dropped its criminal investigation against Goldman in 2012: "Whether the decision by the Department of Justice is the product of weak laws or weak enforcement, Goldman Sachs' actions were deceptive and immoral," Levin said. Goldman's "actions did immense harm to its clients and helped create the financial crisis that nearly plunged us into a second Great Depression;" see http://www.ft.com/cms/s/0/6e032042-e315-11e1-a78c-00144feab49a.html#axzz2O5ePeAlh.

3. In discussing Goldman's practices during the internet/technology boom, Taibbi wrote, "For a bank that paid out $7 billion a year in salaries, $110 million fines issued half a decade late were something far less than a deterrent—they were a joke. Once the Internet bubble burst, Goldman had no incentive to reassess its new, profit-driven

strategy; it just searched around for another bubble to inflate." See M. Taibbi, "The Great American Bubble Machine," *Rolling Stone*, April 5, 2010, http://www.rollingstone.com/politics/news/the-great-american-bubble-machine-20100405.

4. A Chinese wall is a mechanism used to prevent conflicts of interest regarding the use of information. The word *wall* implies that the information cannot get out and is contained. It also implies that there is a line. Often it is a legal line concerning which information can go where, but it is as much an ethical barrier between different divisions of a financial (or other) institution to avoid conflicts of interest. A Chinese wall is said to exist, for example, between the corporate–advisory area and the brokering department of a financial services firm to separate those giving corporate advice on takeovers from those advising clients about buying shares. The wall is created to prevent leaks of inside information that could influence advice given to clients making investments or allow staff to take advantage of facts not yet known to the general public.

5. Goldman acknowledges this confusion in its business standards committee report.

6. http://www.businessinsider.com/goldman-sachs-traders-2010-12.

7. This was a weekly practice from 2006 to 2011. In 2007, Goldman launched a program that allowed research analysts to call a select group of priority clients.

8. A *conviction buy list* is a list of the stocks of companies that Goldman's research analysts believe are extremely attractive for investors to buy.

9. S. N. Lynch and A. Viswanatha, "Goldman to Pay $22 Million to Settle 'Huddles' Case," *Yahoo!*, April 12, 2012, http://news.yahoo.com/goldman-pay-22-million-settle-sec-finra-charges-154759042.html

10. R. Lowenstein, *When Genius Failed: The Rise and Fall of Long Term Capital Management* (New York: Random House, 2000), 172–173.

11. http://www.zerohedge.com/contributed/2012-11-17/greg-smith-vs-goldman-sachs.

12. http://www.sec.gov/litigation/litreleases/lr18113.htm.

13. State of Missouri, Office of Secretary of State, Securities Commission, November 25, 2003, Consent Order, Case No. AO-03-15, http://www.sos.mo.gov/securities/files/goldman_sachs.pdf. Enacted in reaction to a number of corporate and accounting scandals (such as Enron and WORLDCOM), the Sarbanes–Oxley Act of 2002 sets standards for all US public company boards, management, and public accounting firms. The act contains eleven sections, ranging from additional corporate board responsibilities to criminal penalties. The SEC had to adopt dozens of rules to implement the act.

14. State of Missouri, Office of Secretary of State, Securities Commission, November 25, 2003, Consent Order, Case No. AO-03-15.

15. There was already a John L. Weinberg award, which was given to a professional in the investment banking division who best typified Goldman's core values.

16. In this vein, Sørensen and Phillips examine the relationship between organizational size and structural complexity and note problems arising from increasing specialization and fragmentation: "As organizations grow larger, tasks get subdivided into more specialized roles, and an increasing proportion of jobs in the organization is devoted to coordinating between the increasingly elaborate division of labor . . . the average worker in a large firm has less overview over what all of the organization's vital routines are and how they fit together. Nor are they provided with the skills for the integration of the large firm's differentiated skills." See J. Sørensen and D. J. Phillips, "Competence and

Commitment: Employer Size and Entrepreneurial Endurance," *Industrial and Corporate Change* 20, no. 3 (2011), doi: 10.1093/icc/dtr025.

17. Sources for the perception variable discussion include Lulofs (R. S. Lulofs, *Conflict: From Theory to Action* [Scottsdale, AZ: Gorsuch Scarisbrick, 1994]) and Wilmot and Hocker (W. W. Wilmot and J. L. Hocker, *Interpersonal Conflict* 5th ed. [Boston: McGraw-Hill, 1998]).

18. Ellis (*The Partnership—The Making of Goldman Sachs* [New York: Penguin, 2008], 667) wrote that all could be lost—in fact, that all *"would* be lost if the firm squandered its reputation or failed to anticipate, understand, and manage the potential conflicts or failed to excel in its important agency business."

19. A. R. Sorkin, *Too Big to Fail: The Inside Story of How Wall Street and Washington Fought to Save the Financial System from Crisis—and Themselves* (New York: Viking, 2009).

20. Ibid.

21. The business standards committee investigation and report are discussed in detail in chapter 8 as one of the outcomes of Goldman's experience during the credit crisis.

22. See, for example, Sorkin (*Too Big to Fail*) and W. D. Cohan, "Goldman's Double Game," *Businessweek*, March 14, 2012, http://www.businessweek.com/articles/2012-03-14/goldmans-double-game.

23. Ellis, *The Partnership*, 668–669.

24. A. D. Frank, "Goldman Boss Lloyd Blankfein's Testimony Bolsters Case Against Rajat Gupta," *Daily Beast*, June 5, 2012, http://www.thedailybeast.com/articles/2012/06/05/goldman-boss-lloyd-blankfein-s-testimony-bolsters-case-against-rajat-gupta.html.

25. According to court testimony, ironically when then-Goldman board member Raj Gupta wanted to work out an arrangement by which he could stay associated with Goldman and at the same time be associated with the private equity firm Kohlberg Kravis Roberts (KKR), Blankfein said that Goldman had competed with KKR in certain areas and if Gupta worked with both companies it could create a situation of conflict and therefore was not possible. "Mr. Gupta told me he was considering or deciding to accept an offer from a large private-equity group," Blankfein recalled, "to be on their advisory board." The Goldman CEO continued: "I told him that presented certain conflicts for us . . . it created a problem and I did not think it was a good idea." Gupta told Blankfein that he could manage any potential conflicts that might arise while he also consulted with KKR, the private-equity firm first made famous in 1988 by its $25 billion hostile takeover of RJR Nabisco. Blankfein said he decided that Gupta had to give up his Goldman board seat because KKR, while a big customer of Goldman's, also competed with the investment bank, and the conflicts for a director would be too significant to overcome while honoring his "fiduciary duty." So it seems Goldman had decided that Gupta could not "manage conflicts." (See Frank, "Goldman Boss Lloyd Blankfein's Testimony Bolsters Case Against Rajat Gupta.")

26. The conflict issues are often raised by boutique advisory firms as their competitive advantage over larger, full-service firms. Some of the executives I interviewed work at boutique investment advisory firms. They said that because they do not have large trading or financing businesses, they can offer more independent and less conflicted advice. Sorkin (*Too Big to Fail*, 463–464) describes boutique firms as resembling the Wall Street partnerships of the 1970s and 1980s, in that they present fewer opportunities for real or perceived potential conflicts. When Morgan Stanley's independent board members, led by C. Robert Kidder, the lead director, decided to hire an independent adviser, they

chose Roger Altman, former deputy secretary of the Treasury, who founded the boutique investment banking firm Evercore Partners. His role was to advise Morgan Stanley's board on transactions, but within twenty-four hours of being hired, he was advising the board to think seriously about selling the firm. Some people I interviewed raised the concern that some of the boutique firms are publicly traded or have meaningful outside investors or private equity departments that might impact how the firms are managed.

27. The "doomsday scenario" Altman painted during that board meeting had some people convinced that he was interested only in collecting a big fee by advising Morgan Stanley on selling. Others worried that he might pass on information about the company's financial health to his government contacts. Some thought that any advice about selling the firm should come from Morgan Stanley's own bankers. Another concern was Evercore's partnership with Mizuho Financial Group of Japan, a rival of Mitsubishi, which was in negotiations with Morgan Stanley at the time. The main theme seemed to be, "I don't know what this guy [Altman] is up to" (Sorkin, *Too Big to Fail*, 463–464). I mention this story because I find it interesting how banks view each other's conflicts and motivations.

28. William Cohan, quoted at http://www.efinancialnews.com/story/2011-04-14/qa-cohan-goldman-money-power.

29. The categories in which members were grouped are subjective because members have various backgrounds as they have rotated, so although someone may be in one division at the time he/she is on the committee, I asked interviewees with which groups they were most affiliated. I also asked research analysts to independently look at the backgrounds of the various members and make independent judgments, which came out relatively close to my analysis and included information from interviewees.

Chapter 8

1. Goldman's NEOs are currently Lloyd Blankfein (CEO), Gary Cohn (president and COO), David Viniar (CFO), Michael Evans (a vice chairman, global head of growth markets, and chairman of Goldman Sachs Asia), and John S. Weinberg (a vice chairman and co-head of investment banking).

2. "Without question, direct government support helped stabilize the financial system. We believe that the government action was critical, and we benefited from it." Testimony by Lloyd Blankfein, www.goldmansachs.com/media-relations/in-the-news/archive/1-13-testimony.html.

3. R. Swedberg, "The Structure of Confidence and the Collapse of Lehman Brothers," in *Markets on Trial: The Economic Sociology of the U.S. Financial Crisis*, ed. M. Lounsbury and P. M. Hirsch (Bingley, UK: Emerald, 2010), 69–112.

4. My analysis as a sociologist focusing on the organizational factors should not detract from serious questions and concerns raised by many people, such as the Senate Subcommittee on Investigations, chaired by Carl Levin (D.-Mich.), alongside Tom Coburn (R.-Okla.); and several authors including William Cohan, Bethany McLean, Matt Taibbi, and Gillian Tett.

5. In *Too Big to Fail: The Inside Story of How Wall Street and Washington Fought to Save the Financial System from Crisis—and Themselves* (New York: Viking, 2009), A. R. Sorkin implies that Hank Paulson, in his role as Treasury secretary, grasped the true systemic risk at hand only after the Lehman bankruptcy and Bank of America deal for Merrill Lynch. Yet Goldman had been actively trying to de-risk for months.

6. P. Jorion, "In Defense of VaR," *Derivatives Strategy*, April 1997, http://www .derivativesstrategy.com/magazine/archive/1997/0497fea2.asp.

7. J. Nocera, "Risk Mismanagement," *New York Times*, January 4, 2009, http://www .nytimes.com/2009/01/04/magazine/04risk-t.html?_r=1.

8. "Stark's work, however, suggests an alternative conjecture: that it would have taken heterarchical organization to fuse together the two institutionally separate insights needed fully to grasp those dangers. The conjecture is plausible: in particular, Goldman Sachs, reported by several of my interviewees to be more heterarchical in its organization than most other major banks (it was a partnership, not a public company, until 1999), escaped financially almost unscathed. Unlike almost all other banks, Goldman hedged or liquidated its ABS and ABS CDO positions several months before the crisis. However, the systematic, comparative organizational research needed to test the conjecture is, for reasons of access, currently impossible." (See D. MacKenzie, "The Credit Crisis as a Problem in the Sociology of Knowledge," *American Journal of Sociology* 116, no. 6 (2011): 1832.)

9. One of the characteristics Weick ascribes to high-reliability organizations is the "mindfulness with which people in most HROs react to even very weak signs that some kind of change or danger is approaching." He describes HROs as "fixated on failure" and refusing to "simplify reality." See K. E. Weick and D. L. Coutu, "Sense and Reliability: A Conversation with Celebrated Psychologist Karl E. Weick," *Harvard Business Review*, April 2003, 84–90, 123.

10. E. Derman, *My Life as a Quant: Reflections on Physics and Finance* (Hoboken, NJ: Wiley, 2004), 257.

11. J. Nocera, "Risk Mismanagement," *New York Times*, January 4, 2009, http://www .nytimes.com/2009/01/04/magazine/04risk-t.html?_r=1.

12. Sorkin, *Too Big to Fail*, chapter 7. But his actions would have unintended consequences.

13. According to Goldman's 2012 proxy statement, Goldman's board held fifteen meetings. Its independent directors also met thirteen times in executive session without management. Goldman disclosed that its directors meet informally from time to time to receive updates from senior management, and the directors receive weekly informational packages that include updates on recent developments, press coverage, and current events related to its business. Some people I interviewed said that a board position could be almost a full-time position, with selected board members needing to sit in on risk management meetings.

14. U.S. Senate Permanent Subcommittee on Investigations, "Wall Street and the Financial Crisis Anatomy of a Financial Collapse: Majority and Minority Staff Report," 2011, http://hsgac.senate.gov/public/_files/Financial_Crisis/FinancialCrisisReport. pdf.

15. http://www.ft.com/intl/cms/s/80e2987a-2e50-11dc-821c-0000779fd2ac, Authorised=false.html?_i_location=http%3A%2F%2Fwww.ft.com%2Fcms% 2Fs%2F0%2F80e2987a-2e50-11dc-821c-0000779fd2ac.html&_i_referer=#axzz2Rrj0fwk

16. L. Endlich, *Goldman Sachs—The Culture of Success* (New York: Simon & Schuster, 2000), 199.

17. Ibid.

18. Ibid.

19. Endlich, *Goldman Sachs*, 225.

20. William Cohan, *Money and Power: How Goldman Sachs Came to Rule the World* (New York: Doubleday, 2012), 529.

21. http://dealbook.nytimes.com/2012/10/01/the-j-aron-takeover-of-goldman-sachs/.

22. Cohan, *Money and Power*.

23. W. D. Cohan, "Where Blankfein Came From," *Fortune*, April 20, 2011, http://management.fortune.cnn.com/2011/04/21/where-blankfein-came-from/.

24. C. D. Ellis, *The Partnership—The Making of Goldman Sachs* (New York: Penguin Press, (2008), 668.

25. Ellis, *The Partnership*, 670–671.

26. A 2011 review of Cohan's *Money and Power* published in *The Economist* addresses clients' confusion about whether Goldman is an agent or competitor: "Goldman has pushed this envelope further than any other investment banks, believing it had the skill to manage the resulting conflicts." See "Goldman Sachs: Long on Chutzpah, Short on Friends," *The Economist*, April 14, 2011, http://www.economist.com/node/18557354.

27. Ellis, *The Partnership*, 670–671.

28. Goldman had a tradition of mobility of people among departments, divisions, and geographies. Small steps that lead to new practices, and the normalization they entail, are seldom visible or seen as significant by those who work in a department or organization for a long time (see S. Dekker, *Drift into Failure: From Hunting Broken Components to Understanding Complex Systems* [Farnham, UK: Ashgate Publishing, 2011], 180). It helps to have people come in from other areas to bring fresh perspectives that help insiders recalibrate what they consider normal. It also forces insiders to articulate their ideas about running their system. This can be true culturally, as well as from a risk management perspective. In both, an environment that supports rotation of employees and discussion is important.

29. Executives also need to overcome the structural secrecy inherent in the technical language of risk management.

30. M. Taibbi, "The Great American Bubble Machine," *Rolling Stone*, April 5, 2010, http://www.rollingstone.com/politics/news/the-great-american-bubble-machine-20100405.

31. M. Taibbi, "The People vs. Goldman Sachs," *Rolling Stone*, May 11, 2011, http://www.rollingstone.com/politics/news/the-people-vs-goldman-sachs-20110511?page=3.

32. Taibbi, "The Great American Bubble Machine."

33. A *fiduciary* is someone who has undertaken to act for and on behalf of another in a particular matter in circumstances that give rise to a relationship of trust and confidence. A fiduciary duty is the highest standard of care at either equity or law.

34. Goldman is, however, a fiduciary to its shareholders and to the funds it manages for clients. Legislation was proposed (as part of the Dodd–Frank Act) that would impose a fiduciary standard rather than the current suitability standard for those selling products. The intent was to require brokers to put clients' interests first or be held legally accountable. Within a week, that provision was dropped after intense lobbying by Wall Street.

35. However, under the federal securities laws, investment advisers (banks that manage clients' money, such as Goldman's asset management business or private equity business) are bound to a fiduciary standard that requires them to put their client's interests above their own. Conflicts of interest must be disclosed, and self-dealing is generally prohibited.

36. Blankfein "basically [denied] it all" at the hearing. "The political environment we live in now is such that he would rather look like they were as dumb as the other firms on Wall Street. And yet the evidence is overwhelming. They didn't do it nefariously.

They did it because they thought they could make money. And they did. I think they made $13 billion pre-tax in 2007." (See J. Pressler, "Goldman Chronicler William Cohan Is Doing God's Work," *New York Magazine*, April 17, 2011, http://nymag.com/daily/intelligencer/2011/04/william_cohan_is_doing_gods_wo.html.)

37. Goldman did not have a fiduciary responsibility to BP or to Sara Lee (see chapter 1) but still accorded them essentially that level of care.

38. I also heard echoes of the "higher purpose" rationalization (see chapter 9) in the fiduciary responsibility defense offered as an explanation of Goldman's actions.

39. A Goldman spokesman said that until AIG was rescued by the government, the insurer "was viewed as one of the most sophisticated financial counterparties in the world. It wasn't until the government intervened in September 2008 that the full extent of AIG's problems became apparent." The interesting comment is the next one: "'What is lost in the discussion is that AIG assumed billions of dollars in risk it was unable to manage,' the Goldman spokesman added." This is a key ethical issue and source of criticism, so why was Goldman selling it to them? (See S. Ng and C. Mollenkamp, "Goldman Fueled AIG Gambles," *Wall Street Journal*, December 12, 2009, http://online.wsj.com/article/SB10001424052748704201404574590453176996032.html; and http://www.npr.org/blogs/money/2010/04/is_goldman_sorry_it_sold_a_sec.html.)

40. Although the data shows a sudden spike, there were signals and public recognition of changes. For example, there were also rumbles about Goldman's serving its own interests ahead of clients' and questions about conflicts of interest: "Goldman Sachs has engineered many megadeals over the years. But few underscore its influence on Wall Street like the deal it brokered yesterday . . . The surprising merger of Archipelago, an electronic stock market, and the New York Stock Exchange cements, perhaps definitively, Goldman's longstanding role as the premier Wall Street firm, and the one with the most sway over the Big Board's future. . . . But while the merger emphasizes this notion, it also raises longstanding fears among supporters of the auction-based model that Goldman's intent, as the largest user of the exchange, has been to divert order flow from the exchange floor to its own trading desks, a process called internalization." See L. Thomas, "Goldman Seals a Deal, and Its Status," *New York Times*, April 21, 2005, http://query.nytimes.com/gst/fullpage.html?res=9A03EFDE1731F932A15757C0A9639C8B63.

41. "Goldman to Review Its Business Practices," *New York Times*, May 7, 2010, http://dealbook.nytimes.com/2010/05/07/goldman-toreview-its-business-practices/.

42. Endlich, *Goldman Sachs*, 164.

43. "Goldman Sachs Clients Lost in Translation," *London Evening Standard*, January 14, 2011, http://www.this islondon.co.uk/standard-business/article-23914152-city-spy-goldman-sachs-clients-lost-in-translation.do.

44. L. Rappaport, "Goldman Opens Up to Mollify Its Critics," *Wall Street Journal*, January 11, 2011, http://online.wsj.com/article/SB1000142405274870377970457607436028863

5474.html.

45. S. Johnson, "Goldman Sachs: 'We Consider Our Size an Asset That We Try Hard to Preserve,'" *Baseline Scenario*, January 13, 2011, http://baselinescenario.com/2011/01/13/goldman-sachs-we-consider-our-size-an-asset-that-we-try-hard-to-preserve/.

46. R. Teitelman, "Goldman Sachs, Business Standards and the Critics," *Huffington Post*, January 14, 2011, http://www.huffingtonpost.com/robert-teitelman/goldman-business-standard_b_808827.html.

47. J. Carney, "The Banality of Goldman's Business Standards," CNBC, January 12, 2011, http://www.cnbc.com/id/41040099/The_Banality_ of_Goldman_s_ Business_ Standards.

48. Johnson, "Goldman Sachs."

49. Carney, "The Banality of Goldman's Business Standards."

50. Johnson, "Goldman Sachs."

51. Ibid.

52. Carney, "The Banality of Goldman's Business Standards." See also http://www .clmr.unsw.edu.au/article/ethics/embedding-ethics/basis-trust-warranted-goldman-sachs-business-standards-report-assessed: "The failure to articulate and integrate purpose, values and principles within a functioning ethical framework created toxic and socially harmful corporate cultures in urgent need of reform, which an emphasis on technical measures alone will be incapable of addressing. The critical question, therefore, is whether the revised Goldman approach, which covers client relationships, conflicts of interest, structure products, transparency and disclosure, broader governance, and training and development, represents a robust improvement or should be seen as a cynical privileging of symbolism? On this front, the evidence is mixed."

53. http://blogs.reuters.com/financial-regulatory-forum/2013/05/30/goldman-standards-review-reflects-new-compliance-landscape/.

54. S. Craig and P. Lattman, "Goldman's Shares Tumble as Blankfein Hires Top Lawyer," *New York Times*, August 22, 2011, http://dealbook.nytimes.com/2011/08/22/goldmans-shares-tumble-as-blankfein-hires-lawyer/.

55. Greg Smith, "Why I Am Leaving Goldman Sachs," *New York Times*, March 14, 2012, http://www.nytimes.com/2012/03/14/opinion/why-i-am-leaving-goldman-sachs .html?pagewanted=all.

56. I asked some Goldman partners about this survey. They said it was an internal survey and must be taken with a grain of salt. When people fill out internal surveys, they might be concerned about where the information goes and who sees what and from whom; they question the confidentiality. I found this interesting, because some clients I interviewed expressed the same skepticism about Goldman.

57. "Goldman Sachs (GS) Issues Response to Op-Ed Piece in *New York Times*," *Street Insider*, March 14, 2012, http://www.streetinsider.com/Corporate+News/Goldman+Sachs+%28GS%29+Issues+Response+to+Op-Ed+Piece+in+New+York+Times/7268955.html.

58. "Another Ex-Goldman Banker Confesses: The Firm Became 'Toxic,'" *Daily Finance*, March 15, 2012, http://www.dailyfinance.com/2012/03/15/ex-goldman-banker-confesses-toxic-smith-resignation/.

59. When Goldman went public it listed three competitive strengths: "strong client relationships," "distinctive people and culture," and "global reach." It is difficult to argue that Goldman does not still have these as competitive strengths.

60. S. Cruise, "Goldman Sachs' Greg Smith's Letter Prompts Backlash from Clients," *Huffington Post*, March 15, 2012, http://www.huffingtonpost.com/2012/03/15/goldman-sachs-backlash-clients-begins-gain-steam_n_1349576.html.

61. D. McCrum, D. Schafer, and P. Jenkins, "Goldman's Clients Stand by Their Bank," *Financial Times*, March 15, 2012, http://www.ft.com/intl/cms/s/0/db9ae576-6ebd-11e1-afb8-00144feab49a.html.

62. Taibbi, "The Great American Bubble Machine."

63. C. Harper, "Goldman Model Championed by Blankfein Planted Seeds of Distress," *Bloomberg*, July 21, 2011, http://www.bloomberg.com/news/2011-07-22/goldman-sachs-model-championed-by-blankfein-planted-seeds-of-own-distress.html.

64. Nils Pratley, "Muppets of the World Unite," *The Guardian*, March 14, 2012, www.guardian.co.uk/business/nils-pratley-on-finance/2012/mar/14/goldman-sachs-greg-smith-muppets.

65. T. Samuelson, "Goldman Sachs Employee's Op-Ed Doesn't Surprise Some," WYNC, March 14, 2012, http://www.wnyc.org/blogs/wnyc-news-blog/2012/mar/14/goldman-sachs-employees-op-ed-doesnt-surprise-clients/.

66. Cruise, "Goldman Sachs' Greg Smith's Letter Prompts Backlash from Clients."

67. Ibid.

68. www.reuters.com/article/2012/03/16/goldman-apg-idUSL2E8EFCAW20120316.

69. In 2012, in part because Goldman was losing so many financial analysts that it committed to employ for two years to hedge funds and private equity funds after just one year of training, Goldman changed its policy and hired full-time financial analysts right out of school. If the analysts are caught interviewing, it is technically a fireable offense. The New York office's decision came after executives grew frustrated that many graduates weren't staying with the firm after completing the two-year period, and after Goldman fired a handful of analysts for signing on to work at other financial companies in violation of their contracts. In recent years, private-equity firms have become more aggressive in recruiting Goldman analysts, said people in the private-equity industry. The companies used to begin recruiting from Goldman's analyst program in March of the analyst's first year. Recently, some firms advanced their initial overtures to January, when analysts have been working at Goldman for only about six months.

70. I was curious if Goldman's fees had been impacted, so I analyzed Goldman's publicly disclosed sell side advisory M&A fees for $1 billion to $4 billion from 2003 to 2011. I selected this product and range because it is considered "bread and butter" assignments for the M&A department. From 2003 to 2008, the firm had a premium of the percentage of deal size over a selected peer group average each year. But since 2009, the fees have been the average.

71. P. J. Henning, "Is That It for Financial Crisis Cases?" *New York Times*, August 13, 2012, http://dealbook.nytimes.com/2012/08/13/is-that-it-for-financial-crisis-cases/.

72. P. Lattman, "U.S. Goldman Disclosure a Rare Break in Secrecy," *New York Times*, August 10, 2012, http://dealbook.nytimes.com/2012/08/10/justice-department-closes-investigation-of-goldman/.

73. C. J. Levin, "Sen. Levin Statement on DOJ Announcement on Goldman Sachs," August 10, 2012, http://www.levin.senate.gov/newsroom/press/release/sen-levin-statement-on-doj-announcement-on-goldman-sachs.

74. G. Bowley, "$500 Million and Apology from Goldman," *New York Times*, November 17, 2009, http://www.nytimes.com/2009/11/18/business/18goldman.html.

Chapter 9

1. Criticism has been focused on Goldman's arrangement to allow its partners to participate in the $1.5 billion Facebook offer, when some clients were being shut out.

2. C. Harper, "Goldman to Cash Out $1 Billion of Facebook Holding in IPO," *Bloomberg*, May 17, 2012, http://www.bloomberg.com/news/2012-05-17/goldman-to-cash-out-1-billion-of-facebook-holding-in-ipo.html/.

3. M. Dowd, "Op-Ed Columnist; Virtuous Bankers? Really!?!" *New York Times*, November 11, 2009, http://www.nytimes.com/2009/11/11/opinion/11dowd.html.

4. According to J. W. Meyer and B. Rowan ("Institutionalized Organizations: Formal Structure as Myth and Ceremony," *American Journal of Sociology* 83, no. 2 [1977]: 340, doi: 10.1086/226550), "[I]nstitutional theorists believe that the institutional environment can strongly influence the development of formal structures in an organization, often more profoundly than market pressures. Innovative structures that improve technical efficiency in early-adopting organizations are legitimized in the environment. Ultimately these innovations reach a level of legitimization where failure to adopt them

is seen as 'irrational and negligent' (or they become legal mandates). At this point new and existing organizations will adopt the structural form even if the form doesn't improve efficiency." Meyer and Rowan argue that often these "institutional myths" are merely accepted ceremoniously in order for the organization to gain or maintain legitimacy in the institutional environment. Organizations adopt the "vocabularies of structure" prevalent in their environment, such as specific job titles, procedures, and organizational roles. The adoption and prominent display of these institutionally acceptable "trappings of legitimacy" help preserve an appearance of organizational action based on "good faith." Legitimacy in the institutional environment helps ensure organizational survival.

5. John Whitehead, Bob Rubin, Hank Paulson, Jon Corzine, Steve Friedman, and many others have gone on to hold high-level government positions. In addition, Goldman's community service and philanthropy are mentioned often in Goldman's public filings.

6. C. D. Ellis, *The Partnership—The Making of Goldman Sachs* (New York: Penguin, 2008), 664.

7. B. McLean, "The Bank Job," *Vanity Fair*, March 23, 2012, http://www.vanityfair.com/business/features/2010/01/goldman-sachs-200101.

8. http://www.thedailyshow.com/watch/thu-april-28-2011/exclusive william-cohan-extended-interview-pt-2.

9. Stephen Colbert, "Greg Smith's Goldman Sachs Op-Ed," *The Colbert Report* (Viacom), March 14, 2012.

10. W. D. Cohan, "Doing God's Work: How Goldman Became the Vampire Squid," *Institutional Investor*, April 25, 2011, http://www.institutionalinvestor.com/Popups/PrintArticle.aspx?ArticleID=2813008.

11. http://businesshighbeam.com/435607/article-1G1-16396594/inside-goldman-college-cardinals.

12. James Quinn and James Hall, "Goldman Sachs Vice-Chairman Says: 'Learn to Tolerate Inequality,'" *The Telegraph*, www.telegraph.co.uk/finance/recession/6392127/Goldman-Sachs-vice chairman-says-Learn-to-tolerate-inequality.html.

13. William Cohan, *Money and Power: How Goldman Sachs Came to Rule the World* (New York: Doubleday, 2012).

14. McLean, "The Bank Job."

15. L. Endlich, *Goldman Sachs—The Culture of Success* (New York: Simon & Schuster, 2000), 8.

16. See R. S. Kaplan, *What to Ask the Person in the Mirror: Critical Questions for Becoming a More Effective Leader and Reaching Your Potential* (Boston: Harvard Business Review Press, 2011), 15. This attitude seems to have changed in recent years. Gary Cohn has stated that competitive pressures limit how much the firm can cut compensation: "There is enormous pressure out there, even in a market environment like this, for the best people . . . There's always a competitor, or in some cases a client, willing to hire our good people." See also "Goldman's Cohn Warns of Poaching Risks from Further Cuts," *Bloomberg*, May 31, 2012, http://www.bloomberg.com/news/print/2012-05-31/goldman-s-cohn-warns-of-poaching-risks-from-further-cuts.html.

17. Many people have noted that Goldman's political contributions and money spent on lobbying put it in an ethical gray zone. John Fritze noted that Goldman Sachs is "one of the financial industry's most generous political givers"(John Fritze, "Goldman Political Contributions Under Attack, *USA Today*, April 23, 2010 www.intellectualtakeout.org/library/articles-commentary-blog/goldman-political-contributions-under-attack). According to Jonathan Salant, Goldman increased its

lobbying in 2010 when the Senate considered the rewriting of financial regulations (Jonathan D. Salant, "Goldman Doubled Lobbying Expenses Amid Financial Revamp, SEC, Probe," *Bloomberg.com*, July 21, 2010, www.bloomberg.com/news/2010-07-21/goldman-sachs-doubled-lobbying-expenses-amid-financial-revamp-sec-probe.html). Further, Felix Salmon charged that former Secretary of the Treasury Hank Paulson gave insider tips to Goldman employees. Salmon writes, "Paulson was giving inside tips to Wall Street in general, and to Goldman types in particular: exactly the kind of behavior that 'Government Sachs' conspiracy theorists have been speculating about for years. Turns out, they were right" (Felix Salmon, "Hank Paulson's Inside Jobs," *Reuters.com*, November 29, 2011, http://blogs.reuters.com/felix-salmon/2011/11/29/hank-paulsons-inside-jobs/). Madison Ruppert says that Paulson's actions epitomize "the plague upon our economy, and the greater global economic system, that is crony capitalism" (see "Turns Out the 'Government Sachs' Conspiracy Theorists Were Right All Along," December 1, 2011, http://www.activistpost.com/2011/12/turns-out-government-sachs-conspiracy.html).

18. L. Wayne, "The Corridor from Goldman to Washington Is Well Traveled," *New York Times*, December 13, 2002.

19. Ibid.

20. J. Grant, "Goldman Shrinks an Adage; Long-Term Greedy Can't Wait," *Observer*, February 15, 1999, http://www.observer.com/1999/02/goldman-shrinks-an-adage-longterm-greedy-cant-wait/.

21. S. Lohr, "Goldman's Pitch for Deals in Russia," *New York Times*, March 12, 1992.

22. CBS News Investigates, "Goldman Sachs' Revolving Door," *CBS News*, April 7, 2010, http://www.cbsnews.com/8301-31727_162-20001981-10391695.html.

23. M. Lynn, "Goldman Sachs Has Gained Too Much Political Power," *Bloomberg News*, June 4, 2006, http://www.bloomberg.com/apps/news?pid=newsarchive&refer=columnist_lynn&sid=aGS6lvr8ipiw.

24. A. R. Sorkin's *Too Big to Fail* (New York: Penguin Press, 2009) provides a detailed timeline of events that occurred as the financial system teetered on the brink of collapse. It documents a number of phone calls and other communications between Blankfein and Goldman and between Paulson and former Goldman employees, which a few people have pointed to as evidence of Goldman benefiting from its ties to government.

Conclusion

1. According to the *New York Times*, since the close of its May 1999 IPO to September 2011, Goldman's stock has returned nearly 175 percent. The Standard & Poor's 500-stock index over the same period has lost almost 2.9 percent; see http://dealbook.nytimes.com/2011/01/18/study-points-to-windfall-for-goldman-partners/.

2. http://money.cnn.com/2012/07/21/news/economy/dodd-frank/index.htm.

3. Ibid.

4. www.followthemoney.org/press/ReportView.phtml?r=425.

5. P. Weinberg, "Wall Street Needs More Skin in the Game," *Wall Street Journal*, September 30, 2009, http://online.wsj.com/article/SB1000142405274870447150457444359 1328265858.html.

6. Bear Stearns recently agreed to settle a 2009 class action suit brought by its shareholders, who lost most of their investments when the firm started to collapse, the value of their shares falling from more than $170 per share to as little as $2, although J.P. Morgan

paid them $10 per share when it bought Bear Stearns. According to Tom Braithwaite and Tracy Alloway of the *Financial Times*, the $275 million settlement, agreed upon without any admission of wrongdoing, is "a rare example of senior Wall Street figures being held accountable for allegations of misconduct." Certain executives and the firm itself were accused of "misleading investors about the true health of the investment bank . . . [The] company used its misleading models to inflate asset values and revenues and to offer the public artificially low calculations of its value at risk, an estimate of the amount a bank could lose over a single day." The executives' portion of the settlement will most likely be covered by insurance.

7. C. A. Hill and R. W. Painter, "Another View: A Simpler Rein Than the Volcker Rule," *New York Times*, October 28, 2011, http://dealbook.nytimes.com/2011/10/28/another-view-a-simpler-rein-than-the-volcker-rule/.

8. Ibid.

9. According to Jack and Suzy Welch, "In fact, soft culture matters as much as hard numbers . . . And yet, for some reason, too many leaders think a company's values can be relegated to a five-minute conversation between HR and a new employee. Or they think culture is about picking which words—do we 'honor' our customers or 'respect' them?—to engrave on a plaque in the lobby. What nonsense . . . Look, it's Management 101 to say that the best competitive weapon a company can possess is a strong culture. But the devil is in the details of execution. And if you don't get it right, it's the devil to pay." See Jack and Suzy Welch, "Goldman Sachs and a Culture-Killing Lesson Being Ignored," CNNMoney, April 12, 2012, http://management.fortune.cnn.com/2012/04/12/goldman-sachs-culture-values/.

10. A senior financing banker at Goldman, who made partner in 2008, said, "Goldman looks at three things: your commercial effectiveness; your managerial and entrepreneurial skills; and your culture and values. All three are weighted equally and it is the right balance of the three combined that will determine whether you make partner or not." However, another current partner said: "Unofficially, commercial effectiveness is above [the rest]. It helps you stand out." See www.efinancialnews.com/story/2012-11-12/goldman-sachs-protecting-the-partnership.

11. Jack and Suzy Welch wrote that when an employee is not behaving consistently with the principles, there needs to be a public message. "And the only antidote is that Jim and Sally need to be sent home, and not with the usual 'They want to spend more time with their families' BS out of the lawyers and HR, but with the truth. 'Jim and Sally had great numbers,' everyone needs to be told, 'but they didn't demonstrate the values of this company.' We guarantee that such a public 'diss play,' to put it more politely, will have more impact than a hundred 'Our values really, really matter!' speeches by the CEO." See Welch and Welch, "Goldman Sachs and a Culture-Killing Lesson Being Ignored."

12. J.P. Morgan has been criticized recently because the committee responsible for overseeing risks "wasn't up to the task of monitoring the bank's risk." The committee includes, for example, Ellen Futter, head of the American Museum of Natural History, who served on AIG's governance committee just before AIG collapsed. "Other committee members include the CEO of a defense contractor and a man who hasn't worked on Wall Street for 25 years. What the committee's missing that all the other big banks have: people who worked as financial risk managers." (See J. Berman, "JPMorgan Chase Risk Management Committee Missing Bank Directors, Financial Risk Managers," *Huffington Post*, May 25, 2012, http://www.huffingtonpost.com/2012/05/25/jpmorgan-chase-risk-management-committee_n_1546215.html.)

13. According to Jack and Suzy Welch, "An organization's culture is not about words at all. It's about behavior—and consequences. It's about every single individual who manages people knowing that his or her key role is that of chief values officer, with Sarbanes–Oxley-like enforcement powers to match. It's about knowing that at every performance review, employees are evaluated for both their numbers and their values . . ." See Welch and Welch, "Goldman Sachs and a Culture-Killing Lesson Being Ignored."

14. Jack Welch with Suzy Welch, *Winning* (New York: HarperCollins, 2005).

Appendix A

1. Scott A. Snook, *Friendly Fire: The Accidental Shootdown of U.S. Blackhawks over Northern Iraq* (Princeton, NJ: Princeton University Press, 2002), 225.

2. S. Dekker, *Drift into Failure: From Hunting Broken Components to Understanding Complex Systems* (Farnham, UK: Ashgate Publishing, 2011). Johan Bergstrøm ("Listen to Sidney Dekker Lecturing about Drift into Failure," October 10, 2011, http://johanniklas. blogspot.com/2011/10/listen-to-sidney-dekker-lecturing-about.html.) notes, "The drift concept offers the theory of how organizational failure and success emerge in incubation periods not characterized by incomplete interaction, but by non-linear effects of local interactions in environments characterized by goal-conflicts, competition and uncertainties."

3. S. Dekker, *Drift into Failure*, 179.

4. Ibid.

5. Dekker, *Drift into Failure*, 14.

6. Dekker, *Drift into Failure*, 17.

7. Dekker, *Drift into Failure*, 17, 116.

8. Snook points out that the word "drift" implies a subtle movement. He believes that detecting such movement "requires a sensitivity to the passage of time. Single snapshots won't do." (See Snook, *Friendly Fire*, 225.) All explanations assume some passage of time. One of the goals of my study is to extend it further, beyond an event.

9. In *Normal Accidents: Living with High-Risk Technologies* (New York: Basic Books, 1984), Charles Perrow explains a normal accident as normal "not in the sense of being frequent or being expected . . . it is normal in the sense that it is an inherent property of the system to occasionally experience their interaction."

10. Barry A. Turner, *Man-Made Disasters* (London: Wykeham Publications, 1978), 85.

11. Turner, *Man-Made Disasters*, 72.

12. L. Peattie, "Normalizing the Unthinkable," *Bulletin of Atomic Scientists*, no. 3 (1984): 34.

13. E. S. Herman, *Triumph of the Market: Essays on Economics, Politics, and the Media* (Cambridge, MA: South End Press, 1999), 99.

14. Ibid.

15. D. Vaughan, *The Challenger Launch Decision: Risky Technology, Culture, and Deviance at NASA* (Chicago: University of Chicago Press, 1996), 61.

16. Vaughan, *The Challenger Launch Decision*, xiii.

17. Vaughan, *The Challenger Launch Decision*, 39.

18. Normalization differs from Snook in that it starts in a subunit, but the subunit alters the beliefs, understandings, and practices of the whole organization. Also, the normalization of deviance is pushed forward by characteristics such as structural secrecy, organizational culture, and the external competitive environment. NASA organizational culture is changed by the external environment, so NASA, formerly R&D-focused when apolitical and

provided with abundant funding, becomes more like a business organization—competing for scarce resources, making deadlines. The normalization of deviance refers to people making decisions and enacting practices over time so that at the first decision they accepted a technical anomaly that deviated from expectations, then continued to use that as a base, incrementally expanding the amount of deviation they found acceptable. It is agency, shaped by organizational and environmental factors. So what happened at NASA was not drift in the way Snook defines it because drift detaches outcomes from people's action which is different than Vaughan's normalization. From a personal communication with Vaughan, 2013.

19. Vaughan, *The Challenger Launch Decision*, 55.

20. Vaughan, *The Challenger Launch Decision*, 42.

21. Vaughan, *The Challenger Launch Decision*, 238. The compartmentalizing, divisive effects of rapid organizational growth are also evident in the appearance of structural and functional "silos." The more complex an organization's structure becomes, the more likely silos are to emerge, as the result of the division of labor. G. Tett (*Fool's Gold: How the Bold Dream of a Small Tribe at J.P. Morgan Was Corrupted by Wall Street Greed and Unleashed a Catastrophe* [New York: Free Press, 2009]) recognizes such silos as one of the big issues at a large bank, noting that the silos are widely accepted self-contained realms of activity and knowledge that only the experts in the silos can truly understand.

22. Vaughan, *The Challenger Launch Decision*, 67. In the *Challenger* case, Vaughan points out that the NASA culture changed when the politics of the space shuttle program changed. The culture of the organization did not drift slowly over time. The organization culture impinged upon decision making for practices that changed over time, and the normalization of deviance was a cultural belief in the work group that was spread throughout the organization—in relation to one particular component. Snook's argument in practical drift is that the practices drifted over time.

23. Vaughan, *The Challenger Launch Decision*, 273.

24. Vaughan's theory and framework were laid out in her 1985 book, *Controlling Unlawful Organizational Behavior: Social Structure and Corporate Misconduct* (Chicago, University of Chicago Press, 1985). The normalization of deviance and culture and institutional theory in *The Challenger Launch Decision* expanded on that original framework because *Challenger* gave her different data. Diane Vaughan first described structural secrecy in 1983.

25. Vaughan, *The Challenger Launch Decision*, 15. Perhaps Goldman had an advantage over many of its peers in this regard, because it had clear norms in its business principles; problems arose when behavior started to shift away from those norms.

26. Technology, technically, is still an organizational characteristic in Vaughan's framework because the capability is internal to each organization. One also could logically address technology as a separate component within Vaughan's competitive environment category, as everyone was using the same devices to stay in the competition and therefore it became normative, so it fits both those central concepts. However, I believe that technology should be extracted out of organization or competition as its own factor in order to analyze and monitor it more closely. Technology is playing such an important role in organizational change, and is changing so rapidly, that I believe for this case it was helpful to isolate it.

27. There are other sociological processes and theories that I considered for my framework, such as societal pressures. There has been some discussion about whether to include society as a factor in the framework, and if so, how that might be accomplished. Organization scholars have incorporated it as environment or institutions, paring it down from the more global term, *society*. Aldrich wrote *Organizations and Environments*

in the 1970s (Englewood Cliffs, NJ: Prentice Hall, 1979), and A. L. Stinchcombe wrote "Social Structure and Organizations" in 1965 (J. G. March, *Handbook of Organizations* [Chicago: Rand McNally & Co., 1965], 142–193). More recently, Sagiv and Schwartz ("Cultural Value in Organizations: Insights for Europe," *European Journal of International Management* 1 [2007]: 176–190) argue that the surrounding society, the personal value priorities of organizational members, and the nature of the organization's primary tasks influence organizational culture because organizations operate under societal pressure. In other words, organizations must comply with norms and values of societies. Further, organizations consist of individuals who introduce their own value preferences to the organization, which represents the way people select actions, evaluate individuals and events, and explain their actions and evaluations—all of which shape organizational culture. Therefore, frameworks need to account for the possibility of societal pressure as well as the different natures of businesses. Sagiv and Schwartz believe no ethnographer would overlook the important variable of society.

I think this is a very interesting idea and is just one example in which this case study could have been improved. However, I found in this case that it would be challenging for me to have a framework that included society in depth over a long period of time. In 1958, Kroeber and Parsons recommended that culture and social system (society) be analyzed as independent ("The Concept of Culture and Social System," *American Sociological Review* 23, no. 5 [1958]: 582–583). This, of course, was not to say that the two systems are not related, or that various approaches to the analysis of the relationship may not be used. They thought it was often beneficial to researchers to hold constant either cultural or societal aspects of the same concrete phenomena while addressing attention to the other. For this study, I adopted Kroeber and Parsons' recommendations because I found that in my empirical work it was too vague over long periods of time and needed to be broken into its relevant categories.

Appendix B

1. See Diane Vaughan, *The Challenger Launch Decision: Risky Technology, Culture, and Deviance at NASA* (Chicago: University of Chicago Press, 1996); and Diane Vaughan, "The Dark Side of Organizations: Mistake, Misconduct, Disaster," *Annual Review of Sociology* 25, no. 1 (1999): 271–305, doi: 10.1146/annurev.soc.25.1.271.

Appendix C

1. "Goldman Sachs' Revolving Door," CBS News, April 7, 2010.
2. http://www.nytimes.com/2008/10/19/business/19gold.html?pagewanted=all&_r=0.

Appendix D

1. http://www.businessweek.com/1999/99_20/b3629102.htm.

Appendix E

1. J. Creswell and B. White, "The Guys from 'Government Sachs,'" *New York Times*, October 17, 2008, http://www.nytimes.com/2008/10/19/business/19gold.html?pagewanted=all&_r=0.

Appendix G

1. D. Vaughan, "The Dark Side of Organizations: Mistake, Misconduct, and Disaster," *Annual Review of Sociology* 25, no. 1 (1999): 271–305, doi: 10.1146/annurev .soc.25.1.271.

2. Allan Sloan, "An Unsavory Slice of Subprime," *Washington Post*, October 16, 2007, http://www.washingtonpost.com/wp-dyn/content/article/2007/10/15/AR2007101501435. html.

3. Andrew Clark, "Success Shines Unwelcome Spotlight on to Goldman Sachs," *The Guardian*, December 21, 2007, http://www.guardian.co.uk/business/2007/dec/21/ goldmansachs.useconomy.

4. M. Taibbi, "The Great American Bubble Machine," *Rolling Stone*, April 5, 2010, http://www.rollingstone.com/politics/news/the-great-american-bubble-machine-20100405.

5. "Mergers & Acquisitions Review," Thomson Reuters, 2011, http://dmi.thomson-reuters.com/Content/Files/4Q11_MA_Financial_Advisory_Review.pdf.

6. G. Smith, "Why I Am Leaving Goldman Sachs," *New York Times*, March 14, 2012, http://www.nytimes.com/2012/03/14/opinion/why-i-am-leaving goldman sachs .html?pagewanted=all.

Index

Acknowledgments

I would like to thank the faculty, graduate students, and administrators at the Department of Sociology at Columbia University, and in particular Professor David Stark, my thesis adviser and mentor, and Professor Josh Whitford, the director of graduate studies, for their training, support, and advice. In addition, I would like to thank the faculty and administrators, as well as my MBA and Executive MBA students, at Columbia Business School for their encouragement.

I want to thank my agent, Susan Rabiner, who, together with my editor at Harvard Business Review Press, Tim Sullivan, saw my PhD dissertation for what it was—a book not just about Goldman Sachs, but a book that brings business and finance together with sociology to improve the study of management, sociology, and public policy. They understood my vision and helped make it a reality.

Thank you to those I interviewed. I would love to recognize your contributions, patience, and time on an individual basis, but I want to respect your privacy.

Many professionals, professors, students, classmates, research assistants, and friends helped with my training and/or the book. Many thanks to Gary Ashwill, Red Ayme, Peter Bearman, Erin Brown, Soman Chainani, Manu Chander, Sidney Dekker, Helena Ding, Yige Ding, Erin Dolias, Nate Emge, Gil Eyal, Michelle Fan, Stephani Finks, Joe Gannon, Jie Gao, Kyle Gazis, Katrin Giziotis, Angel Gonzalez, Angelito Gonzalez, Simon Gonzalez, Ryan Hagen, Kathryn Harrigan, Charles Harrison, Simon Head, Jon Hill, Gailen Hite, Karen Ho, Paul Ingram, Jane Jacobi, Sam Johnson, El Kamada, Ko Kuwabara, Nan Liu, Emily Loose, Yao Lu, Evangelos Lyras,

Donald MacKenzie, Jeff Madrick, Kinga Makovi, Yarden Mariuma, Joanne Martin, Charles Masson, Debra Minkoff, Carlos Morei, Joy Nee, Olivia Nicol, James O'Shea, Neni Panourgia, Christina Perez, Allison Peter, Damon Phillips, Katherine Phillips, Joyce Plaza, Paula Reid, Ernesto Reuben, Tim Rich, Nan Rothschild, Jonathan Salky, Krista Schult, Hersche Shintre, Hana Sromova, Richard Swedberg, Noriyuki Takahashi, Matthias Thiemann, Mathijs de Vaan, Diane Vaughan, Oliver Wai, Karl Weber, Joanne Willard, Sang Won, Stacy Xing, and Xu Zang.

I would like to thank those who have researched and written about Goldman Sachs over the years, because without their diligent work it would have been impossible to write my PhD dissertation. Many are cited in my work and some are not, but I want to specifically acknowledge a few: Justin Baer, William Cohan, Susanne Craig, Charles Ellis, Lisa Endlich, David Faber, Richard Freedman, Boris Groysberg, Jonathan Knee, Susan McGee, Bethany McLean (who was in my Goldman 1992 M&A analyst class), Gretchen Morgenson, Andrew Serwer, Scott Snook, David Ross Sorkin, Louise Story, Matt Taibbi, Gillian Tett, Jill Vohr, the US Senate Subcommittee on Investigations, and the US Securities and Exchange Commission.

I would like to thank some people who manage to be pragmatic and entertaining at the same time: Stephen Colbert, Jim Collins, Malcolm Gladwell, Vijay Govindarajan, Tony Kornheiser, Michael Lewis, Bill Maher, Roger Martin, Robert K. Merton, Bill Simmons, Jon Stewart, Jack (and Suzy) Welch, and Michael Wilbon. I am sure they never dreamed that they would be acknowledged in a book related to Goldman Sachs, but their work stimulates my thinking.

Last, this book is a result of the love and support of my family and close friends. I didn't specifically acknowledge each and every one of you because I hope that I do that each and every day.

About the Author

STEVEN G. MANDIS worked at Goldman Sachs from 1992 to 2004 in the investment banking, private equity, and proprietary trading areas. He assisted Hank Paulson and other senior executives on special projects and was a portfolio manager in one of the largest and most successful proprietary trading areas at Goldman. After leaving Goldman, he cofounded a multibillion-dollar global alternative asset management firm that was a trading and investment banking client of Goldman's.

During the financial crisis, Mandis was a senior adviser to McKinsey & Company before becoming chief of staff to the president and COO of Citigroup and serving on executive, management, and risk committees at the firm.

Currently, he is an adjunct professor at Columbia Business School. He teaches classes of MBA and executive MBA students on strategic issues facing investment banks and the European financial crisis. In addition, Mandis is a PhD candidate and an honorary Paul F. Lazarsfeld Fellow in the Department of Sociology at Columbia University. He focuses on economic sociology as well as organizational culture and innovation. This book is based on work for his PhD dissertation.

Mandis holds an AB from the University of Chicago and an MA and MPhil from Columbia University.

He was awarded the Ellis Island Medal of Honor, given to children of immigrants who exemplify a life dedicated to community service.